KINDLY SIMILITUDE:
MARRIAGE AND FAMILY IN *PIERS PLOWMAN*

Kindly Similitude is the first study to offer a detailed reading of the many passages in *Piers Plowman* A, B, and C concerned with marriage and family, and to place these passages within the frameworks of contemporary social history, law, theology, exegesis, and literature. The author shows how Langland draws on the nearly universal experiences of familial life both literally and metaphorically to further his expositions of law and love, nature and grace, the image of God in individuals and society, the use of time and material goods, the perversion of right relationships through *covetise*, and doing well in the active life. For Langland, an unmistakably public poet, the marital household is inextricably linked to religious, economic, and political institutions; it reflects and transmits a divine exemplar of community, and plays a fundamental role in creating the society in which he and his audience must live.

This important new critical approach complements the strong current attention to the poem's intellectual and ecclesiological contexts, its concern with epistemology and language, its textuality, and its overall 'clerkliness.'

M. TERESA TAVORMINA is Professor of English at Michigan State University. She is one of the founding co-editors of *The Yearbook of Langland Studies* and a general editor for *Medieval England: An Encyclopedia*.

Piers Plowman Studies

ISSN 0261-9849

Series Editor: James Simpson

Kindly Similitude

Marriage and Family in
Piers Plowman

M. TERESA TAVORMINA

D. S. BREWER

First published 1995
D. S. Brewer, Cambridge

Transferred to digital printing

ISBN 978-0-85991-454-3

D. S. Brewer is an imprint of Boydell & Brewer Ltd
PO Box 9, Woodbridge, Suffolk IP12 3DF, UK
and of Boydell & Brewer Inc.
668 Mt Hope Avenue, Rochester, NY 14620, USA
website: www.boydellandbrewer.com

A CiP catalogue record for this book is available
from the British Library

This publication is printed on acid-free paper

Contents

For my mother and in memory of my father,
who first *kenned me kyndely*
what *trewe wedded libbynge folk* can mean.

Preface

Students of Middle English literature have long recognized the importance of marriage as a subject in Chaucer's poetry, and the high value that Gower attaches to married love. Detailed explorations of marital themes and issues in the works of these poets have been many and profitable. One can hardly come to a genuine understanding of Chaucer's *oeuvre* without taking into account the *Canterbury Tales* marriage group and related materials elsewhere in his poetry; similarly, a full appreciation of Gower must pay significant heed to his 'life-long obsession' with conjugal love.[1]

Piers Plowman scholarship, in contrast, has tended to overlook such domestic elements in Langland's work. Instead, it has focused more – and often very productively – on issues connected to the poet's learning and his ambivalent attitudes toward that learning, or on institutional matters related to 'public policy,' both secular and religious. Thus we have seen excellent studies of Langland's views of *clergie* and of regular and secular clerics; of his intellectual and religious sources and his particular adaptations of those sources; and of his concerns with language, epistemology, and his poetic vocation. We have also seen strong studies of his understanding of good government, of authority both verbal and political, of ecclesiastical and theological controversies, and of the nature of justice and law. This focus on the learned and public contexts of *Piers Plowman* is by no means ill-advised. Langland is deeply concerned with such matters; there are far more records of learned and public life than of domestic life in Langland's time; and many of the books and articles devoted to these topics have greatly advanced our understanding not only of the poem but of medieval English culture in general. Nonetheless, the value and fascinating complexity of these lines of scholarly work may have contributed in part to the relative lack of attention paid to the considerable amount that Langland has to say

---

[1] John H. Fisher et al., 'John Gower,' in J. Burke Severs and Albert E. Hartung, eds., *A Manual of Writings in Middle English*, vol. 7 (Hamden, 1986), 2197.

about the non-clerkly, private world, the everyday life-experience of the vast majority of medieval men and women.

It was a sense of this gap in *Piers Plowman* criticism that drew me into the research for this book. I quickly became convinced that Langland's discussions of marriage are bound up closely with discussions of family – intrafamilial authority, mutual affection and obligations of kin, the educative function of the family, and so on. It also became clear that Langland's specific concerns with respect to marriage and family are not identical with those of Chaucer or Gower, despite undeniable overlaps in the more abstract general issues which they all explore through the marriage theme: Nature, Reason, lawful love, governance, the well-lived secular life. Moreover, the differences in social milieu between the author of *Piers* and the more courtly Ricardian poets means that the sources by which Henry Kelly and others have cast so much light on 'love and marriage in the age of Chaucer' are only partially applicable to marriage and family in Langland's world. Homiletic and penitential literature, yes; Ovid, no. Traditions of Nature and sexuality, yes; the misogynistic and misogamistic traditions, only tangentially. Canon law, yes, but for Langland also English common and customary law; the socioeconomic aspects of marriage, certainly pertinent for Chaucer and Gower, but for Langland crucial. Thus, interpreting Langland's handling of the marriage theme is not a matter of simply applying established questions, methods, and sources to *Piers Plowman*, but also of expanding the universe of discourse to include a wider range of family experience, of paying less attention to some marital issues while introducing and exploring others, and of drawing on some important new sources to make fuller sense of marriage and family as presented in the poem.

No doubt the infrequency of critical commentary on marriage in *Piers Plowman* can be partly explained by the difficulty of constructing the appropriate historical framework for such commentary. Until relatively recently, scholars have had to read the poem's social arguments largely in terms derived from the literary and historical documents of the social elite, terms which tend to make more sense when applied to Chaucer's or Gower's or the *Pearl*-poet's characterization of marriage than to Langland's. While these terms are certainly not unhelpful for understanding Langland's views on the subject, they do need to be supplemented when possible with information on the marital and familial experience of non-elite social groups. Many of the most useful resources for understanding that experience have only become available in the last generation of historical scholarship, with the great burgeoning of family history as a fully developed field of inquiry, concerned not only with the lives of the well-documented upper classes but also of the long-ignored peasantry and townsfolk. Since marriage and its consequences touch on so many aspects of human life, historians of the family have necessarily brought a wide variety of disciplines to bear in their investigations, and syntheses of the multidisciplinary results of these investigations are naturally even younger than the field of family history itself. Fortunately, such studies and syntheses have grown increasingly common, and should enable us to gain a much firmer grasp on questions of marriage and family in *Piers Plowman* and to deepen our understanding of those subjects in the works of Langland's fellow-poets as well.[2]

Thus, one of my two main aims in this book is to set Langland's references to marriage and family within the more comprehensive historical framework that has become available in the last twenty or thirty years. I hasten to add that this project is not conceived as a narrowly defined identification of social parallels to passages in *Piers Plowman*, nor as a mechanical mining of the poem for supposedly pure nuggets of social history. Langland is at best only one sociological informant, and a notoriously cranky one at that; we are more likely to find nuggets of holy fool's gold in his poem than immediately negotiable historical metal. But since social history and its related disciplines are as necessary as literary and intellectual history in coming to grips with much of Langland's poetry, this book attempts to bring some of that social history into critical view. The better we can determine the probable social, economic, legal, literary, religious, and intellectual matrices from which the poet's thinking on the family emerges and at times diverges, the better we will be able to explore and evaluate the nature, degree, and poetic implications of that divergence and of its conforming complement.

---

[2] Useful synthesizing work of recent date and various focus and approach includes David Herlihy, *Medieval Households* (Cambridge, MA, 1985); Barbara A. Hanawalt, *The Ties That Bound: Peasant Families in Medieval England* (New York, 1986); Judith M. Bennett, *Women in the Medieval English Countryside: Gender and Household in Brigstock Before the Plague* (New York, 1987); James A. Brundage, *Law, Sex, and Christian Society in Medieval Europe* (Chicago, 1987); Frances and Joseph Gies, *Marriage and the Family in the Middle Ages* (New York, 1987); Christopher N. L. Brooke, *The Medieval Idea of Marriage* (Oxford, 1989); Shulamith Shahar, *Childhood in the Middle Ages* (London, 1990); Clarissa W. Atkinson, *The Oldest Vocation: Christian Motherhood in the Middle Ages* (Ithaca, 1991); Joel T. Rosenthal, *Patriarchy and Families of Privilege in Fifteenth-Century England* (Philadelphia, 1991); Dyan Elliott, *Spiritual Marriage: Sexual Abstinence in Medieval Wedlock* (Princeton, 1993); Beatrice Gottlieb, *The Family in the Western World from the Black Death to the Industrial Age* (New York, 1993); Barbara Hanawalt, *Growing Up in Medieval London: The Experience of Childhood in History* (New York, 1993); Zvi Razi, 'The Myth of the Immutable English Family,' *Past & Present* 140 (August 1993), 3–44; and for bibliography, Michael M. Sheehan and Jacqueline Murray, *Domestic Society in Medieval Europe: A Select Bibliography* (Toronto, 1990).

Such evaluative exploration is the second and larger goal of the five chapters that comprise this study. I hope that the analyses offered in these chapters will demonstrate the significance of the marital and familial passages in *Piers*, both locally and globally; will convincingly relate those passages to some of the poem's recognized primary themes; and will suggest, in a reasonable first approximation, what Langland thought about marriage, family, and their place in the economy of salvation, and how that thinking developed over the course of his poetic career. Along the way, I have endeavored to keep the poem's language as much in view as possible, attending to its nuances and texture whenever these have borne interestingly on the topics under discussion. Although the historical contexts of the poet's references to families and marriage play an essential supporting role in my argument, I have deliberately focused that argument on the poem itself, subordinating the historical material within the text and restricting much of it to the on-page notes. The study thus offers two distinct but mutually supporting streams of commentary on *Piers Plowman*, one primarily interpretive, the other documentary. It is my further hope that the documentary material will aid and encourage other students of the poem to extend and where necessary correct or qualify the readings of marriage and family in *Piers Plowman* presented here.

My working hypothesis throughout the book is that marriage and family have an important place in Langland's thinking on human social relations and the moral life; furthermore, that they provide him with powerful metaphors for some of his most heartfelt religious beliefs. But they are not central subjects for him in the same way as salvation, truth, justice and mercy, the uses of learning, or repentance for sin; nor as marital relations and married love are for Chaucer and Gower. Often, though by no means always, they arise as means to other ends, as allegories, similes, or examples – another reason for their being only occasionally explored by medieval literary scholars and critics. What makes marriage and family most important for *Piers Plowman* is not simply Langland's direct attention to them for their own sake, though that is certainly not insignificant, but rather his steady habit of turning to them as literal and figurative ways of talking about those matters which *are* on center stage for him. He seems to have seen marriage and family as natural illustrations for all manner of questions, from the right use of temporal goods and the origins of doing well, to the ideal ordering of society and the deepest Christian mysteries. Again and again he draws on them to drive home his points about economics, education, politics, and theology. Moreover, this illustrative function is given added force by the inherent ethical and affective content of marriage and family life, a content which the poem does not overlook. For Langland, marriage and family are – to borrow Robert Bellah's resurrection of Tocqueville's evocative phrase – true 'habits of the heart.' Like his references to agriculture or to eating and drinking, Langland's familial allusions appear so often, so variously, and apparently so spontaneously in *Piers* that they must have been virtually second nature to him, such an intrinsic part of his world-view that he could hardly avoid expressing himself in those terms.

The first three chapters of this book explore Langland's three primary treatments of marriage and family, each of which serves one or more of his larger themes: the marriage of Lady Meed in Chapter 1; the allegorical and literal families described, praised, and castigated by Wit in Chapter 2; and the analysis of the married state as a fruit on the Tree of Charity and as a figure for God the Father or the Trinity in Chapter 3. In these chapters, I seek to show how Langland uses the homely, familiar experiences of kinship and marriage to further his expositions of (*inter alia*) law and love, nature and grace, the use of time and temporal goods, the perversion of right relationships through *covetise*, the principles of like to like and like from like, doing well in the active life, and the loving image of God in human society and individuals. Chapter 4 rounds out the picture presented in Chapters 1 through 3 by collating many of the shorter marital and familial passages in the rest of *Piers*, and analyzing these miscellaneous references under such categories as childhood, sexuality, sibling affections, and aging, rather than attempting to make sense of them *seriatim* across the poem. While most of the themes illustrated by these shorter passages will already be familiar from the three longer treatments of marital and family behavior, at least one such theme – and a major one at that – is expressed only in a string of short passages that build on each other all the way to the climactic Easter Passus itself: the blood-brotherhood and shared nature of Christ and humanity, which make possible the Redemption and the reunion of humankind with God. The brief final chapter synthesizes the results of the preceding four, placing them in the context of Langland's work as a whole. Throughout the book, I also seek to suggest some approaches and directions that future explorations of these complex but rewarding questions might take.

For the full implications of Langland's treatment of marriage and family will not be realized by a single book or the work of only a few critics. The issues at stake and the relevant historical and cultural contexts are too varied to allow for rapid and certain resolution. I have sought to provide a relatively broad survey of the territory involved, but it remains a survey, definitely preliminary, limited by my own vantage points and critical tools and by the extent and variety of the terrain itself. The material requires further scholarly and critical analysis, dialogue, and debate, not unlike that received by Chaucer's marriage group for the last seventy-five years, or that received over the last forty years by Langland's concerns with language, learning, belief, and the individual and societal pursuit of perfection. If this study can help catalyze that dialogue, it will have fulfilled its purpose.

One final aspect of the approach taken to *Piers Plowman* in this study should be mentioned. All three versions are used as a base for discussion, despite the methodological risks of conflating material from the different texts without noting changes in that material from text to text, or of 'adhering too closely to the parallel-text method of reading the poem' and thereby confusing 'rearrangements of material' with 'alterations in doctrine.'[3] The decision also forestalls or at least hinders interpretation of marital and familial themes in one or another version – the B text being the most likely candidate, though C has strong claims as well – taken as a self-contained literary work to be judged on its own merits. However, I believe that the advantages of reading all three texts together outweigh the disadvantages, at least if proper care can be taken to avoid the pitfalls of inappropriate conflation or an inflexible or confusing parallel-text approach. First of all, it seems more interesting to examine the development of Langland's ideas about marriage and family than to restrict oneself to his expression of those ideas at a single point in time. In the last few years, more and more students of the poem have begun to look long and hard at the problem of Langland's incessant revisions, both locally and at large. Although that problem, in my view, is still too large for a detailed comprehensive study, smaller projects on the revisions in particular passus or in the handling of particular topics across the poem should eventually make possible a genuinely synthetic explanation of Langland's revisionary procedures. The comparative analysis offered here, if successful, may someday contribute to such a synthesis.

Secondly, there are several interesting passages on family life or marriage found in only one or another version of the poem; if carefully used, they can broaden our understanding of all three versions, whether they conform or run counter to the passages where they are added or subtracted. Particularly important here are some extensive revisions in C; but at least one A passage (in Wit's speech) goes a long way in

---

[3] E. Talbot Donaldson, *Piers Plowman: The C-Text and Its Poet* (1949; rpt. Hamden, 1966), 137 n. 5, 181.

explaining the seemingly abrupt transitions that occur at the equivalent places in B and C. Even when he is changing his mind, Langland is still the best gloss on Langland. I should add that I have come to believe that Langland's changes in the marriage and family materials of *Piers* are most often shifts of emphasis, rather than downright repudiation of cancelled material, since the gist of the omitted material is often still present elsewhere in the revised version. 'Rearrangements of material' on marriage and family seem to me to be much more common than sharp 'alterations in doctrine.' New lines may expand the poet's argument, but they seldom directly contradict earlier material; instead, the seeds of the revision can often be discovered in the prior version upon careful rereading. As Malcolm Godden observes, Langland's revisions display 'an evident and deep reluctance to destroy what his imagination had conceived at an earlier stage. He respected the autonomy of his poetry, and tended to look for new meaning in the earlier scenes and characters, rather than changing the substance.'[4]

However, for those who are interested primarily in what a particular version of the poem may have to say on marriage and family, I have tried to identify clearly the distinct features of each version in Chapter 5 and in the conclusions to individual chapters – especially in Chapters 1 and 2, where all three texts will be in view throughout the discussion.

A brief note on one of the central terms of this study: in the Middle Ages, the Latin word *familia* primarily meant 'household, retinue'; it could also mean a lineage or kin-group, a 'house' or 'family' in the genealogical sense, but generally did not carry the modern sense

---

[4] *The Making of Piers Plowman* (London, 1990), 5. Godden's analytical strategy is complementary to mine: he focuses consecutively on the A text, then the revisions of A to B and the balance of B, and finally the revisions of B to C; I usually examine all the available versions of a particular passage or episode together. Both strategies will be needed for an eventual full understanding of the poem's making. The still-uncertain status of the Z text and its place, if any, in Langland's composition process has led me to exclude it from the present analysis, though some readers may wish to compare Z's presentation of Meed's marriage with the A, B, and C treatments discussed in Chapter 1.

As my remarks here and throughout the book will suggest, I have not yet been convinced by recent scholarly suggestions that the A text is an abridgment, rather than an earlier version, of B; the data – including the kinds of variation among the versions that both Godden and I examine – seem to me to make more sense under the traditional assumption of an A-B-C order of composition and revision. A detailed presentation of the arguments for the abridgment hypothesis, which became available to me only after the completion of this book, has been presented by Jill Mann, as a plenary address at the International Conference on *Piers Plowman* (Cambridge, 1993) and in her essay 'The Power of the Alphabet: A Reassessment of the Relation between the A and the B Versions of *Piers Plowman*,' *YLS* 8 (1994), 21–50; Mann's discussion impinges most directly on my subject in her comments about differing levels of sexual explicitness in A and B (cf. my discussions of the passages in question in Chapters 1 and 2).

'parents-and-children, conjugal unit.' Middle English *familie* means 'household,' but is very rare. The *MED* lists only one instance, in the *Chester Plays*, the cited manuscript of which is dated 1607, though the original text may date from before 1425; to this we may add Wyntoun's early fifteenth-century use of *famyle*, meaning 'lineage, kindred,' cited in the *OED* and the *Dictionary of the Older Scottish Tongue*. More common in Middle English were the words *familier* (n. and adj.) and *familiarite*, which had such senses as 'intimate'/'intimacy,' 'member of a household,' 'pertaining to members of the household'/'fidelity proper to a household member,' and 'kindly/sociable/courteous.' They overlap to a great extent with the native words *homli* and *homliness* (as suggested by Chaucer's 'famulier foo . . . false hoomly hewe' [*MerT* 1784–85]).

What is central to these definitions is the notion of cooperative, habitual co-residence and the affective bonds created thereby, rather than biological kinship *per se*. But it is also important to note that, in most non-ecclesiastical households, there was a biological family unit at the center of the whole; moreover, this biological core was usually a conjugal unit rather than a complex extended family, especially in the lower and middling ranks of society. A modern nuclear family would have been recognized as a *familia* ('household') in late medieval England, albeit seen as unusual in its exclusion of live-in servants or perhaps a relative or two.

I shall normally use the word 'family' in its modern English senses, referring either to the immediate conjugal family or to larger kin-groupings, including lineages from ancestors to posterity. *Familia*, when it appears, will carry its proper sense of 'household,' but with the understanding that secular households usually had some kind of family group (in the modern sense) at their core. The pun on the modern senses of *family* and *familiar*, though not available in Middle English, is too useful for me to abjure entirely (a partial analogue in Middle English, not easily transferred to Modern English, might be the semantic connections between *kin*, *kinde*, and *kindeli*).

Quotations of *Piers Plowman* are taken from the Athlone editions of the A and B texts, with editorial brackets omitted, and from Derek Pearsall's edition of the C text. Manuscript variants and the readings of other editions are noted when they affect the argument being made. Passages quoted are normally given in the form of the earliest text to include the lines, unless a particular turn of phrase in a later version is important for the discussion at hand.

For the ease of readers who wish to consult the later parallels or near-parallels to the quoted lines, I give line numbers for each text in which the passage appears, beginning with the quoted text and followed by its reflexes in the other versions (if any). If the corresponding passages are genuinely parallel, with only minor differences among them, a comma separates the citations; if the 'parallel' passages have diverged notably from the text quoted, the cited line numbers are set off by a semicolon; now and then, loosely correspondent material elsewhere in the poem is cited, set off by a semicolon and the abbreviation 'cf.'

The Bible is quoted from the Vulgate and the Douai-Rheims translation.

I am happy to acknowledge the assistance of several institutions and many people who have helped enable and improve the writing of this book. The National Humanities Center provided me with a year in which to lay a firm research foundation for the project; Michigan State University provided grants for summer travel and supplementary funds for the year at the National Humanities Center. *Modern Philology* and the *Journal of English and Germanic Philology* published some of my earliest work on marriage and family in *Piers Plowman*, which appears now in expanded form in Chapter 3. Staff members at the Michigan State University and University of Michigan Libraries have been most helpful in supplying essential Inter-Library Loan and Rare Books services. Nicholas Trakul gave invaluable bibliographic assistance in the final stages of preparing the manuscript.

I owe special thanks to Marie Borroff for setting me on the track of medieval nuptial liturgies in the course of research on *Pearl*, and to Steve Barney for keeping me on track in the course of writing a dissertation on those liturgies, related exegesis, and some of their Middle English literary reflexes. Many good friends and colleagues have contributed both wittingly and unwittingly to the development and completion of the book – the late Jack Yunck and Bob Kaske, John Alford, David Benson, Al Shoaf, Mike Twomey, Judith Bennett, Fred Biggs, Fred Robinson, Mary Clemente Davlin, Susanna Fein, A. C. and Sonia Coats, and Elaine Clark, to name but a few. The notes to the text, both literary and historical, reveal how much I owe to the prior work of fellow students of Langland and to those laborers in the fields of family and matrimonial history without whom this book would have been impossible; I record here my deep appreciation of all their work. To Lister Matheson I owe not only ideas and information but also the particularly nurturing environment that has made the last, crucial stages of revision both possible and joyful.

East Lansing
June 1994

Abbreviations and Short Titles

General

AgHR	*Agricultural History Review*
ANTS	Anglo-Norman Text Society
CC	*Corpus Christianorum, Series Latina* (Turnhout, Belgium)
CM	*Continuatio Mediaeualis*
ChauR	*The Chaucer Review*
CSEL	*Corpus Scriptorum Ecclesiasticorum Latinorum* (Vienna)
DTC	*Dictionnaire de théologie catholique*
EETS	Early English Text Society
ELN	*English Language Notes*
Gl.Ord.	*Glossa Ordinaria*
HBS	Henry Bradshaw Society
JEGP	*Journal of English and Germanic Philology*
Kane	George Kane, ed. *Piers Plowman: The A Version* (London, 1960)
K-D	George Kane and E. Talbot Donaldson, eds. *Piers Plowman: The B Version* (London, 1975)
M&H	*Medievalia et Humanistica*
MÆ	*Medium Ævum*
MED	*The Middle English Dictionary*
MLN	*Modern Language Notes*
MP	*Modern Philology*
MS	*Mediaeval Studies*
N&Q	*Notes and Queries*
Neophil	*Neophilologus*
NM	*Neuphilologische Mitteilungen*
OED	*The Oxford English Dictionary* (2nd ed.)
Pearsall	Derek Pearsall, ed. *Piers Plowman: An Edition of the C Text* (London, 1978)
PL	*Patrologiae Cursus Completus, Series Latina*
PMLA	*Publications of the Modern Language Association of America*
PQ	*Philological Quarterly*
RES	*Review of English Studies*
RS	Rolls Series

SATF	Société des Anciens Textes Français
Schmidt	A. V. C. Schmidt, ed. *The Vision of Piers Plowman: A Critical Edition of the B-Text*, new ed. (London, 1987)
Skeat	W. W. Skeat, ed. *The Vision of William concerning Piers the Plowman, in Three Parallel Texts*. 2 vols. 1886; rpt. with additional bibliography (Oxford, 1969)
SN	*Studia Neophilologica*
ST	*Summa Theologica*
SP	*Studies in Philology*
SS	Surtees Society
YLS	*The Yearbook of Langland Studies*

Legal Sources

Corpus Iuris Canonici, ed. Emil Friedberg. 2 vols. Leipzig, 1879–81; rpt. Graz, 1955. Includes the following works cited in this study: *Decretum* = Gratian, *Concordia discordantium canonum*; X = *Decretales Gregorii IX*.

Corpus Iuris Civilis, ed. Paul Krueger, Theodore Mommsen, Rudolf Schoell. 3 vols. Berlin, 1872–99. Includes the following works cited in this study: *Inst.* = *Institutes*; *Dig.* = *Digest*.

Ord. Gloss:	I cite the Ordinary Glosses on the *Corpus Iuris Canonici* and the *Corpus Iuris Civilis* from the 1559–60 and 1566–67 Lyons editions of the two codes.
P & M	Frederick Pollock and Frederic W. Maitland. *The History of English Law before the Time of Edward I*. 2 vols. 2nd ed. Cambridge, 1898; rpt. with new introduction and bibliography by S. C. F. Milsom, Cambridge, 1968.
Bracton	Henry de Bracton. *De legibus et consuetudinibus regni Angliae*. Ed. George E. Woodbine, rev. and trans. Samuel E. Thorne. 4 vols. Cambridge, MA, 1968–77.
Glanvill	*Tractatus de legibus et consuetudinibus regni Angliae qui Glanvill vocatur*. Ed. G. D. G. Hall. London, 1965.
Holdsworth	William S. Holdsworth. *A History of English Law*. 4th ed. Vol. 3. The Mediaeval Common Law: The Rules of Law. London, 1935.
Plucknett	Theodore F. T. Plucknett. *A Concise History of the Common Law*. 5th ed. London, 1956.
Powicke and Cheney	*Councils & Synods with other Documents Relating to the English Church II: 1205–1313*. Ed. F. M. Powicke and C. R. Cheney. 1 vol. in 2 parts. Oxford, 1964.
Wilkins	David Wilkins. *Concilia Magnae Britanniae et Hiberniae*. 4 vols. London, 1737.
CCR	*Calendar of the Close Rolls*, HMSO, 1892–1954.
CFR	*Calendar of the Fine Rolls*, HMSO, 1911–62.
CPR	*Calendar of the Patent Rolls*, HMSO, 1891–1916.
IPM	*Calendar of Inquisitions post Mortem*, HMSO, 1904–70.
CAD	*Descriptive Catalogue of Ancient Deeds*, HMSO, 1890–1915.

1

The Marriage of Meed

The longest single episode of the first Dream in *Piers Plowman* is the attempted marriage and subsequent inquisition of Lady Meed (Passus 2–4 in all versions). In this episode, Langland explores the right use of temporal goods and the right rule of secular society, major themes already laid out in the Prologue and Passus 1. He introduces Reason and Conscience as important characters; they will continue to be significant throughout the work. He considers in detail the corrupting effects of *covetise*, an issue that will arise again and again in the poem. Students of *Piers* have long recognized that these three passus, together with the rest of the first Dream, establish many of the poem's central themes, especially those connected to the social, political, and economic problems of Langland's day.[1]

The primary image through which Langland presents these themes in the Meed episode is that of a marriage: the marriage of a noblewoman, said to be a 'cousin to the king,' and clearly of great political influence throughout the kingdom. The importance of the marital metaphor is signalled early in both the B and C texts. The first thing Will sees when Holy Church shows him 'where [þe false] stondeþ' is Meed in her glory; the first question that comes to his 'rauysshed' heart is no longer simply 'What is þis womman?' as in A.2.15, but 'What she was and whos wif she were' (B.2.18) or 'Whos wyf a were and what was here name' (C.2.17). Although there are long passages within Passus 3 and 4 in which Langland digresses from the initial nuptial context established in Passus 2, the later passus keep returning to the question of whom Meed

---

[1] See, for instance, John A. Yunck, *The Lineage of Lady Meed: The Development of Mediaeval Venality Satire* (Notre Dame, 1963), 284–88; C. David Benson, 'The Function of Lady Meed in *Piers Plowman*,' *English Studies* 61 (1980), 193–205; Anna P. Baldwin, *The Theme of Government in Piers Plowman* (Cambridge, 1981), 55–80 and *passim*; Myra Stokes, *Justice and Mercy in Piers Plowman: A Reading of the B Text Visio* (London, 1984), 99–156; John A. Alford, 'The Design of the Poem,' *A Companion to Piers Plowman* (Berkeley, 1988), 32–39; and James Simpson, *Piers Plowman: An Introduction to the B-text* (London, 1990), 17–60.

shall marry and to her characterization as an all too available female (see for example A.3.5–8, 95–122, 4.8–10, 137–40, B.3.5–8, 106–33, 4.8–10, 161–66, C.3.5–8, 127–69, 4.8–10, 156–61).

As John A. Yunck has pointed out, Langland's depiction of Meed as a pliant and promiscuous female, available to the highest bidder, derives in part from the widespread tradition of medieval venality satire.[2] The allegorical marriages of the devil's daughters – usually a form of estates satire – are another likely literary analogue to Meed's bridal.[3] But Langland's presentation of the problems associated with corrupt reward in terms of a contested marriage also has non-literary roots. In this chapter, I shall propose some of the contemporary social contexts within which Langland and his audience might have visualized Meed's marriage. These contexts are neither exclusive nor exhaustive; they will be confined mainly to matters related in some way to marriage and family, so as to offer a well-focused perspective on the episode and its ruling metaphor which has not yet been very fully explored. As is true of so much of Langland's most effective poetry, the political and spiritual tenor of his argument in the Meed episode is firmly grounded in the material practicalities of its vehicle, a marriage whose social and economic import is high enough to involve the king. Although Langland's primary concern in Will's first Dream is with the corruption of public institutions through duplicitous cupidity, the fact that he satirizes this corruption by way of an allegorical marriage can greatly enrich our understanding of the powerful social critique that introduces his poem. By the end of Chapter 1, we will have seen just how deeply interwoven were the private bonds of literal marriage and the public

[2] *Lineage of Lady Meed*, 289–97. A particularly well worked out marital allegory in this tradition occurs in the *Roman de Fauvel*, ed. A. Lângfors, SATF (Paris, 1914–19). For Langland's possible knowledge of this early fourteenth-century satire, see Roberta D. Cornelius, '*Piers Plowman* and the *Roman de Fauvel*,' PMLA 47 (1932), 363–67, and Yunck, 221–26. In his wide-ranging study *Bribes* (New York, 1984), John T. Noonan, Jr., discusses metaphoric associations of venality and sexuality in a number of cultures (pp. xvii–xviii, 38, 262–63, 319–20, 598–600, 700–702, and *passim*). A new and promising stage in the critical understanding of Meed's gender can be seen in essays by David Aers ('Class, Gender, Medieval Criticism, and *Piers Plowman*') and Clare A. Lees ('Gender and Exchange in *Piers Plowman*'), both in *Class and Gender in Early English Literature: Intersections*, ed. Britton J. Harwood and Gillian R. Overing (Bloomington, 1994), 64–70 and 112–30.

[3] For examples, see Barthélemy Hauréau, 'Les filles du diable,' *Journal des savants* April 1884, 225–28; Paul Meyer, 'Notice du MS. Rawlinson Poetry 241 (Oxford),' *Romania* 29 (1900), 54–72; G. R. Owst, *Literature and Pulpit in Medieval England* (Cambridge, 1933), 93–97; and the *Mirour de l'omme* 205–76, 793–1056, ed. G. C. Macaulay, in *The Complete Works of John Gower* (Oxford, 1899–1902), vol. 1. Henry of Lancaster describes a marriage of the devil and the flesh from which the seven deadly sins are born, but omits the further marrying-off of the sins themselves; see the *Livre de Seyntz Medicines*, ed. E. J. Arnould, ANTS 2 (Oxford, 1940), 88.

bonds threatened by the economic and social transactions personified by Meed. At that point, we will return to the larger figurative and rhetorical implications of Langland's decision to present many of the problems associated with Meed in matrimonial terms.

The Marriage-Making

Meed's Family, Fiancé, and Friends

Meed's marriage reflects many marriages of Langland's day, unions which were often matters of social, legal, and economic interest to a number of people besides the bride and groom.[4] Parental concern for the economic security of offspring can be seen at all social levels, from the peasantry to the aristocracy.[5] Finding an advantageous marriage could lead to such security, as could a generous inheritance or entry into trade, the professions, or the court, so it is not surprising that medieval parents often took an active hand in their children's marriage plans. Moreover, such plans could have significant effects on the social and economic expectations of other people – immediate family members, other relatives, possibly even some neighbors, friends, and associates. A good marriage, in whatever social milieu, brought benefits to family and friends as well as to the spouses. For families within the feudal or manorial hierarchies, marriage arrangements also involved the economic and legal interests of the lords from whom lands were held, and these interests had to be taken into account as well.[6]

[4] For useful overviews, with further bibliography, see Michael M. Sheehan, 'The Wife of Bath and Her Four Sisters,' *M&H* n.s. 13 (1985), 28–34; Elaine Clark, 'The Decision to Marry in Thirteenth- and Early Fourteenth-Century Norfolk,' *MS* 49 (1987), 496–516 (on 'marital decision-making at the village level'); and Sue Sheridan Walker, 'The Feudal Family and the Common Law Courts: The Pleas Protecting Rights of Wardship and Marriage, c. 1225–1375,' *Journal of Medieval History* 14 (1988), 13–31.

[5] Parental concern and affection for children was by no means uncommon in the later Middle Ages. Indeed, contemporary moralists occasionally spoke out against carrying such concern too far, especially in the material realm. For John Bromyard, one of the risks of being a rich parent is that one has 'magnam de prole ditanda uel promouenda . . . sollicitudinem, ex qua sollicitudine frequenter auari, & tyranni fiunt, & propriarum animarum perditores' (*Summa Praedicantium* [Venice, 1586], s.v. Matrimonium, § 4). A Wycliffite treatise notes that many parents 'maken sorowe ȝif here children ben nakid or pore, but þouȝ here children ben nakid fro virtues in soule, þei chargen noþing. And wiþ moche traveile and cost þei geten grete richessis and heiȝe statis and benefices to here children, to here more dampnacion ofte tymes, but þei wolen not gete here children goodis of grace and virtuous lif.' ('Of Weddid Men and Wifis,' in Thomas Arnold, ed., *Select English Works of John Wyclif*, 3 vols. [Oxford, 1869–71], 3:198–99. See also Chap. 2, n. 82 and Chap. 4, n. 3 below.

[6] Elaine Clark vividly depicts this network of interests at the manorial level in 'The Custody of Children in English Manor Courts,' *Law and History Review* 3 (1985), 333–48.

Given the multiple interests of parties other than the bride and groom in many medieval marriages, it was natural that these unions were often entered upon with the assistance of family and friends. Such interventions were intrinsically neither good nor bad: depending on one's judgment of the motives behind a particular marriage, one might have called its arrangement 'bauderye' and 'brocage' or 'gentilesse, / Compassioun, and felawship, and trist' (*Troilus* 3:402–03), but few were likely to question the general practice. Matrimonial decisions that involved kin, allies, and legal superiors were a familiar social reality.

Thus, when Langland describes Meed's marriage, it is socially unsurprising that he includes a number of important relatives and friends of the bride and groom in the nuptial action.[7] They are the 'fader and frendes,' the *parentes, proximi,* and *amici,* whose interests and assistance played a part in so many medieval marriages.[8] Examples of this specialized use of *amicus* appear regularly in medieval marriage liturgies (see those quoted below, pp. 14–16). Several marriage cases cited by R. H. Helmholz in his study *Marriage Litigation in Medieval England* apply the term to people with influence over a person's marriage, including fathers, uncles, masters, and brothers.[9] Humbert de Romans discusses the arranging of marriages in the nuptial sermons of his popular, thirteenth-century *ad status* collection, and notes the importance of the marriage to the spouses' *amici,* whose involvement in

See also Judith M. Bennett, *Women in the Medieval English Countryside: Gender and Household in Brigstock Before the Plague* (New York, 1987), 71–99; for the upper classes, likewise before the Plague, see Scott L. Waugh, *The Lordship of England: Royal Wardships and Marriages in English Society and Politics, 1217–1327* (Princeton, 1988), 15–63; and for London, see Barbara A. Hanawalt, *Growing Up in Medieval London: The Experience of Childhood in History* (New York, 1993), 89–107, 199–222.

[7] Meed's marriage reflects the potential complexity of marital negotiations more clearly than some of the other allegorical marriages to which it is related. In the marriages of the devil's daughters, Satan usually marries his daughter-vices off to the various estates without consulting anyone. See Meyer, 'Notice,' 56–62; Owst, *Literature and Pulpit,* 93–96. In the *Roman de Fauvel,* Fauvel makes his own plans to woo Fortune, and his counsellors flatteringly approve all he intends; Dame Fortune, who has put Fauvel in power, overturns his presumptuous planning and offers him a marriage with her handmaiden Vain Glory instead, to which he quickly assents (*Roman de Fauvel,* Bk. 2). In Gower's elaborate treatment of the marriage of the seven sins, the World asks their grandfather, the Devil, for their hands; the Devil consults only with Sin, his daughter and the mother of the seven sins, before marrying them to the World (*Mirour de l'omme* 793–833). Nonetheless, Langland's presentation of Meed's marriage need not be literally precise in every detail, though it does seem to match social realities more fully than some of its analogues: like those analogues, the episode is aimed primarily at instruction, not at sociologically accurate reporting.

[8] For the English phrase, see E. S. Olszewska, 'Middle English *fader and frendes,*' *N&Q* 20 (1973), 205–07. Cf. also Langland's use of the phrase in the Dreamer's apologia in C.5.35–41, discussed most recently by Ralph Hanna III, *William Langland* (Aldershot, 1993), 18–22.

[9] (Cambridge, 1974), 47n, 49, 200, 207.

the decision is therefore desirable;[10] similarly, John de Burgh includes the 'potentia amicorum' among the secondary causes for matrimony.[11] The term 'next friend' (prochein amy, proximus amicus) was also used more generally to describe a person – often a relative – who assisted a minor in legal actions, or had custody of a minor's inheritance under socage tenure.[12] Thus, given the importance of 'fader and frendes' in medieval marriages, reviewing the role of Meed's proximi amici in her wedding and the roles played by other members of the bridal party will provide a useful point of departure for this chapter.

Constant in all three texts are Meed herself and her fiancé False, who is given the epithet Fickle-tongue in B, Faithless in C. The negotiations for the marriage are carried out by Favel, Liar, and Guile according to the A text, where Favel also enfeoffs Meed and False with the sinful lands that will support them. In B and C, Favel and Liar do the matchmaking, and Guile is said to 'give the charter' in which Favel enfeoffs the spouses (A.2.23–25, 58–68, B.2.42–43, 69–70, 79–104, C.2.43–44, 69–70, 83–108). Simony and Civil – both representing abuses in the ecclesiastical courts – give official assent to the marriage in all three versions.[13]

Another probable constant is the name of Meed's mother: although she is evidently not present at the wedding, all three versions agree on her identity as Amends ('Mendis' in A, 'Amendes' in BC).[14] The formal witnesses to Meed's marriage charter likewise remain more or less the same, beginning each time with Wrong as the first witness, followed by several typical rather than allegorical figures – Munde the Miller, Randolph/Reginald the Reeve, Piers the Pardoner, Bette/Butte the Beadle, traditional types of dishonesty and greed in medieval satire (A.2.72–76, B.2.108–12, C.2.109–13).[15] More interesting changes occur in

[10] See D. L. d'Avray and M. Tausche, 'Marriage Sermons in ad status Collections of the Central Middle Ages,' Archives d'histoire doctrinale et littéraire du moyen âge 47 (1981), 82–85.
[11] Pupilla Oculi (Strassburg, 1514), 123r.
[12] P & M 2:441; cf. Sue Sheridan Walker, 'Widow and Ward: The Feudal Law of Child Custody in Medieval England,' Feminist Studies 3 (1976), 108.
[13] For a careful analysis of the relations among Meed's marriage-brokers, see Gerald Morgan, 'Langland's Conception of Favel, Guile, Liar, and False in the First Vision of Piers Plowman,' Neophil 71 (1987): 626–33. On Civil's close relation to the church courts, see Alexandra Barratt, 'The Characters "Civil" and "Theology" in Piers Plowman,' Traditio 38 (1982), 352–64; Beverly Brian Gilbert, ' "Civil" and the Notaries in Piers Plowman,' MÆ 50 (1981), 49–63.
[14] I follow the lead of the C text, in which Theology calls Amends the 'moder' of Meed; A and B say simply that Meed is 'engendered of' Amends. It is thus possible, though I consider it unlikely, that in AB Langland meant to suggest a dispute between Holy Church and Theology over Meed's father's identity, as over her legitimacy in BC.
[15] Cf. Jill Mann, Chaucer and Medieval Estates Satire: The Literature of Social Classes and the General Prologue to the Canterbury Tales (Cambridge, 1973), 145–52, 160–67. Mann suggests that Chaucer's use of these stereotypes (pardoner, miller, and reeve) may depend in part

the list of informal witnesses – the guests invited to the wedding. In A, these guests include knights, 'comers about,' assize-men, summoners, sellers, beggars, laborers, and the general categories of learned and lewed. In a scene reminiscent of the Prologue, they find lodging in houses, halls, and 'iche feld . . . ful of folk,' pitching 'ten þousand of tentis' in which to await the upcoming wedding (A.2.38–48). The B and C texts offer a slightly longer, more specific guest-list, focused more sharply on venal officialdom: knights, clerks, common people, assize-men, summoners, sheriffs, sheriffs' clerks, beadles, bailiffs, merchants ('brocours of chaffare'), purveyors, victuallers, and advocates. The setting is apparently no longer out of doors; instead, Favel fetches Meed from her bower or chamber (B.2.65; C.2.65), suggesting an interior scene.

Unlike the identity of Meed's mother, Meed's father's name varies curiously in the three texts. In A, he is called Wrong, a name which has already appeared in the poem, clearly identified with the devil, father of lies, violence, and treason (A.1.61–68); False and Meed will eventually dwell with Wrong, according to A.2.71, and he is the first witness of the charter they receive from Favel. In the B text, Meed's father is named False and described as being fickle-tongued, leading to some superficial confusion with his intended son-in-law. In C, his name modulates and multiplies, becoming both Favel 'þat hath a fykel tonge' *and* False, now apparently the son or descendant of Meed's *belsyre* Fickle-tongue (C.2.25, 121).[16] Thus the C text first equates Meed's father with the leading participant in the marital negotiations (a common situation in actual marriages), but then seems to confuse him again with Meed's fiancé, like B.

The apparent inconsistencies caused by these variations in Meed's father's name can be explained in a number of ways. They have been taken as a sign of incomplete revision – Langland making a change at one point without following through on its implications elsewhere.[17]

on their appearance in Langland's poem, although the *Ayenbite of Inwit* had complained of thieving reeves and beadles before Langland (149, 160, 164). She also notes that pardoners are rare in estates satire before Langland and Chaucer; however, the type can be found in English ecclesiastical statutes of the thirteenth and fourteenth centuries, which frequently refer to fraudulent pardoners (*quaestores*). See Powicke and Cheney 352–53, 386, 412, 421, 622–23, 959, 1043, 1113 n. 1; Wilkins 3:84–85.

16 The latter epithet admittedly appears in a subjunctive clause – Theology's assertion that 'Althow Fals were here fader and Fikel-tonge her belsyre, / Amendes was here moder' – but not in such a way that it necessarily implies False is *not* Meed's father. The subjunctive is the expected form after *althow*, whether the conjunction introduces a factual statement ('in spite of the fact that') or one which is contrary to fact or hypothetical ('even if'). See *MED*, s.v. *al-though* 2.

17 Cf. Pearsall, C.2.73n. Detailed discussions of the inconsistencies generated by narrowly literal readings of Meed's parentage will be found in J. J. Jusserand, '*Piers Plowman*: The

Unfortunately, this solution does not adequately account for the *addition* of C.2.121, which calls Meed's father 'False' even though his name had earlier been changed from 'False' to 'Favel,' presumably to avoid the confusion of names created in B. Gerald Morgan makes the interesting suggestion that 'the series of revisions is designed to establish and maintain a distinction between the falseness of Meed by parentage and by marriage' – her parentage signifies that she is intrinsically or 'subjectively' false, erroneous or untrue in herself, while her marriage suggests that she is aimed at a falsely-gained object, 'the corrupt gain that is won by cunning and lying.'[18]

However one interprets the differences in Meed's paternal parentage in the three versions, or deals with the remaining inconsistencies, the similarity of the names must at least serve as a sign of the fundamental similarity of all avatars of falseness. Guile, flattery, lying, fickle tongues, and faithlessness are close kin, morally speaking, so close that they can not be fully distinguished.[19] Indeed, the close spiritual kinship among all these vices and the role that they play in bringing Meed and False together suggests that Langland was imagining Guile, Liar, and Favel as *proximi* to Meed's paternal lineage; moreover, the name and nature of her fiancé False indicate that he too belongs to that lineage. The family is characterized by wrong, deceit, and flattery in all three texts, no matter what name is given to Meed's father. Whether or not Langland intended to suggest father-daughter incest in B or C, the similarities between False, Favel, and Wrong in those texts do leave the impression that Meed is marrying back into her paternal kindred much too closely.[20] If

---

Work of One or Five,' *MP* 6 (1909), 302–05, and John M. Manly, 'The Authorship of *Piers Plowman*,' *MP* 7 (1909), 117–21. Manly argues that C.2.125 (= Pearsall C.2.121) was added before the change of Meed's father's name to 'Favel,' and then forgotten by the time of the name change, but this seems an unnecessarily desperate solution.

[18] 'The Status and Meaning of Meed in the First Vision of *Piers Plowman*,' *Neophil* 72 (1988), 457–58.

[19] On the difficulty of distinguishing some of Langland's allegorical figures, see E. Talbot Donaldson, *Piers Plowman: The C-Text and Its Poet* (1949; rpt. Hamden, 1966), 69–71.

[20] Donaldson, like J. A. W. Bennett, reads the B text's application of 'False' to Meed's father and fiancé as a possible hint of incest (*C-Text*, 69; *Piers Plowman: The Prologue and Passus I–VII of the B Text* [Oxford, 1972], 121). A father-daughter liaison is certainly within the bounds of literary probability; such incest occurs in a similar context in the *Mirour de l'omme*, where the devil first begets Sin, then fathers Death upon her, and finally weds his two children to each other so that they may engender the seven deadly sins, who will eventually be married to the World (cf. *Paradise Lost* 2.727–814 and James 1:15). Non-allegorical tales of father-daughter incest were familiar to medieval audiences as well, from the case of Antiochus and his daughter in the Apollonius legend to the accused-queens tales behind the Constance legend to the *Dux Moraud* story. See Elizabeth Archibald, 'The Flight from Incest: Two Late Classical Precursors to the Constance Theme,' *ChauR* 20 (1986), 259–72; and John Boswell, *The Kindness of Strangers: The Abandonment of Children in Western Europe from Late Antiquity to the Renaissance* (1988; rpt. New York, 1990), 373–78,

we envision these vices as Meed's paternal *proximi* or *amici*, then the social parallel – the letter beneath the allegorical spirit – can be extended even further. Under such a reading, Liar's 'leading' and the 'enchantments' of Favel (whether he is friend or father), can be seen as the efforts of unscrupulous paternal relatives trying to tighten their own family's hold over whatever noble inheritance Meed will receive through her maternal ancestry.

The inconsistencies introduced by Langland's changes in the name of Meed's father are not the only feature of those changes deserving of comment. It is also worth noting that, over the three texts, these paternal names grow increasingly specific as descriptors of Meed's moral origins, though perhaps increasingly limited as forms of evil. The A text's 'Wrong' is probably Satan himself, identified in Passus 1 as Truth's opponent, and the general instigator of human violence and treason as well as deceit. The marriage charter in A encourages such an identification (or at least a very close association) of Wrong and Satan by its clause that Meed and False must yield their souls 'to sathanas to synken in pyne, / Þere to wone wiþ wrong while god is in heuene' (A.2.70–71). In B, the name 'False Fickle-Tongue' for Meed's father suggests verbal wrongs in particular, like those associated with guile, lying, and fawning flattery. C's 'Favel' is yet more specific, focusing on the kind of duplicity that uses fair but insincere speech to gain favors from others, and is thus an even more appropriate name for the progenitor of Meed's complaisant venality. Allegorically and literally, Flattery generates Meed, who inherits her father's talents for smooth talking, as will become evident in Passus 3 and 4. But C still lets us know that Meed's paternal heritage is one of falseness and the fickle or lying tongue – by implication, a heritage that derives ultimately from the Father of Lies himself.

Another variable across the three texts is the question of Meed's birth. In A, it is a simple matter. Theology declares that she is *mulier*, legitimately born of Amends and related to the king: 'a maiden of gode; / She miȝte kisse þe king for cosyn ȝif heo wolde' (A.2.96–97). Since the A text says nothing more about Meed's legitimacy, there seems to be no reason to doubt Theology's claim that Meed has been honorably born

with the suggestion that father-daughter incest may have been perceived as more likely than sibling or Oedipal incest (375, 378).

Not surprisingly, actual instances of paternal incest are rarely recorded; however, one such record appears in the early fourteenth-century Register of Bishop Kellawe of Durham, who excommunicated Sir Ralph Neville 'for the crime of incest and adultery committed with the lady Anastasia his daughter, wife of lord Walter de Faucomberg the younger.' See James Raine, ed., *Depositions and Other Ecclesiastical Proceedings from the Courts of Durham*, SS 21 (London, 1845), 10.

into a noble maternal lineage. Her marriage to the beguiler False, a bastard of diabolic antecedents, is a clear case of disparagement, a social injury from which heirs and heiresses were protected by English law.[21] Thus, in reading A, our initial evaluation of Meed – based on her father's evil nature and the bad company she keeps – is negative; it must then be temporarily modified on the grounds of this new information from Theology. Only with the complaint of Peace will we see incontrovertible, concrete evidence of Meed's perilous likeness to her father Wrong.

In B and C, the question of Meed's legitimacy is not so clear: Theology's claims about Meed's and False's respective births remain the same, but they are seriously undermined by the earlier, presumably authoritative assertion of Holy Church: 'She is a bastard' (B.2.24, C.2.24). The subsequent characterization of Holy Church as a noble lady who is highly and perhaps 'pettishly' conscious of lineage, behavior, and status may have humorous overtones;[22] but it does not in my view give us serious cause to doubt the harsh truth of her accusation, any more than the humor in Study's scolding of Wit devalues her suspicions about Will's motives. It seems most unlikely that, for Langland, the authority of Holy Church herself would be automatically superseded by the objections of Theology, with its sometimes misty subtleties and its readiness to raise objections for the sake of argument – the *videtur quod* tactic (cf. A.11.137–40, B.10.185–88, C.11.129–32).

To be sure, from the abstract plane on which Theology operates, Meed may appear to have genuine claims to legitimate descent from Amends – in other words, to be a legitimate development of the notion of just restitution or fair return. But it can also be argued that Holy Church has more *kynde knowing* than Theology, a more direct apprehension of Meed's dishonorable nature and origin, and that Langland added her remark on Meed's bastardy to raise immediate doubts in readers' minds when Theology makes his claim in B and C. As in the A text, that claim should still lead us to re-examine our understanding of Meed's nature, since it shows that a right-meaning and learned entity like Theology might see potential good in Meed, but the general authority of Holy Church ought to make us at least somewhat uneasy about automatically accepting Theology's analysis at face value.[23] Indeed, the events of the

---

[21] P & M 1:319. See also Walker, 'The Marrying of Feudal Wards in Medieval England,' *Studies in Medieval Culture* 4 (1974), 213–14.

[22] Bennett, *Piers Plowman*, 121; John Norton-Smith calls Holy Church's attack on Meed 'petulant,' in *William Langland* (Leiden, 1983), 57. However, it should be noted that the indignation of allegorical female teachers at their rivals can be traced at least as far back as Lady Philosophy's reaction to the Muses of poetry in the *Consolation of Philosophy*.

[23] Recent arguments for Meed's evil nature (and Theology's consequent error in

following two passus will prove that practice speaks louder than theory, and that even well-intentioned, well-educated human intelligence can give Meed more credit than she deserves.[24]

The B and C texts extend Holy Church's animadversions on Meed's family in at least two other interesting ways. First, they introduce the idea of *kynde* following *kynde* to explain the legacy of bad *mores* which Meed has received from her father. Langland probably came to see this concept as important for his poem during the initial writing of Wit's speech, with its attention to the descent of vice and virtue along familial lines (assuming, as seems likely, that A.10 was composed after A.2). Besides referring to the idea in the BC versions of Holy Church's comments on Meed, Langland expands on it in the B and C revisions of Wit's speech, thereby demonstrating its significance in his thought and suggesting some relationship between Meed's allegorical kinship and the literal kinship ties analyzed by Wit. Here in Passus B.2/C.2, we find the notion expressed thus:

> And Mede is manered after hym as men of kynde carpeþ:
> *Qualis pater talis filius: Bona arbor bonum fructum facit.* (B.2.27–27a)

> And Mede is manered aftur hym, as men of kynde carpeth:
> *Talis pater, talis filia.*
> For shal neuer breere bere berye as a vine
> Ne on a croked kene thorn kynde fyge wexe:
> *Bona arbor bonum fructum facit.* (C.2.27–29a)

The biblical and proverbial maxim 'A good tree bringeth forth good fruit' (Mt. 7:17) was already implicit in Wit's use of seed, root, and fruit metaphors in the A text to describe the familial generation of vices and virtues (A.10.134–38, 155–59, 190–92). When Langland returned to Holy Church's speech in B.2, he asserts the idea explicitly, applying it to Meed in the lines just quoted. Then, in Wit's speech in B.9, he again

judgment) include J. A. Burrow, *Langland's Fictions* (Oxford, 1993), 34–40; Roger Eaton, 'Langland's Malleable Lady Meed,' *Costerus* n.s. 80 (1991), 119–41; and Paula J. Carlson, 'Lady Meed and God's Meed: The Grammar of "Piers Plowman" B 3 and C 4,' *Traditio* 46 (1991), 291–311. For reviews of previous critical positions, see Eaton, 120–21; Carlson, 295–96 nn. 4–7. A more neutral stance is taken by James Simpson, *Introduction to the B-Text*, 43–49, though he concludes his discussion of Meed's ambiguity by observing that in passus 4, she 'enacts her pejorative senses in the trial of Wrong, thereby concluding the debate as to whether or not she can marry Conscience' (48).

[24] Still, the difference between Holy Church and Theology on Meed's birth remains an interpretive crux. Clear resolution of the crux may be facilitated by detailed investigation of the differences and ambiguities in fourteenth-century definitions of bastardy in England. Starting points might include R. H. Helmholz, 'Bastardy Litigation in Medieval England,' *American Journal of Legal History* 13 (1969), 360–83; J. L. Barton, 'Nullity of Marriage and Illegitimacy in the England of the Middle Ages,' in Dafydd Jenkins, ed., *Legal History Studies 1972* (Cardiff, 1975), 28–49; and Chris Given-Wilson and Alice Curteis, *The Royal Bastards of Medieval England* (London, 1984).

adds explicit references to the proverb, first by loosely paraphrasing Mt. 7:17, and then by quoting the preceding biblical verse, 'Numquam [Vulg. *Numquid*] colligunt de spinis vuas nec de tribulis ficus' (B.9.146–55a; Mt. 7:16). Later still, while working on C.2.27–29a, Langland seems to have been influenced once more by the immediately-previous version of Wit's speech, adding two lines in C.2 which virtually translate B.9.155a, 'Numquam colligunt, etc.' He continues working with the idea in C.10.242–42a, which states outright that 'kynde folweth kynde' and supports that statement by quoting both Mt. 7:16 and Mt. 7:17.[25] As we will see in Chapter 2, the concept of *kynde* following *kynde* plays a major role in Wit's explanation of how Do-wel is rooted in actual human wedlock. In the Meed episode, however, the *Talis pater* and *Bona arbor* sayings make a point more allegorical than literal, emphasizing Meed's inherent evil 'manners' by associating them with the obviously evil nature of her progenitor, whether he is called False or Favel.

The second way in which B and C develop Holy Church's remarks on Meed's family is through her sharpening of contrasts between herself and her scarlet-clad opponent, especially the contrasts between their respective pedigrees and matrimonial intentions. In A, Holy Church simply compares her own higher birth and rank with Meed's base origins and ill-gained status at the papal court (A.2.16–21). In B and C we learn specifically who Holy Church's father is, who her leman is, and the quality of her and Meed's respective relationships to their various suitors.

The two later versions differ somewhat on these topics, but not as significantly as they both differ from A's non-treatment of the questions: for instance, B and C respectively describe Holy Church as daughter of 'þe grete god' or as daughter of God the Son (B.2.29; C.2.31). Interestingly, Langland does not take the easiest path in assigning a lover to Holy Church – that is, naming Christ as her leman. Instead, both texts make Leaute her leman (B.2.21; C.2.20). And while we might equate Leaute and Christ in B, the C text seems to block that interpretation deliberately, by calling Holy Church the daughter of *filius dei*.

B and C also differ in the ways they describe the relationship between Holy Church and her other suitors. In B, Langland adventurously suggests that she accepts other lovers, those who are *leel* like her leman

---

[25] A linear development of the motif across and within the three versions is the simplest way to account for these related revisions: A.10 > B.2 > B.9 > C.2 > C.10. However, anyone familiar with the complexities of revision will recognize that revisers do not always follow the shortest or simplest processes in modifying a text, and Langland's 'kynde folweth kynde' passages may have evolved in some other way entirely.

Leaute and merciful like the Lady herself, with her marriage portion of mercy and her right to take it to whatever spouse she chooses:[26]

> [God my father] haþ yeuen me mercy to marie wiþ myselue,
> And what man be merciful and leelly me loue
> Shal be my lord and I his leef in þe heiȝe heuene.
> And what man takeþ Mede, myn heed dar I legge,
> That he shal lese for hire loue a lippe of *Caritatis*. (B.2.31–35)

While one could certainly explicate B's language here in an orthodox way – perhaps with an argument about all *leel* men being incorporated into Leaute as all Christians are incorporated into the Mystical Body – Langland may have decided that the figure was not appropriate in the C text. Perhaps he felt that it makes Holy Church a little *too* analogous to Meed, without sufficiently distinguishing incorporation from promiscuity. In any event, the image shifts from one of marital suit to one of suit for courtly favor:

> y am [*filius dei's*] dere doughter, ducchesse of heuene,
> That what man me louyeth and my wille foleweth
> Shal haue grace to good ynow and a good ende,
> And what man Mede loueth, my lyf y dar wedde,
> He shal lese for here loue a lippe of trewe charite. (C.2.33–37)

Moreover, C changes the clause 'what man takeþ Mede' to 'what man Mede loueth,' perhaps to defuse the sexual or marital connotations of the verb 'to take [a woman].'[27] There will be plenty of language later asserting Meed's promiscuity, and suggesting it here is not essential. The favor in which Holy Church stands with her father is still noted, no longer in terms of her freedom to marry herself but as 'his dere doughter, ducchesse of heuene,' able to grant grace to all good men.

---

[26] The freedom to 'marry oneself' was valued highly enough that women from the top to the bottom of the social hierarchy were often willing to pay higher fees or fines for it, with their own money or the aid of family or friends, either before or after a marriage. See Walker, 'Free Consent and the Marriage of Feudal Wards in Medieval England,' *Journal of Medieval History* 8 (1982), 126, 129; and Judith M. Bennett, 'Medieval Peasant Marriage: An Examination of Marriage License Fines in *Liber Gersumarum*,' in J. A. Raftis, ed., *Pathways to Mediaeval Peasants*, Papers in Mediaeval Studies 2 (Toronto, 1981), 193–246. Given Holy Church's 'dowry' (as I take it) of mercy and her admitted love for Leaute, the traits she seeks in a husband – mercy and *leel* love – are to be expected; as Wit will recommend later, marriages should be based on the attraction of like natures and like virtues. See Stokes, *Justice and Mercy*, 99–103.
[27] On the sexual connotations of B.2.34–35, see Priscilla Martin, *Piers Plowman: The Field and the Tower* (London, 1979), 78.

The Marriage of Meed

The Marriage Ceremony and Charter

Holy Church leaves Will after warning him about Meed's family origins, friends, and promised spouse; she also warns him to stay away from all who belong to or love their 'lordship,' those who place themselves under the patronage of Meed, False, Wrong, Favel, Guile, and Liar. Following her indignation at Meed's prestige in the world, Holy Church's withdrawal from the scene can easily be read as a refusal to sanction the upcoming wedding by her presence. Although Meed and False fulfill the letter of canon law by getting Simony and Civil to assent to their marriage and by celebrating it publicly, the departure of the Lady in white before the ceremony suggests that the true Church cannot countenance its enactment, no matter what her corrupt representatives may do. From a rigorous spiritual perspective – *in foro interno* perhaps – one might say that Meed is not truly marrying *in facie ecclesiae* as canon law demanded, and thus not really entering lawful wedlock at all.

Nonetheless, the union of Meed and False initially appears to meet most of the external canonical requirements for a valid marriage. Both spouses consent to the alliance; ecclesiastical authorities with jurisdiction over marriage agree to it after seeing 'hir boþer wille' (B.2.67–68, C.2.67–68; A implies the same, though more weakly, in 2.51–55).[28] Nor is the marriage in any way clandestine. Indeed, the entire retinue of each party is invited: those that reign with False or are rooted in false life, kin of Meed as well as of False, invited from or by both sides of the proposed alliance (A.2.33–34, B.2.54–55, C.2.55–57). This great rout of folk has been bidden to the bridal in order to 'wytnesse wel what þe writ wolde, / In what maner þat mede in mariage was feffid' (A.2.46–47), or as B puts it, 'to marien þis mayde,' in the sense of participating in the wedding (B.2.57).

As scholars have often noted, the Church's insistence on public celebrations of marriage was an important part of her campaign against clandestine unions.[29] Less frequently discussed is the fact that matri-

[28] Besides being taken to represent simony in general, Sir Simony can be read in particular as the venal abuse of canon law in the church courts; Sir Civil as the corruption of the church courts by concepts and procedures from Roman civil law, and by the greedy self-interest associated with the study of civil law. See Barratt, ' "Civil" and "Theology," ' and Gilbert, 'Civil and the Notaries.' Since the church courts decided the validity of contested marriages, and since Langland says that Simony and Civil give their approval to the marriage after learning the will of the spouses, it does not seem too far-fetched to see these allegorical ecclesiasts as metaphorical equivalents to the local priest. Langland's failure to mention the church door here seems to me no more likely to imply a clandestine marriage than does Chaucer's failure to mention church-door solemnization for the well-witnessed marriage of Griselda. But for a narrower reading of Meed's marriage as clandestine and unpriested, see Bennett, *Piers Plowman*, 128, 131.
[29] On this topic, see the illuminating work of Helmholz, *Marriage Litigation*; Michael M.

13

monial publicity was just as important to secular society, at least in weddings with significant economic implications to the parties involved. In such marriages, it was obviously advantageous to the couple and their families that the terms of the union be witnessed or recorded in such a way as to prevent the abrogation of those terms in the future. (Medieval awareness of this advantage is demonstrated by such texts as the Wife of Bath's Prologue, where marriage at the church door is tantamount to acquisition of dower.) The motive behind the adherence by Meed and False to legal proprieties need hardly be one of devout obedience to the Church or concern for the public avowal of a spiritual bond; the kinds of people they invite to their wedding are far more suited as witnesses to the fact that Meed is married 'more for here richesse' (C.2.80; cf. B.2.76) than as witnesses to a truly virtuous union.

With the publicity of the ceremony demonstrated, the poem moves on to the formalities of the marriage rites proper. The A text, far more than B or C, presents these rites in language overtly parodic of medieval English marriage liturgies. Compare, for instance, A.2.49–56 –

> Þanne fauel fettiþ hire forþ & to fals takiþ
> In foreward þat falshed shal fynde hire for euere,
> And heo be boun at his bode his bidding to fulfille,
> At bedde & at boord buxum and hende,
> And as sire symonye wile segge to sewen his wille.
> Symonye & cyuyle stondiþ forþ boþe
> And vnfolde þe feffement þat fals haþ ymakid;
> Þus begynne þe gomes & gredde wel hei3e

– with the following excerpts from medieval English service books:

> Primo legitur dotalium: deinde detur femina viro, si ambo consenserint. (Parish Missal of Hanley Castle; 13th c.)[30]

Sheehan, 'Marriage Theory and Practice in the Conciliar Legislation and Diocesan Statutes of Mediaeval England,' *MS* 40 (1978), 408–60; and James A. Brundage, *Law, Sex, and Christian Society in Medieval Europe* (Chicago, 1987), 361–64, 440–43, 496–501. Henry A. Kelly places the concern about clandestinity in its literary contexts in *Love and Marriage in the Age of Chaucer* (Ithaca, 1975), 163–242. One can judge the significance of the problem from the official point of view by examining the frequent strictures against clandestine marriages in thirteenth- and fourteenth-century ecclesiastical legislation, available in Powicke and Cheney, *Councils and Synods*, covering 1205 to 1313, and Wilkins, *Concilia*, vols. 2 and 3 for the fourteenth century. Interestingly, clandestinity does not seem to be as major an issue for Langland as lawful but covetous marriage-making. See below, pp. 17–19, 92–99, and 189–90.
[30] Ed. William G. Henderson, in *Manuale et Processionale ad Usum Insignis Ecclesiae Eboracensis*, SS 63 (Durham, 1875), 163.*

Ante omnia ueniant ad ianuas ecclesie sub testimonio populorum qui in thoro maritali coniungendi sunt. et requiratur consensus utriusque a sacerdote. et fiat recapitulacio de dote mulieris . . . et tunc demum detur a patre uel amicis suis. quam uir recipiat in fide dei [et] in su[a] sanam et infirmam quam diu uixerit seruandam. (Sarum Missal A, l. 13th c.)[31]

Ueniente uiro cum muliere ad ecclesiam cum propinquis et amicis et ad hostium ecclesie stantibus inquirat sacerdos primo tam et uiro quam a muliere et eciam a circumstantibus utrum hec conuencio inter illos legittime fieri posset. . . . interroget sacerdos homine[m] ex nomine ita. sic habeas mulierem in legittimam uxorem accipere ita ut eam sicut christianus debet sponsam suam in dei fide et tu[a] tam [in] infirmitate quam in sanitate uelis custodire. quo respondente uolo. Inquirat a muliere utrum uelit hominem illum pro legittimo sponso habere eique per omnia fidem seruare. qua respondente uolo. Propinquus ipsius per manum dexteram tradat eam uiro dicens. Et ego in nomine domini eam tibi trado. Postea sponsus det sponse per cutellum dotem. (Sarum Missal B; e. 14th c.)[32]

Statuantur uir et mulier ante ostium ecclesie coram Deo et populo. . . . Deinde dicat sacerdos cunctis audientibus, in lingua materna. N. Vis habere hanc mulierem in sponsam N. eam diligere et honorare, tenere, et custodire tam sanam, quam infirmam, sicut sponsus debet sponsam, et omnes alias propter eam dimittere, et illi soli adherere, quamdiu vita utriusque vestrum duraverit. Respondit vir. Volo. Iterum dicat sacerdos ad mulierem. N. Vis habere hunc virum N. in sponsum tuum et ei obedire et servire, et eum diligere, et honorare, custodire sanum et infirmum, et omnes alios propter eum dimittere, et illi soli adherere quamdiu vita utriusque vestrum duraverit. Respondeat mulier. Volo. Deinde detur femina a patre suo vel ab aliquo amico. . . . [Dicat vir:] Here Ich N. take ye N. to my weddud wife, to haven and to holden fro þys day forward, for betre, for wors, for rycher, for porer, in syknesse, and in helthe, tyl deth us departe, yf holy chyrche hyt wol ordeyne, and thereto I plyȝth my treuthe. . . . [Dicat mulier:] Ich N. take ye N. to my weddyd hosebound, to haven and to holden fro þys day forward, for betre, for wors, for rycher, for porer, in sekenesse, and in helthe, to be boneyre and buxom in bedde and at boorde, tyl deth us depart, yf holychurch hyt wol ordeyne, and ther to I plyȝth my trewthe. (Pontifical of Edmund Lacy, Bishop of Exeter; l. 14th to e. 15th c.).[33]

[31] Ed. J. Wickham Legg, *The Sarum Missal: Edited from Three Early MSS* (1916; rpt. Oxford, 1969), 413.

[32] *Sarum Missal*, 413. The phrase *per cutellum* here refers to the symbolic delivery of seisin by the handing over of a knife by the donor to the donee; more typical in late fourteenth- and fifteenth-century marriage services was the transfer of silver or gold, usually a coin or coins placed on the service book, and presumably given to the bride. Cf. Gower, *Confessio Amantis* 5.557–61.

[33] Ed. Ralph Barnes, *Liber Pontificalis of Edmund Lacy, Bishop of Exeter* (Exeter, 1847), 257–58. I have silently emended y and z to þ and ȝ where appropriate.

Similar trothplights in English can be found in other fifteenth- and sixteenth-century matrimonial *ordines*.[34] Though they vary somewhat, most of them agree on the woman's promise to be 'buxom at bed and board,' to obey and serve her husband, and on the husband's promise to support his wife. The manuals continue to prescribe that the woman be given 'a patre vel ab amicis' (occasionally by a 'propinquus'), that the dotal agreement be read or that a symbolic transfer of the dowry be enacted, that the wedding be celebrated 'coram publicis et honestis personis ad hoc constitutis' or 'coram deo, sacerdote et populo,' and that the couple's mutual consent is subject to the 'ordaining' of Holy Church.[35]

The A text has given us an unmistakable depiction of the *traditio* of the bride by her *amicus* Favel; the responsibility of the groom to provide and of the bride to obey; the role played by ecclesiastical authorities in instructing couples on these responsibilities and in 'ordaining' the acceptability of a given marriage, albeit for covetous motives here; the 'foreward' which expresses the consent of the various parties to the marriage and the related property settlement; and the public declaration of that settlement.[36] B and C do not offer us such a clear set of allusions to the marriage ceremony, though they do retain the image of Meed being given by her friend or father Favel, and refer more directly to the mutual consent of Meed and False. They may also add a parodic allusion to the troth-plight in the marriage charter: given the matrimonial context, the phrase 'vnbuxome and bolde' (B.2.83, C.2.87) would probably have recalled the bride's promise to be 'boneyre and buxom,'

---

[34] See Henderson, *Manuale . . . Eboracensis*, 26–27 (York), 115*–16* (Hereford), and 167* (St Asaph); and A. Jefferies Collins, ed., *Manuale ad Usum Percelebris Ecclesiae Sarisburiensis*, HBS 91 (Chichester, 1960), 47–48. English trothplights also appear in B.L. MS Add. 30506, ed. Henry Littlehales, *English Fragments from Latin Medieval Service Books*, EETS e.s. 90 (London, 1903), 5–6, and in MS Royal 2.A.xxi (fols. 17a–18a).

[35] According to the Sarum Manual, the bride should be given 'a patre suo vel ab amicis eius' (Collins 47) – the father's friends, not the bride's – suggesting that the *amici* were likely to be from the father's side of the family, at least by the time of the Manual's 16th-c. edition (and probably earlier, given the relative conservatism of these liturgical texts and rituals).

[36] The marriage *ordines* say 'dos' and 'dotalium,' which could strictly refer to the dower from husband to wife, since dower was legally dependent on the church-door ceremony. But the real situation was probably looser, and other grants to the parties could also be declared at the time of marriage. Bracton says that marriage gifts to the couple from the bride's family might be made before, at, or after the nuptials (*De Legibus* 2:77). Medieval references to such gifts seldom say whether they were read at the church door, since their force did not depend on that circumstance; however, one instance where a church door declaration of the marriage gift happens to be mentioned appears in C. N. L. Brooke and M. M. Postan, eds., *Carte Nativorum: A Peterborough Abbey Cartulary of the Fourteenth Century*, Northamptonshire Record Society 20 (Oxford, 1960), 18–19.

though certainly not so strongly as A's 'At bedde & at boorde buxum and hende.'[37]

While it must be granted that B and C do not echo the language of the marriage rite as distinctly as A, we should recognize that they do still present several basic elements of that ceremony: the handing over of the bride, the verification of mutual consent by ecclesiastical authorities, and the public declaration of the marriage settlement, all performed before a crowd of witnesses. However, one important feature of a proper wedding service is missing in all three texts: the inquiry into possible impediments to the union. Fortunately, Theology's unsought but vigorous objection to the marriage will repair this omission, as we will see more fully below.

A number of other interesting new details appear in the B and C passages leading up to the marriage charter. Perhaps the most significant of these occurs in the description of Favel's presentation of the bride. He acts 'as a Brocour,' bringing Meed forth for False like a merchant producing wares, and like a matchmaker who has negotiated the marriage. As noted above, the A text also refers to this matchmaking, showing Favel, Guile, and Liar to be variously involved in the marriage arrangements: Favel forges the union with fair speech, Guile 'begoes' or deceptively persuades Meed to consent to False, and (anticipating the pun in Shakespeare's Sonnet 138) Liar leads them to lie together (A.2.23–25). Although B and C condense and slightly modify the initial reference to the persuasive 'leading' by which the marriage is arranged, they are then much more explicit about the mercenary features of those arrangements when they describe the marriage ceremony and charter. 'Brocours of chaffare' are added to the list of guests invited to witness the marriage; Favel treats Meed as a broker of chaffer might treat a commodity he is offering; Simony and Civil approve the marriage 'at silver's prayer'; the charter itself asserts that she is married more for her wealth than for her virtue or beauty or gentle blood; and 'bargaynes and brocages' are among the territories added to the list of properties in the marriage charter (B.2.60, 66, 68, 76–78, 88, C.2.60, 66, 68, 80–82, 92). Later in C, just before the procession to Westminster, the mercenary quality of Meed's marriage will be mentioned anew: 'To be maried for mone Med hath assented' (C.2.170).

Skeat and Bennett have commented helpfully on the matrimonial connotations of the words *brocage* and *brocour* in Langland's day,[38] but

---

[37] The reversed word order, 'bolde and vnbuxum,' of B.2.83 in MSS R and F may reflect scribal memory of the common liturgical collocation placing 'buxum' second in the alliterative doublet (Add. 30506, Exeter, St Asaph, Sarum Manual).

[38] Skeat 2:34–35; Bennett, *Piers Plowman*, 125.

one or two other lexical details of the words are also worthy of note. Both words first appear in English in the late fourteenth century, and immediately display both their marital/sexual and their mercantile/ larcenous senses. Langland, Chaucer, and Gower are among the first writers cited by the *MED* as using them; Langland's use probably antedates Chaucer's and Gower's. Interestingly, the *MED* citations for the marital senses are, with one exception, taken only from the three Ricardian poets; and for that exception ('brokers,' in *The Assembly of the Gods* 702),[39] the marital/sexual sense is questionable – the editor of the *Assembly* suggests 'receivers of stolen goods' rather than the *MED*'s 'go-between, match-maker, procurer.' Perhaps the use of these terms in marital and sexual contexts was peculiar to late fourteenth-century literary circles, though such a hypothesis would be difficult to establish conclusively.

What can be definitively asserted, however, is Langland's outrage at the use of *brocage* in matrimonial decision-making. In Wit's speech, he inveighs against its contemporary occurrence (A.10.181-201, B.9.158-81, C.10.254-80; see Chap. 2, pp. 92-99 below). Later in B and C, Patience compares giving up all one's wealth for Christ to rejecting familial *brocage* for the sake of a marriage of affection (B.14.262-73, C.16.102-13; see Chap. 4, pp. 188-89 below). To enter a sacramental relationship that should be based on love and on law as though it were a commodity to be chaffered over for the best 'bargayne': such behavior sharply illustrates the infection of human society by cupidity. It also reflects, with a reformer's heightened sensitivity, the actual and common traffic in marriages in medieval England. While that traffic was generally accepted by those whom it affected, and might at times take into account the affections of the potential spouses, it was nonetheless an extremely lucrative business which could be used to make a personal profit, pay off social debts, or show political favor.[40]

[39] Ed. Oscar L. Triggs, EETS e.s. 69 (London, 1896).
[40] See Walker, 'Widow and Ward,' 'Free Consent,' 'Marrying of Feudal Wards,' and 'Feudal Constraint and Free Consent in the Making of Marriages in Medieval England: Widows in the King's Gift,' *Canadian Historical Association Papers* (Ottawa, 1979), 97-110; J. A. Tuck, 'Richard II's System of Patronage,' in F. R. H. du Boulay and Caroline M. Barron, eds., *The Reign of Richard II: Essays in Honour of May McKisack* (London, 1971), 1-20. For the critical importance of advantageous marriages to the upper aristocracy, see G. A. Holmes, *The Estates of the Higher Nobility in Fourteenth-Century England* (Cambridge, 1957), 7-45, and Waugh, *Lordship of England*, especially Chaps. 4-5, pp. 144-231.
Other economic and socio-political aspects of medieval marriage decisions can be seen in the merchet payments made by peasants (J. M. Bennett, 'Peasant Marriage,' and Eleanor Searle, 'Seigneurial Control of Women's Marriage: The Antecedents and Function of Merchet in England,' *Past and Present* 82 [1979], 3-43); in documents like the letter to Robert Hallum, eventual Bishop of Salisbury, seeking his support in the courtship of a wealthy widow (in A. R. Myers, ed., *English Historical Documents IV: 1327-1485* [London,

Marital *brocage* could also involve payments to parties with some claim on the spouses' properties, or fees incurred in marriage litigation or in winning dispensations from matrimonial impediments.[41] In all three texts of *Piers*, Wit's speech will show that Langland saw this intertwining of money and matrimony as evidence that contemporary marriages were based more on 'covetise of catel' than on love and similarity between the spouses. As with the addition of the 'kind follows kind' theme at the start of BC.2, the new BC emphasis on *brocage* in the marriage ceremony reveals how developments in later sections of one text of the poem could influence revisions in the next version.

Two more details of the revised ritual action in B and C should be mentioned. First, both texts describe the charter as being 'read' by Simony but only 'seen' by Civil, perhaps reflecting the fact that matrimonial decisions in the church courts would have been substantively based on canon law, though the details of procedure and form could have been influenced by civil law.[42] Second, the slight primacy which Simony has over Civil here is reinforced in C, where Simony proclaims the marriage charter alone instead of in unison with Civil, as in AB (C.2.74, A.2.56, B.2.74). Civil is still present and can hear the charter in C, of course, but he has a less active role in its promulgation. A related change may be found in Theology's objection to the marriage, addressed originally to Civil in AB, but to Simony in C (A.2.80, B.2.116, C.2.117).[43]

1969], 1193–94; the Stonor, Paston, and Cely correspondences; and the occasional marriage agreements scattered across the *CCR* (e.g., 1354–60: 92–94; 1360–64: 148, 425–27; 1364–68: 263, 501; 1369–74: 555–58; 1377–81: 335, 359; 1381–85: 249–50, 297–98, 442–43), the *CAD* (e.g., 2:301, 418; 3:289, 464–65; 4:357, quoted in *EHD* 4:992–93; 5:470), and other public records. See also n. 46 below.

[41] On court costs in marriage cases, see Helmholz, *Marriage Litigation*, 161–62. For multiple-party involvement in the marriage contract, see for instance the elaborate marriage agreement between Michael de la Pole and Warin de Lisle for the marriage of their respective daughter and son, where several family associates on each side are involved in the arrangements for land and money granted between the parties, and in the penalties for default on either side (*CCR* 1369–74: 555–58). Similar economic, social, and nuptial interdependencies among county gentry are described by Michael J. Bennett, in *Community, Class and Careerism: Cheshire and Lancashire Society in the Age of Sir Gawain and the Green Knight*, Cambridge Studies in Medieval Life and Thought, 3rd ser. 18 (Cambridge, 1983), 26–30.

[42] For instance, notaries, who drew up documents for use in the church courts, had their origins in Roman civil law. The reference to 'sealing the charter by Simony's sight and Civil's leave' (B.2.114, C.2.115; A: 'and notaries' signs') probably reflects the importance of civilian principles and forms in matters of documentary procedure. See Gilbert, 'Civil and the Notaries,' 50–51, 58–61, and C. R. Cheney, *Notaries Public in England in the Thirteenth and Fourteenth Centuries* (Oxford, 1972), 12–14, 40–51.

[43] On developments in the roles of Civil and Simony across the three texts, see Gilbert, 'Civil and the Notaries,' 56–58, and (with some differences) my '*Piers Plowman* and the Liturgy of St. Lawrence: Composition and Revision in Langland's Poetry,' *SP* 84 (1987), 254–55.

Perhaps the most memorable element of the ceremony performed by Meed, False, and their families, friends, and followers is the charter in which the spouses are jointly enfeoffed of ˋthe capital sins. A real fourteenth-century couple might live off the lands granted to them at their wedding, if they had not yet received their inheritances or otherwise acquired their own properties. Allegorically speaking, Meed and False will 'live off' the Seven Deadly Sins, in that those sins will provide a steady stream of folk who support the false and seek Meed's favor in order to hide or further their own wickedness.

The charter of enfeoffment has a number of probable and possible literary antecedents, from the traditional handlings of the Seven Deadly Sins to the charters of Christ and the Devil's letters and charters found elsewhere in medieval religious and satiric literature.[44] It also has antecedents in actual marriage contracts among wealthy late-medieval families, which, as Beatrice Gottlieb points out, 'could be the most important legal documents in their lives, usually far more important than wills, which were less common.'[45] Like the literary charters of the Devil, its primary satirical technique is the imitation of actual legal language and form: 'Wyten & wytnessen' and *Sciant presentes & futuri*; 'to haue & to holde & here eires aftir'; *feffe, sese, graunte*; the long lists of lands and offices or rights given, along with their *purtenaunces*; the *ȝeldinge* of rent after a year; and finally the list of witnesses, date, and seal. All these features of Favel's charter to Meed and False can be readily found in contemporary documents recording the transfer of property rights, whether related to a marriage or not.[46]

---

[44] See Morton W. Bloomfield, *The Seven Deadly Sins: An Introduction to the History of a Religious Concept, with Special Reference to Medieval English Literature* (East Lansing, 1952), 199 and *passim*; Mary Caroline Spalding, *The Middle English Charters of Christ* (Bryn Mawr, 1914), xxxvi–lxii. On the devil's charters, which appear to have been less widespread than the charters of Christ, and the more common devil's letters, see Paul Lehmann, *Die Parodie im Mittelalter*, 2nd ed. (Stuttgart, 1963), 57–70, and Robert R. Raymo, 'A Middle English Version of the *Epistola Luciferi ad Cleros*,' in D. A. Pearsall and R. A. Waldron, eds., *Medieval Literature and Civilization: Studies in Memory of G. N. Garmonsway* (London, 1969), 233–48.

[45] *The Family in the Western World from the Black Death to the Industrial Age* (New York and Oxford, 1993), 73–74.

[46] Many examples of actual land grants can be found in Thomas Madox, *Formulare Anglicanum* (London, 1702); a number of the charters printed here are marriage agreements, granting land to a couple being married (pp. 79–80, 81, 92–94, 99–100). See also S. C. Ratcliff et al., eds., *Legal and Manorial Formularies Edited from Originals at the British Museum and the Public Record Office, In Memory of Julius Parnell Gilson* (Oxford, 1933), 1–11. Extant marriage agreements from the fourteenth century are in Latin and French; around a hundred Middle English marriage agreements, all from the fifteenth century, are listed in the Index of Sources of the *Linguistic Atlas of Late Mediaeval English*, ed. Angus McIntosh et al., 4 vols. (Aberdeen, 1986), 1:59–171. Of these, about a fifth are in print. For

The satirical bite comes of course from the changes made in these familiar forms and phrases. The most important twist is in the kinds of lands and rights granted to the couple: instead of actual pieces of land and familiar feudal rights like the presentation to benefices or the levying of various duties and fees, we have allegorical properties of sin and figurative 'rights' to various wicked activities. The complexity of the catalogue of rights and properties is not atypical of medieval charters; even at the most modest social levels, one can find grants comprising all sorts of bits and pieces of property. What *is* atypical about the grant to Meed and False is the princely quality and extent of the territories they receive – an earldom, a kingdom or county, a castle and lordship, and a town, not to mention their being named 'princes in pride.' The wealth and power that would be involved in an actual grant of this kind could be found only in the very highest social ranks. Indeed, aside from its non-marital nature, the charter investing the Black Prince with the principality of Aquitaine, cited by Skeat in connection with this passage, remains one of the aptest analogues I know for Favel's enfeoffment of Meed and False.[47] A real marriage that brought this much power into the hands of someone as treacherous as False would have been a clear political menace to king and kingdom alike; allegorically, Meed's marriage poses an equally serious and unmistakable threat.

Other twists on standard charter-forms include the type of rent, the expression of the date, and the kinds of witnesses who sign the charter. '3eldinge . . . / Here soulis to sathanas . . . / . . . to wone wiþ wrong [B: in wo] while god is in heuene' (A.2.69–71, B.2.105–07; not in C) is a far cry from simple monetary payments, however large. It is even

---

further discussion of the legal language in the poem, see John A. Alford, *Piers Plowman: A Glossary of Legal Diction* (Cambridge, 1988).

[47] Skeat, 2:34, citing Joshua Barnes' translation of the original Latin and French documents published in John Selden's *Titles of Honor*. The similarities of language can be seen in the following excerpts: 'We therefore . . . , O our most Dear Son, . . . intending by a liberal Recompence to do Honour unto You, who lately in the Parts of Aquitain and Gascogne, while there the frequent Storms of War raged, for our Sakes did not refuse the Summer Dust and the Labour then of our Cares, . . . do convey and grant unto You by these Presents, the Principality of the under-written Lands and Provinces of all Aquitain and Gascogne; Willing and Granting, that . . . You from henceforth be the true Prince [thereof]. . . . [And] We give and grant unto You . . . the City and Castle, and all the Land and Country of Poictou, together with the Fief of Thouars, and the Land of Belleville; . . . the Earldom, Land and Country of Gaure; . . . the City and Castle of Dax and the Town and Castle of St Sever; . . . To HAVE and to HOLD from Us under Liege Homage. . . together with all the Isles thereto belonging, Homages, Allegiances, Honours, ... Jurisdictions, High, Mean and Low, . . . Advousons and Patronages . . . the Duties, Cens, Rents, . . . and all their Rights and Purtenances. . . . Datum sub Magni Sigilli Nostri Testimonio in Palatio nostro Westmonasterii die 19 Mensis Julii, Anno Domini Millesimo, Tercentesimo, Sexagesimo, Secundo, & Regni Nostri Tricesimo Sexto' (Barnes, *The History of that Most Victorious Monarch Edward IIId* [Cambridge, 1688], 620).

farther from the not uncommon practice of asking merely 'a rose at midsummer' or other nominal service for lands granted as a marriage portion. In C, the final dwelling-place of Meed and False comes to sound more like an ironic additional grant than a payment – or rather, a grant which is itself the cost of the charter as a whole: to live forever 'in lordschip with Lucifer, . . . / With alle þe appurtinaunces of purgatorye and þe peyne of helle' (C.2.107–08).[48]

'In the date of the devil' (A.2.77, B.2.113, C.2.114) is more than just a parody of 'anno domini,' since dates on medieval English documents often referred to the authority under whom they were issued, as well as to the year of the Lord. Documents from the king and his officers would be given regnal dates – 35 Edward III, say – while a bishop and his subordinates would refer to the year of the bishop's episcopate. Dating Meed's charter 'in the date of the devil' is an open acknowledgment of the fact that it has been issued under the devil's aegis, rather than any divine, royal, or ecclesiastical authority.

The social quality of the witnesses is likewise skewed from the norm. Not surprisingly, actual charters were generally witnessed by respectable members of the community to which the parties belonged: among the noble class, likely witnesses include knights and upper clergy; among city-dwellers, the mayor, aldermen, clerks, and guildsmen; in a village, the parson and local men of authority.[49] The essential ignobility and venality of Meed's proposed union with False is signalled by the figures who witness their marriage charter: pardoner, beadle, reeve, and miller, stock villains of social satire, along with the allegorical master-villain Wrong, already identified as the satanic lord of the dark Castle of Care. These are hardly suitable witnesses to the marriage charter of a noblewoman 'who might kiss the king for cousin,' but they fit in perfectly with the base and vicious qualities of False's family and of Meed's paternal lineage.

To a lesser extent, Meed's marriage charter parodies the verbal forms of matrimony as well as those of land transfer. The phrase 'to have and to hold' belongs both to the land law and to the marriage service. The A

---

48 Dorothy Jean Burton discusses the relations between Meed's charter and the folk motif of the deal with the Devil in 'The Compact with the Devil in the Middle English *Vision of Piers Plowman*, B.II,' *California Folklore Quarterly* 5 (1946), 179–84. As she notes, C's elimination of the reference to rent greatly weakens the deal with the devil motif by suppressing the cost of the deal; on the other hand, one could argue that C is subtler than A or B, making what looks like Favel's crowning gift be itself the price of the whole. Cf. Stokes, *Justice and Mercy*, 107–08.
49 For examples of witness-lists, see the deeds listed in the *CAD* (including bourgeois examples), the marriage agreements in the *CCR*, and the charters reprinted in Madox, *Formulare Anglicanum*, cited above in nn. 40 and 46.

text evokes the liturgical phrase 'for richer or poorer' in the line 'To be present in pride for pouere or for riche,' although B and C essentially eliminate the allusion in the revision 'To be Princes in pride and pouerte to despise' (A.2.59; B.2.80, C.2.84; the new line shifts the emphasis away from pride as a vice found in poor and rich to pride as a vice more narrowly associated with the rich and powerful.) On the other hand, B and C add the phrase 'vnbuxome and bolde,' with its possible suggestion of the words 'bonayre and buxom' in the bride's troth-plight.

The reading of the document itself also reflects the action of a literal marriage, where the *dos* or *dotalium* would have been read or at least announced and symbolically enacted, usually by the handing over of silver or gold coins in token of the property rights being granted. While the ceremony at the church door was certainly tied to the establishment of the wife's dower rights, the terms *dos* and *dotalium* in the liturgical books may not have referred solely to the dower, or even just to property given by the husband's family to the couple. Many English marriages also involved the granting of property by the wife's family – most often by her father, but sometimes by some other person like a brother, uncle, mother, or guardian – in what was often known as a *maritagium* or marriage gift.[50] Typically, a father would grant the property to the groom 'in marriage with my daughter' or to the bride and groom together. The lands would usually descend to heirs begotten by the couple together, but if there were no issue, they would revert to the wife's family.

In the fourteenth century, at least at the highest social levels, this practice evolved into the provision of a large monetary 'portion' by the bride's father or guardian, while the groom or his family granted a 'jointure' of lands on which the couple would live.[51] Whether or not it technically qualifies as such, Favel's enfeoffment of False and Meed certainly has the flavor of an old-fashioned *maritagium* in land or the more modern jointure. If Langland conceived it as a jointure, as seems historically likely, then we again have the suggestion of overly close relations between the bride's party and the groom's: either as *amicus* or father of Meed, and evidently as an *amicus* of False as well, Favel gives away both the bride and the property which will support her and her husband to be.

As the poem grew into its three versions, the marriage charter grew as well. The largest change occurs between A and B; it consists mainly of

[50] Baldwin, *Theme of Government*, 32, and n. 41 above. On the *maritagium*, see Bracton 2:75–81; P & M 2:15–17, 291–92, 415, 420n; Holdsworth 3:111–12.
[51] Holmes, *Higher Nobility*, 42–43.

the addition and minor alteration of lines describing the rights and properties granted to Meed and False. Only two A lines drop out completely, and even they are replaced by new material on the same subjects, sloth and possibly lust (A.2.65–66; cf. B.2.97–101). The revisions from A to B double the length of the charter, and greatly increase the detail of its list of sins, but they do not change its basic structure or function. The C text revises the charter much less extensively, following B almost exactly for most of the list of sins and making significant changes only at the beginning and end of the document. However, the changes made are interesting insofar as they suggest that the end which awaits Meed and False also awaits their followers, those who pursue falseness and meed in this life. Simony proclaims this shared reward in his remarks before the charter:

> Al þat loueth and byleueth vp lykyng of Mede,
> Leueth hit lelly this worth here laste mede
> That foleweth Falsnesse, Fauel and Lyare,
> Mede and suche men þat aftur mede wayten.   (C.2.75–78)

The natural referent for Simony's 'this' in line 76 is the ensuing charter, with its list of allegorical lands and privileges and the grim country to which they will finally come. To say that the followers of Meed, False, Favel, and Liar will find their 'laste mede' in the charter is a skillful extension of the allegory here. *Ad literam*, we can imagine a newly-wed lord and lady moving onto the lands granted them in marriage, taking with them their servants and retainers and rewarding those *famuli* with the use of some of those lands. *Allegorice*, what we have is a statement of the moral truth that those who use and seek after gifts and favors – people who are almost inevitably enveloped in falseness, flattery, and lies – will be 'rewarded' with pieces of the deadly real estate of sin. And the price of that real estate is no less than the rendering of their souls to Lucifer forever.

The material added near the end of the charter in C (2.101–02, 105–07) also implies that the followers and 'felawschipe' of False and Meed will participate in their slothful despair and ultimate damnation. As in the B text, the spouses have been granted gluttony, particularly as manifested in the tavern sins. However, instead of moving on to the picture of stuporous sitting, sleeping, bedding, and breeding (or perhaps lazily sprawling [*MED* breden v.2 and v.3]) in B.2.93–99, the C text depicts a rowdier scene of noisy fellowship and stumbling drunkenness, a thumbnail forecast of Glutton's behavior in the tavern. Favel grants them the right 'to frete [on fast-days] before noone and drynke / With spiserye, speke ydelnesse, in vayne speke and spene.' Meed and False

24

may follow this jangling fellowship forth, possibly out of the tavern, until they – the couple alone or the whole drunken crew – have fallen into sloth: 'And sue forth suche felawschipe til they ben falle in slewthe' (C.2.100–102).

The next revision also refers to False's comrades, albeit somewhat obscurely: 'This lyf to folowe Falsnesse and folke þat on him leueth, / After here deth þay dwellen day withouten ende / In lordschip with Lucifer, as this lettre sheweth' (C.2.105–07). This new material in C replaces the AB references to Meed and False's heirs receiving the same lands, and may have struck Langland as a better way to talk about the rewards given those who pursue meed and falseness. Like parents and children, lords and followers have a certain similarity of behavior, but there is a more obvious element of free choice in following a wicked lord than in being born to wicked parents, and the participation by such followers in their lord's 'laste mede' is more clearly well-deserved.

The Marriage-Breaking

Theology's Objection

No sooner has Meed's marriage charter been proclaimed to the crowd of assembled witnesses and retainers than it meets with Theology's vehement objections. Theology is in many ways the natural opponent to Meed's marriage, or rather to the two personifications who have given the union an official stamp of approval, Simony and Civil; the ambitious and cupidinous study of the law, especially the civil law, had long been seen as an enemy to theological studies, as Barratt and Gilbert have demonstrated. Moreover, the views of the Church on the nature of marriage had been significantly shaped by the twelfth-century controversy between the disciples of Peter Lombard and the disciples of Gratian, the 'French' and 'Italian' schools of thought on what made an indissoluble marriage. Although the positions of the two sides were certainly not monolithic or simplistic, one can see general tendencies within the theological, French party to stress the more spiritual aspects of marriage – spousal consent in particular – while the canonistic, Italian party gave significant credit to physical or secular elements like actual consummation.[52] Some memory of this history, as well as the long-

---

[52] On developments in the definition of indissolubility, and in the history of Christian marriage generally, see Brundage, *Law, Sex, and Christian Society*; Gabriel Le Bras, 'Mariage,' *DTC* 9/2:2149–62; Edward Schillebeeckx, *Marriage: Human Reality and Saving Mystery*, tr. N. D. Smith (London, 1976), 287–302; Adhémar Esmein, *Le mariage en droit*

standing antagonism between theologians and lawyers, probably underlies Langland's choice of Theology as the spokesman for spiritual over worldly values, and the zealous opponent of Simony, Civil, and the marriage of Meed.

However, Theology has his weaknesses as a defender of spiritual values; he tends to understand those matters in relatively academic, theoretical ways, rather than seeing their practical dimensions in a world all too often ruled by materialistic self-interest, even among the well-intentioned. Unlike Holy Church and Conscience, who respond to Meed with an immediate, instinctive hostility, Theology argues that Meed can be turned to good ends as she was meant to be. And in theory, of course, his position is plausible, just as Meed's own self-defense has its plausible aspects. It is only in practice, at the complaint of Peace, that we will see just how incorrigible Meed's wrong-ful tendencies are.

That complaint, however, is still a passus and more away. Theology's objection makes sense at first hearing, though we should probably be made suspicious by the disparities between his evaluation of Meed and that of Holy Church, especially in their BC disagreement over her legitimacy. The disagreement is never explicitly resolved, and it may be that Langland means us to see it finally as a moot point, given the demonstration of Meed's lawless corruption in Passus 4, and the poet's later argument that mixed marriages between bad and good stock usually give rise to bad offspring (see Wit's speech, A.10.151–56, B.9.126–29, 150–55, C.10.206–07, 237–53). Whether or not Meed was born *illegitime* ('out of wedlock'), she definitely acts *illegitime* ('unlawfully'); by following her father's evil and ignoble *kynde*, she forfeits the right to honorable treatment. Even if an intellectual case can be made for the legitimate origin of unearned material rewards and favors, experience will soon give us a more direct and accurate understanding of Meed's actual operation. For now, however, Theology's assertion of Meed's legitimacy enables Langland to raise the question 'Can Meed be honorably wedded?' and thus to explore Meed's nature more fully than an undisputed condemnation would allow.

Theology's objection is reminiscent of one of the most frequent causes of matrimonial litigation in fourteenth-century England: pre-contract, the impediment of *ligamen*.[53] However, the fact that he does not

---

canonique, 2nd ed., rev. R. Génestal and Jean Dauvillier, 2 vols. (Paris, 1929–35), 1:99–150; Henri Rondet, *Introduction a l'étude de la théologie du mariage* (Paris, 1960), 69–76.

[53] See Helmholz, *Marriage Litigation*, 57–66, 76–77; Michael M. Sheehan, 'The Formation and Stability of Marriage in Fourteenth-Century England: Evidence of an Ely Register,' *MS* 33 (1971), 262–63.

recommend sending the case to the church courts suggests – at least insofar as Langland intended the allegory to reflect contemporary practice, which is admittedly unlikely to reach to an exact literal equivalence – that a fully binding pre-contract is not at issue here. Meed's situation differs somewhat from the cases of pre-contract cited by Helmholz and Sheehan, in that we are only told that she has been 'granted' to Truth, by God or by her mother, not that she has actually contracted marriage with Truth *in propria persona*. To be sure, a marriage arranged by a child's parents or guardian could be taken as a *de futuro* contract providing that the child accepted the arrangement, by explicit consent or by the implicit consent of silence. But by the time of Meed's marriage, Meed's father and various 'friends' have obviously ignored the grant to Truth, and made their own plans for bringing Meed's *richesse* into the power of a husband much nearer their own kind. Since Meed submits willingly to the latter arrangement, it might be difficult to prove her earlier assent to her mother's plans.

Another objection that Theology raises is that, whereas Meed is legitimate, a maiden of good stock, and kin to the king, she is being married to a treacherous bastard, begotten of the devil. If Theology's claims about Meed's birth are valid, then the alliance certainly constitutes a disparagement of Meed – i.e., a marriage to a social inferior, the fear of which was sufficiently high among the English baronage to warrant several statutes providing safeguards against the disparagement of feudal wards.[54] As Ian Bishop notes, 'the king seems to regard [Meed] as a ward of court who is in danger of being 'disparaged' through marriage to the undesirable Fals Fikel-Tonge.'[55] Furthermore, False is a *gilour*, a *faitour*, *faythles*, and *fikel*. English law

---

[54] P & M 1:319. Walker reports that actions for disparagement are relatively rare ('Marrying of Feudal Wards,' 213–14; 'Free Consent,' 128). However, at least some grants of marriages in the king's gift retained the formulaic reminder that any union offered to the heir must be non-disparaging (see CPR 1361–64: 384, 303, 481; CCR 1369–74: 67–68; 1374–77: 268–69, a case of a deaf and dumb heiress). The question of marrying into an 'hault parage' arises in some of the allegorical marriages of the devil's daughters (e.g., the Anglo-Norman 'Mariage des neuf filles du diable' 23–24, 41–43, 151–53, 521–24, ed. Meyer, *Romania* 29:61–69; Gower, *Mirour de l'omme* 823–25, 10081–85 – the latter on the counter-marriage of Reason with the seven virtues, daughters of God). In *The Reeve's Tale* 3942–49 and 3977–86, the theme of marital disparagement becomes a tool for satirizing the social aspirations of 'deynous Symkyn.' Langland himself will advert to disparaging marriages made for money in Wit's speech. The concept of disparagement evidently remained alive, both socially and literarily, although it probably did not come into play in actual marriages with great frequency; a suitor who met sufficiently high criteria of wealth and power was likely to be seen as having sufficient status by those who sought such qualities.

[55] 'Relatives at the Court of Heaven: Contrasted Treatments of an Idea in *Piers Plowman* and *Pearl*,' in *Medieval Literature and Antiquities: Studies in Honour of Basil Cottle*, ed. Myra Stokes and T. L. Burton (Cambridge, 1987), 111.

was sharply aware of the dangers of marrying an heiress to a potential or actual enemy of her lord; when the king licensed widows and heirs in his gift to marry whomever they pleased, the grants sometimes added explicit stipulations like 'of the king's peace and allegiance' or 'of the king's fealty.'[56] In Meed's case, False is undeniably an enemy of God, who, according to Theology, has exercised a species of feudal right over her marriage by granting her to Truth (A.2.84, B.2.120; cf. C.2.125).[57]

Whether we take Meed's marriage as a breach of a prior contract, as a disparagement of Meed's noble maternal lineage, or as an improper union with a known enemy of Meed's rightful lord, it is undeniably a *mésalliance* that must be prevented. And the best prevention of an undesirable marriage is often a wedding with a more suitable and acceptable spouse.

But who has the responsibility and the right to prevent Meed's marriage with False, and to give her to another? It is a commonplace of medieval law, in England and elsewhere, that matrimonial cases are in the jurisdiction of the Church.[58] Hence we find the detailed records studied by Sheehan, Helmholz, and others in the Act Books and Cause Papers of the various diocesan courts, rather than among the rolls of the King's Bench, or other secular courts. We might well expect Theology – who certainly cares about the Church's well-being (A.2.90, B.2.126, C.2.139–40) – to be jealous of her jurisdictional rights too. But he directs Simony and Civil to take the case to London 'þere lawe is yhandlit,' and the subsequent lines show that the law in question is the secular law 'handled' in the king's courts at Westminster.

Part of the answer may lie in Langland's righteous indignation at the corruption in the church courts. This indignation can be seen clearly in Passus 2, thanks to the frequency with which the poet there refers to representatives of those courts. We hear most about Simony and Civil themselves, who 'shenden' Holy Church and (as C.2.247–48 explicitly states) the kingdom as well.[59] On the way to Westminster, they are

---

[56] Bracton 2:255 ('a woman who has an inheritance may not be married, not even, as of right, in the lifetime of her ancestor, without the assent of the chief lord, . . . lest the lord be forced to take the homage of his chief enemy or other unsuitable person'). See also Walker, 'Feudal Constraint,' 101. For examples, see CFR 1356–68: 55, 57; 1377–83: 256–57; CPR 1361–64: 173, 305, 390; 1377–81: 450; CCR 1374–77: 379.

[57] The C text changes Truth's marital arrangements to a plighting of *treuthe* with Amends to wed one of her daughters (not necessarily Meed), if God would grant it, as long as there were no guile involved.

[58] P & M 2:366–68; Helmholz, *Marriage Litigation*, 1–5.

[59] A parallel to Theology's dual concern for church and kingdom in C can be found in Archbishop Thoresby's *Constitutions* of 1368, which condemn the commission of matrimonial cases to untrained judges, often for a 'notabili pecuniae quantitate.' Such deputations of responsibility give grave scandal, to the 'animarum suarum grave

accompanied by summoners, deans, subdeans, archdeacons, registrars, notaries, bishops and their officials, commissaries, and all manner of other clerics and court functionaries. To be sure, the common law and manorial courts are not absolved of venality; Meed, False, and Favel ride to London on non-clerical 'steeds': a sheriff, assize-men, reeves, and the generic 'Fair Speech.' However, these agents of the secular law receive only three or four descriptive verses in each text, while the parade of Simony, Civil, and their comrades-in-corruption takes up anywhere from thirteen to seventeen lines (A.2.128–30, 131–44; B.2.164–66, 167–83; C.2.177–80, 181–93). B and C tighten the link between the church courts and the coupling of meed with falseness by adding further references to abuses in the prosecution of matrimonial and sexual cases. Like A, they speak of the victuals fetched from *fornicatores*, but they also mention the willingness of ecclesiastical judges to overlook 'deuoutrye and diuorses' for silver or the rich adulterers and lovers of lechery ridden by Simony, Civil, the summoners, and the sub-deans (B.2.175–76; C.2.183–84, 187–88).[60]

Even without the abuses that Langland sees in the ecclesiastical courts, both generally and with respect to marriage cases, there are solid rhetorical grounds for trying Meed's case *coram rege*. As has long been recognized, one of Langland's primary concerns in discussing Meed is the problem of right use of *bona temporalia*, the treasure of this world, the things that are Caesar's.[61] The Church had always acknowledged the Crown's jurisdiction over matrimonial cases without spiritual content:

periculum, et reipublicae praejudicium perniciosius'; Thoresby also describes clandestine marriages as 'contrahentibus et reipublicae damnosa' (Wilkins 3:71).

[60] The association of corruption in the church courts with matrimonial cases is another commonplace of the literature of moral complaint; as Gilbert notes, ecclesiastical lawyers had a reputation for 'making divorces' (' "Civil" and the Notaries,' 52). The mid-fourteenth century saw the promulgation of ecclesiastical statutes against false witnesses and crooked lawyers and judges in marriage cases (Wilkins 3:19, 61, 71), and Helmholz notes the ease with which equitable payment of expenses for witnesses could slide into bribery (*Marriage Litigation*, 154–59).

Complaint and reforming legislation, however, are imperfect sources of evidence by themselves, given their prescriptive intent and tendency to focus on worst cases. Helmholz's research leads him to conclude that on the whole, the ecclesiastical courts dealt with marriage cases reasonably honestly, and tended to support the marriage bond rather than undermine it, despite their inability to fully enforce all the strictures of canon law on marriage (*Marriage Litigation*, 189). The accusation that the judicial system 'made divorces' is perhaps understandable in light of the frequency of multi-party litigation, where at least half the claimants involved would probably go away unsatisfied - and, no doubt, often complaining that a 'false divorce' had been made.

[61] See T. P. Dunning, *Piers Plowman: An Interpretation of the A-Text*, 2nd ed., rev. T. P. Dolan (Oxford, 1980), 48–84; D. W. Robertson, Jr., and Bernard F. Huppé, *Piers Plowman and Scriptural Tradition* (Princeton, 1951), 51–58; R. E. Kaske, 'Holy Church's Speech and the Structure of *Piers Plowman*,' in Beryl Rowland, ed., *Chaucer and Middle English Studies in Honour of Rossell Hope Robbins* (London, 1974), 322–24.

cases concerning property, feudal obligations, and other secular aspects of marriage.[62] By sending Meed and False to the royal courts, Theology may be indicating that, although marriage itself is a spiritual matter, his objection to their proposed marriage is finally more temporal than spiritual. Thus, he does not present the arrangement between Amends and Truth as a binding pre-contract (which should have been sent to the courts Christian), and he does not even raise the possibility that Meed and False might be too closely related through her paternal lineage (consanguinity being another ecclesiastical impediment). Instead, for both Theology and the king, the marriage of Meed and False presents a primarily secular problem, the problem caused by the conjunction of material reward and favor with falseness, guile, flattery, and lies, to the clear detriment of the kingdom as a whole. Even if most legal conflicts about marriage went to the Church courts in actual practice, the evident tenor of Langland's allegory – the dangers posed by Meed to the public well-being of the *comune* – leads him to cast the allegory's vehicle as a secular hearing and judgment of the case.

Meed's important role in the political economy of the kingdom is well signified by her depiction as a wealthy kinswoman of the king, and by the figurative interest he has in her marriage whether she is technically his ward or not. Whatever marriage she contracts will be his affair, since it will affect the way her wealth and power operate within the kingdom.[63] Despite the fact that God 'granted Meed to Truth,' it is perfectly appropriate for the king to judge the case, and to find a more suitable husband to rule her, since the king is God's vice-gerent in matters of social governance. As a significant element in English society, Meed requires proper regulation lest she disorder the whole social organism; it is the king's responsibility to provide this regulation. If False is an enemy of God and Truth, he is likewise an enemy of the king;

---

[62] P & M 2:374; see Dunning, *A-Text*, 62–64. Even in areas where Church and Crown theoretically collided, there could be mutual accommodation, as in the matter of bastardy, for which canon law and common law had different definitions. See Helmholz, 'Bastardy Litigation.'

[63] Waugh discusses royal involvement in marriage arrangements, sometimes even in cases in which the king was not the guardian, in *The Lordship of England*, 200–204. As Baldwin suggests, Meed behaves like some powerful noble or noblewoman of Langland's time, using her wealth and persuasive tongue to gain her own ends (*Theme of Government*, 25–27). Meed's adornments and interactions with clerics and city officials in the B and C texts may be a topical allusion to Alice Perrers, as Skeat believed. Her bold self-defense before the king is well within the scope of actual fourteenth-century noblewomen, like Elizabeth Audley, who successfully pled her own case before king and Parliament in 1366, suing her father-in-law for not giving her and her husband everything stipulated in their marriage settlement and winning 2600 marks in compensation and 1000 marks in damages (CCR 1364–68: 237–39, 388).

from the royal perspective as well as the divine, the threat which False poses to kingdom, church, and the human *comune* makes him a thoroughly unsuitable husband for Meed.

Meed before the King

In Passus 3–4, the dramatic action directly pertinent to Meed's marriage frequently gives way to the more general debate on the nature and effects of Meed. The scenes showing Meed's corrupting influence on clerks, city officials, and the law itself, together with the long speeches by Conscience, Meed, and Reason, take up hundreds of lines in the two passus. They contain only occasional reminders of the issue which originally sparked the debate: whom shall Meed marry? However, Langland does not allow us to forget the dramatic context completely. He returns to his 'plot' – the king's attempt to bring Meed and Conscience together – several times in Passus 3 and 4.

The principal scenes that further the 'marriage plot' in these two passus are the opening lines of Passus 3, the subsequent scene in which the king asks Meed and Conscience to consent to each other in marriage (A.3.90–122, B.3.101–33, C.3.127–69), the beginning of Passus 4, and the next to last scene of the Passus, in which Meed's repute thoroughly collapses (A.4.136–40, B.4.160–70, C.4.154–65). There are also other passages in the two passus that reinforce the marital, sexual, and familial context in which Langland first introduced us to Meed. For the moment, however, let us examine those scenes that directly advance the action.

The first eight lines of Passus 3 show us the king's intentions towards Meed. The tone here is quite different from that in which he commanded the arrests of False, Guile, and their companions. Meed is guilty of choosing a marriage partner unwisely, but the king will forgive that guilt if she will marry someone he picks out (or chooses 'by wys men consayl,' in C). Nor is the king indifferent to Meed's own preferences; after she has been made at ease, he will 'apose / What man of þis world þat hire were leuist' (A.3.5–6, B.3.5–6; C.3.6 reads 'þat here leuest hadde'[64]). As Bennett, Pearsall, and others observe, Meed's situation here is something like that of a delinquent ward who has fallen into bad company or followed bad advice, come close to marrying an enemy of the king, but finally been prevented at the last moment; she is now being offered other, more acceptable marriage partners to get her and her property out of harm's way.

[64] On the construction in C.3.6, which probably means the same thing as its AB antecedent, see Pearsall C.3.6n.

This nexus of meed, the system of feudal wardship and marriage, and the question of a choice of marriage partner is not surprising. As noted earlier, traffic in wardships and marriages was an extremely lucrative business in medieval England, as well as a major element in the political patronage system of the day.[65] Wardships and marriages were forms of meed. Yet the system also allowed for a degree of free choice. For instance, the right to refuse a marriage offered by a guardian was recognized, thanks to ecclesiastical insistence on consent in marriage. Conversely, even if a guardian refused permission for the ward's marriage to a particular person, the ward could still validly marry the desired spouse, though usually at the price of a heavy fine.[66] Canonists and secular lawyers knew that 'Invitae nuptiae solent malos proventus habere' and that 'Libera debeant esse coniugia.'[67] In many cases, no doubt, young people simply accepted arrangements made by their families or guardians, more or less willingly as the case may have been; psychological, social, and financial pressures would have encouraged cooperation with the status quo. And common sense could lead to at least some consideration or acceptance of the preferences of those whose marriages were being planned.[68] Thus the king wisely asks both Meed and Conscience if they will consent to be married.

[65] Tuck, 'Richard II's System'; Walker, 'Feudal Constraint,' 'Free Consent,' 'Marrying of Feudal Wards.' Many grants of wardship can be found throughout the Fine and Patent Rolls: e.g., *CFR* 1356–68: 5, 6, 9, 10, 19, 28, etc.; 1369–77: 2, 6, 17, 29, etc.; 1377–83: 2, 8, 10, 26–27, etc.; *CPR* 1361–64: 3, 27, 28, 57, 58, 75, etc.; 1370–74: 34; 1377–81: 31, 186, 502, 526, 537 (the last four being major grants to the king's uncles).
[66] Walker, 'Free Consent,' 126.
[67] 'Invitae': *Decretum* C. 31 q. 2 ante c. 1 and cf. X 4.1.14 (*Ord. Gloss*: 'quia quod quis non diligit, facile contemnit'); 'Libera': X 4.1.17, X 4.1.29, and Bracton 2:257. These aphorisms continue to be quoted by canonists, generally in connection with the *consensus* – for instance, Raymond of Pennafort, *Summa de Poenitentia et Matrimonio cum glossis Joannis de Friburgo* (1603; rpt. Farnborough, 1967), 507–08 (in text and gloss). They reflect an ecclesiastical ideal more than a social reality, but an ideal which could have genuine force if a person wished to resist the ordinary social pressures on his or her choice of partner. See John T. Noonan, Jr., 'Power to Choose,' *Viator* 4 (1973), 419; Helmholz, *Marriage Litigation*, 178, 220; Sheehan, 'Choice of Marriage Partner in the Middle Ages: Development and Mode of Application of a Theory of Marriage,' *Studies in Medieval and Renaissance History* n.s. 1 (1978), 9–13; Charles T. Donahue, 'The Policy of Alexander the Third's Consent Theory of Marriage,' *Proceedings of the Fourth International Congress of Medieval Canon Law* (Monumenta Iuris Canonici, Series C: Subsidia, vol. 5), ed. Stephan Kuttner (Vatican City, 1976), 251–81; and Brundage, *Law, Sex, and Christian Society*, 260–78, 331–38, 351–55, 430–43, 494–503. Donahue's essay contains a fascinating series of eighteen 14th-century English marriage cases, described in illuminating detail.
[68] See Gottlieb, *The Family in the Western World*, 52–56, on the issue of 'love or policy' in marriage decisions at all social levels. Karl P. Wentersdorf notes that Edward III eventually supported the clandestine and consanguineous marriage of the Black Prince to Joan of Kent, despite the negotiations already under way to betroth the Prince to Margaret of Flanders; see 'The Clandestine Marriages of the Fair Maid of Kent,' *Journal of Medieval History* 5 (1979), 217–18. At less exalted levels, English church courts seem to have been readier than their continental counterparts to value the spouses' preferences over parental

Although it can be useful to think of Meed as a king's ward, with the implications that such a circumstance has for her marriage plans, it must be remembered that she does not qualify as such a ward under a rigorously literal and legal definition. We hear nothing about her parents' death (insofar as such 'death' can be meaningful for allegorical personages); indeed, in A and C, her father Wrong or Favel witnesses or grants the marriage charter. In the C text, Theology says that Meed can't be married without her mother, which suggests that Amends may be alive as well. Even if Amends is dead, her husband should retain control over their daughter's marriage.[69] But Meed's economic and political importance in the realm means that the king could take a justifiable interest in her marriage anyway. The principle that heiresses should not marry enemies of their lord retains its moral and political force, even when the parents of the heiress are alive (see n. 56 above). And since neither Meed's father nor her mother accompanies her to Westminster, one could well argue that the king is the only authority left to arrange a proper marriage for Meed. In any event, Langland seems to have felt comfortable with an allegory that was suggestive of royal wardship without conforming rigidly to all the legal details thereof. While he can be quite precise about the technical letter of the law, the spirit of the law is far more important to him, and the spirit of English laws of royal wardship clearly give the king a stake in Meed's marriage, given her figurative characterization as wealthy noblewoman in addition to her symbolic value as a representation of economic and social reward.

When the king summons Meed, he leaves her in no doubt as to how she has erred: though she has a history of unwise behavior, accepting False as a spouse is the worst thing she has ever done.[70] C expands on this accusation quite interestingly, showing a king who still treats Meed more courteously than her true nature warrants – it is a king's 'kynde' to

---

arrangements; see Donahue, 'The Canon Law on the Formation of Marriage and Social Practice in the Later Middle Ages,' *Journal of Family History* 8 (1983), 144–58. But family pressures were still quite strong in England, and apparently much stronger than constraints imposed by feudal lords and guardians, which could usually be relieved by paying a suitable fee (Walker, 'Free Consent,' 124–25; Clark, 'Decision to Marry,' 499).

[69] This would be true even if Meed's royal kinship and her inheritance comes to her from Amends; see Bracton 2:259.

[70] Baldwin suggests that the intensity of the king's response is more suited to a case of ravishment of ward than to a case of disparagement (*Theme of Government*, 33). For an example of an actual response to the ravishment and unlicensed marriage of a royal ward, see *CCR* 1360–64: 349–50, describing the eloignment of Margaret Blount by William de Keynes, who sold her marriage to Walter atte More, who then married her; William and Walter had to pay the king £240, but no mention is made of any penalty being imposed on Margaret, a minor whose lands and marriage had been granted by the king to Prince Lionel.

be courteous – but who has a fuller understanding of Meed's misdeeds and a greater readiness to punish her if she should not reform.

> [He] lacked here a litel whith for þat she louede gyle
> And wilned to be wedded withouten his leue
> And til Treuthe hadde ytolde here a tokene fram hymsulue;
> And saide, 'Vnwittiliche, woman, wroft hastow ofte
> And monye a gulte y haue the forgyue and my grace graunted
> Bothe to the and to thyne in hope thow shost amende,
> And ay the lengur y late the go the lasse treuthe is with the,
> For wors wrouhtestou neuere then now, tho thow Fals toke.'
> (C.3.130–37)

Langland describes Meed's history of misbehavior more specifically here than in A or B, and additionally notes the failure of the king's past lenience as a method of rehabilitation. The new lines also tie the scene more closely to Theology's claim that Truth had promised to marry Meed or (in C) one of Amends' daughters, if God would allow it (C.2.124–25). Not only should Meed have obtained the king's leave for her marriage, but she should have waited to hear from Truth as to his will in the matter. A nearby revision in C reveals the treasonable quality of Meed's alliance with False more fully: instead of simply killing the king's father herself 'þoruȝ false behest,' Meed is said to have committed the crime together with False (A.3.116, B.3.127; C.3.162).

The king goes on to warn Meed that he will imprison her 'as an ancre' if she does not reform, so as to make an example of her to 'alle wantowen women' and to teach her 'to louye treuthe and take consail of resoun' (C.3.140–44). His threat suggests that he is concerned about her proclivities to promiscuity, just as a guardian might worry about the possible incontinence of an heiress in his custody.[71] The warning also gives us some notion of what should happen to Meed once she has been shown to be a 'queynte comune hore,' and has been taken by a sheriff's clerk as she tries to leave the hall at Westminster. If she were deprived of

---

[71] In late twelfth- and thirteenth-century legal theory, an heiress could be deprived of her inheritance for incontinence. See Glanvill, 7.12, 17; less clearly stated in Bracton 2:255. I have been unable to find references to this punishment being put into practice, however; it is not even mentioned in the discussions of escheat or wardship in P & M, Holdsworth, or Plucknett. Isabella, the mother of Edward III, retired to Castle Rising in Norfolk after the trial and execution of Mortimer in 1330, her paramour and co-conspirator against Edward II, but retained a generous allowance and the freedom to move about the countryside (McKisack, *Fourteenth Century*, 102). On the other hand, sixteen years earlier in France, two daughters-in-law of Philip the Fair were in fact imprisoned for having adulterous affairs, presumably because their relationship to the king was not as powerful as Isabella's to Edward III; ironically, Isabella may have been the source of Philip's information against her sisters-in-law. See Charles-Victor Langlois, *Saint Louis, Philippe le Bel, les derniers Capétiens directs* (Paris, 1911; rpt. Paris, 1978), 217–21.

her estates and made to live 'as an ancre,' then she would indeed be unable to mainprise wrongdoers anymore.

The king then offers Meed to Conscience – a development that seems a bit strange, since we know Truth has a claim on her. It may be that Conscience is, as Pearsall suggests, Truth's proxy; proxy marriages were not uncommon in the Middle Ages, especially among the nobility, and the legal aspects of such marriages were discussed by contemporary canonists.[72] Figuratively, such a proxy relationship could be read as indicating that Conscience is the representative of Truth within each soul, and the very means by which the soul knows Truth. Alternately, it may be appropriate to think of the situation as typological in some sense: on the divine plane, permission for the marriage between Truth and Meed has been granted by God; on the social and political plane we have permission for a marriage between Conscience and Meed, granted by the king. The demands of narrative would also have contributed to the change in partner. By having the king offer Meed to Conscience, Langland sets the stage for Conscience's single-minded refusal of the union, and avoids the complications of having the refusal come from Truth, who has already consented to Meed – explicitly in C by pledging faith with Amends, implicitly in AB by receiving God's 'grant.'[73] Once again, though, the legal situation is rather loosely defined; strict legal accuracy and rigidly consistent allegory were evidently not essential to Langland's poetic intentions here.

However one interprets the substitution of Conscience for Truth as a possible husband for Meed, it is clear in all three versions that Meed is perfectly willing to agree to whomever the king proposes, though she phrases her answer more subjunctively than an attentive listener might like: 'Unless I be completely at your command, have me hanged!' (A.3.101–02, B.3.112–13, C.3.147–48) And of course, her sincerity here is cast into grave doubt by her equal, earlier willingness to accept offers of help against Conscience from the clerks and friar who woo her favors (A.3.18, 41, B.3.19, 42, C.3.20, 43).

If the king must ask Meed whether she wishes to marry Conscience, so also must he seek the consent of Conscience to the marriage. Marital consent must be mutual. Meed's complaisant response to the proffered marriage, which momentarily raises the hope that her operation might

---

[72] E.g., Raymond of Pennafort, *Summa*, 515; de Burgh, *Pup. Oc.*, 124r, 125v.

[73] The C text may give Truth a way out by having him simply promise to marry one of Amends' daughters. John de Burgh discusses the nature of a pre-contract to marry one of several daughters, indicating that such agreements were within the realm of possibility; he says that a man who pre-contracted marriage in this way could refuse the daughter eventually offered by the parents, but if he did so, the whole agreement was nullified (*Pup. Oc.*, 124r–v).

be regulated by Conscience, is immediately countered by Conscience's moral outrage at the very proposal of a union with her. His reasons for refusing her can be seen as falling in two main categories: her promiscuous lechery (A.3.109–22, B.3.120–33, C.3.155–69) and her corruption of the courts (A.3.123–56, B.3.134–69, C.3.170–214). She undermines both love and law in the realm. She herself is metaphorically 'wanton,' by being available to all comers, 'tykil of hire tail, talewys of hire tunge, / As comoun as þe cartewey to knaue & to alle, / To monkis, to mynstrelis, to myselis in heggis' (A.3.120–22, B.3.131–33; C.3.166–69, adding the line 'Lyggeth by here when hem lust lered and lewed'). No refined, courteous bower-bird here: Meed perverts the ideal of love for all men into an indiscriminate depravity.[74]

Corruption of the courts, of course, is not necessarily connected with matrimony, but Langland seems to have found it so, at least in the church courts.[75] Thus, Conscience points out the clerical concubinage that Meed maintains, along with the whoredom and bastardy that inevitably follow in its wake, and her work as a go-between in the 'coupling' of clergy and covetise. Still, these references to marital and sexual abuses in the church courts take up only a small part of the second half of Conscience's response to the king. In contrast, the entire first half of his rejection of Meed is predicated precisely on the matrimonial metaphor: what man would want a wife whose sexual morals are so corrupt that she even lies with lepers, who teaches wives and widows to be as promiscuous as herself? The misogynist spectre of the procuress – La Vieille, Dame Sirith, Celestina, and their like – looms into view here. Compared to Meed, there 'Is not a betere baude. . . / Betwyn heuene & helle, & erþe þei3 men sou3te' (A.3.118–19, B.3.129–30, C.3.165–66).

As the debate between Meed and Conscience continues, the question of their marriage recedes into the background, and the focus of the debate shifts to Meed's political, economic, and moral aspects. Passus 4, however, returns to the dramatic action, with the king's command 'Sessiþ.' Though he appears willing to respect Conscience's rejection of Meed as a wife, he still hopes to reconcile the two of them, and have loyal service from them both. And, with Reason's assistance, he still wants to find someone to wed Meed. It is the unexpected entrance of Peace, with his bill of complaint against Wrong, that forestalls the discussion with Reason of whom Meed should marry. Fortunately, Meed's response to Peace and to Wrong finally gives the king

---

[74] In this regard, Meed's activity is much like that of Lechery in the marriages of the devil's daughters; Satan usually marries her to no single estate, but prostitutes her universally, making her common to all.
[75] See above, p. 29 and n. 60.

unmistakable evidence of her incorrigibility and leads to her condemnation by Reason and the righteous members of the *comune*. As the C text adds, 'Thorw Wrong and his werkes there was Mede yknowe' (C.4.71).

Langland ultimately resolves the king's dilemma along with the marriage plot by reporting the judgment passed by 'alle riȝtfulle' and 'þe comune': Meed is a 'muche wrecche,' a 'mansed sherewe,' and a 'queynte comune hore' (A.4.136, B.4.160, 166, C.4.161).[76] As for her marriageability, Love's scornful comment best expresses what all have come to see:

> Whoso wilneþ hire to wyue for welþe of hire godis,
> But he be cokewald ycald, kitte of my nose.
> (A.4.139–40, B.4.163–64, C.4.158–59)

Thus she is unfit to be a wife to any of the king's trusted servants, and must be removed from 'maistrie' within the realm, as Reason has proved.

These uncompromising judgments close the case on Meed's marriage, by showing her utter undesirability as a mate. However, the question of what happens to Meed after the conclusive decision seems to have given the poet some difficulty; at least, he tries three different solutions to the problem. In A, Meed is simply never mentioned after Love's verdict. In B, she is followed by a summoner and a *sisour*, after which a sheriff's clerk reviles 'al þe route' (i.e., the followers of Meed) for never having let him in on the profits. Meed appears finally in B as the object of the king's stern gaze, during his declaration that henceforward she shall have no power over the law (B.4.165–81). C modifies B by having Meed try to leave the hall with the summoner and *sisour*, and having the resentful sheriff's clerk cry out to have her arrested but not imprisoned; as in B, the king promises that Meed shall have no more power to mainprise those who corrupt his law (C.4.160–75). Aside from these brief references, Langland does not trouble himself with specifying Meed's final disposition in detail. Far more important than the particulars of Meed's punishment is the fact that Reason and Conscience will now help rule the kingdom.

Although the scenes discussed above constitute the principal treatments of Meed's figurative marriage in Passus 3 and 4, other lines in these passus reinforce the marital theme in subtler ways. Even when he is discussing Meed's behavior and merits in relatively general terms,

---

[76] On 'queynte comune hore,' see A. V. C. Schmidt, '*Lele Wordes* and *Bele Paroles*: Some Aspects of Langland's Word-Play,' *RES* n.s. 34 (1983), 149–50.

Langland periodically reminds us of marriage, sexuality, and family. Some of these reminders operate at the allegorical level, and pertain to Meed herself; others reflect literal fourteenth-century abuses.

We have for instance the wooing of Meed by the justices and clerks who come to her bower, treat with her intimately, and promise to help her fight Conscience and (in B and C) wed where she will. She in turn promises to 'love hem lelly,' like a lady of romance. As if called forth by these sexually suggestive negotiations, a friar-confessor appears, promising to shrive Meed of all manner of lechery, be her bawd (in A and B),[77] and help her overpower Conscience. In B and C, she in turn woos the friar, asking him to give easy forgiveness to lecherous lords and ladies. She 'woos' the mayor too, with phrases like 'for my love,' but not about sexual matters. These private negotiations here at the start of Passus 3 prepare us to take Conscience's accusations seriously, and in my view cast serious doubt on arguments that Meed is morally neutral. At least in terms of what Meed actually does, leaving aside questions of how she might be or ought to be, Langland seems to view her ready availability to anyone as an intrinsically negative trait. Certainly the sexual metaphor in which he presents that availability implies a moral judgment being passed, a judgment that will eventually be confirmed by Conscience, Reason, and the whole of the righteous *comune*.

Set against Meed's actively flirtatious interactions with the men who come to her chamber, the repetition of the epithet 'Meed the Maid' comes to take on a particularly ironic cast. The phrase initially appears at the beginning and the end of Passus 2, once on Holy Church's lips, and once on Will's (A.2.16, 196, B.2.20, 237, C.2.19, 250). In Passus 3, however, it achieves much greater prominence – A.3.1, 4, 35, 76, 94, B.3.1, 4, 36, 87, 105, C.3.1, 4, 39, 115 – and then completely disappears as soon as the debate with Conscience begins.[78]

Another sexually suggestive image arises when Meed accuses Conscience of giving cowardly counsel in the French wars:

> ȝet I may, as I miȝte, menske þe [Conscience] wiþ ȝeftis,
> And maynteyne þi manhod more þan þou knowist.
> . . .

---

[77] The readings *baudekyn* and *baude* in B.3.41 and 46 have little manuscript support; all manuscripts read *bedeman* in line 41 (like C), and all but two have *brocour* in line 46, with *baude* and *on hande* in the two exceptions. The Kane-Donaldson emendations assume censorship of a text originally like A (K-D, 156–57). But given Langland's several added references to *brokours* and *brokage* elsewhere in B, Schmidt's retention of *brocour* in line 46 seems preferable. C uses *bedman* and 'to bere wel here ernde' in the lines parallel to B.3.41 and 46, though Conscience still calls Meed a bawd later on.

[78] Gerald Morgan offers an excellent analysis of Langland's application of the term 'maid' to Meed in 'The Status and Meaning of Meed,' 452–53, 458.

[I] bateride [the king] on þe bak, boldite his herte,
Dede hym hoppe for hope to haue me at wille. . . .
Mede makiþ [a king] be louid & for a man holde.
(A.3.171–72, 186–87, 199, B.3.184–85, 199–200, 212, C.3.229–30, 267)

Meed defends herself against Conscience by attacking his 'manhood' as well as his courage; *she* could maintain that manhood if he were interested in her, more than he can know. In A, she hints at having seduced the king himself, making him merry and bold; in the parallel B lines, she claims instead to have made all the king's *meynee* merry, bold, and hopeful of 'having her at will.' It is hard to know which is worse – making the king 'hop for hope' of having her, or making his whole army do so. In all three versions, she promises the king that she can give him a manly reputation, and this offer may also carry sexual implications, given Meed's nature and the military campaigns to which she has been alluding. Connections between sexual virility and martial success were part of Langland's culture, as they are in many cultures, our own included. Thomas Bradwardine, in the *Sermo Epinicius* delivered before Edward III and his nobles after the victory at Crécy in 1346, warned his audience against the superstition that military success depended on sexual prowess:

> These soldiers of the goddess Venus, these servants of Aphrodite, these knights of Epicurus ascribe merit, victory, or triumph to their audacious bravery. But they say that none can be brave unless he is amorous or loves amorously, that none can bear himself with exceeding vigor unless he loves exceedingly. But how impious is this vanity, how false and mad this insanity!
>
> And so these amorous knights, soldiers of the love-goddess, serve the devil, and are of his retinue; they follow his banner. And they serve him in two things especially: In pride, for they strive greatly in war that they might make for themselves a name next to the name of the great ones of the world, nay that they might make for themselves a name that is above every name, that they might thus be seen to transcend others in name and in fame, and alone to be worthy of a knightly name. Lo, the execrable pride before God! And why ultimately do they seek such a name? That they might be loved more amorously by foolish women! Lo, the abominable lechery before God![79]

One suspects that Bradwardine and Langland might have had similar responses to the *fin' amour* notion that an 'encrees of hardynesse and myght / Com[eth] of love, his ladies thank to wynne, / That altered his spirit so withinne' (*Troilus* 3.1776–78).

---

[79] Heiko Oberman and James A. Weisheipl, eds., 'The *Sermo Epinicius* ascribed to Thomas Bradwardine (1346),' *Archives d'histoire doctrinale et littéraire du moyen âge* 33 (1958), 323–24 (my translation).

Even Peace's complaint, which seems at first to be an interruption of the matrimonial question 'Who should wed Meed?' turns out to have sexual and familial implications. Wrong's crimes include attacks on Peace's family and household, the rape or abductions of maidens, wives, widows, and servant girls, as well as the more economically oriented violence perpetrated against Peace, his serving men, and his property. Nearly half of Peace's bill deals with sexual crimes against members of his household.[80] Meed's willingness to maintain Wrong by offering Peace a 'present of pured gold' shows her 'vnsittyng soffraunce' of all sorts of crime, including sexual sin. She encourages not only consensual lechery and the damage it does to family and society, but also sexual violence, which even more clearly breaks the social and familial peace.

Other lines and phrases in Passus 3–4 harmonize with the marital metaphor that operates throughout the Meed episode, though taken alone they would not call attention to matrimonial issues. Many of these are related to families in one way or another: Meed's reference to the 'brolles' of the king's blood, whom he could endow with the spoils of war;[81] Conscience's exemplum of Saul and Agag, demonstrating, among other things, the punishment of children for the sins of their fathers (a topic to which Langland frequently returns); the proper discipline of children seen in Reason's vision of a Meed-free society; perhaps even the repetition of the word 'amends' in the description of Wisdom's and Meed's response to Peace – appearing four times in 16 lines or less, it may be meant to remind us of Meed's maternal lineage, and show how that lineage has been corrupted. C's long addition in Passus 3 contains several references to family, from the disinheriting of the offspring of traitors to a familial metaphor of *relacions rect* to the notion of grammatical *kynde* or genus.[82] The C text creates a further link between Meed and sex when Conscience defines Meed as payment

---

[80] For contemporary analogues to the bill or petition brought by Peace to the king's court, see Baldwin, *Theme of Government*, 40–45. Wrong has literally and figuratively broken the king's Peace, which represents 'the law and order for which the king was directly responsible' (Baldwin, 43). Thus, in both his name and his deeds, he embodies the legal notion of *tort*, an essential term in the language of criminal suits (< Lat. *tortum*, 'twisted'; as Langland may well have recognized, *wrong* derives from the same root as *wring*).

[81] On the king's distribution of military spoils, see James Simpson, 'Spiritual and Earthly Nobility in *Piers Plowman*,' *NM* 36 (1985), 472–76.

[82] See Priscilla Martin, '*Piers Plowman*: Indirect Relations and the Record of Truth,' in *Suche Werkis to Werche: Essays on Piers Plowman in Honor of David C. Fowler*, ed. Mícheál F. Vaughan (East Lansing, 1993), 171–79. D. Vance Smith places C's grammatical metaphor into the context of medieval philosophical analyses of relationship (familial, economic, and Trinitarian relationships all being among the pertinent medieval examples) and connects those analyses to notions of genealogy, origin, and history in the poem; see 'The Labors of Reward: Meed, Mercede, and the Beginning of Salvation,' *YLS* 8 (1994), 127–54.

before performance, *pre manibus,* and compares such payment to the money taken in by whores and false leeches (C.3.292–303). As we shall see, many of these minor references to marital and familial mores will be picked up later in the poem and explored in greater detail.

Conclusions

Much of the material pertinent to Meed's marriage in Passus 2 through 4 appears in all three versions of *Piers Plowman.* The central concepts remain fairly constant: to 'knowe þe false,' as Will desires, is to see first that falsehood most often operates by allying itself intimately with material reward or meed; second, that meed itself has roots in falsehood and its kindred vices, and so possesses certain natural proclivities toward deceitful ends; and third, that the union of falsehood and meed is supported by all manner of covetous men, but especially by officers of the church courts and the secular government. The alliance poses a fundamental threat to the kingdom; Meed's indiscriminate availability to any cause, even false and wrongful ones, makes the acceptance of her *maistrie* extremely hazardous to a well-ordered realm. The marriage metaphor allows Langland to express his outrage at the workings of meed in powerful terms, likening them to abuses of a sacramental bond, of feudal faith and duty, and of sexual propriety – abuses that are blasphemous, treasonable, and obscenely scandalous.[83]

As Langland revised his text, he left the marital matter of these three passus essentially unchanged in its general content and narrative functions; occasionally, however, he did refine or expand on that material, and shift some of its emphases, in order to render it more expressive of his thought. I have referred in passing to a number of these changes earlier in this chapter, but a review of the more significant patterns of revision may be helpful here. The most noteworthy revisions in marriage-related passages in the Meed episode seem to occur between the A text and the B text, and are then retained in C. Some of these A to BC revisions are carried still further in C, which also contains some interesting, mostly isolated revisions of its own.

One of the important revisions in BC is the addition of passages that state or employ the idea of moral similarities within families – the 'kynde followeth kynde' principle. These additions heighten the reader's suspicions of Meed; they also link the Meed episode with Wit's speech,

---

[83] For a similar analysis of the aptness of the marital metaphor to Langland's institutional critique in passus 2–4, see Simpson, *Introduction to the B-Text,* 50–53.

which focuses on the same theme more fully in regard to literal families. Besides Holy Church's direct assertion of the principle, there are several revisions that derive from it: (1) the increasing specificity of Meed's father's name from A to B to C, which allows us to understand her nature more fully; (2) the BC claim that Meed is a bastard, implying that she descends from a scorner of wedlock; (3) Will's question in BC about whose wife Meed may be, since husbands and wives can also be said to share one *kynde*; and (4) the BC contrast of Meed's father and lover with those of Holy Church.

Another change from A to BC is the shift of scene and 'supporting cast' at Meed's wedding, where an apparently indoor setting near her bower or chamber replaces the tent-filled field with its proud pavilion, and the guest-list comes to represent venalities of a more specifically official and mercantile stripe. While fields and pavilions could certainly be found in or near towns, the BC versions of Meed's marriage appear to stress urban and curial *gilours* and activities more than A does. The redirected satire supports the natural biographical conjecture that Langland may have had greater experience of London, with its commerce and its courts, by the writing of B.[84] He pays increased attention to *brocours* and *brocage* at several points. Fairly or not, *brocours of chaffare* are linguistically associated with the sort of *brocage* undertaken by Favel in procuring Meed for False, as well as with the more asexual *bargaynes and brocages* in the borough of Theft.[85]

In similar fashion, B and C sharpen the attack on abuses in the courts, especially the ecclesiastical courts, and especially on the abuses surrounding marriage and morals cases. This sharpening can be seen in the added reference to divorces, adultery, and lechery in the descriptions of the steeds ridden by Simony and Civil; it may also explain the increasing primacy of Simony over Civil in the charter scene and in the C version of Theology's objection. Related BC additions include the promise of the justices who visit Meed to help her 'be wedded at [her] will,' and Meed's request to her confessor at Westminster, seeking mild penances for lechery among the nobility.

Finally, a change which occurs between B and C as well as between A and B is the slow but steady deterioration in Meed's character – Langland colors her a little more darkly each time.[86] Thus, in BC, we find

---

[84] On Langland's familiarity with the capital, see Caroline M. Barron, 'William Langland: A London Poet,' in Barbara A. Hanawalt, ed., *Chaucer's England: Literature in Historical Context* (Minneapolis, 1992), 91–109.

[85] The majority manuscript reading at B.3.46 – 'brocour' rather than K-D's 'bawd' – may be part of this pattern of revision as well; see n. 77 above.

[86] In addition to the features noted here, the meed-mercede distinction and grammatical metaphor also contribute to the harsher presentation of Meed in the C text, as Robert

Holy Church's assertion of Meed's bastardy and likeness to her father, and Meed's request to the friar for the gentle treatment of lechery; when Meed is judged by the *comune* at the end of Passus 4, she is called a 'muche wrecche' in A, a 'mansed sherewe' and 'hore' in B, and a 'queynte comune hore' in C. In the C text, the king rebukes Meed not merely for having taken False, as in AB, but also for loving guile, marrying without his leave, offending Truth, and ignoring previous mercies. He threatens imprisonment both as punishment for her and as an example for all wanton women – presumably those who, as Conscience has said in all three texts, have been taught by Meed to commit lechery for the sake of gifts. And it is C alone that identifies Meed with the *pre manibus* payments demanded by harlots, whores, and false leeches. Occasionally a negative aspect of Meed's character disappears in the later versions – e.g., the friar's offer to be her bawd is dropped in C, and may or may not belong in B – but on the whole, Langland keeps loading his language against her rather than for her. One might even argue that if the friar *has* dropped his offer to be Meed's bawd, then her initiation of the request for kindness to noble lechers is all the more reprehensible.

Although other revisions of the marriage material in the Meed episode could be pointed out, considerations of space and significance lead me to pass over them here.[87] A good deal of Langland's major rewriting in the Meed episode occurs in non-marital passages, mainly in Passus 3: e.g., the millenarian vision added to Conscience's remarks at the end of BC.3; and the much-studied grammatical metaphor in C.3. The revisions in the marriage-related passages run more to moderate shifts in emphasis than to radical recasting of ideas. But they are by no means perfunctory modifications; they carry genuine poetic force in themselves, and will help to connect the first Dream more closely with later developments in the poem.

As students of *Piers Plowman* have long recognized, the marriage of Lady Meed is first and foremost a satirical allegory against venality. The focus of this chapter notwithstanding, I do not read the Meed episode as being *primarily* about the institution of marriage or about specific literal marriages. Yet the satire and the allegory are much enriched by the

Adams demonstrates in 'Mede and Mercede: The Evolution of the Economics of Grace in the *Piers Plowman* B and C Versions,' in Edward Donald Kennedy et al., eds., *Medieval English Studies Presented to George Kane* (Woodbridge, 1988), 217–32.

[87] A change from A to BC for which I have no explanation yet is the omission of most of the linguistic echoes of the marriage liturgy found in A. It would also be interesting to work out more clearly what Langland is doing in the revisions at the end of Passus 4.

repeated connections between the figurative action and actual fourteenth-century English marriages, especially but not only among the upper classes. While the tenor of the allegory addresses itself to disorder in the public structures of society – corruption and guile in greedy justices, advocates, royal and ecclesiastical officers, merchants, clerks – its vehicle is busy suggesting similar disorders in society's most basic private bond – unholy, faith-breaking marriages based on greed and procured by lies, guile, and flattery. Nor can the two levels be kept separate. Corruption in the church courts includes the purchase of crooked lawyers and false witnesses in order to break up valid marriages or make invalid ones, as well as payments for the condoning of adultery, concubinage, and bastardy. Corruption among the king's retainers includes the buying and selling of marriages, even against the interests of crown and kingdom, and the giving of sex for gifts under the name of courtesy. Lady Meed may be allegorically promiscuous, but meed itself draws many widows, wives, lords, and ladies to literal promiscuity. Corruption in the *comune* includes marriages by *brocage*, as Langland will demonstrate further in Wit's speech. To be sure, much of the anti-venality satire in the Meed episode has nothing to do with marriage, but when it does, it mingles levels of representation in the complex and powerful way that characterizes some of Langland's most energetic poetry.

In so far as Meed's marriage is like real marriages of Langland's day, it is most like the marriages of the aristocratic upper classes. At this high level, scandalously obvious *brocage* for the sake of property or political power may have been more noticeable than anywhere else in society; here too, economic and political factors may have had a particularly heavy weight in comparison to personal preferences. But similar considerations also affected marriages at lower social levels, as can be seen in documents ranging from the Stonor or Paston letters to the various records of manor, village, or small town life, documents which testify to the frequent connections (positive and negative) between marriage and property in those communities.[88] Still, most of us find it much easier to be scandalized by the crimes of the great than to see those crimes in operation at our own lower levels, where the stakes are smaller and our own interests are in play. For rhetorical impact, Langland may have chosen to use an extreme case in his initial

---

[88] For examples of the latter, from the late 13th century to the mid-15th, see J. A. Raftis, *A Small Town in Medieval England: Godmanchester 1278–1400* (Toronto, 1982), 15–23, 42, 217–18; Zvi Razi, *Life, Marriage and Death in a Medieval Parish: Economy, Society and Demography in Halesowen 1270–1400* (Cambridge, 1980), 50–69, 135–36, 145–49; J. M. Bennett, 'Peasant Marriage,' 209–11, 227–29, 231–39, and *Women in the Medieval English Countryside*, 100–141.

presentation of the problem of covetous marriages. By doing so, he could prepare his readers to be receptive to the topic when it appears again in Wit's speech, treated in more detail and as a more ubiquitous fault.

Whatever Langland's reasons for choosing a marriage as the central metaphor in his analysis of Meed, the choice is apt in so many ways that it can justly be called brilliant. I have spoken of medieval marriage as a private bond, which indeed it was, grounded ultimately in the mutual consent of two individuals. But it was a private bond with significant public ramifications, and those ramifications stretched much farther than the public dimensions of modern Western marriage. The multiple interests that marriage brought into play contributed largely to these public aspects of marriage; family, neighbors, friends, associates, patrons, and lords might all have some stake in a marriage, in various emotional, economic, legal, social, and political ways. The Church was always involved by right, although that right was not always respected *de facto*. Moreover, as the principal institution whereby society attempts to regulate sexuality and generation, marriage channels powerful human drives; thus, in all cultures, it tends to become enormously value-laden and to give rise to strong feelings quite apart from the personal affections that may exist between spouses. As Georges Duby has remarked,

> Through the *copulatio*, the door opens upon the dark, mysterious, and terrifying domain of sexuality and procreation - that is, upon the realm of the sacred. As a result, marriage stands at the intersection of two orders, the natural and the supernatural.[89]

Louise Fradenburg describes 'the idea of marriage,' especially royal marriage, in similarly compelling terms: like the Incarnation, she says, marriage

> is a site of crossover, between change and fixity, identity and difference, freedom and constraint, pleasure and sacrifice. . . . For sovereignty, the importance of the marriage metaphor lies in its power to express bonds between differences as intense - as important, as necessary to preserve - as that between native and foreigner, male and female, body and head, sovereign and subject. The legal fiction of the king's two bodies is in fact intimately linked to the legal fiction of marriage as its conceptual obverse; each creates a fictive body, the one a multiplication of a singularity, the other a unification of a multiplicity.[90]

[89] 'Le mariage dans la société du haut moyen âge,' in *Il Matrimonio nella Società Altomedievale*, 2 vols. (Spoleto, 1977), 1:16.
[90] *City, Marriage, Tournament: Arts of Rule in Late Medieval Scotland* (Madison, 1991), 84, 86, 87.

Au carrefour; 'a site of crossover.' Because marriage, like meed, touches and is touched by so many areas of human experience, the marriage allegory allows Langland to display Meed's workings in a wide variety of connections – spiritual, judicial, economic, feudal, courtly, and sexual. The ravishment and unlicensed marriage of a feudal ward could threaten the orderly devolution of social authority and of property, violate ecclesiastical and spiritual laws, and trespass on the rights of many other people. So too the unlawful union of Meed and False threatens the welfare of kingdom, church, and individuals. Because marriage is so powerfully invested with societal significance, Langland can draw on his readers' likely outrage at gross marital abuses so as to intensify their response to his main target, the misuse of meed throughout the realm. Furthermore, while meed and marriage both intersect extensively with other aspects of existence, they also intersect with each other. The constant interplay between the figurative characterization of meed and the literal characterization of marriage in Passus 2 through 4 enlivens our understanding of the former and deepens our understanding of the latter, clinching them even more tightly together.

Indeed, Langland's depiction of Meed's allegorical marriage to False necessarily depends on the poet's ideas about the nature of literal marriage. The union of Meed and False is an affront to the very foundations of the sacrament, which are also the foundations of the ideal, meed-free society envisioned by Conscience and Reason: *leaute*, honest law, and love. We know from the start of BC.2 that Meed is a mocker of Leaute. The only law she knows is that which can be bought and sold. The only forms of love she seems to understand are lechery, cupidity, or the 'lovedays' on which law is so easily sold for love of meed (A.3.145–49, B.3.155–60, C.3.192–97). In contrast, when Conscience predicts Reason's millenarian rule, he specifies love, *louȝnesse*, and *leaute* as its masters instead of Meed, and he includes a reformed law among its features (A.3.267, B.3.291, C.3.443). I suspect that it is the importance of *leaute* in this non-marital passage of A which led to the naming of Leaute as the leman of Holy Church in B and C, to her complaint that Meed mocks and slanders Leaute before the keepers of the law, and to the addition of several new references to *leaute* and *leel* love and law in B and C.[91]

---

[91] On this triple concept so central to the poem, see Patricia M. Kean, 'Love, Law, and *Lewte* in *Piers Plowman*,' *RES* n.s. 15 (1964), 241–61. Kean focusses her discussion on the B text, noting that the ideas she is concerned with 'are present . . . [but] not much developed in A,' and that C's treatment of those ideas is 'a matter of some interest,' though beyond the scope of her essay (241n2). A complete analysis of the development of

A society clearly grounded in love, *leaute*, and lawfulness remains a relatively remote ideal throughout the poem, though the duty to strive for that ideal is never diminished. (Will's second Dream will reveal just how hard it can be to achieve among the fair field of folk.) In good marriages, however, these qualities can be much nearer one's grasp. The lawfulness of honest wedlock is declared in the liturgy; spouses take each other 'pro *legitimo* sponso' and 'pro *legitima* sponsa' – as lawful wedded husbands and wives. Furthermore, mutual love and loyal fidelity can at least be reasonably approximated in marriage, if not achieved in unswerving perfection. And the familial model underlies many medieval social structures, from the households of lords (often called *familiae*), to monasteries and convents ruled by father-abbots and mother-abbesses, to the paternal authority of kings, bishops, and popes and the maternal authority of Holy Church herself. Good marriages and mutually supportive families offer hope for society, and a counter-example to the anti-values signified by the marriage and self-serving *familia* – whether family, friends, or followers – of Meed and False.

As an early episode of Langland's poem, the three passus on Lady Meed naturally set the stage for many subsequent developments of theme and action. For instance, the paradoxical combination of divine *mercede* and divine meed – the reward given to humanity *juxta opera sua* together with the gift of unearnable grace – will underlie both the recurrent question of the salvation of just pagans and the luminous description of the Passion and Redemption in the Easter Passus.[92] Passages related to marriage are no exception to this phenomenon of 'foretastes.' The charter of sins anticipates the Confession of Sins in the second Dream; the problem of marriages by *brocage*, marriages *for* meed instead of the marriage *of* Meed, will be an important element in Wit's treatment of literal marriages, as will the principle of kind following kind. The ideal of a rule by love, law, and *leaute* will reappear frequently throughout the poem, not least in Wit's definition of marriage as doing well by living in law and love. And the notion of family as a positive model for society, while still in embryo here, will begin to emerge in Piers's love for his own family and workers; it will continue maturing through the poem and reach full stature with Christ's liberation of his 'bloody brethren' from Hell.

the *leaute* theme across all three texts, including its appearance in the Trajan scene, would be most welcome.

[92] C. David Benson discusses the ways in which Meed ironically foreshadows the unearned gift of the Redemption in 'The Function of Lady Meed,' 198–205; see also Stokes, *Justice and Mercy*, 142; and James Simpson, 'Spirituality and Economics in Passus 1–7 of the B Text,' *YLS* 1 (1987), 92–93.

2

Do-wel in this World

In Will's second Dream, references to marriage and family are relatively scattered, at least in comparison to the extended marital metaphor operating throughout the Meed episode. As Chapter 4 will demonstrate, illuminating vignettes of familial relationships do occur in the second Dream, but these brief pictures are sharply subordinated to its main narrative line, from the Confession of the Sins through the plowing of the half-acre to the Pardon scene. Will's search for Do-wel, by contrast, brings familial and marital topics into prominence once more, on both the literal and the metaphoric planes. Because discussion of these matters is most thorough in the first long didactic monologue of the third Dream – Wit's discourse on the nature of Do-wel in A.10/B.9/C.10 – this chapter will focus on that discourse.[1]

Wit's special concern with familial behavior appears from the very start of his speech, in the figure he uses to describe the relations among the three Do's, Anima, Kynde, Inwit, and the senses and limbs. Anima is protected by interior faculties whose relationships are partly described in family terms, both in the modern sense of family as kin and in the larger medieval sense of *familia* as household. Anima herself is Kynde's betrothed, soon to be kin to him through marriage, the beloved chosen one for whom he will eventually send or come. The discussion of the proper use of Inwit leads to further commentary on the physical and spiritual responsibilities of families, including the family of the Church, for their weaker members. Finally, Wit offers a detailed analysis of the merits

---

[1] An excellent discussion of the pertinence of these familial references to the poem is given by Joseph S. Wittig, ' "Piers Plowman" B, Passus IX–XII: Elements in the Design of the Inward Journey,' *Traditio* 28 (1972), 211–29. See also D. W. Robertson, Jr., and Bernard F. Huppé, *Piers Plowman and Scriptural Tradition* (Princeton, 1951), 112–20; Robert W. Frank, Jr., *Piers Plowman and the Scheme of Salvation: An Interpretation of Dowel, Dobet, and Dobest* (New Haven, 1957), 51–54; Britton J. Harwood and Ruth F. Smith, 'Inwit and the Castle of Caro in *Piers Plowman*,' *NM* 71 (1970), 648–54; and Harwood, *Piers Plowman and the Problem of Belief* (Toronto, 1992), 57–63.

of matrimony in itself and the flaws in actual marriages as they are all too often practiced. In both its degree of detail and its length, this final portion of Wit's speech is the most complete discussion of literal marriages in the poem, and it will therefore receive particularly close attention in the pages below.

A general rationale for Wit's frequent references to households, families, and marriage in his discussion of Do-wel can be found in Will's repeated request for 'more kynde knowyng' of Do-wel, Do-bet, and Do-best.[2] The brief explanations offered by Thought or the friars do not satisfy the Dreamer; he wants to know where the three Do's dwell and how they operate 'on þis erþe' (A) or 'among þe peple' (B). Wit's answer is 'more kynde' in a number of ways. He speaks in some detail of man's nature or *kynde*, from the internal economy of the soul and its sensory and psychological faculties, to the appropriate fulfillment of one's social kind or status, and finally to the procreation of good and evil human kind through good and evil marriages. He presents human nature as the image of the divine nature, of the *kynde* of Kynde himself.

He casts his answer in terms of immediate and everyday experience: on earth and among the people, the three Do's will be found nearby, within each individual's nature and within each individual's most natural and personal relationships. And he establishes the notion of loving union through likeness of *kyndes*, a concept which will play a major role in Langland's treatment of the Redemption later in the poem.

Marriage and family life are highly suitable metaphors and examples for Wit's 'kinder' explanation of doing well, better, and best. They are already 'kind' in themselves: affective, extremely common, experientially concrete, virtually innate to the species, closely related to the physical generation of humankind and the moral generation of human nature. On earth and among the people, they are 'familiar' and 'native' in the radical senses of those words.[3] Medieval civilians and canonists regularly cited

---

[2] The best treatments of the full implications of the phrase 'kynde knowyng' are Hugh White's *Nature and Salvation in Piers Plowman* (Cambridge, 1988), pp. 41–59, and Mary Clemente Davlin's work, especially her 'Kynde Knowyng as a Major Theme in *Piers Plowman* B,' *RES* n.s. 22 (1971), 1–19, and 'Kynde Knowyng as a Middle English Equivalent for "Wisdom" in *Piers Plowman* B,' *MÆ* 50 (1981), 5–17. On the iconographic and intellectual backgrounds of the identification of Kynde and God, see Davlin's 'A Genius-Kynde Illustration in Codex Vat. Pal. Lat. 629,' *Manuscripta* 23 (1979), 149–58, and Brian Tierney, 'Natura id est Deus: A Case of Juristic Pantheism?' *Journal of the History of Ideas* 24 (1963), 307–22. See also Britton J. Harwood, 'Langland's *Kynde Knowyng* and the Quest for Christ,' *MP* 80 (1983), 242–55; and James Simpson, 'The Role of *Scientia* in *Piers Plowman*,' in *Medieval English Religious and Ethical Literature: Essays in Honour of G. H. Russell*, ed. Gregory Kratzmann and James Simpson (Cambridge, 1986), 49–65.

[3] Several senses of the ME noun *kinde* relate directly to marriage and family; see *MED*, s.v. *kinde* n., 10–13, 14a. Its other meanings are more generally related to nature, creation, inborn qualities, and the human race as a whole (senses 1–9, 15). Similarly broad

matrimony and the upbringing of children as examples of human institutions established by natural law.[4] Even more importantly, for Langland, parental *kyndes* are a major factor in determining the moral *kynde* of children – i.e., in determining whether those children will do well in this world. Wit shows that Do-wel, Do-bet, and Do-best are intrinsic to man's nature as it was originally created by God; 'Increase and multiply' was a part of that creation, as were Caro and Anima. Indeed, the literal experience of family life, with its procreative and educative functions, is so central to Langland's view of human nature that he uses it as a model for the psychological and social dimensions of that nature as well.

Before discussing Wit's remarks in detail, it will be useful to outline their general structure and content as these features unfold within and across the three texts. The easiest way to present such an analysis is in tabular form (see Figure 1).

As this outline demonstrates, Wit builds his discourse around two essentially fixed elements: the allegory of the Castle of Caro with which the speech begins, and the history of Cain, Seth, Noe, and contemporary marriages with which it ends. Though Langland tinkers with these passages in each version of the poem, altering occasional subtopics, examples, and details, it seems clear that he had no doubts about their indispensability in Wit's discussion of Do-wel. Such is not the case for Wit's treatment of the divine image in man or of human social responsibilities. These elements vary significantly from one version to the next, suggesting that the middle section of the speech was a continuing area of dissatisfaction and experimentation for the poet. Nonetheless, the seeds of the new material can be found in the earlier forms of these passages, despite the major changes between the texts. Comparisons of all three texts will help explain the more obscure connections and abrupt transitions of the later versions, as well as indicating certain developments in Langland's thinking on marriage, family, and related issues.

applications of the various senses of *kinde* (adj.) and *kindeli* (adj. and adv.) also occur throughout Wit's speech.

[4] *Inst.* 1.2.pr. = *Dig.* 1.1.1.3 (quoting Ulpian); *Decretum* D. 1, c. 7 (quoting Isidore, *Etym.* 5.4). See Tierney on distinctions made by the glossators on differences among various definitions of natural law, including these passages ('*Natura id est Deus*,' 309–16), and more generally Rudolf Weigand, *Die Naturrechtslehre der Legisten und Dekretisten von Irnerius bis Accursius und von Gratian bis Johannes Teutonicus*, Münchener Theologische Studien: Kanonistische Abteilung 26 (Munich, 1967), 78–85, 283–306; Jeremy Cohen, '*Be Fertile and Increase, Fill the Earth and Master It*': *The Ancient and Medieval Career of a Biblical Text* (Ithaca, 1989), 271–305; and Pierre J. Payer, *The Bridling of Desire: Views of Sex in the Later Middle Ages* (Toronto, 1993), 66–68, 129–30, 179–80.

Michael W. Twomey discusses the relation of natural law to marital procreation in a vernacular context in 'The Anatomy of Sin: Violations of *Kynde* and *Trawþe* in *Cleanness*' (Diss. Cornell, 1979), 72–85, and Kurt Olsson demonstrates its importance for Gower in 'Natural Law and John Gower's *Confessio Amantis*,' *M&H* n.s. 11 (1982), 229–61. Cf. pp. 80–82 below.

FIGURE 1: A STRUCTURE FOR WIT'S SPEECH

(Italicized line numbers represent passages so radically revised as to constitute new treatments, albeit of the same topics. They generally omit large portions of the material in the preceding version of the poem, and often add significant amounts of new material. In A.10.76–130/B.9.95–109α/C.10.187–201a, the revisions become still more profound; even the topics under discussion are changed.)

A.10	B.9	C.10	General content
THE INTERIOR HOUSEHOLD			
1–63	1–67	127–81	**The Castle of Caro; right ordering of human faculties**
1–24	1–24	127–49	Inhabitants of Caro
25–41α	*25–53*	*150–57*	Creation of world; God's image in man
42–54	54–60	170–73	Relation of Anima and Inwit
55–63	*61–67α*	*158–69*	Abuse of Inwit or of God's image
		174–81	
THE SOCIAL FAMILY			
64–130	68–109α	182–201a	**Duties of care for others and obedient steadfastness in one's vocation**
64–75	*68–94α*	*182–84*	Care of infants, fools, and other dependents by family and church
76–130	—	—	*Timor domini*; following conscience; holding humbly to one's calling
—	*95–109α*	*185–86*	*Timor domini* (B); not wasting speech or time; do-best as right use of time in speech and 'trewe tidy. . .trauaille' (B)
—	—	187–201a	Pastoral responsibilities of prelates
TREWE WEDDED LIBBYNGE FOLK			
131–215	110–201	202–300	**Do-wel = right use of marriage**
131–38	110–20	202–05	Marriage as source of saints
139–64	*121–33α*	206–19	Cain and his cursed offspring
165–77	134–45	220–31	Noe
—	*146–55α*	232–42a	*Filius non portabit. . .*
178–81	156–58	243–53	Cain and his seed (reprise and transition)
182–215	159–201	254–300	Contemporary marriages
—	*182–86α*	281–87	Marriage as remedy for fornication
216–18	**202–10**	**301–07**	**Recapitulation of Do's**

The Interior Household

The Castle of Caro

In answering Will's questions about the location and operation of Do-wel, Do-bet, and Do-best, Wit follows the reasonable expository strategy of beginning at the beginnings. In order to explain the three Do's, he analyzes their sources in the psychological and social givens of human nature as originally created by God. He starts his lesson in the psychological realm, by offering Will the allegory of the Castle of Caro, with its complex household of interdependent kinsfolk and retainers.

The explanation provides important new information about Do-wel from its opening words on. 'Sire Dowel. . .' is clearly a man of some worth, as the honorific *sire* suggests. His possession of a castle implies significant power and status, an implication confirmed by the later reference to him as 'duk of þise marchis' (A.10.11, B.9.11, C.10.137). His dwelling is indeed 'not a day hence,' for as we are about to see, he lives within the individual human being, 'man with his soule.' Already, Will's wanderings in search of Do-wel begin to look a bit misguided. Like charity, Do-wel begins at home; like Holy Church's *treuthe*, it is *kyndely* rooted in each person's heart (B.15.322–35, C.17.55–63; A.1.130, B.1.142, C.1.141).

The information that Do-wel's castle has been created from earth, *eir*, wind, and water prepares us for a scene of origins, in which the primary constituents of human nature – both matter and spirit – will be examined.[5] Those constituents have been 'wittiliche enioyned,' and the adverb suggests that Wit has the capacity and authority to expound this 'enjoining.' He is a reliable guide within the limits of his expertise, which is more or less limited to matters accessible to natural human intelligence. Although a number of critics have found Wit's teaching unsatisfactory in various ways – often for being mechanical in its metaphors, incomplete, or disunified – I hope to show that there is actually a good deal of moral depth and sound practical instruction in his discourse, and that its parts are more related and its metaphors richer than has sometimes been thought.[6]

---

[5] For reasons to interpret *eir* as a manifestation of the element fire, see Wittig, 'Design,' 217 and n. Or perhaps *eir* refers to the aether, which was sometimes taken as having both airy and fiery qualities (*MED*, s.v. *ether* n., 2), as Skeat suggests (2:138); against this view, see John Norton-Smith, *William Langland* (Leiden, 1983), 107–08.

[6] On the limitations and value of Wit's teaching, see Philomena O'Driscoll, 'The *Dowel* Debate in *Piers Plowman* B,' *MÆ* 50 (1981), 18–29. Harsher critics of Wit include S. T. Knight, 'Satire in *Piers Plowman*,' in S. S. Hussey, ed., *Piers Plowman: Critical Approaches*

The castle built by Kynde is not named until later in the passus, but its material and inhabitants leave no serious question as to its equivalence to the human body or flesh.[7] Wit's allegorical equation of the castle and the human body contrasts interestingly with the friar's recent comparison of the body to a one-man boat tossed upon the sea. The boat-simile emphasizes human weakness, instability, and isolation; the castle-allegory implies man's potential nobility, steadfastness, and strength in community. Both views have their merits, but the latter seems more in tune with Langland's own socially oriented vision.

To the political and aristocratic connotations of Do-wel's title and castle, Wit now adds overtones from the romance tradition, by introducing Anima as the 'lemman þat [Kynde] louiþ lik to hymselue' (A.10.6, B.9.6, C.10.132). Her enclosure in the castle recalls a wide range of analogues, from the enclosed beloved of Canticles to some versions of the Christ-Knight allegory to legends of kings' mistresses.[8] It echoes the beginning of some versions of the Christ-Knight allegory, which Langland will employ (with significant changes) in the Harrowing of Hell episode.[9] It must be noted, however, that the term 'lemman' here does not hint at any illicit quality in Kynde's relation to Anima.[10] Rather,

---

(London, 1969), 296–97; Mary Carruthers, *The Search for St. Truth: A Study of Meaning in Piers Plowman* (Evanston, 1973), 87–89; and Norton-Smith, *Langland*, 108–09. Elizabeth Kirk calls the castle metaphor 'mechanical,' but defends it for the way its details 'suggest the human realities of love, protection, defense, and future liberation'; see *The Dream Thought of Piers Plowman* (New Haven, 1972), 108.

[7] On the widespread metaphor of the body as castle, see Roberta D. Cornelius, *The Figurative Castle: A Study in the Medieval Allegory of the Edifice* (Bryn Mawr, 1930), 14–36; Pearsall lists a number of the more striking analogues to Langland's allegory, including passages in *Sawles Warde* and the *Chateau d'Amour* (C.7.232n). See also Wittig, 'Design,' 216–19, and Michael H. Frost, 'Symbolic Buildings in *Piers Plowman*: A Reading' (Diss. SUNY-Binghamton, 1984), 89–97. An elaborate working out of the image of the body-castle under attack by the devil can be found in Henry of Lancaster's *Livre de Seyntz Medicines*, ed. E. J. Arnould, ANTS 2 (Oxford, 1940), 64–84, where the hands, feet, and senses are given a crucial role in defending the body's central tower and treasury, the heart and soul.

[8] E.g., 'fair Rosamond' Clifford, reputed mistress of Henry II, to whom Langland probably refers in B.12.47. At Woodstock in the reign of Edward III, there was a chamber in a house beyond the park wall known as 'Rosamond's bower,' and Ranulph Higden relates the story of Henry building such a chamber to protect Rosamond from Eleanor of Aquitaine (*Polychronicon* 7.22; RS 41:8, 52–55). See Virgil B. Heltzel, *Fair Rosamond: A Study of the Development of a Literary Theme*, Northwestern University Studies in the Humanities 16 (Evanston, 1947), 4–6.

[9] Cf. Nicholas Bozon's *Vn rey esteit iadis ke aueit vne amye*, discussed by R. A. Waldron, 'Langland's Originality: The Christ-Knight and the Harrowing of Hell,' in *Medieval English Religious and Ethical Literature: Essays in Honour of G. H. Russell*, ed. Gregory Kratzmann and James Simpson (Cambridge, 1986), 67–73.

[10] For licit senses of *lemman*, especially with religious connotations, see *MED*, s.v. *lemman* n., 1a, d, 2. Langland refers positively to allegorical lemans elsewhere in the poem as well: e.g., B.2.21, C.2.20; B.14.303; B.18.102, C.20.115; for a negative use, B.20.156, C.22.156. See also Chap. 4, p. 179, below.

it reveals the power of his affection for her; she is his sweetheart, his darling, his one true love. Indeed, Wit implies that there is a promise of marriage between them by saying that Kynde will eventually send for Anima or come for her himself. Until that time, however, she will be in the protective keeping of Do-wel and Inwit, with the assistance of their families and household.[11] The threats to the love affair are not those of broken secrecy and scandal, but rather that a jealous, rival prince might seduce or ravish Anima away from her true lover. Once again, as for Meed, we find the suggestion of wardship over an attractive woman of high status; this time, however, the lady appears to be in the hands of more trustworthy guardians, at least as long as they regulate their household wisely.

Important to Wit's characterization of Kynde's love for Anima is the phrase 'lik to hymselue,' since it can be taken to modify either 'lemman' (Anima is a leman like Kynde himself) or 'louiþ' (Kynde loves Anima as he loves himself). Although the two possibilities are logically distinct, they may well not be mutually exclusive; as we shall see, love and likeness go hand in hand for Langland. In fact, the ambiguity of the phrase 'lik to hymselue' may be intended precisely to unite the two syntactic possibilities.

Within this chivalric allegory of lords, castle, leman, and so on, Do-wel plays a major role. He is a duke of the marches, and thus an extremely powerful royal vassal, with regalian rights in his marcher lands. He is probably to be seen as a close kinsman of his liege lord Kynde; real English dukes were generally of the blood royal until the late 1390s – the sons of Edward III, or his cousin Henry of Lancaster, for instance. Do-wel controls and protects crucial territory on the boundary of the kingdom. When loyal to his ruler, he is one of the staunchest supports of the realm; if loyal to his own interests first, as the marcher lords often were, he could be one of the most dangerous men in the land.[12] Though the castle certainly connotes strength and stability, as noted earlier, it remains a border-castle, one that must be ready for

---

[11] Affianced minors often lived with the families of their future spouses; a feudal guardian might also place his or her ward, betrothed or not, in the care of a third party with no interest in the ward's marriage. See Sue Sheridan Walker, 'The Marrying of Feudal Wards in Medieval England,' *Studies in Medieval Culture* 4 (1974), 209; 'Widow and Ward: The Feudal Law of Child Custody in Medieval England,' *Feminist Studies* 3 (1976), 106.

[12] As were such families as the Mortimers, Bohuns, Despensers, and other marcher lords under Edward II; see May McKisack, *The Fourteenth Century: 1307–1399* (Oxford, 1959), 58–67. If Langland grew up in Worcestershire, as his dialect indicates, or if his father was a tenant of the Despensers, then the young William may have learned at first or second hand of the strategic position, power, and rebellious tendencies of the marcher lords. For a good account of the March and its lords, see R. R. Davies, *Lordship and Society in the March of Wales* (Oxford, 1978).

attacks by the envious *princeps huius mundi.* By its very nature, humankind is situated in the borderlands – between spirit and matter, heaven and earth, the Tower of Truth and the *donjon* of Wrong. Castle Caro has been built and manned by Kynde, but its name echoes that of the earlier Castle of Care, and its final allegiance is still at issue.

Do-wel's protection of Anima is aimed primarily outward, against the wiles of the proud pricker of France who seeks to win her away from Kynde. Satan's 'enuye' toward Anima can be understood in a number of mutually reinforcing ways. If we take him as a rival suitor for Anima's affections, then his 'envy' of her can be seen as a sort of amorous jealousy, roughly equivalent to an envy of Kynde's possession of her.[13] Given the high rank of Kynde, Do-wel, and Anima suggested by the allegory, such jealousy could easily be seen as having political dimensions as well, representing the 'feudal' or even 'national' enmity between Satan and God. Gaining a foothold in Anima's affections would be a major victory for the Princeps-Huius-Mundi in his war against Kynde.[14] Part of Do-wel's duties as Anima's protector is to prevent her willing or unwilling *raptus* – a not uncommon experience for medieval English wards, even after their marriages were arranged.[15] From a different perspective, Satan can be said to envy Anima herself, since she has replaced him in Kynde's affections, as illustrated by the traditional notion of humanity filling up the seats of the fallen angels and by the common identification of envy as Satan's major motive for tempting Adam and Eve.

[13] Cf. Pearsall, C.10.133n.

[14] I suggest no particular political topicality here; the reference to the marches is general, not specifically Welsh, and the French origin of the Princeps-Huius-Mundi is sufficiently explained by the general English animosity toward France during much of the fourteenth century. (Though it is interesting to note that in 1377, there was some concern over French support of a Welsh invasion in Pembrokeshire; see Davies, *March of Wales*, 74n and CCR 1374–77: 487.) An intriguing mirror-image of Langland's princely and Gallic Adversary occurs in Gerson's 'Le profit de savoir quel est péché mortel et véniel,' where Satan's temptations of the soul are compared to embassies from the King of England to the Queen of France urging her to betray her lord and husband (*Oeuvres*, 7/1:387–89).

[15] See Walker, 'Marrying of Feudal Wards,' 218–22; and 'The Feudal Family and the Common Law Courts: The Pleas Protecting Rights of Wardship and Marriage, c. 1225–1375,' *Journal of Medieval History* 14 (1988), 19–21. In the former essay, Walker cites a case of an abduction by night of a minor heiress in the King's custody, from Warwick Castle (*CPR* 1317–21:39). In the mid-1330s, Ralph Stafford kidnapped the young heiress Margaret Audley from her parents' house and married her. Later, perhaps through Edward III's intervention, Stafford and Hugh Audley were reconciled enough for Audley to settle his daughter's inheritance (valued at over £2000/yr.) on Stafford; see *CPR* 1334–38:298; 1343–45:140). Less fortunate were the abductors of Margaret Blount, a royal ward, in 1362; the offense cost the perpetrators £240 (see Chap. 1, n. 70). *Raptus* also occurred lower down in the social hierarchy. A familiar example is the abduction of Chaucer's father John in 1324, for which his kidnappers were imprisoned and fined £250; Cecilia Chaumpaigne's *raptus* may also have involved some form of abduction.

The external protection which Do-wel offers to Anima is certainly necessary to her well-being, a *sine qua non*, but it is evidently not sufficient. She needs guidance, service, and protection within the castle, as well as external defense. Do-wel's active outside role is complemented first of all by the service given to Anima by Do-bet and the teaching given her by Do-best (the latter in BC only). The allegory of a noble household unfolds more clearly as we learn that Do-bet is Do-wel's daughter and that Do-best is a high-ranking ecclesiastic attached to the household in some way (a 'bishop's peer,' perhaps meant to suggest a royal confessor or counsellor). According to A, Do-bet helps with the 'keping' of Anima; her service to Anima could well be envisioned as that of a lady-in-waiting somewhat older than her mistress and noble in her own right, more like a governess or duenna than a serving maid. Thought's earlier definition of Do-bet in terms of service, gentleness, and generous altruism harmonizes nicely with Wit's picture of a duke's daughter whose *leel* constancy would make her an ideal companion and chaperone to the king's betrothed.[16] Similarly, Do-best's role as spiritual leader and teacher, obeyed even by Do-wel and Do-bet, fits well with Thought's definition of Do-best as a bishop who fearlessly governs his flock.[17]

The three Do's have additional help in their task of keeping Anima safe. The castle has a constable as well as a duke, and while Do-wel guards the surrounding marches, the constable Inwit and his clutch of warrior sons defend the castle proper. If Langland has a strictly consistent allegory of a marcher lordship in mind, then we should probably envision Inwit as being set in place by Do-wel, the marcher duke. On the other hand, the description of Caro as a castle made by Kynde, and the suggestion that Inwit, like grace, is given to Anima

[16] Norton-Smith suggests 'Lady Companion' as Do-bet's role (108). The ME word 'damysel' (L. *domicella*, OF *damoiselle*) frequently but not always means an unmarried woman, usually but not always young, and sometimes specifically in service to a high-born lady; see *MED*, s.v. *damisele* n., 1, 2. Chaucer's wife Philippa, for instance, was a *damoysele* of the Queen and of John of Gaunt's second duchess, Constance of Castile (*Chaucer Life-Records*, ed. Martin M. Crow and Clair C. Olson [Oxford, 1966], 67–87). On the role of 'mistresses' in the upbringing and chaperonage of young noblewomen, see Nicholas Orme, *From Childhood to Chivalry: The Education of the English Kings and Aristocracy 1066–1530* (London, 1984), 26–27, and cf. Chaucer's remarks in the *PhyT* 72–92. Actual mistresses of young noblewomen were likely to be married or widowed already. Whatever the social equivalent to Do-bet's function, her office of 'kepyng' Anima (A.10.15) does imply some authority over her lady. Some A-text scribes (MSS T, Ch, H2) alter Do-bet's relationship with Do-wel from 'daughter' to 'sister,' perhaps to make her seem older and thus a better 'keper' of Anima.

[17] The failure of the A text to define Do-best here may indicate, as Frank suggests, an incomplete working out of Do-best's meaning by the poet, remedied in BC (*Scheme*, 39). Or perhaps a line was lost from the A archetype, as occasionally happened in B (cf. K-D, 78–79, 81, 84–85, 90, 210).

directly by God, may allow us to imagine Inwit's constableship as an even more honorable office granted directly by Kynde. As Richard Firth Green has pointed out, the constableship of a royal castle in England was a prestigious and valuable appointment, an important sign of the king's favor.[18] The honor and military importance of such a constableship is taken for granted, not only in Wit's discourse, but also in other psychological castle-allegories of Langland's time: thus, in the *Summa Praedicantium*, Bromyard describes Reason as the *constabiliarius* of the soul-castle, while Gower's *Traitié* on married love speaks of the soul 'dont sur le corps raison ert conestable' (I.7, 14, 21).[19]

Further defense of Castle Caro is provided by the senses and limbs rightly used: See-*well*, Go-*well*, and so on.[20] These five wits, like Anima, are under the governance of the constable Inwit, the natural moral intelligence given to human beings so that they might control their affections, senses, and deeds. Even granting the spiritual authority of Do-best's teaching and counsel, Inwit's constableship gives him official command within the castle. He 'kepiþ hem alle,' and is charged with preserving '*caro & anima* / In rewele & in resoun'; 'aftir þe grace of God þe grettest is Inwyt' (A.10.16, B.9.17, C.10.142; A.10.50-51; A.10.48, B.9.60). As we shall see, Inwit's allegorical custody of Anima also provides Langland with a natural bridge into his discussion of familial and social obligations to persons still in their moral nonage.

Do-wel's castle, like real medieval castles, houses a relatively complex community of kin, allies, and retainers, united by blood, loyalty, and duty.[21] Only a dozen or so inhabitants of the castle are identified, but the idealized sketch of their relationships is broadly analogous to the large

---

[18] *Poets and Princepleasers: Literature and the English Court in the Late Middle Ages* (Toronto, 1980), 27, quoting Sir John Fortescue's fifteenth-century treatise on *The Governance of England*, Chap. 17. A number of fourteenth- and fifteenth-century instances of such appointments are given by Charles Plummer in his notes to Fortescue's work (1885; rpt. Westport, CT, 1979), pp. 326-37.

[19] *Summa Praed.* (Venice, 1586), s.v. 'Anima,' § 13; Gower, *Works* 1:379-89.

[20] As Pearsall points out, Langland's divergence from the usual list of the five purely sensory wits here is not without parallel elsewhere in Middle English (C.10.144n). Cf. *Cursor Mundi* 24000; *Castle of Love* 1173 (ed. Kari Sajavaara, *Mémoires de la Société Néophilologique de Helsinki* 32); John Audelay's 'De quinque sensus' (ed. Ella Keats Whiting, EETS 184, p. 184); and Chaucer's *Melibee* 971-72, 1420-24. An even closer analogue appears in the castle-body allegory of the *Livre de Seyntz Medicines*, where sight, hearing, smell, mouth (speech and taste), hands, and feet defend the soul within the heart. Authorial decisions to include hands, feet, and speech among the outer wits are quite suitable in contexts where choices among good and bad bodily acts are at stake, since a number of those acts do not fall readily under the senses properly defined.

[21] Recent discussions of the social, military, and religious dimensions of late medieval castle communities may be found in M. W. Thompson, *The Rise of the Castle* (Cambridge, 1991), 131-78, and N. J. G. Pounds, *The Medieval Castle in England and Wales: A Social and Political History* (Cambridge, 1990), 152-275.

households of fourteenth-century magnates, though one must allow for the more self-interested motives and greater organizational complexity in actual noble *familiae*.[22] By allegorizing the virtuous capacities and basic faculties of the individual in terms of a chivalric household, Wit implies several important things about individual human nature. For instance, the high rank of all the inhabitants of Caro reveals an intrinsic nobility in human nature; their hierarchical relationships of governance and support remind us that well-ordered faculties are essential to the moral defense of soul and body.

In some cases, the type of kinship between certain personifications reflects the nature and degree of their relation to each other. The five wits, for instance, are very closely related to Inwit; as the A text explains, Inwit is the 'beginner' and encourager of right use of the senses (A.10.52–53).[23] Furthermore, all of these faculties are meant to support each other dutifully and lovingly, like loyal members of a noble *meynee*. Do-best cannot exercise his guiding and correcting function if Do-wel does not protect the castle from external enemies. Do-wel and Inwit complement each other in external and internal defense, the one protecting Anima and Caro from Satan's assaults and wiles, the other from any waywardness that Anima might fall into on her own. In order to keep Caro and Anima safe for their liege lord, each of the human faculties must fulfill the purpose for which it was created by Kynde.

Inwit and the Image of God

Will responds to Wit's allegory of Do-wel's *meynee* with questions about the name of the castle (A) and the nature of Kynde. These questions give Wit a chance to gloss his previous answer in less metaphorical language,

---

[22] On such households, see Kate Mertes, *The English Noble Household 1250–1600: Good Governance and Politic Rule* (Oxford, 1988); Green, *Poets and Princepleasers*, 3–37; David Starkey, 'The Age of the Household: Politics, Society and the Arts, c. 1350–c. 1550,' in *The Later Middle Ages*, ed. Stephen Medcalf (New York, 1981), 225–90.

[23] On the significance of relations within Inwit's family, see Robertson and Huppé, *Scriptural Tradition*, 107–08; Randolph Quirk, 'Langland's Use of *Kind Wit* and *Inwit*,' *JEGP* 52 (1953), 185–88; Harwood and Smith, 'Inwit and *Caro*,' 648–54; Wittig, 'Design,' 217–19; Norton-Smith, *Langland*, 108–09; Ernest N. Kaulbach, '*Piers Plowman* B.IX.: Further Refinements of Inwitte,' in M. A. Jazavery et al., eds., *Linguistic and Literary Studies in Honor of Archibald A. Hill*, 4 vols. (The Hague, 1979), 4:103–10. The import of Wit's remark that Inwit's sons were born 'of his first wife' remains for me uncertain. Previous glosses on the 'first wife' include 'the old law' (Robertson and Huppé, 108), the unfallen will (Harwood and Smith, 652), the inferior reason or prudence (Wittig, 217–19), and the unfallen flesh (Pearsall, C.10.144n); Norton-Smith suggests that Inwit fathers two families, first the outer wits mentioned here and second the 'inward wits' (108). For James Simpson, Inwit represents the higher reason or wisdom (with Wit the inferior reason or prudence), and his first wife is the body on whom the senses are engendered (*Piers Plowman: An Introduction to the B-text* [London, 1990], 102).

and to provide new information. He immediately confirms what has already been implied: Kynde's identity as God the Creator, the Father and first of all things. Henceforth, any uses of the word *kynde* in the poem will bear at least a potential relationship to the Kynde that is God. The reference to Kynde as father enriches the familial metaphors for the Do's, Anima, and the senses, sanctifying those metaphors by extending them from the human realm to the divine. In addition, Wit again calls attention to the importance of origins, evoking the whole panorama of creation, from the eternal 'gynnynglessness' of God, to heaven and hell (*lisse* and *peyne*), to light and the angels, to all things and all beasts (or 'al þat forth groweth' in C), and finally to humankind itself (A.10.25–32, B.9.25–31, C.10.150–56).

In all three texts, Wit goes on to assert and discuss the creation of man in God's image and likeness, although the discussion takes notably different turns in each version. The mention of man's likeness to God harks back to Kynde's love for Anima, 'lik to hymselue,' and looks forward to the importance of likeness between marrying couples later in Wit's speech. All three texts explain this divine 'mark and shape' rather loosely, but there is a consistent suggestion that it is closely associated with the human possession of life and soul, and perhaps even some element of divinity proper.[24] Thus we have the 'gost of [the] godhed' breathed into Adam at creation; the 'lif þat ay shal laste'; Anima herself as the human soul and life-force; and Anima and Inwit together as the affective and morally rational aspects of the human spirit. The Lady Anima is indeed like her divine Lover, for she is a 'goost of þe godhede of heuene,' a spirit that will live forever in man and in all his *lynage* – the whole family descended from Adam and ultimately from the Father-Creator Kynde (A.10.32–41a, B.9.31–53, C.10.156–69).

A number of minor and major revisions occur in the B and C versions of this section of Wit's discourse. The B and C texts, for instance, omit Will's question about the name of the castle where Anima dwells, although the castle still obviously signifies the body or flesh. The C text also omits the point made in AB that God created human beings by word and work, instead of simply using his word as he had for all other creatures. In fact, the whole discussion of man's creation in God's image is sharply abridged in C, though the main point persists. On the other hand, B and C spend more time than A on the abuse of the divine

---

[24] On the image of God as a theme in the poem, see Barbara Raw, 'Piers and the Image of God in Man,' in Hussey, *Critical Approaches*, 143–79; and Daniel Maher Murtaugh, *Piers Plowman and the Image of God* (Gainesville, 1978). Cohen discusses exegetical views of the *imago dei* and its relation to dominion over nature and over physical aspects of human nature, including reproduction, in 'Be Fertile and Increase,' 224–43.

likeness by ungodlike behavior. But the most interesting and difficult revision here is a complex and ambitious passage in B (9.35–46), well described by Pearsall as a 'more adventurous disquisition' than its C replacement (C.10.157n).

The new B lines evidently grow out of A's remark that God created humankind by his work as well as his word (A.10.33–35, 40). In the second half of the B revision, Langland develops this idea by means of the troublesome pen and parchment simile for the creation of man (B.9.39–46), an image which has been explored by a number of critics in recent years.[25] The comparison makes at least two important points about the creation of human beings: first, that God employed more care and thoroughness in making man than for any other creature; second, that the creation of humankind reflects the several operations of the divine persons – work/might, word, and life mirroring Father, Son, and Spirit.

Less attention has been paid to the first half of the new passage in B, in which Langland expands the description of human origins to include the creation of Eve from Adam's rib:

> And al at his wil was wrou3t wiþ a speche,
> *Dixit & facta sunt,*
> Saue man þat he made ymage to hymself,
> And Eue of his ryb bon wiþouten any mene.
> For he was synguler hymself and seide *faciamus*
> As who seiþ, 'moore moot herto þan my word oone;
> My my3t moot helpe forþ wiþ my speche.' (B.9.33–38)

The explanatory clause here – 'For he was synguler . . .' – can be read as applying to the creation of Adam and Eve just described as well as to the following pen and parchment simile. The shaping of Eve from Adam's rib is clearly an example of God 'working' to create. Furthermore, the mention of Eve's creation may be intended as an example of God's reflection in 'man þat he made ymage to hymself.' The Deity is both singular in nature and plural in persons; so too the human race, even at its first moment in Adam and Eve (especially as portrayed in Gen. 1:26–27, the *Faciamus* and *imago dei* passage). Humanity reflects deity in its plurality of persons of one kind, a point that will be adumbrated later in the B text and worked out fully in C. Moreover, says Wit, Kynde 'seide

---

[25] Murtaugh, *Image*, 16–22; A. V. C. Schmidt, *The Vision of Piers Plowman: A Critical Edition of the B-Text*, new ed. (London, 1987), 277, 327–28, and 'Langland's Pen/Parchment Analogy in *Piers Plowman* B.IX.38–40,' *N&Q* 27 (1980), 538–39; Penn R. Szittya, 'The Trinity in Langland and Abelard,' in *Magister Regis: Studies in Honor of Robert Earl Kaske*, ed. Arthur Groos et al. (New York, 1986), 207–16; and Harwood, *Piers Plowman and the Problem of Belief*, 61 (with attention to 'word,' 'wit,' and 'work').

faciamus / As who seiþ, "moore moot herto þan my word oone; / My my3t moot helpe forþ wiþ my speche." ' Since God created Eve to be a help like unto Adam (*adiutorium simile sibi*, Gen. 2:18), we might at least consider the possibility that Langland was toying with a still richer notion: that the co-operation of the divine persons in human creation finds its image in the mutual help of man and woman in human procreation.

Such a reading of B.9.33-38 is admittedly speculative. The passage is too brief and receives too little support from A or C to allow interpretive certainty for a reading that may be as 'adventurous' as the lines themselves. In any case, Langland drops the material in the C version of Wit's speech. Still, it is worth remembering that a more extended statement of a similar idea will appear later in both the B and C texts, when Abraham compares the Trinity to the grades of chastity and to marriage itself (see Chap. 3, pp. 140-63 below).

In this first part of Wit's speech, human *kynde* is presented mainly in terms of the individual. To be sure, these terms are representative; Wit is speaking of generic Man, not a man. But Man is depicted as an individual body and soul, having particular, personal faculties of mind, sensation, and action. Human membership in society is suggested, but indirectly, in the image of the figurative household. Before moving on to discuss doing well in literal social contexts, Wit briefly re-invokes the castle allegory so as to deepen his exposition of the individual's responsibility for his own well-doing.

The allegory is most vividly recalled in A.10.38-63: we are reminded that Inwit and the other wits are 'enclosed' in castle Caro; Inwit is personified further as an 'ally' of Anima, heaven's *lemman*, suggesting a possible in-law or kinship relation between them.[26] Anima and Inwit have special dwelling places within the bodily castle – a 'home in the heart' and a 'bower in the brain' respectively; and Sir Princeps Huius Mundi appears again as the lurking enemy eager to gain power over men's souls. In B.9.50-60 and even more in C.10.170-73, the household conceit is less elaborate, but the general metaphor is still revived in the line 'Inwit and alle wittes enclosed ben þerInne' (B.9.54, C.10.170; cf. A.10.42).

All of the versions provide further information on the relation between Anima and Inwit; they all connect Anima with the heart and thus with affective behavior, and link Inwit to a rational self-rule over

---

[26] See *MED*, s.vv. *allie* n., 2; *allien* v., 2; *alliaunce* n., 2, 3. 'Allie' in A.10.47 is a conjectural emendation, but an attractive and plausible one: three MSS have the meaningless 'halle' (a homoeographic error according to Kane, p. 133), the other ten (followed by Knott-Fowler) have the relatively colorless word 'help.'

Anima's affective tendencies. Again, the A text makes these points more vividly than either B or C. In A, Inwit is characterized as a desired ally to Anima, a help to her, a wise governor who keeps both '*caro & anima* / In rewele & in resoun' (A.10.47-51). The only way that Inwit's own *bremenesse* can be overthrown is if the blood – the heart's humor, and thus a suitable sign of excess in the affective faculties – should grow 'wantoun & wilde, wiþoute any resoun.' The phrase 'wantoun & wilde' carries interesting connotations of an ungoverned, willful childishness; in the medieval period and later, the two adjectives were often applied, together or separately, to unruly children (*OED*, s.vv. *wanton* a., 1a, and *wild* a., 6a, b, 7a, b). A dozen lines later, Langland will have Wit advise adults who are rearing children to 'witen hem [the children] fro wauntounesse' (A.10.66-67; see below, pp. 67-68). The A-text discussion of Inwit's responsibility for Anima warns us that when blood, heart, and ungoverned affect overpower brain, head, and reason, the ensuing subversion of moral order is as dangerous and unacceptable as if an incompetent but rebellious minor were to defy his or her lawful guardian, repudiating the wise counsel and defense required against an enemy ever ready to attack.[27]

The B and C texts are much flatter and more concise in their treatment of Inwit's governance of Anima. B still shows the lady 'walking and wandering' throughout the body and making the heart her particular 'hoom and hir mooste reste'; Inwit, on the other hand,

> is in þe heed and to þe herte he lokeþ
> What *anima* is leef or looþ; he let hire at his wille,
> For after þe grace of god þe gretteste is Inwit. (B.9.56-60)

C drops the image of the perambulating lady, observing simply that Anima lives 'by loue and by leute,' and that life (presumably still a synonym for Anima as in AB) 'lyueth by inwit and leryng of Kynde; / Inwit is in the heued and *Anima* in herte' (C.10.171-73).

Although A had certainly recommended that Inwit rule Anima, it also granted the soul some decision-making power of her own, calling her a *ledere* in 10.46; B, on the other hand, has Anima led by Inwit, though apparently he at least 'lokeþ what' her desires may be. In C, Anima's leadership or preferences are not mentioned at all; we may note, however, that her guidance now seems to come from the warmer, affective qualities of love and *leute* as well as from Inwit and the teaching of Kynde.

---

[27] See Walker, 'Proof of Age of Feudal Heirs in Medieval England,' *MS* 35 (1973), 310, on minor heirs disputing their guardians' rights to take seisin of their lands.

These seemingly small changes in the relation between Anima and Inwit may reflect a growing conservatism in Langland's estimate of the instinctive, non-rational side of human nature.[28] In each revision, the lady Anima loses small increments of leadership or influence, and the importance of Inwit's rational self-control grows correspondingly larger. Indeed, over the three texts, Langland will lay greater and greater stress on the wickedness of abusing Inwit and reason. The affective dimension is not bad in itself – Anima supplies the breath of life as well as the heart's impulses, and both love and *leute* have strong affective components – but it must be rationally governed. The changes that the poet makes in this passage need not mean a change in his basic position on the issue, but they certainly indicate a shift in what he felt needed to be emphasized most in his discussion. Later in the poem, toward the end of the search for Do-wel, the name Anima will be claimed by a more authoritative, less anthropomorphic, entity whose nature comprehends a far wider range of faculties than the Anima of Wit's speech. Here, however, Langland distributes those faculties among different personifications so as to illustrate their relative roles more clearly, and perhaps also to illustrate Will's growth in wisdom from the 'fragmented' beginning to the more integrated end of his interior quest. It is only when one achieves proper self-governance through the right balance of Inwit and Anima (or head and heart, wit and will, law and love) that the heart can truly become the 'heiȝe welle' and fountainhead of *kynde knowyng*, the throne room of Charity, and the garden wherein God plants Trewe-love.[29]

From Inwit's governance of Anima, Wit's discourse moves easily into commentary on misgovernance through the abuse of Inwit. For children and fools, Inwit is naturally undeveloped or lacking, and they are not to be blamed for that lack.[30] But those who drown their Inwit in ale, as the A text puts it, have voluntarily overthrown the faculty which should

---

[28] Bruce Harbert gives a more detailed analysis of the C text's greater emphasis on reason, in contrast to the will, in 'A Will with a Reason: Theological Developments in the C-Revision of *Piers Plowman*,' *Religion in the Poetry and Drama of the Late Middle Ages in England*, ed. Piero Boitani and Anna Torti (Cambridge, 1990), 149–61.

[29] On the special connection of *kynde knowing* with the heart – suggesting depth and intimacy, and a particular relation to the inner nature of the knower – see White, *Nature and Salvation*, pp. 49–50, 53.

[30] The age of reason or discretion, like the age of majority, varied according to context, social class, and author; 7, 12, 14, and 21 were among the common transition points from one moral or legal state to another. Cf. *Decretum*, C.22 q.5 cc. 14–16 (*Ord. Gloss:* 'haec aetas [before discretion] nescit quid agat'), and X 5.23. See also the authorities cited by Thomas N. Tentler on the proper age for confession, in *Sin and Confession on the Eve of the Reformation* (Princeton, 1977), 70, n. 1. On leniency toward idiots and lunatics guilty of crimes in medieval England, see Nigel Walker, *Crime and Insanity in England*, vol. 1, The Historical Perspective (Edinburgh, 1968), Chaps. 1 and 2. See also n. 32 below.

protect them from the prince of this world, and they will be held responsible for betraying their obligations to Kynde. Drunkards are Langland's favorite example of Inwit abused; his disgust at excessive drinking and related sins can be seen in Glutton's graphic confession earlier in the poem. Given its particular tendency to impair judgment and rational inhibitions, drunkenness is an excellent concrete instance of the way sin undermines God's creative and redemptive intentions, destroying his divinely given and redeemed image by turning men bestial and devilish.

B's description of misruled Inwit is much harsher than A's. The later text shows such misrule to be equivalent to serving Satan, and thus making one's soul 'lich þe deuel' instead of like the God who is Love. The A text had spoken first of blood overpowering brain, almost as though such an event might be involuntary, a physiological superfluity or imbalance; in contrast, B immediately focuses on more intentional behavior: Woe worth the man who *misrules* his Inwit! To A's example of drunken sots with drenched Inwit, B adds 'glubberous' gluttons: 'Their god is their stomach,' 'They serve Satan,' 'Their soul is like the Devil.' By directing their worship away from God in an especially disgusting way (like the Pardoner's Flemish rioters), these gluttons and drinkers have warped their God-given divine likeness into a likeness to Satan. The B text makes the important point that likeness and image manifest themselves in action. The image of God – the ghost from the Godhead given to each human being, the lady Anima rightly governed by Inwit – is revealed in the living of a good life. Doing well and the divine image are inextricably intertwined, which is why Wit has answered Will's questions about the Do's with so much information about Anima, Inwit, and God's image in man:

> And alle þat lyuen good lif are lik to god almyȝty
> *Qui manet in caritate in deo manet &c.* (B.9.65–65a)

The C text expands still further on the misuse of Inwit and the obscuring effects of sin on God's image. It adds some of the most infamous cases of Inwit lost 'thorw lykerous drynke' (Lot, Noe, Herod; C.10.176–79). It also describes how the soul's similitude to God is destroyed by other sins, from lechery, suicide, and greed to the root sin of putting a creature before God, of loving and believing 'on catel more then on Kynde' (C.10.168). The new version recalls a key issue from the beginning of the poem: the right use of worldly *tresour* and heavenly *tresour*. The misrule of Inwit in B becomes misspending in C (B.9.61, C.10.174); the emphasis has shifted slightly, from good governance to proper use. Finally, C amplifies Inwit's importance by characterizing it in language previously applied to Truth: 'goddes oune goed, his grace and his tresour' (cf. 'when all treasures are tried, Truth is the best'). To have Inwit is to have 'tresor ynow of Treuthe' – treasure from Truth and also treasure composed of truth within oneself (C.10.180–81). No longer is Inwit said to be 'greatest *after* grace' (cf. A.10.48, B.9.60; my emphasis); rather, in C it appears to be a part of God's grace itself. Like grace, love, and the life without end given by God, Inwit is an aspect of the soul's likeness to her Creator, a likeness that can be clouded over or lost through sin.

Wit's lesson on Do-wel thus begins with the fact that all mentally competent adults possess Inwit and the three Do's (or the three degrees of power to do well, to de-nominalize the language) as part of their basic nature. They thus have the innate capacity and duty to employ those faculties in protecting their souls. The A text makes the claim most fully:

> Ac iche wiȝt in þis world þat haþ wys vndirstonding
> Is chief souereyn ouer hymself his soule to ȝeme,
> And cheuisshen hym for any charge whan he childhod passiþ,
> Saue hymself fro synne, for so hym behouiþ;
> For werche he wel oþer wrong, þe wyt is his owene.
> Þanne is dowel a duc þat destroyeþ vices,
> And sauiþ þe soule þat synne haþ no miȝt
> To routen ne to resten ne roten in þin herte. (A.10.71–78)

In the process of revision, the explicit assertion in these lines drops out of B, though it may be implied by the biblical tag, 'Et dimisi eos secundum desideria eorum' (B.9.67a; Ps. 80:13). God forsakes those who desire evil, letting them follow their own free will and giving them, in a sense, what they've been asking for. As C says in connection with the same psalm verse, 'God wol nat of hem wyte bute lat hem yworthe' (C.10.163–64a). Moreover, like A, the C text openly affirms the essential self-sovereignty of individuals, albeit more briefly and with an acknowledgment of the importance of physical as well as mental competence: 'Euery man þat hath inwit and his hele bothe / Hath tresor ynow of Treuthe to fynden hymsulue' (C.10.180–81).

To sum up the first section of Wit's discourse: the interior duchy and the interior household are under the defense and guidance of the natural faculties set in each person by the Creator. Every 'man with his soule' contains within himself the royal officers who can keep, *ȝemen*, and *fynden* the strategically vital fief and beloved leman entrusted to them by Kynde. To betray this trust is to destroy the very likeness of God itself. The political aspects of the metaphor look back to the commonwealth of the Visio, and to its miniature reflection in Thought's definitions of the Do's as a realm ruled by a king (A.9.90–100, B.8.100–

110, C.10.99-105), but Wit's allegory operates on a somewhat smaller and more personalized scale. He presents right action in figurative terms more suited to the private governance and society of a large household than to the public affairs of a kingdom (although public duties are not completely irrelevant for Do-wel's household). As the passus approaches its conclusion, we shall see still homelier, *kyndere* expressions of doing well, in the little societies of married couples and their immediate offspring.

The Social Family

Helping the Helpless

Between Wit's discussion of the inhabitants of Caro and his analysis of the merits of matrimony and the defects in contemporary marriages lies a passage which varies greatly from each version of *Piers Plowman* to the next (A.10.64–130/B.9.68–109α/C.10.182–201a; cf. Figure 1 above). However, two principal features of this portion of Wit's speech are common to all three texts and important for the purposes of this study. First, Wit's remarks always pertain in one way or another to the material and spiritual obligations that human beings have to one another through kinship or calling. Second, the rhetorical function of those remarks always includes the introduction of marriage as a major example of doing well in this world.

The revisions in this middle section of Wit's speech have a number of effects. Most importantly, the three texts emphasize different kinds of social responsibilities, directing our attention to different classes of people and kinds of duty (e.g., from more or less ordinary Christians to the leaders of the Church, and from duties toward nearby people or in daily work to a world-wide spiritual mission). Furthermore, as the various revisions modulate each version of the speech into the next, they gradually redefine the kind of well-doing exemplified by ideal marriage. Thus the nature of marital virtue is presented in somewhat different terms in each text, with inevitable consequences for the interpretation of each text taken alone. On the other hand, most of the revisions that occur in the middle section of Wit's discourse do not contradict the prior version(s) of the passage in any obvious way. Hence, I shall be reading Langland's deletions and additions of material more often as a reflection of his changing preoccupations than as a sign of major changes in his basic views; evidence for significant alterations in his beliefs should be more striking than the revisions I shall be discussing here.[31]

Wit's discussion of Inwit and Anima in the A text has presented the implicit image of a minor under tutelage, an image which leads smoothly into a typical Langlandian qualification: infants, and idiots likewise, do not possess reason and thus cannot be held accountable for their actions – though those actions may be wicked in themselves:[32]

> In ȝonge fauntes & folis, wiþ hem failiþ Inwyt. . . .
> Ac in fauntis ne in folis þe fend haþ no miȝt
> For no werk þat þei werche, wykkide oþer ellis.
> Ac þe fadir & þe Frendis for fauntis shuln be blamid
> But þei witen hem fro wauntounesse whiles þei ben ȝonge.
> (A.10.58, 64–67)

Although the two later versions of the poem do not explain the implications of a 'failing' in one's Inwit as clearly as A, they too bring up the fact that 'fauntes and fooles' lack the faculty and go on to discuss the ways in which society is responsible for the care of these and other helpless persons. In the A text, Wit emphasizes the duties of immediate family and near relatives: the 'fadir & þe Frendis' are responsible for warning children away from 'wauntounesse' during their youth.[33] The word looks immediately back to 'wantoun' in line 57 (describing the Inwit-balking effects of 'blood . . . bremere þanne brayn'), and it may be used here with some of its etymological force of 'undisciplined, ill-reared' (OE *wan-togen*). Even if the root sense of the word was lost to Langland, he would very likely have known the common application of

---

[31] For a good example of significant shifts in Langland's views on a topic, see E. T. Donaldson's discussion of Langland's changing ideas on beggars and minstrels, in *Piers Plowman: The C-Text and Its Poet* (1949; rpt. Hamden, 1966), 130–55.

[32] Under English law, idiots who were heirs were given guardians; lunatics could be absolved of the penalties for crimes committed during a period of madness; and minors could claim exemptions from lawsuits until they came of age. See Bracton 2:324, 384, 4:177, 308; P & M, 1:481, 2:438–44, 480; Barbara Hanawalt, *Crime and Conflict in English Communities, 1300–1348* (Cambridge, MA, 1979), 125–28 (children), 145–50 (the 'insanity plea'); Richard Neugebauer, 'Treatment of the Mentally Ill in Medieval and Early Modern England,' *Journal of the History of the Behavioral Sciences* 14 (1978), 158–69; and Nigel Walker's *Crime and Insanity*, vol. 1 (n. 30 above).

Care of orphans was also a matter of communal and legal concern, as shown by Elaine Clark in 'The Custody of Children in English Manor Courts,' *Law and History Review* 3 (1985), 333–48, and by Sue Sheridan Walker, 'Widow and Ward: The Feudal Law of Child Custody in Medieval England,' *Feminist Studies* 3 (1976), 104–16 (also in *Women in Medieval Society*, ed. Susan Mosher Stuard [Philadelphia, 1976], 159–72). See also Brundage, cited in n. 35 below.

[33] See Chap. 1 n. 8 above on the phrase 'fader and frendes.' In at least some communities, the *proximi amici* were also expected to care for lunatics, and to 'ensure that they come to no harm or loss and that they do not harm to others' (Walker, *Crime and Insanity* 1:30, quoting fourteenth-century Bristol Borough Customs).

the term to children, meaning 'unruly, naughty' and often collocated with 'wild' as in line 57 (see p. 62 above).

Langland now has Wit take an interesting step, from the moral guidance owed children by their families to the physical support and protection owed by the Church to those who lack the material or psychological capacity to care for themselves.[34] As in the description of the defense of Caro and Anima by the Do's and the wits, we again find the verb 'keep'; when Inwit and the Do's cannot function, then the Church should give her aid:

> And ȝif þei ben pore & cateles, to kepe hem fro ille,
> Þanne is holichirche owyng to helpe hem & saue
> Fro folies, & fynde hem til þei ben wise. (A.10.68–70)

Line 70 seems to allow for the care of fools as well as for children without families; in B, Langland will draw the Church's mantle over other dependent and helpless persons too, albeit at some cost to the original logic of his argument about a childish lack of wisdom and Inwit. But the implication will remain: the Church is itself a family, with family responsibilities to its members. Until children and other dependents achieve the capacity for moral and economic independence, they should be given instruction against *wauntounesse*, protection against folly, and material support by parents, relatives, guardians, or churchmen – the senior members of their physical and spiritual families.

The B text expands significantly on the issue of familial responsibility to the weak and helpless. The new lines (B.9.68–94*a*) move in a direction that is different from, though not incompatible with, that of A's discussion. Where A starts with the obligations of the natural family and moves on to analogous responsibilities in the Church, B focuses on spiritual families throughout – not merely the institutional church but also the far more personal relationship of godparents and godchildren. Both texts insist on moral and physical support for children, fools, and other socially helpless persons, of course, but B modifies A's position in some interesting ways. First, it pays more attention to physical care for the needy, especially by the Church. Second, B's definition of 'needy' has expanded and made explicit A's phrase 'pore & cateles,' so that poor widows and poor maidens as well as orphans and madmen are counted among those who 'lakken Inwit.'[35] Apparently, lacking Inwit

---

[34] On the care of children abandoned by their natal families, see John Boswell, *The Kindness of Strangers: The Abandonment of Children in Western Europe from Late Antiquity to the Renaissance* (1988; rpt. New York, 1990), with a relatively optimistic reading of the care given foundlings by those who reared them, whether religious or lay.

[35] On the support of infirm widows, as prescribed in B, see Elaine Clark, 'Some Aspects of Social Security in Medieval England,' *Journal of Medieval History* 7 (1982), 310–11. Clark

here means more than just not having attained the state of moral discretion; Langland seems to have a broader concept in mind, something more like 'being unable to care for oneself.' He recognizes that individuals can not always control the economic factors that reduce them to poverty – a fact which, as this passage suggests, almost certainly affected women more than men. Like his notable C-addition 'þat most neden aren oure neyhebores' (C.9.71–161), Wit's comments here in B demonstrate Langland's unremitting compassion for the genuinely needy.

However, the B text does not omit teaching as an important duty to those in need. The Church should still 'helpe . . . and saue, / And fynden' those who lack Inwit, but she should give them *loore* as well (B.9.69–73). Wit insists equally strongly on the *loore* owed by godparents to godchildren:

> Godfader and godmoder þat seen hire godchildren
> At myseise and at myschief and mowe hem amende
> Shul purchace penaunce in purgatorie but þei hem helpe.
>
> (B.9.77–79)

While 'amending misease and mischief' might include supplying physical needs, the following lines show that instruction in God's law is the main concern here:

> For moore bilongeþ to þe litel barn er he þe lawe knowe
> Than nempnynge of a name and he neuer þe wiser. (B.9.80–81)

By focusing on godparents instead of the 'fadir & þe Frendis,' the B text does not so much deprecate the natural obligations of blood kindred as it shows how those important duties extend to the bonds of spiritual family. The godparent relation is a personalized, cameo version of the relation of the Church to each Christian. Like the baptismal sponsors at a christening, Holy Church 'underfongeth at the font' her spiritual children (cf. A.1.74, B.1.76, C.1.73; B.11.118, C.12.51).[36] If individual

notes that medieval old-age pension arrangements 'rendered any dereliction of duty to the old a matter of public concern and communal review, of possible censure, even of intervention' (311). James Brundage discusses the still largely unstudied question of the Church's responsibility for widows, orphans, and indigent persons in 'Widows as Disadvantaged Persons in Medieval Canon Law,' in Louise Mirrer, ed., *Upon My Husband's Death: Widows in the Literature and Histories of Medieval Europe* (Ann Arbor, 1992), 193–206; see also Barbara Hanawalt's 'The Widow's Mite: Provisions for Medieval London Widows,' in the same volume, pp. 21–45.

[36] For godparents' actions during the baptismal ceremony (including the *levatio* from the font), and for their responsibilities to their godchildren, see A. Jefferies Collins, ed., *Manuale ad Usum Percelebris Ecclesiae Sarisburiensis*, HBS 91 (Chichester, 1960), 35–43, and references there to de Burgh, canon law, and other sources; William G. Henderson, ed., in *Manuale et Processionale ad Usum Insignis Ecclesiae Eboracensis*, Surtees Society 63 (Durham,

godparents have obligations to their children in God, then *a fortiori* so does the Christian community and especially its episcopal leadership. The jump from godparents to prelates after B.9.77–81 is not as broad as it may seem at first, though it does move rather abruptly from spiritual back to physical needs.

Yet another intriguing revision in the B text, and perhaps the most prophetic of things to come in C, is the specific attention paid to prelates in B.9.82–94a. If bishops spend the Church's silver, the *patrimonium Christi*, on japers instead of on needy beggars, then they are no better than Judas, the larcenous keeper of the apostles' funds (cf. Jn. 12:6, 13:29). Frivolous wasters of the 'family heritage,' they are *unkynde* in a wide range of senses: unnatural, unloving, rejecters of the bonds of kinship, even ungodly (since God is Kynde). The word *kynde* and its derivatives occur three times in these fourteen lines, suggesting Langland's desire to integrate the new passage with the rest of Wit's speech. The poet also indicates the origin of the spiritual bond of *kynde* by the repetition of *cristene, cristes,* and *christi,* identifying Christendom as a kin-group. Membership in that group begins with christening (whence the importance of godparents) but carries responsibilities far beyond the mere 'nempnynge of a name.'[37] In comparison to the shameful treatment of needy Christians by the leaders of the Christian family, says Langland, the close family and community ties among the Jews are a model of the loving fulfillment of natural duties to one's helpless kin and co-believers.[38]

This discussion of the responsibility of prelates to use 'cristes good' for the good of the poor also relates the B version of Wit's speech more fully

1875), 16–22 (York), 151*–54* (St Asaph). Barbara Hanawalt discusses the place of godparents in the lives of medieval families, and suggests that they played a relatively passive role, at least as far as tangible outcomes are concerned; see *The Ties That Bound: Peasant Families in Medieval England* (New York, 1986), 246–48. See also Joseph H. Lynch, *Godparents and Kinship in Early Medieval Europe* (Princeton, 1986), a work which focuses on the early Middle Ages, but often looks forward to later periods as well; and Louis Haas, 'Social Connections between Parents and Godparents in Late Medieval Yorkshire,' *Medieval Prosopography* 10/1 (Spring 1989), 1–21.

[37] In England, it was the godparents who named children at baptism, and they gave their own names to same-sex godchildren very frequently (perhaps in as many as 80 to 90 per cent of all baptisms). See Philip Niles, 'Baptism and the Naming of Children in Late Medieval England,' *Medieval Prosopography* 3/1 (Spring 1982), 95–107, and Michael J. Bennett, 'Spiritual Kinship and the Baptismal Name in Traditional European Societies,' in *Principalities, Powers, and Estates: Studies in Medieval and Early Modern Government and Society,* ed. L. O. Frappel, 1–13 (Adelaide, 1979).

[38] Using thirteenth-century eyre rolls, Zefira Entin Rokeah makes a strong case that unnatural deaths of English children, whether deliberate or due to negligence, were not uncommon among Christians but were virtually unheard of in Jewish families; she also cites other studies of strong family ties in medieval Jewish culture. See 'Unnatural Child Death Among Christians and Jews in Medieval England,' *Journal of Psychohistory* 18 (1990), 181–226 and nn. 146–47.

to several of the poem's recurrent themes: the right use of *bona temporalia*, especially by the Church; the concern for the good of the *comune*; the contrast between giving to the true poor and spending money on worldly entertainment. And thanks to the generally familial context of the passage here, we learn that these questions can also be seen in terms of family bonds and obligations. For Langland, these social duties should not be a burden but rather the expression of mutual love and support based on underlying kinship.

In C, a different sort of prelatical responsibility comes to the fore. 'Frendes' are still advised to support and protect children and idiots, and the Church is still urged to assist in these obligations, so as to help prevent beggary and the misspending of speech, time, and tangible goods:

> Ac fauntokynes and foles þe which þat fauten inwit,
> Frendes shal fynde hem and fram folye kepe
> And holy churche helpe to, so sholde no man begge
> Ne spille speche ne tyme, ne myspende noyther
> Meble ne vnmeble, mete noþer drynke. (C.10.182–86)

But this advice has been condensed from thirty-odd lines in B to a mere five in C, in order to give room and emphasis to the needs of a different group of people: 'oure enemyes,' especially those who are still non-Christian (an idea that may have struck him in reviewing his B-text reference to Jewish families):

> And thenne dede we alle wel, and wel bet ʒut to louye
> Oure enemyes enterely and helpe hem at here nede.
> And ʒut were best to ben aboute and brynge hit to hepe
> That alle landes loueden and in on lawe bileuede. (C.10.187–90)

Perhaps Langland had come to feel that his emphasis on duties to kin involved a moral oversight. By stressing the importance of caring for natural and spiritual kin in A and B, he leaves himself open to charges of ignoring the Christian counsel 'Love thine enemy.' In C, the imbalance is redressed, both by reducing the discussion of duties to families and fellow Christians, and by labelling those duties as Do-wel and loving one's enemy as Do-bet. But Do-best combines the two ideals by encouraging bishops to work zealously toward the end 'That alle landes loueden and in on lawe bileuede.' Even at the cost of their own goods and lives, 'prelates and prestes and princes of holy churche' bear the apostolic responsibility of converting the heathen. We will examine this responsibility further in the next section, but for now may simply note its effect of turning enemies into members of the Christian family.[39] By

---

[39] Langland's abiding interest in problems relating to the salvation of the unbaptized is

bringing about universal and mutual affection, and well-ordered, supportive relationships, Do-best ideally can create a society in which all interactions would in fact be familial, based on shared love and law. The Christian message, which the Church should be preaching to all nations, holds out hope for social harmony as well as for individual salvation.

Standing Fast in One's Station

The most drastic revisions in Wit's speech occur in the B and C reflexes of A.10.76–130. Here one finds wholesale replacement of topics, and the omission of several brief but appealing images, from hints of the schoolroom and of proverbial teaching by unlettered parents to the ragged root, rough brier, and sweet red rose of the three Do's. The B text already differs drastically from A, though some relationships between the two can still be seen; C bears only faint traces of its predecessors, woven into its much-changed discussion of prelatical obligations. Yet profitable comparisons of the three texts can still be made, for the content of the A text is not totally lost in B, nor that of B in C. Despite the major revisions between the versions, the combination of their changing emphases and tenuous continuities helps more than it hinders us in understanding the intent and implications of each version of Wit's speech.

One of the primary aims of A.10.76–130, in my view, is an analysis of Do-wel as the humble and steadfast fulfillment of one's station in life and Do-bet as the meek sufferance of tribulations, whether sent by God or inflicted by other people. Wit's actual definition for Do-wel in these lines is 'dred of god'; he refers to Do-bet both as *dred* or *doute*, and as sufferance. Thus the first two Do's tend to shade into each other, but as Wit goes on discussing them, they become somewhat more distinguishable, mostly in terms of their relative activity and passivity. Do-wel (like

traced by G. H. Russell, 'The Salvation of the Heathen: The Exploration of a Theme in *Piers Plowman*,' *Journal of the Warburg and Courtauld Institutes* 29 (1966), 101–16, and Gordon Whatley, 'The Uses of Hagiography: The Legend of Pope Gregory and the Emperor Trajan in the Middle Ages,' *Viator* 15 (1984), 54–55, 60–63. Michael R. Paull discusses related B to C revisions in 'Mahomet and the Conversion of the Heathen in *Piers Plowman*,' *ELN* 10 (1972), 1–8. As all of these critics point out, the poet's interest in the spiritual fate of Saracens and Jews is tied to his deep concern over corruption and tepidity among Christian clergy, who fail in their duties of learning and love to believers and unbelievers alike. On the intensification of this concern from B to C, see also my '*Piers Plowman* and the Liturgy of St. Lawrence: Composition and Revision in Langland's Poetry,' *SP* 84 (1987), 245–71, particularly 268 n. 35; and 'The Chilling of Charity: Eschatological Allusions and Revisions in Piers Plowman C.16–17,' in Robert R. Edwards, ed., *Art and Context in Late Medieval English Narrative: Essays in Honour of R. W. Frank, Jr.* (Cambridge, 1994), 51–77.

the duke of the marches) goes out and performs his duties in fear of the Lord; Do-bet (in some ways like Anima's loyal *damysel*) is meek and mild, a kind of suffering servant.

In the A text, Wit realizes his definitions of Do-wel and Do-bet through several concrete examples. These examples connect very nicely to his previous injunctions on the teaching of children, for they frequently refer to parental and schoolroom instruction. They also underscore the concern of Will's third dream with learning, suggesting the familial and grammar-school roots of the more advanced *clergye* that will be encountered and interrogated later in the dream; some of Will's problems with his later instructors can be seen as a sign of his failure to understand some of Wit's teachings, especially concerning humility and sufferance. The biblical phrase *timor domini* occurs most often by far in Proverbs and Ecclesiasticus, both of which provide traditional lore in the form of a father's instruction to his son.[40] In fact, Wit's own exposition of Do-wel and Do-bet as honest work, humility, the following of conscience, and long-suffering runs along lines quite similar to the advice given in the two Wisdom books.[41] Wit also links the consoling rod and staff of A.10.87 (= Ps. 22:4) with the schoolroom ȝarde in line 85. Later, he quotes the staple grammar-school author Cato,[42] and then glosses the moralist in lines that have a suspiciously schoolmasterly ring:

> Catoun counseilliþ – tak kep of his teching –
> *Cum recte viuas ne cures verba malorum*,
> But suffre & sit stille & sek þou no ferþere,
> And be glad of þe grace þat god haþ Isent þe. (A.10.97–100)

In addition to these schoolroom *dicta*, we find a piece of the proverbial *leryng* given by unlettered men to their children, together with a similar

---

[40] The phrase *timor Domini* (or *Dei*) appears fifteen times in Proverbs, twenty-nine times in Ecclesiasticus, and five times each in Tobias and the Psalms; it appears eighteen other times in the rest of the Bible, never more than three times in any single book. See Boniface Fischer, ed., *Novae Concordantiae Bibliorum Sacrorum Vulgatam Versionem Critice Editam*, 5 vols. (Stuttgart, 1977).

[41] Mary Clemente Davlin notes a number of parallels of form and content between *Piers Plowman* and the Wisdom literature of the Old Testament, including their common social and moral concerns, their mix of styles, frequent use of satire, proverbial lore, and word play; see 'Piers Plowman and the Books of Wisdom,' *YLS* 2 (1988), 23–33.

[42] On other appearances of Cato in *Piers*, see Andrew Galloway, 'Two Notes on Langland's Cato: *Piers Plowman* B I.88–91; IV.20–23,' *ELN* 25 (1987), 9–12, with a list of all references to Cato in all three texts at 10 n. 7. Gerald Morgan interprets the Cato-allusion at the start of Passus 4 as a figure for 'the integral part of prudence called by Aquinas *docilitas*, that is, a receptiveness to teaching,' and a similar reading would work well in Wit's speech too. See 'The Meaning of Kind Wit, Conscience, and Reason in the First Vision of *Piers Plowman*,' *MP* 84 (1987), 357.

adage of more learned origins: 'selde mosseþ þe marbil þat men ofte treden' and 'Qui circuit omne genus in nullo genere est,' both of which warn against aspirations to social mobility.[43] In light of Will's appetite for unlimited knowledge and his rolling-stone, foot-loose tendencies, Wit's comments here on holding firmly to one's own social kind have a particularly pointed quality.[44] Finally, as the culmination of his lesson on humility and social stability, Wit invokes the teaching of the Epistles and Gospels; from scenes of childhood instruction, he moves to precepts for adults and the gifts which God grants to people who observe those precepts:

> Poule þe apostel in his pistil wrot it
> In ensaumple þat suche shulde not renne aboute,[45]
> And for wisdom is writen & witnessid in chirches:
> *In eadem vocacione qua vocati estis state.*
> ʒif þou be man maried, monk, oþer chanoun,
> Hold þe stable & stedefast & strengþe þiseluen
> To be blissid for þi beryng, ʒe, beggere þeiʒ þou were.
> Loke þou grucche nouʒt on god þeiʒ he gyue þe litel;
> Be paied wiþ þe porcioun, pore oþer riche.
> Þus in dred liþ dowel, and dobet to suffre,
> For þoruʒ suffraunce se þou miʒt how soueraynes ariseþ,
> And so leriþ vs luk þat leiʒede neuere:
> *Qui se humiliat exaltabitur &c.*
> And þus of dred & his dede dobest arisiþ,
> Which is þe flour & þe fruyt fostrid of boþe.
> Riʒt as a rose, þat red is and swet,
> Out of a raggit rote and a rouʒ brere

---

[43] The nearest presently-known analogue to the Latin sentence 'Qui circuit' occurs in Higden's *Polychronicon* 1.60 (RS 41:2, 168–72), which emphasizes its applicability to socially ambitious clerics who seek advancement by shifting from one social role to another as circumstances dictate. See John A. Alford, 'More Unidentified Quotations from *Piers Plowman*,' MP 81 (1984), 279.

A similar attack on clerics who imitate the behavior of other estates occurs in Thomas Wimbledon's sermon 'Redde rationem villicationis tue,' ed. Ione Kemp Knight, Duquesne Studies, Philological Series 9 (Pittsburgh, 1967), 78. John M. Bowers notes Langland's general concern over the members of various estates failing or refusing to fulfill their ordained social duties, in *The Crisis of Will in Piers Plowman* (Washington, 1986), 106–09.

[44] 'Selde mosseþ þe marbil. . .' is an early variant of the now more familiar 'A rolling stone gathers no moss' (Whiting M372). It is worth noting, however, that Langland's version of the proverb focuses on the movement of human feet across a fixed stone rather than the movement of the stone itself as preventing moss from growing on the stone (whether for good or ill); I am grateful to Professor Michael Twomey for this insightful observation.

[45] On 'renne aboute' as a pejorative phrase, see the examples given in MED s.v. *rennen* 1c(a), 'to run here and there, run wildly or helter-skelter; also *fig.*; . . . go about one's business; . . . crowd hastily around; . . . keep changing occupations; . . . dance in a ring.' Cf. Langland's own further use of the phrase in B.6.148, where 'Robert Renaboute' probably refers to someone in religion who moves from one place to another, like the ambitious clerics condemned by Higden (n. 43 above), or like the wandering hermits suggested by Schmidt (*B-Text*, 322, following Bennett).

Springeþ & spprediþ, þat spiceris desiriþ,
Or as whete out of weed waxiþ, out of þe erþe,
So dobest out of dobet & dowel gynneþ springe
Among men of þis molde þat mek been & kynde.
For loue of here lou3nesse oure lord 3iueþ hem grace
Such werkis to werche þat he is wiþ paied.   (A.10.109–30)

The notion of sovereignty arising from sufferance highlights and helps relieve a certain tension in the preceding sections of Wit's discourse. On the one hand, he has argued for the sovereignty of the well-formed individual conscience, no matter what others may say, yet he has also argued for meekness and sufferance. But arrogance about one's conscientious behavior or meekness so yielding as to do wrong under social pressure would defeat the aims of Do-wel and Do-bet alike. It is only through the Christian paradox of exaltation by way of humility that true sovereignty of spirit can be achieved. Thus we see here an early, A-text hint of the great theme of Patience which will blossom in the B and C versions of the poem. *Patientes vincunt*: Through sufferance, sovereignty.

According to the A version of Wit's speech, then, Do-best grows out of honest, God-fearing, steadfast (i.e., place-keeping) work in one's proper station and long-suffering meekness, *lou3nesse*, and *kyndenesse*. Those who humbly fulfill their God-given nature and tasks will receive the grace to do well and please God. And whom does Wit offer as the 'formest & ferst' example of this honest, *kynde*, grace-bearing fulfillment of vocation? None other than 'folk þat ben weddit / And lyuen as here lawe wile' (A.10.131–32).

In B.9, the schoolroom and the proverbial lore of unlearned parents disappear entirely, although – as noted above – B emphasizes the didactic responsibilities of Inwit, the Church, and godparents to those in their care at least as much as, and sometimes more than, the A text does. A's definitions of Do-wel and Do-bet as the fear of the Lord and sufferance are modified in B, becoming servile fear of God and filial fear respectively. As Wit points out, dreading God on account of love is better than dreading him for fear of his vengeance; the grounding of Do-bet in love is thus clearer in B than it had been in A. Insofar as Thought has already associated Do-bet's meekness with love in both the A and B texts, it is probably a mistake to think that Langland saw A's 'to ben ywar for betyng of þe 3arde' and B's 'no3t for drede of vengeaunce' as irreconcilable opposites. The '3arde' of A, after all, is equated with the comforting rod and staff of Ps. 22:4. Nonetheless, the two texts do emphasize quite different aspects of the lamb-like, suffering service which characterizes Do-bet.

In place of A's disquisition on the fulfillment of one's station in life, B offers an attack on misspent time and speech. By calling speech 'God's gleeman,' Wit relates this complaint to the B text's immediately-preceding tirade against bishops who spend Christ's patrimony on japers; the passage also calls to mind the contrast between good and bad minstrels of which Langland is so fond.[46] The references to God as faithful father and to wasted speech as a 'gedelyng' or vagabond look both backward and forward within Wit's discourse: back to the paternal nature of Kynde and to Will's wanderings and forward to the 'gedelynges' born out of wedlock or conceived outside of the lawful times.

In B, Wit defines Do-best as the constant refraining ('by daye and by ny3te') from the waste of time and language. We can easily translate this negative definition into its positive equivalent: to do best is to use time and language in morally profitable work and speech, being true of hands and tongue, and imitating the God who created humankind by word and work. The notion is reminiscent of A's approval of people who 'gather moss' by doing the work to which they are called, and not pridefully gadding about, although the B text appears to focus more on the non-wasteful use of time whereas A is more interested in obedience and humility. In spite of the different focus of its exposition, B's final bridge into the discussion of contemporary marriages would fit perfectly well at the equivalent point in A (10.129–30, quoted above):

> To alle trewe tidy men þat trauaille desiren,
> Oure lord loueþ hem and lent, loude oþer stille,
> Grace to go to hem and ofgon her liflode:
> *Inquirentes autem dominum non minuentur omni bono.* (B.9.107–09α)

At this point in B, as in A, Wit turns to honest wedded folk as his best example of the 'true, tidy workers' whom God aids and rewards with grace for doing well. Langland's choice of the word 'tidy' may connote more than just a general approbation of moral character; in its root sense, it means 'timely' or 'seasonable,' and seems a particularly appropriate appellation of those who waste neither time nor language (cf. *OED*, s.v. *tidy* a., 1a). It also anticipates the subject of timely sexuality which will appear in a few lines.

---

[46] Ecclesiastical statutes against clerics supporting *histriones* were repeatedly promulgated in medieval England, frequently in language echoing that of Peter Cantor's *Verbum Abbreviatum*: 'Item Hieronymus, Paria sunt histrionibus dare et demonibus immolare.' See Powicke and Cheney 63, 151, 204 n. 1, 271, 348, 407, 565, 1013; Wilkins 3:60. For further backgrounds to Langland's views on minstrels and japers, see B.Pr.33n in Bennett's edition; Pearsall, C.Pr.35n; Skeat's notes to the several passages cited in Pearsall's note; and Donaldson, *C-Text*, 136–55.

As for the C text, it almost completely eliminates references to the fear of God, honest work, and well-spent time from this section of Wit's speech. Instead, C develops other themes already present or hinted at in B: the prelatical duties discussed above and the importance of love in doing well, better, and best. After briefly mentioning the duties of kinsmen and the Church in caring for the helpless and preventing the waste of time, speech, or earthly goods (C.10.182–86), Wit thoroughly redefines the three Do's. To do well is to love and help one's kin; to do better is to love and help one's enemies; to do best is to convert all lands to love and a single law.

Do-best again takes on a particularly episcopal cast, like that which it bears in Wit's allegory of Caro and in Thought's comments on the Do's. There are suggestions of this connection in B's remarks on helping the needy and doing best by not wasting time; the *unkynde* bishops are shown as wasting their time and Christ's goods on japers, and thus failing to do best. 'Perniciosus dispensator est qui res pauperum christi *inutiliter consumit*' (B.9.94α; my emphasis). But C makes the episcopal obligation to do best much clearer. The A text's concept of steadfastly fulfilling one's calling has been thoroughly transmuted, its focus redirected from the vocations of the Christian flock – 'man maried, monk, oþer chanoun' – to the vocations of Christian shepherds – 'prelates and prestes and princes of holy churche' (A.10.113; C.10.196).

Another innovation in the C text lies in its new definitions of the Do's. The fulfillment of social and spiritual duties is no longer shown as springing from fear, not even from the loving filial fear mentioned in B, but from love: love for kin, love for enemies, and universal love. No doubt Langland still believed Solomon's 'soþ tale,' *Inicium sapiencie timor domini* (A.10.81–81α, B.9.96α), but his stress now falls on lawful deeds done for love. For all Christians, and especially for bishops, it 'were best to ben aboute and brynge hit to hepe / That alle landes loueden and in on lawe bileuede'; like Christ, a bishop should be willing to lose his *catel* and his life so that 'lawe sholde loue wexe.' Neither death nor poverty should prevent Christian pastors from 'wend[ing] as wyde as þe worlde were / To tulie þe erthe with tonge and teche men to louye' (C.10.189–99). This sort of wandering is a most profitable spending of time. It turns speech into the divine gleeman and 'spire of grace' that B declares it should be, but all too often is not.[47]

---

[47] On the rich wordplay in B's phrase 'spire of grace,' see R. A. Shoaf, ' "Speche þat spire is of grace": A Note on *Piers Plowman* B.9.104,' *YLS* 1 (1987), 128–33, and Mary Clemente Davlin, *A Game of Heuene: Word Play and the Meaning of Piers Plowman B* (Cambridge, 1989), 58–60. Priscilla Martin discusses the abuse of speech denounced by Wit in B; see *Piers Plowman: The Field and the Tower* (London, 1979), 61–64, as does A. V. C. Schmidt, *The*

It is important to note that the pastoral duties which Langland describes here are not totally divorced from the responsibilities of the ordinary Christian. From peasant to Pope, no one is justified in misspending God's gifts of Inwit, speech, time, or material goods. Both the ordinary Christian and the prince of the Church must beware of placing *catel* and *covetise* before Kynde, love, and eternal life – an admonition that will have special application to matrimony, as we will soon see. Moreover, the love that should send Christian pastors forth on their apostolic mission is itself the message that they are carrying to all men. They should be teaching love, because love brings God's sustaining aid: Wit has already told Will that the person with Inwit and health has 'tresor ynow of Treuthe to fynden hymsulue,' but now he also promises that 'ho-so loueth . . . god wol nat laton hym sterue / In meschief for defaute of mete ne for myssyng of clothes' (C.10.181, 200–201).

Having passed efficiently from loving pastors to the flock they are instructing in love, the C text is ready to move on to its discussion of contemporary marriages. It retains B's Latin line, 'Inquirentes autem dominum non minuentur omni bono,' but now applies it to those who are rewarded by God for living in love, instead of for their honest work or their humble acceptance of their station. Once again, marriage will be Wit's example of the well-doing upon which God sends his grace, but the reason for that grace is here revealed as the love that animates lawful wedlock:

> Ho-so lyueth in lawe and in loue doth wel,
> As this wedded men þat this world susteyneth.   (C.10.202–03)

Trewe Wedded Libbynge Folk

The Right Use of Marriage

The most complete discussion of literal human marriages in *Piers Plowman* occurs in the final section of Wit's discourse. It is a section whose general content and organization seem to have satisfied Langland throughout his poetic career, though his continued modifications of its local expression indicate that it remained an area of active interest and creative involvement across that career as well. Comprising roughly 40, 45, and 55 per cent of Wit's speech in A, B, and C respectively, this analysis must be taken as the poem's central statement

Clerkly Maker: Langland's Poetic Art (Cambridge, 1987), 10–11 and 16–20 (the latter with reference to Ymaginatif's speech as well).

on marriage. Other literal references to marriage are briefer; figurative uses of marriage or references to marriage in the abstract, however lengthy or sublime, are necessarily grounded in its concrete, literal qualities. Speaking through Wit, Langland describes marriage as it can be rightly used and as it is all too often abused. Together, the norm and the actuality reveal the poet's strong belief in the potential sanctity of marriage and in the indispensability of good marriages to a God-fearing society.

In each text, Wit introduces marriage as a primary example of Do-wel, with whatever nuances he has given to that concept in the immediately preceding material. As we have seen, these nuances shift, but in no way contradict each other; all of them can be taken as facets of Langland's understanding of marriage. Lowliness, steadfast work, and living 'as their law will' characterize married folk in A; *trewe* working and winning characterize them in B; and living in love and law in C. All three texts associate doing well in marriage with the reception of divine grace; the C text even suggests that those begotten in lawful wedlock (*leel legityme*) can actually claim grace by right, as paradoxical as that may seem. (Cf. A.10.129-32, B.9.107-11, C.10.200-203, 208-10.)

By linking marriage and grace, Wit's discourse reflects a relatively recent development in sacramental theology. The assertion that matrimony is a positive source of grace like the other sacraments did not gain widespread theological currency until the late thirteenth century; previously, marriage had been viewed as providing at best a remedial grace mitigating the sexual act.[48] The kind of grace that Wit speaks of here operates in both the spiritual and material realms: it helps people perform deeds that please the Lord (A) and produce saintly children (ABC), and it also helps provide them with *liflode*, food, and clothing (BC). *Inquirentes autem dominum* – those who do well, but especially those in lawful wedlock – *non minuentur omni bono.*[49]

[48] Le Bras, 'Mariage,' *DTC* 9/2:2207-2214: 'Dès la seconde moitié du XIIIᵉ siècle, en effet, l'opinion que le mariage confère la grâce est généralement considérée comme sûre. . . . [Le mariage est] efficace au même titre que les autres sacrements' (2213). Cf. Albertus Magnus, *De Sacramentis* 9 q.1 a.6 (*Opera Omnia* [Münster, Westf., 1951-], 26:159), and Aquinas, *In quatuor libros Sententiarum* 4.26 q.2 a.3 (*Opera Omnia*, [Parma, 1852-73; rpt. New York, 1948-50] 7/2:922); de Burgh, *Pup. Oc.*, 122r. For a more detailed picture of this development, see Seamus P. Heaney, *The Development of the Sacramentality of Marriage from Anselm of Laon to Thomas Aquinas* (Washington, 1963), 72-136; Edward Schillebeeckx, *Marriage: Human Reality and Saving Mystery*, tr. N. D. Smith (London, 1976), 327-38.

[49] As a look at the Psalter will show, the lack of want described by this verse results directly from a saintly fear of the Lord (Ps. 33:10-12); Langland may have added the verse to B because of its association with the *timor domini* theme earlier in Wit's speech, following the method of concordance elucidated by John A. Alford in 'The Role of the Quotations in *Piers Plowman*,' *Speculum* 52 (1977), 80-99. Langland's views on the grace given to those who 'seek the Lord' and thereby do well, especially in marriage, fit with his general

Furthermore, Langland sees marriage as the source of all members of an idealized social world. As the A text puts it, marriage is 'þe rote of dowel.' The world stands and is sustained through lawful wedlock (A.10.133, B.9.111, C.10.203), firstly because in all classes of society, virtuous individuals spring from virtuous marriages, and secondarily because those individuals will go on to sustain the world by their honest work and winning. In the natural order of things, those who do well will have been born in wedlock of good parents, whose good *kynde* will be passed on to their children and is already manifested by their participation in the institution of marriage.

As the poem develops from one text to the next, it uses increasingly honorable and saintly examples to support its claim that honest marriage is the origin of Do-wel. In describing the *confessours* who come from folk of wedded *kynde*, the A text offers a fairly comprehensive list of all the major estates: religious (maidens, nuns, monks, anchorites, clerks); military (kings, knights, barons); and laboring (burgesses and bondsmen). The B text, which has already moved away from A's emphasis on humility as part of Do-wel, tends to focus more on 'honorific ranks of society,' both secular and spiritual: kings, knights, emperors, clerks, maidens, and martyrs.[50] In C, the general category 'confessors' is altered to 'confessors and martyrs,' a change which intensifies the suggestion of sanctity already present in the term 'confessors'; in addition, the specific examples of virtuous classes born in wedlock are completely limited to the religious domain: 'prophetus and patriarkes, popes and maydenes.' Interestingly, this catalogue of the best fruits of marriage focuses largely on spiritual leaders – the patriarchs before the Law, prophets under the Law, and popes under the New Law. Given C's earlier additions on the spiritual duties of prelates – confessing Christ's message even at the cost of martyrdom – the revised catalogue is quite appropriate, and underscores the thoughtful interrelatedness of the revisions in Wit's speech.

Finally, Langland conceives of ideal human marriage as being deeply in tune with nature in general and with ideal human nature in particular. He is not unusual in doing so, since medieval theology, philosophy, and legal theory commonly associated marriage and child-rearing with the natural law applicable to humanity at large. One of the

---

tendency to a 'semi-Pelagian' theology, as described by Robert Adams, 'Piers's Pardon and Langland's Semi-Pelagianism,' *Traditio* 39 (1983), 367–418.

[50] Although more MSS read 'cherles' here in place of 'clerkes,' both K-D and Schmidt adopt the minority reading. As Schmidt explains, '*clerkes* fits well in a list of what are surely honorific ranks of society' (*B-Text*, 278). Even with 'cherles' in the line, however, the classes listed in B are less varied and on the whole higher than those in A.

earliest canons in Gratian's *Decretum* quotes Isidore on the *ius naturale* thus:

> Ius naturale est commune omnium nationum, eo quod ubique instinctu naturae, non constitutione aliqua habetur, ut uiri et feminae coniunctio, liberorum successio (*var.* susceptio) et educatio, communis omnium possessio et omnium una libertas, acquisitio eorum, quae celo, terra marique capiuntur; item depositae rei uel commendatae pecuniae restitutio, uiolentiae per uim repulsio. (D.1 c.7, quoting Isidore, *Etymologies* 5.4)

The *Institutes* and *Digest* of Justinian similarly derive marriage from the natural law:

> Ius naturale est, quod natura omnia animalia docuit. nam ius istud non humani generis proprium est, sed omnium animalium, quae in caelo, quae in terra, quae in mari nascuntur. hinc descendit maris atque feminae coniugatio, quam nos matrimonium appellamus, hinc liber-orum procreatio et educatio. (*Inst.* 1.2.pr.; *Dig.* 1.1.1.3)

Theologians of marriage tended to stress the specific act of divine institution when discussing the origins of marriage, but they too recognized the education of children 'ad cultum dei' as part of the intrinsic and natural *bonum prolis* which characterizes matrimony.[51] Again we may see Langland as grounding his third Dream, with its lengthy examination of the value of learning and education, in the natural roots of such education, beginning as it must with the early instruction of children by the precepts and example of parents, guardians, and their representatives.

The passing on of human nature through marriage is a logical consequence of the extremely common medieval notion of kind following kind, found in sources ranging from the Bible to vernacular and Latin proverbs to theological and philosophical texts.[52] Thus,

---

[51] Cf. n. 4 above; see also Rudolf Weigand, 'Die Lehre der Kanonisten der 12. und 13. Jahrhunderts von den Ehezwecken,' *Studia Gratiana* 12 (1967), 443–78, and John T. Noonan, Jr., *Contraception: A History of Its Treatment by the Catholic Theologians and Canonists* (Cambridge, MA, 1965), 279–82. The notion that the *bonum prolis* includes more than simple reproduction begins with Augustine himself: 'in prole [attenditur] ut amanter suscipiatur, benigne nutriatur, religiose educetur' (*De Genesi ad Literam* 9.7; *PL* 34:397); this expanded definition was guaranteed even wider circulation by its inclusion in the *Sentences* of Peter Lombard (4.31.1). Thus, de Burgh observes that the principal cause of marriage is the 'susceptio sobolis educande ad cultum dei' and later modifies Augustine's remark to 'amanter suscipiatur, debite educetur, et religiose instruatur' (*Pup. Oc.*, 122v–123r). For Aquinas, paying the marriage debt 'ut proles ad cultum Dei procreetur, est meritorius' (*In IV lib. Sent.* 4.26. q.1 a.4; *Opera*, 7/2:920).
[52] See for instance, Mt. 7:16–17; Ecclus. 11:30, 23:32–35, 30:3–4, 40:15; Wis. 4:3–6. Whiting, A169, F685, F689, I24–25, T465, T469, T472 (trees, grafts, fruit); K29–30, K32, K34, K36–37 (*kynde*); F75–77, F80, M720, S463 (parents and children); and others. Walther,

Bromyard notes that children are like their parents by a 'naturalis similitudo' and by 'morum imitatio,' and that adulterous conceptions incline children 'ad paterna crimina' even before their birth.[53] Canonists and theologians knew a definition of nature as the 'vis insita homini ex similibus similia procreans,' which was variously misattributed to Boethius or Aristotle.[54]

Good people will enter marriage in order to have children, and in marriage will pass on their good *kynde*; wicked people will pass on their wicked *kynde* to children born out of wedlock or in wedlock but from untimely sex or in marriages undertaken for *unkynde* reasons. Both the B and C texts use arguments from nature to justify the unforgiving implications of this model of moral development, which visits the sins of the parents on the children. Getting good offspring from evil parents and evil couplings, the texts assert, is about as likely as getting sweet apples from a graft on a sour tree; sowing seed in a field which has been set aside for fallowing, besides being contrary to the commands of one's lord, will damage the natural fertility of the field (B.9.150–55α, C.10.206–10, 215–18).

What Wit provides us with here is the natural, divinely-established 'production plan' for Do-wel's continuing presence among human beings, the dynamic process whereby Do-wel is constantly regenerated along with the species. After God's initial creation of Adam and Eve with the natural capacity to do well, as described in the first part of Wit's speech, it is marriage which enables that capacity to be physically and morally transmitted from one generation to the next. Rational adults, whose Inwit gives them the capacity for moral sovereignty, need to have been instructed and cared for in childhood by their physical and spiritual families, as the law of nature itself intends. But the very existence of children in supportive families presupposes a still earlier foundation or root: procreation within lawful marriage, an institution in which social and moral obligations are observed and developed. As the rest of the speech will demonstrate, when this production plan is not properly followed, the outcome is a dysfunctional, anti-social, and deeply unnatural state of affairs; it constitutes a subversion of divine intention so offensive to God as to warrant catastrophic annihilation, in these last days as much as in the days of Noe.

23209–58 (*Qualis/Qualiter*); 29639b–42 (*Similis*); 30972–97 (*Talis/Taliter*); and others cross-referenced to these entries, not all of which are related to genetic likenesses.
[53] *Summa Praed.*, s.vv. 'Filiatio,' § 3, and 'Adulterium,' § 4.
[54] See Albertus Magnus, *De bono* 5 q.1 a.1 obj.12 (*Opera*, 28:260, v.82n and analogues cited there). Cf. Dante, *Convivio* 4.23: 'Every effect, so far as it is an effect, receives the likeness of its cause so far as it is possible to retain it' (trans. William W. Jackson [Oxford, 1909], 272).

Marriage at Mischief

From Cain to Noe

The primary argument for *trewe* marriage as the *formest* instance of Do-wel is that it gives rise to those who do well. Conversely, bad marriages and untimely or extramarital sexuality give rise to those who do evil. From wicked marriages and sinful sexual practices are born 'fals folk & feiþles, þeuis and leiȝeris,' the kin of Cain, false heirs, foundlings, *gadelynges*, wasters, wanderers, wolfsheads or outlaws, all manner of cursed wretches. Near the end of Wit's speech, all three versions warn that children not born in wedlock rightly used will 'aȝens dowel . . . don euele' (A.10.139, 209-13, B.9.121-22, 195-99, C.10.294-98).

Given Langland's didactic and satiric purposes in *Piers Plowman*, it is unsurprising that Wit spends much more time reproaching imperfect marriages than rhapsodizing over the ideal form of the sacrament. Still, the ideal remains well in view, as the opposite of the negative behavior excoriated by Wit. By demonstrating the evil outcomes of bad marriages past and present – what A and B speak of as *meschief* and *maugre* (A.10.181, B.9.158) – Langland seeks to draw his audience much closer to lawful and loving marriage, the root of Do-wel.[55]

Wit's first example of marriage *at meschief* is the story of Cain and his seed, the accursed lineage whose wickedness brought the Flood upon the world. The curse upon Cain and his kind is a constant motif in Wit's telling of the story; forms of the word 'curse' appear frequently in each version of this passage (A.10.140, 146, 148, 154, 155, 170, 172, 178; B.9.123, 139, 141, 157; C.10.212, 217, 225, 227, 245).[56] Cain's accursedness had received detailed analysis from commentators on Genesis throughout the Middle Ages.[57] Its manifestations were said to include, *inter alia*, his outlawed, wandering life; the infertility of the earth under his tillage; a constant fear of the violence which he himself had brought among men; and finally his death at the hands of Lamech. The outlaws,

---

[55] On 'meschief' as a legal term, see Twomey, 'Anatomy,' 49-51.
[56] The epithet 'cursed' for Cain is common enough in ME for the Chester-cycle Cain to say 'whether I bee in house or hall, / "cursed Cayne" menn will me call' (ed. R. M. Lumiansky and David Mills, EETS s.s. 3 [London, 1974], 40). Cf. *Cursor Mundi* 1052: 'Cain þe curst, þat ful of care.'
[57] On the nature of the curse on Cain, see Bede, *In Gen.* 2.4.11-16 (CC 118A:78-81); Peter Comestor, *Historia Scholastica* 27 (PL 198:1077-78); *Biblia Sacra cum Glossa Ordinaria . . . et Postilla Nicolai Lyrani [ac Moralitatibus]*, 6 vols. (Douai and Antwerp, 1617), 1:119-22; Hugh of St Cher, *Opera Omnia in Universum Vetus et Novum Testamentum*, 8 vols. (Venice, 1600), 1:7v; Nicholas of Lyra, *Postilla* and *Moralia*, in *Biblia Sacra cum Glossa*, 1:114, 118-22. Literary treatments of Cain are discussed by Oliver F. Emerson, 'Legends of Cain, Especially in Old and Middle English,' PMLA 21 (1906), 831-929; Ruth Mellinkoff, *The Mark of Cain* (Berkeley, 1981); David Williams, *Cain and Beowulf: A Study in Secular Allegory* (Toronto, 1982).

wanderers, thieves, liars, wretches, and other false folk born outside of good marriages are all clearly of Cain's moral *kynde*, despite the physical extermination of that bloodline in the Deluge.

For Langland, the nature and cause of the curse on Cain and his offspring are complex. To begin with, he roots the curse in the sinful intercourse of Adam and Eve during a 'cursid tyme,' apparently equivalent to the forbidden intercourse of Christians during the closed times of the Church year (cf. B.9.187–90, C.10.288–90).[58] Adam and Eve's first sexual 'werk' is 'untidy,' unprofitable in its abuse of the time set aside for spiritual work; proper sexuality in marriage is timely work, like that praised earlier in B.9.99–109 and C.10.185–86. Commenting on this passage, Wright claimed that a 'popular' medieval legend has Cain being born 'during the period of penance and fasting, to which our first parents were condemned for their breach of obedience.' However, subsequent editors have apparently not been able to adduce any very close analogues to Wit's description of Cain's conception, and some of its details may well be original with Langland.[59] Cain was sometimes referred as 'malignissimus' and 'malignus,' terms fairly transparently derived from *maligenus* = 'misbegotten,' and such adjectives could have led any writer on Cain to invent his 'cursed engendering' (cf. A.10.148, 'Caym þei hym callide, in cursid tyme engendrit').[60] Whatever sources Langland may have had for the idea, making the curse begin

---

[58] See John A. Alford, *Piers Plowman: A Glossary of Legal Diction* (Cambridge, 1988), s.vv. 'out of time,' 'untime.' For detailed discussion of these forbidden times, see James A. Brundage, *Law, Sex, and Christian Society in Medieval Europe* (Chicago, 1987), 91–92, 154–63, 198–99, 242, 451–53, 508, 601, 604; and n. 66 below.

[59] *The Vision and Creed of Piers Ploughman*, 2nd rev. ed., 2 vols. (London, 1856), 2:533. As Schmidt's note to B.9.121 suggests, this 'common' legend is not readily traced. The Bible itself implies God's approval of Cain's conception, since Eve declares, 'Possedi hominem per Deum' (Gen. 4:1). I have not been able to find any exact parallel to Wit's assertion in the various ME legends of Adam and Eve, the ME Biblical paraphrases, the mystery plays, or Josephus's *Jewish Antiquities*. Comestor's description of Adam's begetting of Cain outside Paradise, 'jam reus et ejectus,' indicates simply that no procreation had occurred in Eden, and applies equally to Adam's later offspring (*Hist. Schol.* 25, PL 198:1076).

The closest 'analogues' I know for Langland's description of Cain's conception appear in some narratives descended from the 'Vita Adae et Evae' (ed. R. H. Charles in *Apocrypha and Pseudepigrapha of the Old Testament*, 2 vols. [Oxford, 1913], 2:136–38), like the ME 'Canticum de Creatione' and the Wheatley 'Life of Adam and Eve.' In these stories, Eve ceases her penance early, tricked by Satan and physically exhausted; Adam, however, completes his penance, at which point Eve, three months pregnant and sorrowing for her weakness, leaves him until her labor begins. But there is no hint in these narratives that the act of conception had been forbidden before their penance, and angels come at Adam's prayer to bless Eve and help her give birth to Cain, so the analogy is not very strong.

[60] *Malignissimus*: Josephus, *Antiq. Jud.*, 130, widely retailed in the *Hist. Schol.* 25 (PL 198:1076), 'Cum enim esset malignissimus, ut etiam avaritiae consuleret suae primus terram incoluit.' Cf. 1 Jn. 3:12, 'Cain ex maligno erat, et occidit fratrem suum. . . . Opera eius maligna fuerunt.'

with Adam and Eve reinforces his earlier point about the origins of children's moral nature in parental *kynde* and deeds.

Another reason for the curse on Cain's offspring is the fact that they were born of forbidden couplings between Cain's line and Seth's line. Langland follows one of the most common interpretations of Genesis 6:1–7, according to which the descendants of Seth ('the sons of God') and of Cain ('the daughters of men') intermarried, against God's command to Seth; these miscegenations produced the lustful and violent race destroyed by the Flood.[61] Thus, the mixed Sethite-Cainite line is accursed for the sin of the Sethites, who coupled their own *kynde* with *Caymes kynde*, as well as by the curse that descends through Cain's blood. By mismating themselves to the Cainites, the Sethites disobeyed God's command, just as Adam and Eve had disobeyed by conceiving Cain 'in untyme'; furthermore, by wedding good seed with bad, the miscegenation violated the natural precept that like should be mated to like. That the outcome was evil is no surprise for Langland. He does not believe in hybrid vigor in the moral realm, nor in improving evil stock by crossing it with good, as can be seen in his depiction of Lady Meed. The good stock of Amends fails to overcome the evil of Wrong/False/Favel; bad seed drives out good. Both B and C note that an apple grafted to a sour trunk is unlikely to taste sweet (B.9.152–53; C.10.206–07; cf. Chap. 1, pp. 10–11, above, and Chap. 3, p. 120, below).

Finally, the curse on Cain and his offspring stems from Cain's own sins. Langland does not mention these sins directly, perhaps because they were so well-known as to go without saying and because they are not immediately related to marriage. Yet they seem to have been part of his thinking in this section of the poem, to judge by the way he describes the nature of those who are begotten out of time or out of wedlock, and the way he describes the *unkynde* unions of contemporary couples. The most visible of Cain's sins was, of course, the murder of his brother – the archetypally violent, treacherous, and *unkynde* crime, which makes him the spiritual father of all outlaws and vagabonds, 'fals folk & feiþles, þeuis and leiȝeris.'[62]

Just as important, however, is Cain's *covetise*: not merely as the general *radix omnium malorum* but also as his particular, besetting vice. His very name means 'possessio,' 'getting,' in both the reproductive and economic senses.[63] The mystery plays about Cain and Abel

---

[61] Bede, *In Gen.* 2.6.1–2 (*CC* 118A:99); *Hist. Schol.* 31 (*PL* 198:1081), citing ps.-Methodius; *Gl. Ord.*, 1:139–41; Hugh of St Cher, *Opera*, 1:9r–v.
[62] On the legal collocation 'false and faithless' (*falsus et infidelis*), see Alford, *Glossary*, 54.
[63] Gen. 4:1; Josephus, *Antiq. Jud.*, 130 (Cain as *avarus*); Ambrose, *De Cain* 1.3 (*CSEL* 32/ 1:340; '[Cain] omnia sibi adquireret'); Jerome, *Liber Interp. Hebr. Nom.* (*CC* 72:63; Cain =

consistently reminded medieval audiences that Cain's covetous retention of his best crops led to the unsatisfactory sacrifice which God
rejected, and thus to his wrathful envy and murder of Abel. He was also
the first builder of cities and the ancestor of Tubalcain, who invented
metalworking – activities which, according to biblical commentators,
reflect and support the human tendencies to greed and warfare. For
example, in the *Historia Scholastica*, Peter Comestor attributes Cain's
city-building to his fear of the rapine which men had learned from him.[64]
The C-text revision of the story of the Sethites suggests that *covetise* also
led to their marriages with Cain's children: the command that Seth
breaks is 'that for *no kyne catel ne no kyne byheste* / [Should he] soffre his
seed seden with Caymes seed his brother' (C.10.248–49; my
emphasis).[65] And in all three texts, Langland will soon identify *covetise* as
the radical disorder in the infertile, wrathful, mismatched, and faithless
marriages he sees around him.

Several of the accursed sins which infect the line of Cain are drawn
together nicely by a homely simile added in the C text, the comparison
of Cain's conception to the sowing of a fallow field against its lord's will.
Fallowing was essential to the continued productivity of medieval fields,
as limited as that was; sowing a *leye-land* might generate a larger short-
term return, but in the long term it would exhaust the land entirely,
rendering it incapable of producing anything but weeds. Thus, sowing
'in untyme' would have been a clear example of a greedy, short-sighted
misuse of natural goods. It works against nature instead of with her.
And if such sowing were also 'aȝeynes [the] lordes wille,' then the act of
disobedience violates the social order as well. Similarly, sexual sowing
out of time – during a woman's menses or pregnancy or during a period
of penance and prayer – was considered to be *unkynde*, and thus counter
to God's law. It was seen as giving rise to moral and physical monsters,
disrupting the order of God, nature, and society. Langland's explanation of the origin of evil-doers runs parallel, in the spiritual realm, to the

---

'possessio uel adquisitio.' *Gl. Ord.* (Interlinear), 1:113–14 (Cain signifies those 'qui
terrenas divitias ambiunt, et quantum in se est possident'); Lyra, *Postilla*, 1:115 ('Et Cain
agricola: ex cultura terrae querens lucra'). For Hugh of St Cher, the giants born from
Cain's line are so named from the word *ge*, 'earth,' since they mystically signify those who
love and glory in worldly things (*Opera*, 1:9r–v). Cain's avarice was frequently represented
as an unwillingness to tithe properly; for vernacular examples, see Emerson, 'Legends of
Cain,' 838–51.
[64] *Hist. Schol.* 28 (PL 198:1078); similarly, Remigius of Auxerre, *In Gen.* 4 (PL 131:71);
Rupert of Deutz, *In Gen.* 4.10 (CC-CM 21:294); Lyra, *Post.*, 1:123–24. For violence, robbery,
and tyranny in Cain's line, see also Josephus, *Antiq. Jud.*, 131; Hugh of St Cher, *Opera*,
1:8r; Lyra, *Post.*, 1:141–44.
[65] On the relation of Seth's name and the seeding metaphor here, see Thomas D. Hill,
'Seth the "Seeder" in *Piers Plowman* C.10.249,' YLS 1 (1987), 105–08.

medieval medical belief that physically monstrous offspring would be born from intercourse during pregnancy or the menstrual period.[66] To do well in marriage and to produce children who will do well, couples must live in wedlock, obey God's and nature's laws in their marriage, and not seek to use marriage as a means toward inordinate pleasure or profit. Then the world will be sustained, just as the manorial community is sustained by the moderate and rightly-ordered use of its fields.

By the time the Sethite-Cainite miscegenations had proceeded for several generations, so that 'all flesh had corrupted its way upon the earth,' the only remedy was the Deluge. Having used the story of Cain's offspring as an example of how sinful couplings lead to wickedness, Langland has more or less committed himself to some mention of the Flood by which that wickedness was punished. Only the obedient Noe and his passengers in the Ark are saved when God drowns the world 'for mariages makynge þat men made þat tyme,' washing 'clene awey þe cursid blood þat caym haþ ymakid (C: þat of Caym spronge)' (C.10.244; cf. A.10.178-81, B.9.156-57; A.10.169-70, B.9.138-39, C.10.224-25). Wit makes the relation of the Flood to his discussion of marriage quite clear – it is both punitive and purgative. In the C text, he even goes so far as to offer a startling modification of God's words in Gen. 6:6-7, 'Penitet me fecisse hominem' (A.10.162, B.9.133α), changing them to the English lines 'Me forthynketh / Þat y man made *or matrimonye soffrede*' (C.10.250-51; my emphasis). The institution of marriage is an essential part of the creation of mankind, and both mankind and marriage must be rehabilitated through the Flood.

In addition to the direct links that Wit points out, there are other connections between marriage and the story of Noe, connections which make this segment of Wit's speech still more pertinent to the themes of marriage and family. First of all, the humans and animals who were saved in the Ark were saved *in couples*, as mating pairs, so that the world could be regenerated after the Deluge. Gender is an essential feature of the Ark's passenger-list. All flesh entered the Ark as male and female. And on leaving the Ark, all flesh received once again the Edenic blessing

---

[66] See Robert of Flamborough, *Liber Poenitentialis*, ed. J. J. Francis Firth (Toronto, 1971), 198, 236-39, 243 (on spiritually forbidden times); 197-98, 237-38, 243 (on 'naturally' forbidden times of pregnancy, menses, and childbirth, and the risks of monstrous births). Likewise Thomas of Chobham, *Summa Confessorum*, ed. F. Broomfield (Louvain, 1968), 336-39, 364-66; John de Burgh, *Pup. Oc.*, 128v-129r; *Decretum*, C.33 q.4. The origins of the medieval notion of periodic marital continence are discussed by Jean-Louis Flandrin, *Un temps pour embrasser: aux origines de la morale sexuelle occidentale (VI°-XI° siècle)* (Paris, 1983); and Pierre J. Payer, 'Early Medieval Regulations Concerning Marital Sexual Relations,' *Journal of Medieval History* 6 (1980), 353-76. For the later periods, see Tentler, *Sin and Confession*, 208-20; and Payer, *Bridling of Desire*, 98-110.

of fertility, 'Increase and multiply upon [the earth]' (Gen. 8:17; repeated for humanity in Gen. 9:1 and 9:7).[67] Even the oft-forgotten sevens of the clean beasts were generally taken to comprise three pairs for generation and one beast for sacrifice after the Flood.[68] Hence, Wit speaks of Noe entering the Ark with his wife, his sons, and their wives; likewise, he says that Noe saved 'of iche beste a couple' (A) or 'oonliche of ech kynde a couple [C: payre]' (A.10.167, 175; B.9.136, 144; C.10.222, 230). The BC revision in this last line, changing 'beste' to 'kynde,' helps call attention once again to the theme of *kynde* running throughout Wit's speech.

The Ark is not just a collection of couples from which animate life will be reborn. It also contains a family, headed by a figure often seen as typifying the married state.[69] A fairly common exegetical observation is that Noe represents Christ protecting his *familia* in the safety of the Church; he is also said to signify prelates guiding their ecclesiastical families.[70] Familial order in the Ark is an important theme in the mystery plays about the Flood: the well-known disobedience of Noe's wife usually has to be overcome, and often contrasts with the filial obedience of Noe's children.[71] Given Wit's earlier remarks on the responsibilities of parents, guardians, or prelates to their dependents, the more general duty of humble fulfillment of one's station, and the well-known interpretation of the Ark as the ecclesiastical hierarchy of care and governance, it seems impossible to separate Langland's reference to the Flood from his familial model of social order. Unlike the friar's comparison of the human condition to a lone man in a frail boat, the Ark represents human nature as being communal, ordered, and protected

[67] Commentary on the persistence of Gen. 1:28's blessing of fertility even after the Fall and the Flood can be found in Ambrose, *De Noe* 3.6 (*CSEL* 32/1:416); Bede, *In Gen.* 2.9.1-3 (*CC* 118A:131); Bruno d'Asti, *Expositio in Genesim* 9 (*PL* 164:183); and *Hist. Schol.* 23 (*PL* 198:1074); Lombard, *Sent.* 4.26.2-3. For additional commentary on the initial blessing and its persistence, see Cohen, '*Be Fertile and Increase*,' 245-70. See also Chap. 3, pp. 129-35 below.

[68] Cf. Lyra, *Post.*, 1:153-54; also noted earlier, e.g. by Remigius of Auxerre *In Gen.* 7 (*PL* 131:76).

[69] For Noe as a type for the married man, see Morton W. Bloomfield, '*Piers Plowman* and the Three Grades of Chastity,' *Anglia* 76 (1958), 247. He was also taken as a type for *rectores* or *continentes* by many commentators.

[70] Such interpretations can most readily be found in commentaries on Gen. 6-9, Mt. 24:37-39, Lk. 17:26-27, and 1 Peter 3:20. See Augustine, *Contra Faustum* 12.14 (*PL* 42:262); Isidore, *Quaestiones in Vetere Testamento*, 7 (*PL* 83:230); Rabanus Maurus, *In Gen.* 2.6 (*PL* 107:515); Remigius of Auxerre, *In Gen.* 6 (*PL* 131:75); Peter Damian, *Collectanea in Librum Genesim* 12 (*PL* 145:998-99); *Gl. Ord.*, 1:143, 5:403, 922, 6:1332-34; Hugh of St Cher, *Opera*, 1:9v-10r, 6:237v-238r; Lyra, *Mor.*, 1:140, *Post.*, 6:1331. For ps.-Hugh of St Victor, Noe ruling the ark can also signify the rational intellect ruling the soul (*Alleg. in Vet. Test.* 1.13-14, *PL* 175:641-43; cf. Inwit and Anima).

[71] Noe's wife is recalcitrant in the Towneley, York, Newcastle, and Chester Noe plays, but not in the N-Town or Hegge cycle. Cf. *MilT* 3538-43.

by God's command and care. The world is still a storm-tossed sea, but the ship is well-built and can be well-governed if all aboard fulfill their duties.

We have seen Wit's suggestion that part of the reason for Cain's ill-doing was his unseasonable begetting, during a time when Adam and Eve should have been doing penance. Later in the passus, Wit will admonish contemporary married couples to refrain from sex at forbidden times (in case they had not inferred as much from the case of Cain). This aspect of the right use of sex and marriage – timeliness, due proportion, subordination to spiritual pursuits – is exemplified by the shipboard life of the Ark's passengers. As exegetes had observed from early on, Genesis reports that 'Noe went in and his sons, his wife and the wives of his sons with him'; after the Flood, however, God told Noe, 'Go out of the ark, thou and thy wife, thy sons and the wives of thy sons with thee' (7:7, 8:16). This change in wording was regularly taken to mean that in the Ark, males and females did not mingle sexually, but did penance for the sins that had brought on the Flood;[72] for Langland, presumably, those sins would run from Adam and Eve's incontinence to the corruption of all flesh in Noe's day. However, when the waters receded and the second age began, God let Noe know that it was once more a 'tempus amplexandi.'[73] By noting that forty days must be fulfilled before the flood would have washed away Cain's accursed blood (A.10.169–70, B.9.138–39, C.10.224–25), Langland reminds us of the cleansing penitential function of the time spent in the Ark, and of the need of all sinners – husbands and wives included – to set aside the appropriate time, such as Lent and other seasons, for doing penance.

Thus the story of the Ark supports a number of themes already operating in Wit's speech: sexuality and families as the source of earthly life, familial order as an analogue for social and ecclesiastical order, timeliness and proportion in marital sexuality, and divine punishment for abuses of marriage. It also serves as a warning that the punishment for abusing the 'root of Do-wel' is no ordinary penalty – the evils that merited the judgment of the Flood in the past may merit the judgment of fire in the future. The prophetic association of the Flood with the Last

---

[72] Ambrose, *De Noe*, 21 (*CSEL* 32/1:467–69); Remigius of Auxerre, *In Gen*. 7 (*PL* 131:76); *Hist. Schol*. 33, 35 (*PL* 198:1083, 1085); *Gl. Ord.*, 1:155–56; Hugh of St Cher, *Opera*, 1:10v; Lyra, *Post.*, 1:155, 163–64.

[73] Biblical commentators sometimes concord these lines in Genesis with Eccles. 3:5 and 1 Cor. 7:5, and use all three passages as justifications for periodic marital abstinence. See Bruno d'Asti, *Exp. in Gen*. 8 (*PL* 164:182); *Gl. Ord.*, 3:1768; Hugh of St Cher, *Opera*, 1:10v, 3:79v, 7:89r; Lyra, 3:1768, 6:245. Similarly, canon law and the pastoral manuals often use the language of Paul ('vacare orationi') and sometimes of Ecclesiastes ('tempus amplexandi'; 'abstinere ab amplexibus') in prescribing the timely use of marital sexuality.

Judgment was made by Jesus himself; interestingly, in juxtaposing the two judgments, he briefly mentions marriage too:

> And as in the days of Noe, so shall also the second coming of the Son of man be. For as in the days before the flood, they were eating and drinking, marrying and giving in marriage, even till that day in which Noe entered into the ark, and they knew not until the flood came, and took them all away; so also shall the coming of the son of man be. (Mt. 24:37–39; cf. Lk. 17:26–27).[74]

Wit's characterization of the Flood as a punishment for corrupt antediluvian marriages gives apocalyptic overtones to his subsequent attack on similarly corrupt contemporary marriages. Like the lecherous affairs and covetous divorces that accompany Antichrist's legions in the poem's final passus, these *unkynde* mismatings point ominously to an impending Doomsday.

Filius non portabit . . .
Wit's emphasis on the transmission of parental guilt and vice to children implies a rather deterministic view of human moral capacities, not entirely in tune with Christian concepts of free will and grace. Those concepts make it seem unjust that 'þe barn [abouȝte] þe belsires giltes, / And alle for hir forefadres ferden þe werse' (B.9.146–47, C.10.232–33). Between writing A and B, Langland evidently decided to acknowledge this dissonance, and at the same time to clarify and justify Wit's position with analogies from nature and (in C) the common law. As a number of passages in *Piers* reveal, Langland generally accepts the wide-spread folk belief 'Like father like son.'[75] We have already seen the BC revisions in the Meed episode that reflect this idea; in addition, Truth's pardon describes beggars who cripple their bastard children and lead them into a life of dishonest beggary, suggesting that parental example is at least a partial cause of such legacies of character (A.8.72–81, B.7.90–99, C.9.166–74). To some extent, the notion would have been borne out by social experience, although modern eyes would be more likely to see its origins in environmental factors than in family genetics.[76]

---

[74] While commentaries on these two passages tend to be brief, they generally do take care to observe that the Deluge was a punishment for the intemperate use of otherwise licit things like food and marriage, not a judgment against those things in themselves. Cf. Ambrose, *De Noe* 21.76 (*CSEL* 32/1:468), quoted in *Gl. Ord.* 5:403, 922; Hugh of St Cher, *Opera*, 6:237v–238r.

[75] Although the saying has a written source (the Athanasian Creed, where it refers to the identical nature of the first two persons of the Trinity), the general notion in its desacralized form is extremely common, as are the constructions 'Such x such y' and 'Like x like y.' See Whiting, F80, H655, L455, M408, M720, P135, P136, P403, T465, W186, W614, as well as entries listed in note 52 above.

[76] The possibility that certain socioeconomic classes or particular families may have been

For Langland, the natural course of events is that 'kynde folweth kynde' (C.10.242); worse yet, bad *kynde* tends to overcome good *kynde* if the two are mixed. This expression of natural law necessarily applied to the whole human race in the pre-Mosaic period, when men lived under the law of Kynde alone. But it was not suspended by the advent of the old law or the new, merely modified in appropriate contexts. Christ himself said 'Numquam [Vulg. numquid] colligunt de spinis vuas nec de tribulis ficus' (Mt. 7:16; B.9.155α; cf. C.10.242a). Apples grafted onto elders were still sour (B);[77] the rule of attainder and 'corruption of blood' still held in English common law (C).[78] Since one of Wit's major themes has been the relation of the three Do's to *kynde*, his naturalistic, 'genetic' view of vice and virtue is perfectly fitting here at the start of Will's quest for Do-wel, Do-bet, and Do-best. Furthermore, it makes good rhetorical sense to exhort parents to do well for their children's sake as well as their own. The biblical verse 'Filius non portabit iniquitatem patris' can too easily become an excuse for shrugging off moral obligations, as Dame Scripture notes later in B.10.113–18. Far better to urge parents to do well themselves and to teach their children to do well, so that good trees will bear good fruit as nature asks.

Wit does not entirely ignore a person's potential to escape a vicious moral legacy from his parents. The remark in B that one 'selde' sees a son who does not 'savor after his sire' still allows for that possibility, rather like Imagynatif's quibble on '*vix* saluabitur.' The inheritance of a felon's heir was 'at þe kynges wille' (C.10.239), so the king could, and in

---

'bastardy-prone' has been tentatively suggested for the early modern period by Peter Laslett, and may also apply in the Middle Ages; see 'Long-Term Trends in Bastardy in England,' in *Family Life and Illicit Love in Earlier Generations: Essays in Historical Sociology* (Cambridge, 1977), 149. Barbara Hanawalt documents the frequency with which criminal partnerships were based on identifiable kinship relations (*Crime and Conflict*, 192–95), as does James Given, *Society and Homicide in Thirteenth-Century England* (Stanford, 1977), 43–49, 154–60, 176–81.

[77] Medieval treatises on grafting did at times speak of grafting apples on elders, for the sake of creating a particularly red fruit; but this seems to be an artificial, internal coloration, as it is mentioned together with the insertion of blue dyes in the trunk so as to achieve blue apples. See the grafting treatise in J. O. Halliwell's *Early English Miscellanies*, (London, 1855), 67–68. In more practical treatises or parts of treatises, one finds the advice that imps of the desired fruit should be grafted to stock that is as close as possible to the fruit itself. See Alicia M. Tyssen-Amherst, 'A Fifteenth Century Treatise on Gardening,' *Archaeologia* 54 (1894), 161; W. W. Skeat, ed., *The Book of Husbandry by Master [Anthony] Fitzherbert*, English Dialect Society 37 (London, 1882), 88–90; M. C. Seymour et al., eds., *On the Properties of Things: John Trevisa's Translation of Bartholomaeus Anglicus De Proprietatibus Rerum: A Critical Text*, 2 vols. (Oxford, 1975) 17.2 (2:889); W. L. Braekman, 'Bollard's Middle English Book of Planting and Grafting and Its Background,' *SN* 57 (1985), 32–33. I owe Professor Lister Matheson thanks for providing me with some of these references.

[78] On escheats for treason and felony, see P & M 1:351–52, 476–78, 2:500–02, and Bracton 2:335, 366. Cf. *MED*, s.vv. *atteinen* v., 4, and *atteinten* v., 2.

practice sometimes did, leave it with the heir or return it.[79] All three texts will conclude their final condemnation of misbegotten offspring with the important qualification 'but ȝif god giue hem grace here to amende' (A.10.215, B.9.201, C.10.300). But the qualification is only a brief foretaste of Langland's later and more extensive explorations of the saving power of grace given to sinners. Here in Wit's speech, he is much more interested in the grace which can be claimed 'by law,' by those who do well and seek the Lord in their proper calling, of whom 'trewe wedded folk' are the model.

Contemporary Marriages

The intermarriages of the Cainites and Sethites, undertaken against God's command, brought disaster to their lineage, from the curse on their blood to the penalty of the Deluge. Langland sees contemporary families as making similarly ill-wrought marriages for their children – mismatched, covetous, against divine command – and thereby inviting similarly disastrous outcomes. According to A and B, the children of Seth and his sister

> were maried at meschief as men do now here children. (A.10.181)
>
> þei wroȝte wedlokes ayein þe wille of god.
> Forþi haue þei maugre of hir mariages þat marie so hir children.
> (B.9.157–58)

> For summe, as I se now, soþ ·for to telle,
> For coueitise of catel vnkyndely be maried.
> A carful concepcioun comiþ of such weddyng
> As fel of þe folk þat I before shewide. (A.10.182–85, B.9.159–62)

The C text makes the same point structurally, by placing the story of the Sethites' miscegenation with Cain's posterity immediately before the material on contemporary marriages (instead of before the Noe passage as in AB), and by making God's command that 'goode sholde wedde goode' apply both to Seth and to contemporary people. Alas, says Wit,

> fewe folk now folweth this, for thei ȝeue her childrene
> For coueytise of catel and connynge chapmen. (C.10.254–55)

The Bible, the Old Testament apocrypha, and medieval exegetes and historians identify the major sins before the Flood as lust (the sons of God were attracted by the beauty of the daughters of men), violence (the

---

[79] Edward III was 'seldom disposed to visit the sins of guilty fathers upon their children,' and he eventually returned the confiscated lands of several convicted traitors to their offspring (McKisack, *Fourteenth Century*, 255–57).

giants and 'mighty men' of those days were said to have been especially savage), and unnatural sexuality of homosexual and bestial sorts. Langland, however, takes a somewhat different slant on the situation, by focusing more on covetousness, the ancestral vice of Cain's lineage.[80] This focus is sharpest in C, where God explicitly warns Seth against mingling his seed with Cain's for *catel* or *byheste*, but all three texts suggest the cupidity of antediluvian wedlock by comparing it with covetous modern marriages.

Because of *covetise*, contemporary parents ignore the natural – and thus divine – law that like should wed like. Instead, they arrange loveless marriages between young and old for the sake of material gain, marriages that can only yield 'carful concepcioun.' These unions of the fertile young with impotent (*feble*) old men or barren widows are unnatural in their frustration of the reproductive drive as well as in their mixing of different kinds. Like Cain's accursed tillage, they produce no true fruit, unless one counts the joyless jealousy, bedtime wrangling, foul words, *cheste*, and *choppes* between the two spouses. (One can imagine what Langland would have thought of the Wife of Bath's marital career.) Like Cain, such couples are false and faithless: perhaps as adulterers, as A.10.210 suggests with its mention of 'false heirs,' but certainly as breakers of the troth-plight in the marriage ceremony:

> In gelosie, ioyeles, & ianglyng a bedde,
> Manye peire siþen þe pestilence han pliȝt hem togidere.
>
> (A.10.190–91, B.9.169–70)

The strife, jealousy, and greed of these marriages violate the promises made by all married couples to love, honor, obey, and cherish.[81] The C text highlights the allusion to the trothplight in the marriage service, by expanding the AB phrase 'pliȝt hem togidere' to 'plyhte treuthe to louye.' It then continues with the harsh new judgment 'Ac they lyen lely, here neyther lyketh other,' with its mordant oxymoron of 'leal lying,' its possible ironic play on the sexual sense of 'lying together'

---

[80] Ambrose, *De Noe*, 21.76 (*CSEL* 32/1:468; intemperance, lust, gluttony as causes), quoted in *Gl. Ord.*, 1:164; Rupert of Deutz, *In Gen.* 4.16, 25 (CC-CM 21:300, 310; 'petulantem atque . . . lasciuientem mundum recentem [Deus] corripuit,' 'feruentiore uoluptatis tempore superuenit [diluuium]'). Hugh of St Cher says flatly that the cause of the Flood was *luxuria* and later cites ps.-Methodius on the unnatural sexual practices of Cain's offspring (*Opera*, 1:9r). Lyra describes the line of Cain as *raptores et luxuriosi* and attributes the Flood to 'carnalia peccata . . . fraudes et rapinas . . . peccat[a] contra naturam'; even the beasts and birds are said to have coupled without regard for *genus* or species (*Post.*, 1:142, 144). Cf. the ME *Gen. and Ex.* 527–54 and *Cursor Mundi* (Trin.) 1563–82. See nn. 63–64 above on Cain's avarice and the violence of his offspring, and Twomey, 'Anatomy,' 31–33, on the unnatural lusts of the antediluvians.
[81] For English and Latin troth-plights, see Chap. 1, pp. 14–16.

(C.10.269-70; cf. A.2.25 and p. 17, above), and the dual sense of *lyketh* suggesting both disaffection and dissimilarity.

These unkind, loveless marriages are lawful enough if the couple themselves consent, but that doesn't make them good marriages or a root of Do-wel. Just as lawless couplings, outside of marriage or the proper time, have mischievous outcomes, so too do lawful but unloving unions. Even if these unions are arranged by parents out of a concern for their children's economic security, too much attention to material goods alone could well create unhappy and sinful marriages. Wit's exhortations are well in line with the warnings of late medieval moralists like Jean Gerson, who castigated parents for striving after their children's worldly welfare at the cost of their own or their children's spiritual well-being.[82] They also fit with popular prejudices against marriages between unlike partners.[83] In Langland's view, Christian couples and their parents need to keep love in mind when making marital decisions, and love is most likely to spring from similarity between the two parties. Thus maidens should wed maidens, and widowers wed widows, despite the fact that this strategy may not set young people up in the world as quickly as others might. Even when *kyndes* are alike, the motive for marriage should be love, not land (B); the C text more practically asks that love be 'more þe cause then lond oþer nobles.'

Nor was this ideal of love and likeness as the basis for matrimony a new-fangled one in Langland's day, despite the ever-present realities of economic and social motives in the arranging of marriages. Guibert of Tournai (d. 1288), in a massive *ad status* sermon collection which gained a considerable circulation, defends a position very similar to Langland's; married love, he says,

> ought to be formed in such a way that the motives for it are pure, so that the husband and wife should not love each other or be joined in marriage for the sake of some temporal gain, or a beautiful figure (*forme*), or to gratify their lust, but so that they may live together (*vivant*

[82] Bromyard warns that marriages arranged for wealth instead of love will be plagued by strife, adultery, or infertility (*Summa Praed.*, s.v. 'Matrimonium,' §§ 10–12). A Wycliffite text denounces 'myȝtty men' who 'marien here children, where þat here herte consentiþ not wilfully, but feynen for drede. For comynly þei loken alle aftir richesse and worþinesse to þe world, and not after goodnesse of virtuous lif' (*Select English Works of John Wyclif*, ed. Thomas Arnold, 3 vols. [Oxford, 1869–71] 3:191–92). And Gerson tells the story of two wealthy parents who, upon having a long-prayed-for first child, 'commencerent a pansser comment il seroit avancé comme les autres, et soubstrayrent incontinent leurs mains des bonnes oeuvres qui souloient faire, pour les reserver a leur enfant' (*Oeuvres*, 7/1:323). See also Chap. 1, n. 5.

[83] Whiting, B363, C401, L551, N127, M254, J14, L18. Many other proverbs simply assert the likeness that should exist between spouses. Cf. Ecclus. 13:19–20. Mirk's *Festial* advises that 'by Goddys ordynaunce, a man schal takon a wyf lyke of age, lyk of condicions, and lyk of burth; for þereos þese ben acordyng, it is lyk to fare wel, and ellys not' (290).

simul (!)) happily and decently, so that God may receive honour, and
the marriage yield fruit for the service of God. . . . For when they are
equal (*pares*), then they live in peace; but when they have got married
for the sake of a dowry or for something temporal they always quarrel.
So if you want to get married, marry an equal.[84]

As Langland notes in A and B, such marriages of like *kyndes* please God,
who will send grace and livelihood to those who do well in this way.[85]
Or, as B and C have already put it, 'goode sholde wedde goode, þou3
þei no good hadde; / "I am *via & veritas*," seiþ crist, "I may auaunce
alle" ' (A.10.197–201, B.9.176–81, C.10.276–80; B.9.163–64, C.10.252–53).

An historically interesting feature of Wit's attack on mismatings for
land or money is the claim that these miscegenations have linked 'many
peire siþen þe pestilence,' especially in the light of recent studies of the
short- and long-term effects of the Black Death on English marriage and
fertility patterns. The situation Wit describes, with often-barren
marriages of land-hungry young men to wealthy widows, obtained
more certainly in the earlier fourteenth century.[86] After the Plague, a
sharp increase in available land, marriages, and births and a decline in
marriages to widows occurred in many communities, but the baby boom
was largely cancelled by later plagues which struck children especially
hard (e.g., in 1361–62 and 1368–69) and left a population seriously
depleted in its reproductive age-cohorts, not to mention the depletion of
heirs.[87]

Despite seemingly favorable conditions of land availability, higher
wages, and fewer mouths to feed, this population apparently failed to
recover until the sixteenth century, suggesting continuing high
mortality, low fertility, or both. Some historians argue that economic
conditions in fact did encourage early marriages for both men and
women, with consequent increased birth rates, and that the explanation

[84] Quoted by D. L. d'Avray and M. Tausche, 'Marriage Sermons in *Ad Status* Collections
of the Central Middle Ages,' *Archives d'histoire doctrinale et littéraire du moyen age* 47 (1981),
115 (exclamation point original).
[85] A. V. C. Schmidt discusses Langland's semantic plays on notions of good, God, grace,
goods, *covetise*, and *kynde* vs. *unkynde* desires and couplings in *The Clerkly Maker: Langland's
Poetic Art* (Cambridge, 1987), 134–41. See also his '*Kynde Craft* and the *Play of Paramorez*,'
1986 Bennett Memorial Lectures, ed. Piero Boitani and Anna Torti (Tübingen, 1987), 105–24,
and White, *Nature and Salvation*, 96–97.
[86] See M. M. Postan, *The Cambridge Economic History of Europe*, vol. 1, rev. ed. (Cambridge,
1966), 563–65; J. Z. Titow, 'Some Differences Between Manors and Their Effects on the
Conditions of the Peasantry,' *AgHR* 10 (1962), 6–13; Zvi Razi, *Life, Marriage and Death in a
Medieval Parish: Economy, Society and Demography in Halesowen 1270–1400* (Cambridge,
1980), 63, 66; Jack Ravensdale, 'Population Changes and the Transfer of Customary Land
on a Cambridgeshire Manor in the Fourteenth Century,' in R. M. Smith, ed., *Land, Kinship
and Life-Cycle* (Cambridge, 1984), 197–225.
[87] As Schmidt points out in his note to B.9.169, citing Postan's *The Medieval Economy and
Society: An Economic History of Britain in the Middle Ages* (1972; London, 1975).

for the continued population decline must lie in the recurrent attacks of plague and other diseases throughout the fifteenth century.[88] Others cautiously suggest that late medieval marital practices may have been such as to depress the birth rate directly – perhaps through contraceptive activity in marriage, delayed marriages, or first marriages of young men to widows, all aimed at establishing a much stronger economic safety-net before seeking offspring.[89] Langland might have found the latter analysis plausible, but would no doubt have used harsher language about the economic security-motive, viewing it as covetous in itself and *unkynde* in its frustration of procreation. For Langland, working and winning is one thing, but being so solicitous for earthly acquisition that one despairs of God's providence and acts against the natural order is quite another (though modern readers may sympathize with such a response to the grim uncertainties of the 'golden age of bacteria'). 'Goode sholde wedde goode, þouȝ þei no good hadde; / "I am *via & veritas*," seiþ crist, "I may auaunce alle." '

Langland's outrage at infertile, covetous, cross-generational marriages may derive from pre-Plague social practices and the complaints of pre-Plague moralists, despite his belief that such marriages are the result of the Plague.[90] Even so, whatever English nuptial patterns were like in the

---

[88] Razi and Ravensdale give evidence of a decrease in the age of first marriage for men and women in first two generations after the Plague, at least in the communities they have examined (*Life, Marriage, Death*, 135–38; 'Transfer of Customary Land,' 220–23). Similarly, Hanawalt's work on coroners' rolls suggests an increase in the numbers of children in village households after the Plague ('Childrearing Among the Lower Classes of Late Medieval England,' *Journal of Interdisciplinary History* 8 [1977], 5). A more general argument is mounted by John Hatcher, *Plague, Population and the English Economy 1348–1530* (London, 1977).

[89] Karl F. Helleiner, 'The Population of Europe from the Black Death to the Eve of the Vital Revolution,' *The Cambridge Economic History of Europe*, vol. 4 (Cambridge, 1967), 69–71; Edwin B. DeWindt, *Land and People in Holywell-cum-Needingworth: Structures of Tenure and Patterns of Social Organization in an East Midlands Village 1252–1457* (Toronto, 1972), 188–93, 205; Bruce M. S. Campbell, 'Population Pressure, Inheritance and the Land Market in a Fourteenth-Century Peasant Community,' in Smith, ed., *Land, Kinship and Life-Cycle*, 99–100, 128–29. For detailed discussions of the complexities of the problem, see Richard M. Smith, 'Hypothèses sur la nuptialité en Angleterre aux XIIIe – XIVe siècles,' *Annales: Économies Sociétés Civilisations* 38 (1983), 107–136, and Christopher Dyer, *Lords and Peasants in a Changing Society: The Estates of the Bishopric of Worcester, 680–1540* (Cambridge, 1980), 218–35.

[90] P. P. A. Biller documents clerical concern over marital infertility caused by contraception, perhaps in response to economic pressures before the Plague, in 'Birth Control in the West in the Thirteenth and Early Fourteenth Centuries,' *Past and Present* 94 (1982), 20–25. Biller's list of moralizing complaints about infertility includes Bromyard's fulminations against covetous marriages punished by God with sterility, cited above in note 82. Attacks on covetous, cross-generational marriages appear after the Plague as well; the Wycliffite treatise 'Of Weddid Men and Wifis' warns that marriage 'shulde not be maade bitwixe a ȝonge man and an olde bareyne widewe, passid child-berynge, for love of worldly muk, as men ful of coveitise usen sumtyme, – for þan comeþ soone debat and avoutrie and enemyte, and wast of goodis, and sorowe and care ynowȝ. . . . Many

1350s and 1360s, some widows and widowers – rich ones especially – would still find young partners, though perhaps fewer than before. Even a minority of scandalous cases could trigger the righteous indignation of a poet concerned more with highlighting abuses as he saw them than with calmly analyzing them in their full statistical and social-historical context, were that full context any more available to him than to us. Though the A text postdates the 1361–62 plague, it is doubtful whether its attack on infertile, cross-generational marriages implies any suspicion of the population decline about to begin anew; the traditional criticism of such marriages accounts for the attack well enough. But by the time the C text was in process, Langland might have had at least some sense of the dying out of families and net fertility decline which had started to affect the English population, and the increased vehemence of Wit's remarks on the subject of 'unkynde' marriages may partly reflect such awareness.

Whether or not Langland had noticed or worried about the increasing failures of family lines for lack of offspring, his intensified ire at mismatched, covetous marriages is unmistakable in the C text. In AB, he speaks against marriages across age lines and, to a lesser extent, marriages across moral lines like the Sethite-Cainite unions. In C, he broadens the field to include differences in social status, parentage, beauty, and sexual desirability, using a rhetoric of extremes to drive home his outrage at marriages made by the rich for the sake of further wealth:

> Of kyn ne of kynrede counteth men bote litel
> And thogh she be louelich to loken on and lossum abedde,
> A mayde and wel ymanered and of gode men yspronge,
> Bote she haue oþer goed haue wol here no ryche.
> Ac lat here be vnlouely and vnlossum abedde,
> A bastard, a bond oen, a begeneldes douhter,
> That no cortesye ne can, bute late here be knowe
> For riche or yrented wel, thouh she be reueled for elde
> Ther ne is squier ne knyhte in contreye aboute
> That he ne wol bowe to þat bonde to beden here an hosebonde
> And wedden here for here welthe and weschen on þe morwe
> That his wyf were wexe or a walet ful of nobles. (C.10.256–67)

The reference to knights and squires strongly suggests that the main new issue here for Langland is disparate status; 'kyn and kynrede' are the only certain difference between these gentlemen (whose age and

hote and coragious men wolen not take a pore gentil womman to his wif in Goddis lawe, and make here a gentil womman, and save here owene soule, but lyven in þe develis servyce . . . and abiden to have a riche womman for muk' (*Select English Works* 3:191).

97

appearance are unspecified) and the rich but lowborn women he accuses them of marrying. The manners, beauty, and *lossumnesse* of unmarried maidens of good birth and the age, ugliness, and immorality of marriageable wealthy women merely add fuel to the satirical fire. In contrast to A and B, however, we are no longer in the realm of social probability. This is the language of hyperbolic complaint, akin to the world-upside-down imagery of Thomas of Erceldoun's prophecies, which foretell lads (knaves) wedding ladies among other forms of social chaos before the end of the Scottish wars.[91] As we have already seen, economically motivated marriages between young people and old widowers or widows were familiar enough in late medieval England, though maybe not as common as Langland contends; so too, within reasonable limits of disparity, were socially asymmetric but economically advantageous marriages.[92] Similarly, among the various economic sub-groups in village communities, marriage within one's economic group was by far the most common practice, and most especially so among the most substantial peasant families, who thereby consolidated and preserved property and power.[93] Moreover, throughout the peasantry, distinctions of free and villein tenure seem to have been less significant than the chance of gaining good land, whether by marriage, tenancy, or other means; economics outweighed legal status in any number of situations.[94] However, the likelihood of a knight or squire marrying himself or his son to an old, loathsome, bastard villein, however rich, is virtually nil.[95]

[91] The earliest version, in MS Harley 2253, may be found in Rossell H. Robbins, ed., *Historical Poems of the XIVth and XVth Centuries,* (New York, 1959], 29, 261n ('a common complaint of the moralists'). Several later adaptations of the prophecy retain this line in some form. See Israel Gollancz, ed., *A Good Short Debate between Winner and Waster* (London, 1930), lines 15–16 and n.; J. A. H. Murray, *The Romance and Prophecies of Thomas of Erceldoune,* EETS 61 (London, 1875), xxxvi, xxxix, 44–45. Cf. Whiting, L18, 'A lad (*low fellow*) to wed a lady is an inconvenient (*misfortune*).'

[92] For some typical ways in which marriages of interest could gradually aid the upward social and economic mobility of knightly, gentry, and professional families, see P. J. Jefferies, 'Social Mobility in the Fourteenth Century: The Example of the Chelreys of Berkshire,' *Oxoniensia* 41 (1976), 324–36.

[93] Edward Britton, *The Community of the Vill: A Study in the History of the Family and Village Life in Fourteenth-Century England* (Toronto, 1977), 17–19, 52–54; J. A. Raftis, *A Small Town in Late Medieval England: Godmanchester 1278–1400* (Toronto, 1982), 214–16.

[94] Postan, *Cambridge Economic History,* 1:610–17; DeWindt, *Holywell-cum-Needingworth,* 153–54. However, there is also evidence for some favoring of free over villein suitors by women acquiring licenses to marry in Ramsey Abbey villages; see Judith M. Bennett, 'Medieval Peasant Marriage: An Examination of Marriage License Fines in *Liber Gersumarum,'* in *Pathways to Medieval Peasants,* ed. J. A. Raftis, Papers in Mediaeval Studies 2 (Toronto, 1981), 211.

[95] *The Wife of Bath's Tale* applies the same rhetoric of improbable extremes, for quite different purposes, to the marriage of the young knight to the loathly lady. Interestingly, canon law presumed that alleged clandestine marriages between obvious social unequals

But even if the C text's hyperbolic scenario here is not a very accurate social sketch, it does suggest which traits Langland thinks ought to make a nubile woman attractive to a potential husband, especially one marrying for the first time. Certainly, wealth should not be very important. Instead, the most desirable features in a bride will be legitimate birth in a good, free family; good manners, maidenhood (probably virginity *and* youth, at least for a young husband), and a lovely appearance; and, interestingly enough, being 'lossum abedde.' In similar manner, one can see or infer the traits of a desirable husband for such a woman: also a maiden (so ABC), not 'an old feble' (AB), and likewise of good family and behavior, since 'kynde sholde wedde kynde.' With these qualities, the spouses' natures will easily give rise to honor and love; it will be easy for them to live in law and love, bringing forth good offspring.

Þat Iche Man Haue a Make

Having come to the end of his attack on covetous marriages between unlike kinds, Wit concludes his discussion of marriage with some brief remarks on sexuality. In so doing, he returns to the theme of sexuality in due season, recalling (explicitly in BC) his previous explanation of Cain's evil nature as the result of untimely intercourse between Adam and Eve. Sexuality should be restricted to the monogamous structure of formal marriage; it is not to be used 'as betwyn sengle & sengle' but according to the 'lawe [that] haþ ygrauntid / Þat iche man haue a make in mariage of wedlak / And werche on his wyf & on no womman ellis' (A.10.206-08). The clause 'þat iche man haue a make in mariage of wedlak' echoes a biblical *locus classicus* on marriage, Paul's advice in 1 Cor. 7:2, 'Bonum est ut unusquisque uxorem suam habeat propter fornicationem,' quoted in the B and C versions of this passage. It is also reminiscent of commentaries on Mt. 19:1-6 and Mk. 10:1-9, the standard Gospels for the nuptial Mass, which traditionally observed that God created humankind as 'masculum et feminam,' one male and one female, cleaving unto each other, to show that marriage should be a permanent relation between one man and one woman, not for one man and many women or one woman and many men.[96] The B text refers

were not bona fide, on the grounds that the socially superior party (usually the man) would not have been serious and that the socially inferior party would have known it because of the disparity of rank. See R. H. Helmholz, *Marriage Litigation in Medieval England* (Cambridge, 1974), 132-33; de Burgh, *Pup. Oc.*, 126v.

[96] See especially Mt. 19:4-5, Mk. 10:6-7. Typical comments are those of Jerome, *Comm. in Math.* 3.725-33 (CC 77:165-66), quoted by Bede, *In Marcum* 3.642-50 (CC 120:558); Chretien de Stavelot, *Expos. in Matt.* 62 (PL 106:1412-13); Gl. Ord. (Interl.), 5:314-16, 585-86; Aquinas, *Comm. in Matt.* 19 (*Opera* 10:174-75). Cf. ParsT 921.

specifically to the divine institution and approbation of matrimony, juxtaposing that reference with Paul's divinely-inspired words: the right use of marriage 'likeþ god almy3ty, / For he made wedlok first and þus hymself seide: / *Bonum est vt vnusquisque vxorem suam habeat propter fornicacionem'* (B.9.193–94α).

Unlike the two later texts, A does not refer directly to the remedial purpose of marriage – 'propter fornicationem' – and it thus projects a less pessimistic view of sex than the Pauline verse or B and C. Langland apparently decided that A's warning against extramarital sex was not stern enough, for in B he adds both the full Pauline statement and several lines to the same effect:

> And euery maner seculer man þat may no3t continue
> Wisely go wedde and ware þee fro synne,
> For lecherie in likynge is lymeyerd of helle.
> While þow art yong and yeep and þi wepene yet kene
> Wreke þee wiþ wyuyng if þow wolt ben excused:
> *Dum sis vir fortis ne des tua robora scortis;*
> *Scribitur in portis, meretrix est ianua mortis.* (B.9.182–86α)

The only real amelioration of the sexual pessimism in these B lines comes in the subsequent observation that rightly used marriages please God, who created marriage first (9.193–94α). The C text relieves the severity somewhat more, altering line B.9.186 to read 'Awreke the þerwith on wyfyng, for godes werk y holde hit' (10.285). While C still sharply condemns sex outside of marriage, it gives marital sexuality more credit than B – no longer describing the conjugal debt as a way for youthful male sexual drives to 'be excused,' but lauding it as God's work. (At this point in the poem, as often elsewhere, Langland is clearly envisioning a primarily male audience.)

Unlike sex outside of marriage, which is always untimely, marital sexuality has its appropriate times. All three texts remind spouses (A) or husbands (BC) not to work 'in vntyme,' as Adam and Eve did in engendering Cain. There should be no 'bedbourd,' no 'dede derne,' at forbidden times, which usually included times of penance, festal solemnity, and certain biological periods.[97] Thus Haukyn's fornications are made all the worse by the fact that he and his partners have shown no *mesure* when they

---

[97] For specific 14th-century English rules about times for marital abstinence, see de Burgh, *Pup. Oc.*, 128v–29r: 'In festiuitatibus solennibus, tempore ieiuniorum, et processionum conuenire carnaliter non debent coniuges, quia huiusmodi solennis est veneratio exhibenda.' The physical periods for abstinence – during the menses, during pregnancy, and before the woman's churching – are matters of counsel more than command; although the debt may be sought at these times, says de Burgh, the 'tutior' path is to avoid intercourse. See also nn. 58 and 66 above.

to þe werke yeden,
As wel fastyng dayes as Fridaies and forboden ny3tes [C: heye-festes
euenes],
And as lef in lente as oute of lente, alle tymes yliche.
Swiche werkes with hem were neuere out of seson
Til þei my3te na moore. (B.13.347-51; cf. C.6.181-85)

Marriage makes sexual *mesure* easier; analogies between the seven sacraments and the seven virtues often associate marriage with Temperance.[98] But Langland's prescription for the right use of marital sexuality goes beyond a temperate observance of suitable times; the partners must also be 'clene / Of lif & of loue & of lawe also' (A.10.202-05, B.9.187-92; cf. C.10.288-93). Corruption in the B archetype of the 'life, love, law' verse (the manuscripts read 'Boþe of/in lif and of/in soule and [also] in parfit charite') forces Langland to rephrase its C successor to read 'clene of lyf and in loue of soule and in lele wedlok,'[99] but the fact that he reunites the word *lyf* with *loue* and the concept of *leaute* shows how important this threefold condition for saintly procreation was to him. Given all the things Wit has said about marriage, the triple cleanness he envisions may be glossed as follows: cleanness of life – completion of one's due penance for past sins; cleanness of love – love of one's mate, based on likeness of *kyndes*; cleanness of law or *lele* wedlock – willing obedience to the divinely instituted laws of matrimony. To be sure, constant fulfillment of all these conditions will not be possible. But they can be striven for, and the recurring penitential seasons of the Church give men and women the chance to keep closing the gap between the actual and the ideal. Like the field lying fallow, which regenerates its fertility while not being worked, the married couple who 'ad tempus vacant orationi et iterum revertantur' (1 Cor. 7:5) will refresh and invigorate the spiritual crop they bring forth. Through deeds and children alike, they will engender Do-wel, Do-bet, and Do-best.

Finally, all three texts conclude with the vehement condemnation of offspring gotten other than in lawful wedlock, and a brief coda recapitulating the three Do's (A.10.209-18, B.9.195-210, C.10.294-307).

---

[98] De Burgh, *Pup. Oc.*, 2v; Aquinas, *ST* 3 q.65 a.1 (*Opera*, 4:285). Cf. Frances G. Godwin, 'An Illustration to the *De Sacramentis* of St Thomas Aquinas,' *Speculum* 26 (1951), 609-14.
[99] K-D 404; 79 ('confusion of *l* and long *s*' in *loue/soule* corruption), 87 (*in parfit charite* 'more emphatic' than *of lawe also*). Schmidt suggests reading 'Of lif and in love of soule, and in lawe also,' commenting that 'the A/C *l*-phrases, with legal sense, support rejection of Bx as scribal explicitness prompted by failure to grasp sense. Langl.'s point seems to be that as well as freedom from canonical sin a couple must have the right spiritual attitude (mutual love) and be married without impediment if intercourse is to be pleasing to God. A X 206-8 is plainer' (*B-Text*, 98, 278).

The misbegotten are characterized as doers of evil, enemies of Do-wel, the devil's servants. As we have seen, the nature of their wickedness shows them to be spiritual descendants of Cain. They also have a share in the lineage of Lady Meed, and particularly in the final legacy of that lineage: 'aftir here deþ day [they] shuln dwelle wiþ þe [devil].' The escape clause, 'But ʒif god giue hem grace here to amende,' reminds us that none are absolutely predestined to damnation, but even its salient final position in Wit's marital discourse can hardly counter the preceding hundred lines devoted to the thesis that *kynde folweth kynde*.

Conclusions

Wit's speech lays elementary but necessary groundwork for Will's continuing education through the rest of his search for Do-wel. In arguing this point, I diverge to some extent from a number of fine critics of the poem, who see Wit as providing little help to Will. For instance, James Simpson's splendid recent study, *Piers Plowman: An Introduction to the B-Text*, suggests that Wit's speech is irrelevant to Will's needs at this point in the poem, since Piers has already given Will the example of abandoning marriage and work in the world (112). Yet Will's encounter with the very-much-married Haukyn/Activa Vita, his return to his family after the Harrowing of Hell dream, and his comments about his wife's sorrow about his impotence in the final passus indicate to me that he (like the aged Piers, though with less virtue *in via*) must still live through his active, married life before reaching the kind of crisis that will enable or force him to leave the world behind. The example of Piers, like the authoritative teaching of Holy Church, gives Will something to aim for; but he can only reach that goal by way of experience – seeing much and suffering more – and that experience must begin at the beginning.

To be sure, Wit's views on what it is to do well, and where doing well has its roots and dwelling are by no means a complete definition; they need to be complemented by the explications that Will is going to receive from his several other teachers. But to say that Wit's instruction is elementary or incomplete is not to say that it is incorrect or trivial (save as grammar, rhetoric, and logic were 'trivial' in medieval universities). His teaching, like Abraham's near the beginning of Will's journey through salvation history, provides an essential foundation for the subject at hand: in Wit's case, the origins, nature, and circumstances of doing well; in Abraham's, the fundamental mysteries of faith.

It is in terms of this foundation-laying that we should evaluate the content and method of Wit's speech. He offers beginning points for

Will's search for Do-wel, not endpoints; so too, marriage and family are beginnings rather than ends in *Piers Plowman*. But we must recognize that family life is a beginning point which continues to support the good that springs from it, just as Do-wel must continue in order to support Do-bet and Do-best. The foundation offered by marriage and family must be carefully laid and then carefully built upon, like the internal 'domestic economy' of the soul and body, made in God's image but quite capable of marring that image if not properly governed. Of course, for Wit's teaching to be useful to Will and to the poet's audience, it needs to be received and understood in the right spirit – accepted humbly and assimilated judiciously, as only a part of the wisdom offered by the poem, not as the whole of that wisdom. As Philomena O'Driscoll notes, 'the principle constantly important in the Dowel debate . . . [is that] the part must not be taken for the whole.'[100] 'Audiatis alteram partem' (C.4.188) is a maxim as important for Will and the reader as for the Visio king. The fact that Wit's speech doesn't seem to do Will much good has more to do, in my view, with Will's own resistance to the conversion of heart and action than with faulty teaching from Wit.

As the previous sections of this chapter have aimed to show, Wit's seemingly disunified discourse can be seen as having certain unifying elements after all, perhaps more than are usually recognized. The passus could be viewed as a kind of triptych, whose primary subject is the origins and nature of doing well, and whose panels depict the Castle of Caro, the social family, and the married state proper. It is further unified by repeated references to metaphorical and literal families and households, and by a consistent interest in the multiple manifestations of *kynde*. And all manner of smaller themes and images can be found playing across the passus, adding their own connecting links to the whole.

Although Will may have simplistically taken an action for a person or thing by seeking 'where Dowel dwellith,' as Carruthers and others have argued, I would defend Wit against the charge of encouraging the Dreamer in this simplification.[101] All three panels of his triptych display *doing* well in various modes: (1) as it originates in the individual who maintains the right relations between his various faculties and acts so as to preserve the divine image which they reflect; (2) as it is fostered by

---

[100] 'The *Dowel* Debate,' 28.
[101] The accusation has become a critical commonplace; among many others, see Carruthers, *St. Truth*, 81–82, 86–89; David Mills, 'The Rôle of the Dreamer in *Piers Plowman*,' in Hussey, *Critical Approaches*, 194–95; Maureen Quilligan, 'Langland's Literal Allegory,' *Essays in Criticism* 28 (1978), 100–02; Martin, *The Field and the Tower*, 46.

adults fulfilling their social duties to teach and support their physical and spiritual families; (3) as it originates in and is fostered by honest wedded couples, lawfully and lovingly producing children who take after their parents by nature and example.

The first and third of these panels remain relatively stable in all three versions of the poem, but the second undergoes a fair amount of change. Whereas the middle section of the passus plays a fairly clear bridging role in the A text, its reflexes in B and C sometimes submerge earlier connections among its parts, making the later texts more difficult to follow than A at this point. However, if we examine some of the major patterns of change in Wit's speech as a whole, we can see that the revisions in the middle section do serve coherent poetic purposes, even though they tend to obscure some of the structural and logical links within the passus.

In the first section of the passus, at least two passages undergo substantive change. The lines on the creation of man in God's likeness, by God's work *and* word, evidently left Langland unsatisfied at least twice, yet were important enough for him to retain some form of the passage in each revision and to pick up on its ideas elsewhere in the passus. For instance, in the C text, where the work-and-word mode of human creation is not mentioned, the importance of using time (working) and words profitably is still noted in the section on social duties. A second point at which significant revision can be traced is in the explanation of Anima's relation to Inwit; here we may note the poet's increasing emphasis on Inwit's control over Anima and on Inwit's spiritual worth as part of the divine image in man. Thus, as the three versions develop, this passage gives higher and higher relative priority to reason and law over the affections and love, in a common enough head-over-heart order.[102] As we have seen, however, the C text rebalances the books later in the passus, by way of its new definitions of the Do's and new details in the marriage discourse.

For the middle panel of Wit's triptych, it is more helpful to consider overall trends in revision than to look at revisions in particular passages.

---

[102] The metaphoric relations among the psychological personifications in *Piers* could be the starting point for a very interesting analysis of the poem based on recent, psychoanalytically-oriented critical approaches like Lacan's or Kristeva's. The interplay of adult and child (or legal minor) figures, and of male and female figures, combined with the themes of authority, hierarchy, power and protection, and training in adult action and use of language, provides highly promising material for such approaches. Looking at the poem from one or more of those perspectives, while not within the scope of this study, may someday tell us much that is new about Langland's understanding of the development of self and language within an inescapably social and in many ways familial context.

These trends run parallel for several important topics, three of which are especially worthy of note: (1) social obligations and vocation; (2) word and work in the human family; and (3) law and love as the basic principles of doing well. Each of these topics represents some aspect of Do-wel, especially as achieved through an active life in the world. Changes in their treatment from A to B to C move us along a spectrum of shifting but related examples of how to do well; their differences are in the degree and direction of emphasis, not in the kinds of goodness being depicted.

With respect to social obligations and vocation, we find A focusing on familial duties to immediate kin and on the vocations of ordinary Christians who support the *comune* by working in any state of life. B puts its emphasis on godparents and bishops, especially on the negative example of bishops who selfishly refuse to fulfill their episcopal vocation. In C, the stage goes almost entirely to the bishops, but now with positive descriptions of the way they can be fulfilling their vocations, preaching and dying for the faith. But the focus on prelates in B and C in no way absolves other Christians of duties to their physical and spiritual families or to their vocation; the basic type of obligation is the same, and higher rank merely broadens the scope of one's duties.

As for the theme of works and words, which links the actions of good men to the divinely creative activity seen earlier in the passus, we find these concepts exemplified in A mainly by the physical, worldly work of the ordinary good person, and by the teaching passed on in families and in schools. Through that teaching, Langland implies, young people are enabled to become contributing members of society who do well in their own right. In B, we hear of responsibilities for spiritual teaching by godparents and the Church. We also encounter the overt injunction against waste of speech and time – shorthand for a whole slew of related pairings throughout the poem, from the virtues of being true of tongue and true or tidy of hands and work, to the vices of being fickle-tongued and an undeserving beggar or waster. And finally, in C, we find the positive enjoining of prelates to employ their word and work 'to tulie þe erthe with tonge,' teaching the heathen and all men the law of Christ's love, a verbal task as laborious and as crucial to human welfare as the plowing to which it is compared.[103]

All well-doing rests on law and love. Failing either of them, there is no doing well. But Do-wel may be characterized in terms that are more law-

---

[103] On the association of agricultural work and preaching, see Stephen A. Barney, 'The Plowshare of the Tongue: The Progress of a Symbol from the Bible to *Piers Plowman*,' *MS* 35 (1973), 261–93. Elizabeth Kirk demonstrates the innovative quality of Langland's use of the plowing metaphor in 'Langland's Plowman and the Recreation of Fourteenth-Century Religious Metaphor,' *YLS* 2 (1988), 1–21.

like or more love-like, depending on the context. The middle section of Wit's speech in the A text tends to stress obedience to the law: fear of the Lord, fear of the rod in school, keeping one's place, humility, sufferance, hard work, and so on. As Langland's thinking developed across his poetic career, he gradually changed this section to focus more on loving obedience and finally on love itself. From fear of the Lord and meek sufferance in A, to servile fear and filial fear in B, to love of kin and of enemies in C: these are Wit's changing definitions of Do-wel and Do-bet in this section. Do-best grows likewise: from being undefined at this point in A, to B's negative definition of not wasting time and speech, to C's powerful vision of a universal love under which enemies have become kin: 'That alle landes loueden and in on lawe bileuede. . . . for lawe sholde loue wexe' (C.10.190, 195). Law is not obliterated by love in this vision, but fulfilled by it, much as love comes to be the fulfillment of the law under which married couples agree to live until death's departing. And love is a work so pleasing to God that he will provide all necessary goods for those who seek him in love: *Inquirentes autem dominum non minuentur omni bono.*[104]

Taken together, the patterns of revision sketched here tend to universalize and spiritualize Wit's discussion of social responsibilities. This process virtually redefines the whole notion of family, and hints at a redefinition of vocation which will appear more clearly at the end of the poem, in Kynde's description of the work, or 'craft,' most pleasing to God: 'Learn to love and leave all other' (B.20.208, C.22.208). The local, secular bonds of laypersons to kin and calling gradually give way to broader, more spiritual obligations, seen especially but not exclusively as they apply to churchmen. The growing emphasis in B and C on the duties of spiritual leaders – bishops, Inwit, perhaps even the 'bishop's peer' Do-best – could have engendered a corollary emphasis on rigid obedience to the law they enforce, were it not for the simultaneous underscoring of love as a complementary principle. Instead of embodying this principle early on, in Anima's affective but fallible urges, the later texts keep it in store till fairly late in the passus; thus Langland avoids a premature tempering of the sterner remarks on misruled or misspent Inwit in B and C. And in the C text, of course, Wit's comments on the three Do's as three kinds of lawful love yield a very satisfactory bridge into his discourse on the lawful love of marriage.

We come at last to the third panel in Wit's triptych, the marriage discourse proper. As with the Castle of Caro section, this part of the

---

[104] Norton-Smith observes that in Wit's speech, 'marriage and work are the clearest images to emerge of Dowel' (*Langland*, 108).

passus remains relatively stable over all three versions of *Piers Plowman*. The only sizable additions are the BC lines on children bearing their parents' guilt and those on marriage as a remedy for fornication, the details of which have already been discussed. Both additions color the section with a darker view of human nature, especially its capacity to control instinctive or 'genetic' impulses; this increased mistrust in some ways matches the increasing subordination of Anima to Inwit in the Castle of Caro passage. However, it must be observed that both additions expand on material already in A; they are not startling developments, though they may reflect a growing awareness on Langland's part, based perhaps on greater life-experience, of human frailties. But while we may allow for the possibility or plausibility of such an attitude-shift, we must not think of it as a shift into a rigidly condemnatory stance, given the way C ameliorates its sexual pessimism by some striking positive comments on marital sexuality (even *lossumnesse abedde*) as a good thing, 'godes werke.'

Despite the two somewhat pessimistic additions to his discourse on marriage, Wit unmistakably attaches greater value to the ideal of marriage with each revision of the poem. The increments of added worth are relatively small – usually just a line or a phrase here or there – but their combined presence indicates that pessimism is by no means Langland's primary response to the matrimonial estate. For instance, in each revision, he increases the honor and sanctity of the classes named as offspring of honest wedlock. Both B and C add examples from nature and references to *kynde* which reinforce the point that marriage is an institution established by the Creator in his role as Kynde. In all three texts, marriage is said to receive the grace granted to those who do well, but the mode of doing well stressed in A is that of humble work and following one's law, in B that of seeking God by working and winning and not wasting time, and in C that of seeking God by living in law and in love. Both B and C also add the stipulation that marriages, even those between like parties, should be motivated by love rather than wealth.

The C text goes even further than B in depicting and praising a marital ideal of love and affection, and in dispraising marriages that pervert that ideal. The hyperbolic contrast between the virtuous and physically attractive poor maiden and the ill-mannered, repulsive rich crone paints a romanticized picture of an ideal mate, desirable both on her own merits and in contrast to the alternative. Sex in marriage, though sometimes remedial, is also 'God's work.' At several points, C heightens its attacks on *covetise* and links modern marriages and the miscegenations of the first age more tightly with each other and with *covetise*, thus placing higher value on well-wrought marriages by condemning ill-made ones still more sharply.

Wit's comments on marriage, real and metaphorical, do not operate in isolation. The condemnation of covetous marriages, made by *brocage* without consideration of virtue or the potential fruitfulness of body and soul, connects his speech back to the Meed scenes in the First Dream. Like Meed's union with False, such marriages are arranged 'by þe fadres wille and þe frendes conseille, / And . . . assent of hemself' (B.9.117–18), but hardly with the approval of God or Holy Church. Similarly, Wit's remarks on children's *kynde* likeness to their parents resonates with the 'Talis pater talis filia' passage at the beginning of the Meed episode in BC.

Wit's speech also has an important role to play as a part of the Third Dream, despite the apparent abandonment of problems facing actual marriages and families in favor of a more individualized cognitive quest focused on problems of learning, authority, and belief – though even here, relationships among most of his instructors are figuratively familial.[105] But besides continuing to meet allegorical relatives through-out this vision, the Dreamer will face questions of metaphorical and real matings just before the end of the Dream, as he is tempted into relationships with Fortune's maidens (who function in a sense as 'false wives' to Will[106]) and then contemplates the differences between animal and human reproduction. As Steven Kruger has recently observed, Will's panoramic vision of the world from the mountain of Middle-earth – a vision granted by Kynde, the Creator and builder of Do-wel's castle Caro – reveals

> the universal marriage of 'higher' and 'lower' forces, a view of the divine plan working in the physical world. [Kynde] demonstrates how the ideas in the mind of the Creator manifest themselves in a life of eating, nest building, and (especially) reproduction. Without referring explicitly to Rechelesnesse's argument or to the problem of 'kynde knowyng,' Kynde's mirror presents a paradigm of how the abstract and concrete – idea and matter, the doctrines of Christianity (Clergie) and Christian works in the world – should ideally be united. The mirror gives access to knowledge of both an abstract plan and the workings of that plan in the 'kynde' world of matter.[107]

Finally, we may look forward to the transition from Will's interior quest to the beginning of his experience of biblical history, his vision of

---

[105] For recent commentary on the significance of the figurative relationships between Wit, Study, Scripture, and Clergy, see Harwood, 'Dame Study and the Place of Orality in *Piers Plowman*,' *ELH* 57 (1990), 6–7; and Simpson, *Introduction to the B-Text*, 104–07.
[106] I am indebted to Kimberly Keller for this observation.
[107] 'Mirrors and the Trajectory of Vision in *Piers Plowman*,' *Speculum* 66 (1991): 86.

the Tree of Charity and his encounter with Faith. As we will see in Chapter 3, these episodes look back to Wit's discussions of Anima, her home in the heart, the *imago dei*, and marriage, as the poem rises toward its emotionally powerful climax in the Easter passus. And we will also see how later portions of the C text explicate, even more fully than Wit's discourse, the honor due to *kynde* and fruitful marriage.

3

Þe Trinite It Meneþ

At the end of Wit's speech, Will has made little visible progress in achieving the right frame of mind and heart for understanding what it is to do well, better, and best. However, the events of the next several passus will begin to convert his *affectus* in ways that will give him some degree of 'kynde knowyng' by the end of his encounter with Patience and Activa Vita. Analyses of this change have been ably provided by a number of scholars, and need not detain us here.[1] The remainder of the Third Dream and to a lesser extent the Activa Vita episode contain occasional references to family, marriage, and generation – we encounter, for example, allegorical spouses and lemans, the redeeming 'bloody brotherhood' of Christ and humankind, the important puzzle of rational sexuality occurring between animals more often than between men and women, and the effect of Haukyn's literal or figurative family on his moral life. However, like the family references in the latter part of the Visio, these passages are not concentrated heavily at any particular point, and I shall withhold discussion of them until Chapter 4.

The third and last major analysis of matrimonial and familial issues in *Piers Plowman* arises in another passus of beginnings: B.16/C.18, 'primus de Dobet' according to some manuscripts and critics, the passus in which Will sees the Tree of Charity, gets a quick sketch of Christ's life up

---

[1] See, among others, Stella Maguire, 'The Significance of Haukyn, *Activa Vita*, in *Piers Plowman*,' *RES* o.s. 25 (1949), 97–109; Robert Worth Frank, Jr., *Piers Plowman and the Scheme of Salvation: An Interpretation of Dowel, Dobet, and Dobest* (New Haven, 1957), 34–77; Elisabeth M. Orsten, '*Patientia* in the B-Text of *Piers Plowman*,' *MS* 31 (1969), 317–33; Elizabeth D. Kirk, *The Dream Thought of Piers Plowman* (New Haven, 1972), 127–58; Joseph S. Wittig, ' "Piers Plowman" B, Passus IX–XII: Elements in the Design of the Inward Journey,' *Traditio* 28 (1972), 211–80, and 'The Dramatic and Rhetorical Development of Long Will's Pilgrimage,' *NM* 76 (1975), 59–66; Britton J. Harwood, ' "Clergye" and the Action of the Third Vision in *Piers Plowman*,' *MP* 70 (1973), 279–90; Philomena O'Driscoll, 'The *Dowel* Debate in *Piers Plowman* B,' *MÆ* 50 (1981), 18–29; David G. Allen, 'The Dismas *Distinctio* and the Forms of *Piers Plowman* B.10–13,' *YLS* 3 (1989), 31–48.

to the Crucifixion, and meets Faith typified by Abraham.[2] However, the poet's argument here, including his references to the married state, has now shifted to higher planes. Matrimony is linked with the two other grades of chastity in the description of the fruits on the cosmological Tree of Love; it thus appears clearly in its role as one of the basic states of life available to the human race. Further, it is presented as a reflection of the Trinity itself within humankind – in conjunction with the other grades of chastity in B, and by itself alone in C. Once again, in laying groundwork for a major section of his poem – here, groundwork concerning love in action and the loving relations of the Trinity – Langland casts his views partly in marital terms, terms which combine the familiar and the sacred, the actual and the ideal.

Unlike the passages treated in Chapters 1 and 2, where the three texts offer more or less similar materials on marriage and family, the presentation of these topics in B.16 is thoroughly revised and greatly expanded in C.18. Indeed, the two references to marriage in B.16 are little more than passing allusions, their dozen or so lines of relatively minor importance in the passus at large. In C, on the other hand, both allusions are enlarged and explored at significant length, displaying what I consider important changes in the ways Langland was thinking about the whole passus.

Before examining the matrimonial and other fruits of Charity, we should recall how Will has come to the Tree. In both the B and the C texts, he has been speaking with his soul, or rather an ideal version of that soul. Students of *Piers Plowman* B have come to call this interlocutor Anima, although that is only the first of many names by which the creature identifies himself, and neither it nor any other name is used by Will in addressing or referring to this being 'wiþouten tonge and teeþ.' In C, Will's new teacher is specifically introduced and addressed as Liberum Arbitrium, but he also gives himself all the names claimed by B's 'Anima,' with the new epithet 'Liberum Arbitrium' added to the list between Love and Conscience.[3]

---

[2] I avoid the labels '(Vita de) Dowel' and '(Vita de) Dobet' in the following discussion, since their authorial origin is dubious. For the most recent statement of the evidence and arguments, see Robert Adams, 'Langland's *Ordinatio*: The *Visio* and the *Vita* Once More,' *YLS* 8 (1994), 51–84, and works cited therein. However, this cautionary tactic should not be taken as a denial of the gradual but unmistakable modulations of poetic focus and technique accomplished by the speeches of Anima and Liberum Arbitrium. Those speeches bring the Dreamer from the contemporary scene against which the Banquet and Activa Vita's confession take place to the much wider stage on which the pageant of salvation history unfolds. The Tree of Charity, with its clear Edenic connotations, marks the completed entry into the new realm of vision, and the theft of its fruit initiates the soteriological action of the next three passus. Cf. Elizabeth D. Kirk, *Dream Thought*, 159–60.

[3] The matter of Anima/Liberum Arbitrium's names is of more than passing significance to

The C text's introduction of this complex psychological entity as Liberum Arbitrium is a most salient revision. By adding the name 'Liberum Arbitrium' and giving it pride of place in C, Langland alters our sense of Will's new guide so as to emphasize traits proper to a being so named – freedom, choice, judgment. Moreover, the new name provides a smoother transition into the Tree of Charity scene, where the B text had rather abruptly introduced Liberum Arbitrium as Piers's lieutenant in the 'herber of herte' (B.16.16–17, 46–52). Modern readers of the poem often regret the loss of Piers Plowman from the Tree-scene in C, and the excision of B's riddling description of Anima in favor of the plain 'Liberum Arbitrium, leader of Activa Vita.' Still, those losses and the renaming of Anima help unify this transitional section of *Piers Plowman*, thanks to the notable extension of Liberum Arbitrium's active presence in the poem, running now through three passus (C.16.157– 18.181). As a 'leader' of Activa Vita, that minstrel-waferer apprenticed to Piers but all too like the still-imperfect Dreamer, Liberum Arbitrium can be read as an ideal 'Peres prentys.' He is also an ideal version of Will himself – 'free Will' itself, authorized and dignified further by the Latin translation of the English phrase. Under his leadership, Activa Vita and Will can become their best selves, through the understanding of charity which enables one truly to do well, better, and best.[4]

It would be a mistake, however, to think that C's Liberum Arbitrium is doing vastly different things from B's Anima. Both of them provide recapitulatory closure to the intellectual and moral quests of the Third and Fourth Dreams.[5] They roughly synthesize the faculties dissected into separate personifications in Wit's speech – the senses; the quickening life force and will; knowledge, conscience, and reason; the powers (especially in C) of defending, enduring, and governing –

Will's passage into the study of Charity and salvation history. See James Simpson, *Piers Plowman: An Introduction to the B-Text* (London, 1990), 183–84; Anne Middleton, 'William Langland's "Kynde Name": Authorial Signature and Social Identity in Late Fourteenth-Century England,' in *Literary Practice and Social Change in Britain, 1380–1530*, ed. Lee Patterson (Berkeley, 1990), 44–47; and my 'The Chilling of Charity: Eschatological Allusions and Revisions in Piers Plowman C.16–17,' in *Art and Context in Late Medieval English Narrative: Essays in Honour of R. W. Frank, Jr.* (Cambridge, 1994), 51–77.

[4] On Liberum Arbitrium, see especially Donaldson, *Piers Plowman: The C-Text and Its Poet* (1949; rpt. Hamden, 1966), 180–96; A. V. C. Schmidt, 'Langland and Scholastic Philosophy,' *MÆ* 38 (1969), 134–56; and Britton J. Harwood, '*Liberum Arbitrium* in the C-Text of *Piers Plowman*,' *PQ* 52 (1973), 680–95.

[5] In C, the Fourth Dream apparently continues up to Will's meeting with Abraham, though Langland's inconsistent or incomplete revision of the poem's dream structure here makes his ultimate intention uncertain. Cf. Pearsall, C.18.179n; Robert W. Frank, Jr., 'The Number of Visions in *Piers Plowman*,' *MLN* 66 (1951), 211–12. However, the first half of C's Fourth Dream (up to the appearance of Liberum Arbitrium at C.16.157) functions very much like the Fourth Dream in B, which stops just before Anima's appearance.

thereby indicating that Will has progressed at least to the point of recognizing the aspects of the soul in their unified complexity. In their aspect as *lele loue* or *Amor*, both Anima and Liberum Arbitrium have an intimate understanding of charity and the heart's country, major topics in their lessons to Will. This understanding in turn suggests their kinship with Kynde's beloved Anima, whose favorite dwelling is in the heart, the organ identified by Holy Church as the *heiʒe welle* and fountainhead of *kynde knowyng* itself. Both of them also lay great stress on the clergy's responsibilities to teach love and faith and generally display the moral leadership characteristic of Inwit. Thus, in B and C alike, the appearance of the integrated and idealized soul harks back to the psychological allegory at the start of Wit's speech. The new Anima, or Liberum Arbitrium, is a soul that knows itself well, and hence is able to do well, to rightly exercise a well-ordered, authentically *liberum arbitrium*. What more suitable leader to introduce Will to the land of Love within the self, the human race, and salvation history?

As noted earlier, B.16/C.18 takes us back to basics and beginnings, but on new levels. Aside from the sketch of Christ's life in the middle of the passus, its primary biblical context is the book of Genesis, especially its chapters on Eden and the Fall, and its chapters on Abraham. Here again we find a parallel with Wit's discourse, which drew on the first book of the Bible for the stories of Creation, Cain's seed, and Noe. But where Wit's speech focused primarily on natural, rationally accessible aspects of Creation and procreation, B.16/C.18 stresses theological issues and revealed truths: sin, the Fall, the promise of salvation, faith in the Trinity. In addition, the passus opens with Will asking a more advanced question – what is charity and where can it be found? As with his similar questions about Do-wel and Company, the first answer is again, 'inside oneself.' Indeed, with its overtones of domestic privacy, B's *herber* of heart *amyddes mannes body* (B.16.14–15) corresponds quite well to the metaphor of the heart as Anima's favorite chamber or bower inside Caro. Both images suggest a pleasurable and intimate space, naturally analogous to the linked biblical images of the *hortus conclusus* and *thalamus*. The enclosed, interior *hortus* is suggested even more strongly in C.18.4–5, '*Cor-hominis* . . . / Erber of alle *pryuatees* and of holynesse' (my emphasis in line 5).

But the full answer to Will's question expands far beyond the self alone. As he and we come to see, it extends to all the manifold expressions of charity within humankind and across history. To be sure, charity grows within the loving individual, whose moral life is supported and protected by the Trinity against the world, flesh, and devil. But it also grows within the human race, seen in terms of three loving states of life and in terms of our common descent from Adam, subjection to death, and salvation by Christ. As Will discovers, Love can be understood metaphorically as a cosmological and fruitful tree, rooted in *kynde* and reaching up to Grace, a 'ful trie tree' that mirrors the triune Godhead in many ways, not least in the *kynde* estate of matrimony.[6]

The Fruits of Charity

Let us turn then to the first allusion to matrimony in B.16/C.18. Piers or Liberum Arbitrium describes the fruits on the Tree as the three degrees of chastity – marriage, widowhood, and virginity.[7] This description (B.16.67–78, C.18.58–110) is one of the few places in *Piers Plowman* where Langland openly refers to the traditionally preferred status of virginity over widowhood, and widowhood over marriage.[8] Normally, he pays only occasional attention to the life of virginity or contemplative withdrawal from the world. Although he recognizes the high spiritual value of such a life, he prefers to focus on the more common, secular aspects of human experience. He vigorously seeks the spiritual values that should underlie the social bond, politics, marriage, and the self-knowledge that leads to action. Even when he recommends leaving the world behind in patient poverty and unsolicitous *rechelesnesse*, he

---

[6] For the rest of this chapter, the distinct notions of marriage and family will usually be subsumed under the single terms 'matrimony,' 'marriage,' or 'married state,' since Langland's focus in this passus is on the married state as a relatively unified concept. One could even say that part of his point about matrimony here is that its threefold, familial multiplicity is essentially still a unity.

[7] Useful studies of the Tree of Charity and the grades of chastity include Morton W. Bloomfield, '*Piers Plowman* and the Three Grades of Chastity,' *Anglia* 76 (1958), 227–53; Ben H. Smith, Jr., *Traditional Imagery of Charity in Piers Plowman* (The Hague, 1966), 56–73; A. Joan Bowers, 'The Tree of Charity in *Piers Plowman*: Its Allegorical and Structural Significance,' in Eric Rothstein and Joseph Anthony Wittreich, Jr., eds., *Literary Monographs* 6 (Madison, 1975), 1–34, 157–60; Mary Clemente Davlin, 'A Genius-Kynde Illustration in Codex Vat. Pal. Lat. 629,' *Manuscripta* 23 (1979), 149–58; Peter Dronke, 'Arbor Caritatis,' in *Medieval Studies for J. A. W. Bennett, Aetatis Suae LXX*, ed. P. L. Heyworth (Oxford, 1981), 207–53; Robert Adams, 'Piers's Pardon and Langland's Semi-Pelagianism,' *Traditio* 39 (1983), 377–85; Frederick M. Biggs, ' "Aungeles Peeris": *Piers Plowman*, B 16.67–72 and C 18.85–100,' *Anglia* 102 (1984), 426–36; Malcolm Godden, *The Making of Piers Plowman* (London, 1990), 122–27, 198–200. Also of interest, though based on more restrictive interpretive assumptions than the readings suggested here are David Aers, *Piers Plowman and Christian Allegory* (London, 1975), 79–109, and Margaret E. Goldsmith, *The Figure of Piers Plowman: The Image on the Coin* (Cambridge, 1981), 58–71.

[8] Other references to the three grades or to the value of continence include B.12.33–39 (married men, religious, and maidens to do well through *leaute*); C.4.46–48 (Wrong commits sexual crimes against a wife, widow, and maiden); C.16.346 (Sts Edmund and Edward were chaste all their lives). In A.7.233 and B.6.249, but not the parallel C passage, Actif and Contemplatif are cited by Hunger as equally suitable ways of 'working' for a living as Kind Wit and Christ require.

seldom identifies such endeavors specifically as a life of religious vows, virginity, or contemplative withdrawal. Langland generally chooses to praise charity in action; Mary Magdalen's 'best part' is poverty, not the traditional contemplation (B.11.250–55α, C.12.134–38a). He is more likely to decry hypocritical, loveless celibacy than to praise a cloistered virtue: 'Chastite wiþoute charite worþ cheynid in helle' (A.1.168, B.1.188, C.1.184).

Nonetheless, when Langland steps back to create the sublime vision of the Tree of Charity, simultaneously personal, historical, and transhistorical, he is perfectly ready to acknowledge that the crop of the Tree bears the sweetest fruits, 'Maidenhode, Aungeles peeris' (B.16.71; cf. C.18.90).[9] Having begun the whole scene with a tree of virtues, whose fruits of good works have no special hierarchical order, Langland here shifts the picture to one in which the fruits are virtuous states of life for which a traditional ranking was already available. Although the three grades of chastity can be externally defined and ranked by their relative use of sexuality, they are more essentially characterized by the directions in which a personally focused love can be aimed and expressed in this world. Marital, vidual, and virginal chastity – each with its characteristic bonds of affection, fidelity, and sexual *mesure* – are fruits of love in very real and similar ways. All three grades are meritorious because they are forms, in the strong sense, of love. What makes virginity most meritorious, and most angel-like, is the fact that it addresses itself to loving God most directly. (As we will see below, the C text is clearer on this point than B, in its comment that both maidens and martyrs are nearest to God in heaven because of their close service to him on earth – it is the service, not the asexuality or even the physical and spiritual integrity, that the poet says God honors.)

But Langland is interested in more than the simple fact that the three degrees of loving chastity serve God in various degrees of perfection. In both texts, the fact that all three fruits fall into death is an important feature of the whole scene; that fall is handled similarly in B and C, though there are some interesting minor differences which we will examine later in this chapter. In the C text, the poet's attentions are drawn to another important issue as well: the relationships and

---

[9] As Biggs observes, the dream-within-a-dream device in B may provide an eschatological perspective from which human nature appears in an ideal form – virginity, in his reading (' "Aungeles Peeris," ' 435–36). However, in C, where the inner dream is no longer part of the narrative structure, the transtemporal aspects of the Tree are more thoroughly interpenetrated by references to such temporal matters as *kynde*, growth, the variable descent of offspring, and the ripening fall through age into death; the interrelations of time and eternity, nature and grace, active and contemplative are thus shown to be more inextricably interwoven than we might have seen in B.

respective merits of these three forms of love. Their six-line description in B.16.67–72 explodes outward into forty-some lines in C, one of the largest blocks of new material in the whole passus. Most of this section and the next will focus on C's much-expanded treatment of matrimony and the other grades of chastity, but a few paragraphs on B's handling of the subject will provide a useful base for the rest of the discussion.

The Fruits of the Tree in B

The depiction of the fruits in B, though brief, is nevertheless instructive. Marriage, the lowest on the tree, is 'moist' and can be taken if Piers (or perhaps anyone) has need. Its moisture may suggest the literal fluids of sexuality and birth; or it may refer to a metaphorical softness of texture that will rot more quickly than a firm-fleshed fruit, just as the marriage bond dissolves with death while virginity partakes of eternity.[10] Continence, later called widowhood (B.16.76), is 'neer þe crop' like a 'kaylewey bastard.' Skeat's explication of 'kaylewey bastard' as 'bastard Cailloux pear' – i.e., a variety of sweet pear that has perhaps been grafted or cultivated – has not to my knowledge been superseded. As he notes, Cailloux pears were relatively expensive, both when purchased as fruit and as grafts for orchards.[11] Taking *bastard* as 'grafted, cultivated' is less certain, but continence can arguably be viewed as a life of deliberate celibacy grafted onto a prior state of openness to sexual commerce.[12]

Virginity has the greatest number of defining traits: growing at the top of the tree, the cleanest fruit and soonest ripe, 'angels' pears/peers,'[13] never subject to the swellings of desire or pregnancy or to the loss of its sweetness. Perhaps the most interesting feature of maidenhood is that it is 'kynde fruyt.' Hugh White suggests that

---

[10] Dronke points out possible positive connotations for the fleshly moisture of matrimony, noting an analogous reference to the 'apples of [God's] madescent (*saftigen*) humanity' in the *Revelations* of Mechthild of Magdeburg, a phrase which he glosses as 'apples rich with the sap of Christ's human nature' ('Arbor Caritatis,' 219).

[11] 2:237. Cailloux pears (fruits or slips) are among the costliest items among the medieval garden accounts cited by Alicia M. Tyssen-Amherst, *A History of Gardening in England*, 3rd ed. (New York, 1910), 34–36, and John Harvey, *Mediaeval Gardens* (Beaverton, OR, 1981), 80–84.

[12] In his EETS edition of *Piers*, Skeat notes the French *bastardiere*, meaning 'nursery, wherein young trees are set to be afterwards removed'; see *The Vision of William Concerning Piers Plowman*, Vol. 4: Notes, EETS 67 (London, 1877), 377.

[13] The 'pears/peers' pun was recognized by Skeat (EETS 67:377, C.19.90/B.16.71n). Biggs reviews the traditional assimilation of virginal integrity to the angelic state in ' "Aungeles Peeris," ' 426–31; see also John Bugge, *Virginitas: An Essay in the History of a Medieval Ideal* (The Hague, 1975), 30–35.

Langland may be making a point about the absolute naturalness of virginity (elsewhere. . .he associates *kyndeness* with the motions of the flesh), but the force of *kynde* may simply be 'genuine' (as a mark of approbation) with *kynde* perhaps standing in opposition to *bastard* describing a lesser fruit in the previous line.[14]

Alternately, if Skeat's notion of continence as a grafted pear is correct, then 'kynde' may mean 'natural' in the sense of 'innate, characteristic' – something that is a lifelong choice, not a matter of second thinking (*MED*, s.v. *kinde* adj. 1). Or maybe the adjective here simply means 'kind, gracious, genuine, pure' (*MED*, s.v. *kinde* adj. 2b, c, 5, 6).

Will's desire to 'savor' of this fruit – now identified as apples, despite the earlier mention of pears – gives us more information on the three grades of chastity (or love).[15] From top to bottom, all of them are under the death sentence that resulted from Adam's desire to savor the apple of knowledge, and all of them cry out, weep, or 'ma[k]e a foul noise' as they fall from the Tree. No matter which state of life one chooses to experience, no matter how spiritually fair that state may be, death must come to everyone in that estate (though it does sound as if death is most grievous to those in the married state). And before the Redemption, all members of all three estates were grabbed up and hoarded by the *rageman* apple-thief Satan, suffering spiritual as well as physical death.

Adam's taste of the fruit of knowledge prevents his descendants from tasting the fruit of life, even if their will and works are good, until Christ himself comes to 'savor' the knowledge of death. Will's desire to know the 'sauour' of Charity is good in itself – a desire for *sapientia* rather than *scientia* – but it is frustrated for the moment because of Adam's craving for the apples of that other Tree, a craving which has subjected the fruits of Charity (Adam's saintly offspring with their good works) to death in body and soul. Only *Filius dei*, jousting in Piers's arms, can win back the fruit stolen by the devil, or lay the Eucharistic feast that can satisfy Will's spiritual hunger. The two yearnings for two kinds of fruit are

---

[14] *Nature and Salvation in Piers Plowman* (Cambridge, 1988), 42 n. 6.

[15] Langland was probably more interested in getting both the Edenic suggestion of 'apple-tree' and the play on 'angels' pears/peers' than in preserving a careful picture of a single type of fruit tree. Moreover, the 'eclecticism' (Smith) and 'disorderly conventions' (Dronke) of medieval tree-symbolism would have certainly allowed for shifting images, if in fact there is such shifting here. But there may not be: ME 'appel' can be used generically, for any fruit, so the mention of both pears and apples need not be particularly inconsistent. It is also possible to graft pears or apples onto each other, since the two species are taxonomically close, and compound grafting of 'diuerse frutes in oon stok' to yield trees 'half peris and half apples' was not unknown in fourteenth-century England; see W. L. Braekman, 'Bollard's Middle English Book of Planting and Grafting and Its Background,' *SN* 57 (1985), 32, 24.

superimposed here much as the Trees of Death and Life are super-imposed in the great medieval hymns of the Cross.[16]

By naming specific Old Testament figures as fruits that have dropped from the Tree, Langland completes the transmutation of those fruits from general human virtues to particular virtuous humans, by way of the three grades of love and chastity. We move from 'þe fruyt Charite' to the three grades of chastity (which can be seen both as different modalities of love, and as states of life which include all loving men and women), to all the individual saints 'boþe grete and smale' before Christ's coming, and inferentially to all those who follow Christ in time as well. No longer do we see humankind divided into the economic and socio-political estates found elsewhere in the poem. The three grades of chastity are available to everyone in the social hierarchy, and each in its own way gives physical embodiment to their common inner form – a sturdy, fruitful love whose varieties can provide *saulee* to the heart-hungry Will once Christ has conquered Hell (cf. B.16.11).

The Fruits of the Tree in C

Most of the foregoing observations on the fruits of charity and chastity in B apply equally well to C. However, the content of C's passage on the three grades of chastity is much enlarged, and some of its emphases are altered; moreover, revisions elsewhere in the Tree scene have implications for the three grades as well. Pertinent revisions at the beginning of the scene involve a more explicit definition of the fruits of the Tree, a more direct acknowledgment that the Tree is or includes God's image, and an earlier clear mention of the Trinity's relationship to the Tree.

In comparison to Anima, Liberum Arbitrium defines the fruits of the Tree more fully and its other parts less so. Of B's root of mercy, trunk of *ruþe*, leaves of leal words and the Church's law, blossoms of buxom speech and benign looks, and additional names of Patience and Poor-Simple-of-Heart for the Tree, C retains only loving looks and speech, in slightly altered form (B.16.5–8; C.18.10–11). But to these brief mentions of love in thought and word, the C text adds a much fuller description of love in action, which B had simply called 'þe fruyt Charite' (16.9). From

---

[16] Adams gives a sensitive reading of the positive aspects of Will's desire to eat of the fruit of the Tree, to which these comments are deeply indebted; he makes the interesting suggestion that Will wants to know 'what savior' as well as 'what savor' the fruits of Charity have ('Semi-Pelagianism,' 381–82).

The descriptions of that fruit earlier in the scene as a *saulee* above all others (B.16.11) or as 'Cristes oune fode, / [Which] solaceth alle soules sorwful in purgatory' (C.18.14–15) reinforce Adams' argument for seeing positive as well as negative connotations in Will's desire to taste Piers's or Liberum Arbitrium's fruit.

the Tree, says Liberum Arbitrium, and perhaps also from 'louely lokynges' and 'Benigne-speche,'

> cometh a goed fruyt, þe whiche men calleth werkes
> Of holynesse, of hendeness, of helpe-hym-þat-nedeth,
> The whiche is *Caritas* ykald, Cristes oune fode,
> And solaceth alle soules sorwful in purgatory. (C.18.12–15)

What was implicit in B – that the fruit Charity is the *works* of charity – is made explicit here; furthermore, the fruit is no longer just a *saulee* desired by Will (B.16.11), but 'Cristes oune fode.' It is the food by which he comforts souls in purgatory, presumably because one's good works and the good works of all the saints expedite the passage from purgatory to heaven. 'Cristes oune fode' may also mean the food which Christ desires – 'to do the will of him that sent me, that I may perfect his work' (Jn. 4:34) – the works which Liberum Arbitrium, image of God's will in man, cultivates and protects on the Tree of Love.[17] These revisions enable us to recognize more immediately that the three grades of chastity involve the good works of active love, and are not just fixed or passive states of life. They also prepare us to see the three fruits as a treasure-hoard of nourishment worth recapture by *Filius Dei*.

Liberum Arbitrium also refers to the Tree as an 'ympe . . . hihte *Ymago-dei*,' growing graciously 'euene in þe myddes' of *Cor-hominis*, a country which is the 'erber of alle pryuatees and of holynesse.' Its name, he says, is Trewe-loue, and it has been 'set' by the Trinity. While the 'erber' *Cor-hominis* descends to C from B's 'herber of herte,' the rest of these descriptive phrases are new. They emphasize the mystery and holiness of the heart, a fitting site for God's (Trinitarian) image, and the involvement of grace in the Tree's growth ('graciousliche hit growede'). In C, the heart is a garden, as in B, but a large enough one to be called a country as well; the location of the Tree in that garden is made more precisely Edenic – not merely 'amyddes mannes body' but '*euene in þe*

---

[17] The references to 'Cristes oune foed' in C, to Will's desire for *saulee* in B, and to his yearning to taste of the Tree later on in BC, are clearly related to the larger patterns of food and drink imagery throughout the poem, and link the Tree of Charity scene with such passages as the appearance of Hunger at the plowing of the half-acre; the Banquet scene; Hawkin's wafering and Patience's offer of spiritual victuals; and Christ's hunger and thirst for souls in the Harrowing of Hell. On food and drink in *Piers*, see A. C. Spearing, 'The Development of a Theme in *Piers Plowman*,' RES n.s. 11 (1960), 241–53; Elizabeth Lunz, 'The Valley of Jehoshaphat in *Piers Plowman*,' *Tulane Studies in English* 20 (1972), 1–10; Jill Mann, 'Eating and Drinking in *Piers Plowman*,' *Essays and Studies* 32 (1979), ed. Dieter Mehl, 26–43; A. V. C. Schmidt, 'Langland's Structural Imagery,' *Essays in Criticism* 30 (1980), 311–25; and, at the literal level, R. W. Frank, Jr., 'The "Hungry Gap," Crop Failure, and Famine: The Fourteenth-Century Agricultural Crisis and *Piers Plowman*,' YLS 4 (1990), 87–104.

myddes' of the heart, as the Trees of Life and of Knowledge were traditionally said to be at the center of Eden ('in medio paradisi,' Gen. 2:9). The change from B's 'benigne lokynge' to C's 'louely lokynges' may also play on the biblical description of every tree in Eden as *pulchrum visu*, suggesting 'lovely-looking' as well as 'loving looks.' 'Trewe-loue' calls to mind the primacy of Truth and Love throughout the poem, from Holy Church's speech on. None of these points really contradicts Anima's initial picture of the Tree, and some had been expressed later in B.16 (e.g., the Trinitarian image), but Liberum Arbitrium brings them forward much sooner in C.18.

However, one important feature of Liberum Arbitrium's preliminary description of the Tree has no antecedent at all in B: its nature as an 'ympe,' a sapling or a grafted tree. Given Langland's earlier references to imps and grafting, the sense 'graft'/'grafted tree' seems to be the right one here (cf. B.5.137–43, 9.150–55α; C.10.206–07).[18] Love is the 'graffe of grace,' according to Holy Church in C.1.200 (not in AB), and the Tree of Trewe-loue can be seen as a long-delayed development of this metaphor. Wit's warnings in B and C against grafting sweet apple-shoots onto sour stocks do not apply here; sin is not in the stock of human nature as created by God, but rather in the effects of the three winds which attack the Tree. Man's fundamental *kynde* is good, and is imprinted with – or rather, engrafted with – the *Ymago-dei*. We are wild apples, not elders, and take grafts of like *kynde* most *kyndely*. Questions of human and divine *kynde* are introduced implicitly in the grafting metaphor here; they will be explored in much greater detail throughout the C version of this passus, especially in the new material on the three grades and on the similarity of marriage to the Trinity.

With respect to the Trinity's relation to the Tree, Liberum Arbitrium makes the point much sooner than Piers does in B, and will expand on it more fully in discussing the three grades. His first line notes that the Trinity has 'set' (a standard word for planting saplings, slips, or grafts in

---

[18] I follow recent scholarship in reading 'ympe' here as referring to grafting (e.g., Smith, *Traditional Imagery*, 59–62; Murtaugh, *Piers Plowman and the Image of God* [Gainesville, 1978], 26–27n; Pearsall, C.18.7n), but the differing interpretation offered in Skeat's notes should be mentioned: the word can simply mean a young shoot or slip of a tree, cut from its parent stock and planted separately. However, while Skeat glosses the word as 'sapling, young tree' in his notes, his glossary gives the definition 'graft, shoot' and cites this line as an instance. The *MED* follows Skeat's notes, not his glossary (s.v. *impe*, n. 1c). Fruit trees need to be propagated from slips or grafts because they usually do not retain desired varietal traits when grown from seed. For more general discussions of the literary symbolism of grafted trees in the Middle Ages, see Sharon Ann Coolidge, 'The Grafted Tree in Literature: A Study in Medieval Iconography and Theology,' Diss. Duke, 1977, with special reference to *Piers* on pp. 68–77; and Seth Lerer, 'Artifice and Artistry in *Sir Orfeo*,' *Speculum* 60 (1985), 94–97 and nn. 10–17.

ground or stocks) the Tree, and he reveals the nature of the three 'schoriares' which support and protect the Tree as soon as Will asks what they are:

> Bote thenne toek y hede,
> Hit hadde schoriares to shuyuen hit vp, thre shides of o lenghe
> And of o kyne colour and kynde, as me thoghte,
> Alle thre yliche long and yliche large.
> Moche merueyled me on what more thei growede,
> And askede eft of hym of what wode they were?
> 'Thise thre shorriares,' quod he, 'that bereth vp this plonte,
> Bytokeneth trewely the trinite of heuene,
> Thre persones indepartable, perpetuel were euere,
> Of o will, of o wit; and herwith y kepe
> The fruyt of this fayre tre fro thre wikkede wyndes,
> And fro falling þe stok, hit faile not of his myght.' (C.18.19–30)

In the B text, where Will originally asks only about the purpose of the three 'piles' (B.16.24: 'whi stonde þise piles here?'), the issue of their nature and the express naming of the Trinity are withheld until *after* Piers has explained their protective function in 16.25–52:

> 'Ac I haue þou3tes a þreve of þise þre piles,
> In what wode þei woxen and where þat þei growed,
> For alle are þei aliche longe, noon lasse þan ooþer,
> And to my mynde, as me þinkeþ, on o more þei growed;
> And of o greetnesse and grene of greyn þei semen.'
> 'That is sooþ,' seide Piers, 'so it may bifalle.
> I shal telle þee as tid what þis tree highte.
> The ground þere it groweþ, goodnesse it hatte;
> And I haue told þee what hi3te þe tree; þe Trinite it meneþ.'
> (B.16.55–63)

Besides this change in the point at which the Trinity and the Tree are associated, a few other related continuities and revisions are worthy of note. B's Tree grows in goodness (probably with the familiar chime on 'God-ness') and it 'meneþ' the Trinity; similar points are made in C.18.7 by saying that the Tree 'grows graciously' (with the echo of 'grace') and that it is called *Ymago-dei*. In both B and C, the three *schoriares* serve simultaneously as stakes or planks supporting the stock, as a defense against the worm-bearing winds that attack flower and fruit, and as weapons against vandals and thieves. In C, however, the use of all three planks by Liberum Arbitrium against the world, the flesh, and the devil is a trifle more symmetrical than the defense described in B, where Piers uses the first two planks and Liberum Arbitrium uses the third. In a literal garden, of course, one would hardly pull up the stakes supporting a tree to fight off vandals, much less brandish them against the wind, but Langland's metaphor is not so rigidly constrained.[19]

In C, as in B, Will is curious about the wood from which the planks come, their common 'more,' and their identical length, size, and color. The repetition of 'yliche' and the 4-stave alliteration in C's 'Alle thre yliche long and yliche large' heightens the impression of parallel and identical qualities in the three planks. The change of the more sensuous line 'And of o greetnesse and grene of greyn þei semen' (B.16.59) to the plainer phrase 'of o kyne colour and kynde' (C.18.21) was probably driven by a decision to add the term 'kynde' to the passage, with a consequent need for alliteration on /k/. While the loss of the attractive color-detail in B is regrettable, I hope to show in the following pages that the implications of C's new stress on *kynde* more than make up for that loss.

One Kind, Two Lives, Three Degrees

One Kind

Langland begins his expanded, C-text discussion of the grades of chastity by asserting the common *kynde* of all three types of fruit on the Tree of Love. Even before Liberum Arbitrium defines those three degrees as virginity, continence, and marriage, he re-identifies the Tree as the tree of Adam's descendants, emphatically all of one kind (C.18.59, 62, 70; cf. 57) but varying naturally among themselves.[20] The repetitions of 'kynde' link the passage back to earlier treatments of the subject, notably Wit's speech and Will's vision of natural sexuality in C.13. More immediately, the word recalls the three *schoriares*, of one kind and growing from one root; unlike the Trinity, however, 'oure kynde' fares in such a way as to vary widely within itself. Liberum Arbitrium's emphasis on 'kynde' also prepares us for the recurrence of the term in Abraham's comparison of the Trinity to matrimony.

---

[19] Medieval horticultural treatises sometimes speak of protecting new grafts and saplings from the wind in various ways, by pruning, setting up windbreaks, or sticking other boughs around the newly set plants; see *The Book of Husbandry by Master [Anthony] Fitzherbert*, ed. Walter W. Skeat, English Dialect Society 37 (London, 1882), 90, and W. L. Braekman, 'Bollard's Book,' 32. The walls of an enclosed garden would have had a similar protective function for the fruit trees planted therein.

[20] It was an exegetical commonplace that Eve was created from Adam so that all humanity might originate from one individual, and thus be as closely kin as possible, whereas all other animals were simultaneously created as males and females: Ambrose, *De Paradiso* 10.48 (*CSEL* 32/1:306); Augustine, *De Civ. Dei* 12.22 (CC 48:380), and *De Bono Coniugali* 1 (*CSEL* 41:187); Rabanus Maurus, *In Gen.* 1.7 (PL 107:461); Gl. Ord., 1:34; Nicholas of Lyra, *Post.*, 1:34, concording on Acts 17:26, 'fecitque [Deus] ex uno omne genus hominum.'

Other effects of this initial passage include a heavier emphasis on parallels between Genesis and the whole Tree of Charity scene – the references to apple-trees, and to Adam and his apples, make Will's later desire to savor the fruit an even clearer reminder of Adam's apple-tasting. Furthermore, the transmutation of the Tree from a tree of individual virtue to a genealogical tree of Adam's descendants comes sooner in the passage and is more overt; the Tree now unmistakably represents all humankind, from the beginning to the end of time. And while 'kynde' in these opening comments mainly carries this sense of 'species, race, lineage,' it is also related to that aspect of human nature which urges us on to reproduce, 'asking' married folk to 'follow the flesh,' as Liberum Arbitrium will soon put it. One other change later in the vision of the Tree may also be connected to this new stress on 'kynde,' namely the change in the figure who shakes down apples for Will: no longer Piers, not even Liberum Arbitrium, but Elde, whose role as the unlovely but effective ally of Conscience, Kynde, Holiness, and Death against Antichrist, Pride, Fortune, Lechery, Covetise, and worldly Life will become unmistakable at the poem's end.[21]

Although Will has already noticed three degrees of fruit on the Tree, Liberum Arbitrium's initial description of that fruit presents it dichotomously: some apples, those growing on the sunny side and top of the tree, are sooner ripe, sweeter, tastier, greater, soothfast and large; those on the shady northern or lower boughs are late-ripening, less sweet, less savory, variable and little (C.18.64–70; cf. 75, 85).[22] (Langland's use of this horticultural image is not unique; Henry of Lancaster makes a similar point about the Virgin Mary being the best fruit on the vine of Jesse because she was on the highest branch, nearest to the warmth of divine love.[23]) The dichotomy of better and worse, whether intended or not, is about to be echoed in Liberum Arbitrium's opposition of the asexual grades of chastity to the sexual grade, virginity

---

[21] Elde and Holiness have already been briefly allied against Fortune, worldly Life, Lechery, Pride, and Covetise in B.11/C.11–12; see Chap. 4, pp. 206–07 below.

[22] Line 60 – 'Ac somme ar swettore then somme and sonnere wollen rotye' – is puzzling in light of lines 65–66, as Pearsall observes; however, I do not fully understand his comment that 'the contradiction is resolved in [line] 100' (C.18.66n). Perhaps line 60 is slightly elliptical and, following Bloomfield's paraphrase, means that 'some are sweeter than others and some rot sooner' ('Three Grades,' 251).

[23] *Le Livre de Seyntz Medicines*, ed. E. J. Arnould, ANTS 2 (Oxford, 1940), 144–46. Later, Henry compares Christ outstretched on the Cross to the best and reddest rose at the top of a rose-tree, blooming most expansively from the heat of the Father's love (155). The parallel between Langland and Lancaster need not be a matter of common literary sources; it is far more likely the result of common experience with actual fruit- and flower-bearing plants, since the sunnier parts of plants often do have better and earlier flowers and fruit. Cf. Roy Genders, *The Complete Handbook of Fruit Growing* (London, 1976), 12–13, 67, 80–81; Genders notes that pears need even more sunshine and warmth than apples.

and widowhood as lives of contemplation vs. marriage as the life of action. While this complication confuses Will, and has exasperated a number of critics, I believe that it can be understood as part of a larger pattern of C-text revisions, generally related to the tensions between the Active Life and the call to renunciation of the world, direct service to God, and perfection.[24]

Two Lives in Three Degrees

Liberum Arbitrium begins his actual specification of the fruits on the Tree with a threefold catalogue: 'weddede men and wedewes and riht worthy maydones.' As Bloomfield pointed out some years ago, the lines that follow hint at a traditional parallel between the persons of the Trinity and the three grades of chastity, Father/Son/Spirit and marriage/ widowhood/virginity. The parallel is laid out a little more fully in Abraham's discussion of the Trinity in B, where the Father and Son are directly compared with marriage and widowhood. Here in C, we merely find the Spirit linked to 'riht worthy maydones . . . monkes and monyals, men of holy churche,' the fruits which grow on the sunny top of the tree nearest the 'hete of þe Holi Goest.'[25] However, the poet may have felt that his earlier depiction of the Tree as a Trinitarian *Ymago-dei* would enable readers to complete the comparison between the three grades and the persons of the Trinity if they so wished.

After virginity, we find widowhood and marriage, described in fairly traditional ways. What distinguishes the widowed state is the fact that its members were once married, literally or perhaps figuratively, by being wed to worldly duties and joys.[26] In electing continence, they forsake 'here ownere wil,' not least in the sexual realm but also in other matters. In its direct attention to God's will, then, this state is more pleasing to him than following the desires of the flesh, even when those fleshly desires are *kynde* and fruitful and contained within lawful wedlock.

---

[24] Donaldson, for instance, argues that 'we could do without' the passage, in which he feels the C poet 'smear[s] his own [canvas]' in revising B (*C-Text*, 190); somewhat more tolerantly, Pearsall calls the new material 'rather confusing,' and the dreamer's question 'at first puzzling' (C.18.76n, 81n). Of the handful of other critics who have commented on C.18, most slide quickly over these 40-odd new lines on the three degrees and two lives.

[25] See Bloomfield, 'Three Grades,' 250–52.

[26] The *ordo vidualis* was often associated with non-monastic clerics, as Bloomfield points out ('Three Grades,' 246); the sorrow of losing a spouse translates readily into the penitential sorrow with which one gives up worldly attachments. Whether Langland was thinking primarily of literal widows vowed to continence, clerics, or both seems to me to be a moot point since both groups are supposed to turn away from the world.

So far, so good – traditional material, traditionally handled. But Langland draws in another tradition to liven things up, and to give himself a chance to comment more fully on the relative merits of the grades of chastity. I refer of course to the mention of the two lives – contemplative and active – along with the three grades. The two continent degrees of virginity and widowhood are called 'lyf of contemplacioun' while marriage is labeled '*Actiua* lyf.'[27] It is this last labeling which I think gives us a clue as to what Langland is doing in this passage. The dramatic rearrangements, deletions, and additions of material on the active life and on the 'rechelesse' renunciation of worldly attachments constitute some of the most striking revisions in the whole C text, and I believe that the introduction of the contemplative-active ranking here is closely related to those revisions.

Recall that Liberum Arbitrium is the 'ledere' of Actif, né Haukyn the Active Man, for whose love Anima described the Tree to Will in the B text.[28] In C, Actif loses his personal name and much of Haukyn's concreteness, largely due to the transplantation of some 120 lines to the Confession of the Sins in C.6–7, and the outright loss of another 200-plus lines, including the moving scene of Haukyn's own repentance. Haukyn's self-defense, 'Vxorem duxi' (B.14.3α), is transferred to the end of C.7, where 'oen . . . Actif' excuses himself from the pilgrimage to Truth because of his duties to his wife. Contemplacioun, on the other hand, is willing to follow Piers in care, famine, and want. (Given the occasional similarities between Haukyn and Will in B, it is intriguing to note that the wife of 'oen . . . Actif' bears the same name as Will's wife Kitte.) Recall also that another large addition in C is Rechelesnesse's encomium on perfect poverty, the kind of life that Contemplacioun accepts and which, in both texts, Patience will preach to Activa Vita and Will. Will's somewhat embarrassed, 'autobiographical' defense of his life and acknowledgment of its imperfection (C.5.1–104) also relates to these themes, insofar as it depicts him as being unprofitable in worldly

---

[27] The reclassification of the three degrees in terms of the two lives is unusual but not totally unprecedented. Aquinas associates marriage and virginity with the active and contemplative lives respectively, though without mentioning widowhood (*Summa Theologica*, 2-2, q.152 a.4; *Opera* 3:507).

Bromyard at one point divides the three grades of chastity in a two-fold manner, distinguishing the 'magnus meritus' of marriage from the 'maior meritus' of the two continent estates rather as Liberum Arbitrium does here (*Summa Praed.*, s.v. 'Matrimonium,' § 3).

[28] Haukyn the Active Man may himself have a partial precursor in a brief passage in A, where Scripture defines Do-wel as 'a wel lele lif . . . among þe lewide peple; / Actif it is hoten; husbondis it vsen' (A.11.182–83). In the parallel B passage, Langland drops the reference to 'Actif,' perhaps out of a decision to explore the experiential difficulties of Do-wel and *Activa Vita* in depth later in the poem.

activities and yet nowhere near perfect in spiritual work – partly because of his continued involvement in the world, the married state (C.5.2), and the ambiguous activity of poetry-making.

Though we may not like the depersonalization of Haukyn, it can hardly be called a careless revision. Perhaps Langland felt that the Deadly Sins material was too distracting or too extreme, that it made Activa Vita seem *too* negative for this stage of Will's education. But he obviously was not uninterested in the problems of the active life, or he would not have added new references to it at crucial points in the poem – e.g., at the pilgrimage to Truth, at the introduction of Liberum Arbitrium, or in the description of the Tree of Charity.[29] In fact, it could be argued that C's expansion of B's brief description of the three grades of chastity is motivated at least as much by an interest in the tension between Activa Vita and the Vita Contemplativa – honest, fruitful work in the world vs. a holy insolicitude or even a total abandonment of the world – as by the Trinitarian image reflected in the three grades.[30] Though the fruits of love grow in three degrees, the most significant difference between them is two-fold: to serve God 'as in heuene' or 'as kynde asketh.'

Ac Bothe Two Ben Gode

Will is understandably perplexed by the seeming incommensurability of three fruits and two lives, and seeks clarification: 'sethen þer aren but tweyne lyues / That oure lorde alloweth, . . . / Why groweth this fruyt in thre degres?' Authoritative and learned commentators have usually taken Liberum Arbitrium's response as a general encomium on virginity, which pays only momentary attention to the other fruits.[31] Such a position is certainly defensible, especially given the high

---

[29] A fuller treatment of Langland's revisions of material on the Active Life, perfection, insolicitude, and poverty is beyond the scope of this study, but would be very much worth doing. Such an analysis would need to build on Donaldson's remarks on Rechelessnesse and Liberum Arbitrium (*C-Text*, 169–98); Bloomfield's studies of the theme of perfection in the poem (especially *Fourteenth-century Apocalypse*); T. P. Dunning, 'Action and Contemplation in *Piers Plowman*,' in Hussey, *Critical Approaches*, 213–25; Anne Middleton, 'The Idea of Public Poetry in the Reign of Richard II,' *Speculum* 53 (1978), 94–114; John M. Bowers's discussion of the physical and spiritual work-ethic which the poem opposes to sloth, in *The Crisis of Will in Piers Plowman* (Washington, 1986), 66–67, 105–06, 121–28; and Malcolm Godden's brief discussion of Active/Contemplative tensions as developed in the C-revisions (*Making of Piers Plowman*, 187–90, 199–201).

[30] Hugh White connects the tension between the two lives with the poem's developing valuation of *kynde wit*'s capacity to lead to salvation, moving initially from a positive to a negative view, and finally to a tempered and significantly redefined optimism (*Nature and Salvation*, 33–38).

[31] So Skeat; Pearsall; Bloomfield, 'Three Grades'; Biggs, ' "Aungeles Peeris." '

significance of virginity in Christian eschatology and as a path to individual perfection. However, I would like to propose a rather different reading of Liberum Arbitrium's answer to Will, a reading that I have come to prefer in light of Langland's general presentation of marriage, the active life, and the other degrees of chastity throughout the poem. The passage is a difficult one in a number of ways, and the interpretation offered here may not answer all those difficulties to the satisfaction of all readers, but it resolves enough of them to warrant serious consideration.

In my view, Liberum Arbitrium's answer is intended as an explanation of the relative worth of the three grades which will first show that the essential criterion for evaluating them is the degree to which they serve God directly and secondly affirm the positive sanctity of marriage in spite of the existence of the higher grades. An affirmation of matrimony's value fits in very well with the value placed on lawful and loving marriages elsewhere in the poem, especially in Wit's speech. An even stronger endorsement comes later in C.18, when Abraham presents marriage alone as an emblem of the Trinity, instead of comparing the Trinity to all three grades of chastity as in B. Unfortunately, Liberum Arbitrium's response to Will's question suffers from a small but confusing knot of semantic, syntactic, and textual ambiguities, which have hindered readers from completely grasping Langland's argument there. The following pages will suggest one way of unravelling that knot, and argue that Liberum Arbitrium explains the gradation of the fruits of Trewe-loue in a more balanced way than he is usually given credit for.

'Why does this fruit grow in three degrees?' asks Will. 'For a good reason,' says Liberum Arbitrium:

> 'Here beneth y may nyme, yf y nede hadde,
> Matrimonye, a moist fruyt, þat multiplieth þe peple.
> And thenne aboue is bettere fruyt (ac bothe two ben gode),
> Wydewhode, more worthiore then wedlok, as in heuene.
> Thenne is Virginite, more vertuous and fayrest, as in heuene,
> For þat is euene with angelis, and angeles pere.
> 91 Hit was þe furste fruyte þat þe fader of heuene blessed,
> And bad hit be, of a bat of erthe, a man and a maide,
> In menynge þat the fayrest thyng the furste thynge shold honoure,
> 94 And þe clennest creature furste creatour knowe.
> In kynges court and in knyhtes, the clenneste men and fayreste
> Shollen serue for þe lord sulue, and so fareth god almyhty.
> Maydones and martres ministrede him here on erthe
> And in hey heuene is priueoste and next hym by resoun,
> And for þe fayrest fruyte byfore hym, as of erthe,
> And swete withoute swellynge, sour worth hit neuere.'
>
> (C.18.85–100)

The central difficulties in this passage lie in line 91-94, where the referents of 'furste fruyte' and 'furste thynge' are not immediately clear, and where the syntactic function of 'Hit was' and the subject-object relationships of lines 93 and 94 are ambiguous. Furthermore, the word *creatour* in line 94 can mean either 'Creator' or 'creature'; indeed, some C manuscripts, including the copy-text for Pearsall's edition, actually read *creature* at this point (though Pearsall emends *creature* to *creatour* based on the readings of other manuscripts).

The most important problem to solve in these lines is the identity of the 'furste fruyte' in line 91. This identification depends in turn on the interpretations given to the phrases 'the fayrest thyng' and 'the furste thynge.' Lines 89, 95, and 99 firmly establish that the fairest thing is virginity, *pace* Skeat who takes it to be man.[32] But the proper gloss for 'the furste thynge' is not obvious from the text alone: Skeat, followed by Pearsall and Biggs, takes it as God, the Prime Cause. Bloomfield takes it as 'the first thing [the] creator acknowledged,' but his paraphrase of the passage preserves the ambiguities of its original, making it difficult to determine what this first-acknowledged thing actually is.[33]

The first thing and the fairest thing, however, are not defined by line 93 alone. Whatever the first thing is, its relationship to virginity – that is, to the fairest thing – must be signified by lines 91-92: 'It was the first fruit that the father of heaven blessed, and commanded to be of a lump of earth, a man and a maid, as a sign (*in menynge*) that the fairest thing the first thing should honor' (C.18.91-93, with the syntactic ambiguities preserved). In order to understand how this *menynge* works, we need to know what the 'first fruit' is. The most common gloss here – that the first fruit is virginity – postulates that by blessing Adam and Eve at the moment of their creation, God was blessing the virgin state as well.[34] This analysis yields the apparently plausible *menynge* that the fairest thing, virginity, should honor the first thing, God, because he blessed it as the first fruit.

---

[32] Skeat, 2:237; Biggs tentatively suggests that it might mean Eve, honoring Adam as first (human) creature, but his alternate gloss, 'the virgin state of Adam and Eve' fits better with the referents of 'fayrest' in 89, 95, and 99 (' "Aungeles Peeris," ' 434).

[33] Skeat, 2:237; Pearsall, C.18.93n; Biggs, ' "Aungeles Peeris," ' 434. See also Bloomfield, 'Three Grades,' 252, where both the first fruit and the fairest fruit are clearly identified as virginity, while the blessing on the first fruit seems to be equated with the creator's acknowledgment of the 'furste thynge,' apparently resulting in virginity honoring itself in line 93.

[34] Bloomfield, 'Three Grades,' 252; Pearsall, C.18.93n; Elizabeth Salter and Derek Pearsall, eds., *Piers Plowman*, York Medieval Texts (Evanston, IL, 1967), 148; Biggs, ' "Aungeles Peeris," ' 434-35.

But there are several reasons *not* to identify the 'furste fruyte' as virginity. For one thing, if the first fruit *were* virginity, then Liberum Arbitrium's answer to Will would be devoted almost entirely to virginity, creating an exceedingly lopsided explanation of the relation between the two lives and the three degrees. It is not surprising that Pearsall puts the qualifying phrase 'ac bothe two ben gode' in editorial parentheses – under his interpretation, the remark seems to lead to little else in Liberum Arbitrium's answer. To be sure, lopsided explanations are possible with Langland, but a heavy stress on virginity here would not match Langland's general lack of interest in virginity and positive treatment of marriage elsewhere in the poem; such an emphasis needs explanation itself.[35] A second objection: if Langland does mean to praise virginity from line 89 on, then we need to explain the allusion to Adam and Eve as 'a man and a maid' in line 92. Perhaps Langland is simply allowing for male and female virgins, as in line 74 ('monkes and monyals'); nonetheless, the phrase does seem to emphasize the sexual differences of our first parents, rather than pointing to their initial virgin state.

The third and most important objection to taking the first fruit as virginity derives from the first three chapters of Genesis, the text in whose terms the Tree of Charity is described in both the B and the C texts. Several of the allusions to Genesis have been noted above; one could also add that Liberum Arbitrium's task of 'keeping' the Tree is like Adam's assignment to 'dress . . . and keep' the Garden, and that the three planks shoring up the Tree are a motif drawn from the legends of Adam's life after his expulsion from Eden. Now Genesis says nothing about a divine blessing on virginity, but it very clearly proclaims God's benediction on marriage: 'Male and female he created them. And God blessed them, saying "Increase and multiply, and fill the earth" ' (Gen. 1:27–28). In Western exegesis, this blessing was commonly taken as part of the institution of marriage, and as proof that marriage and sexual procreation were part of God's plan for man even before the Fall; had Adam and Eve not sinned, sexual reproduction would have taken place in Eden, but without the infection of lust.[36] '*Crescite*: Fecunditatem sexus

---

[35] Bloomfield's analysis is colored somewhat by his interest in the theme of perfection, especially as expressed in the religious state; while Langland's concern for perfection in the Christian life is undeniable, more recent studies of the poem suggest that the locus of that concern is primarily in the life of more ordinary Christians, either lay or clerical (cf. Middleton, 'Public Poetry'). Biggs takes a different tack, arguing that the Tree of Charity scene collapses the angelic, pre-lapsarian and eschatological states of humanity so as to show Will whence men fell and whither they should seek to return (' "Aungeles Peeris," ' 435–36).

[36] The primary authority on this issue for Christian exegesis was Augustine, especially in

accipite,' says the *Glossa Ordinaria*: 'Receive the fertility of sex.' It goes on to observe that

> Although the manner of the creation [of man and woman] is not explained [at Gen. 1:27–28], the fact that they were created is properly reported here, so that the divine blessing might be suitably introduced, saying as it were, 'Increase and multiply, for the multiplication of human beings is carried out through the union of male and female.' Therefore marriage, which the heavenly blessing established for the sake of propagation, is not to be condemned, although virginity is preferred.[37]

Other comments in the *Glossa* are less literally oriented, or less favorable to matrimony; most memorable perhaps is Jerome's 'Nuptiae terram replent, virginitas caelum' (*Gl.Ord.* 1:35–36, adapted from *Adv. Jov.* 1.16, *PL* 23:246). But it is worth remembering that for Langland, filling (or sustaining, or multiplying) the earth through matrimony is no bad thing, being necessary for the generation of all the saints. His views on marriage, as I have indicated in Chapter 2, place him much more in the mature Augustinian tradition than the Hieronymian.[38] Indeed, as we will see, in the matter of comparing marriage to the Trinity, he is even willing to go beyond Augustine in the value he sets on marriage. (Interestingly, a number of the arguments made by Jovinian in favor of marriage and attacked by Jerome recur in later, favorable treatments of the sacrament by orthodox theologians, especially the examples of married holy men and women in the Old Testament. Jerome's polemic, though memorable, may have had a deeper influence on anti-feminist and anti-matrimonial satire than on more sober theological analyses of marriage.)

Theologians noted that marriage was the only sacrament instituted before the Fall; even after the Fall, the blessing of fecundity did not fail,

---

his later writings; as Jeremy Cohen notes, 'Augustine offered the single most extensive and influential contribution to the Christian career of Gen. 1:28' (*'Be Fertile and Increase, Fill the Earth and Master It': The Ancient and Medieval Career of a Biblical Text* [Ithaca, 1989], 246). See also Elizabeth A. Clark, ' "Adam's Only Companion": Augustine and the Early Christian Debate on Marriage,' in *The Olde Daunce: Love, Friendship, Sex, and Marriage in the Medieval World*, ed. Robert R. Edwards and Stephen Spector (Albany, 1991), 15–31 and 240–54. A number of influential medieval theologians extended some of Augustine's claims for the prelapsarian value of marriage and sexuality even further: cf. Cohen, 245–70; Pierre J. Payer, *The Bridling of Desire: Views of Sex in the Later Middle Ages* (Toronto, 1993), 18–41; and Michael Müller, *Die Lehre des hl. Augustinus von der Paradiesesehe und ihre Auswirkung in der Sexualethik des 12. und 13. Jahrhunderts bis Thomas von Aquin* (Regensburg, 1954), 19–32, 275–318.

[37] *Gl. Ord.*, 1:34–35. The Marginal Gloss continues with passages from *The City of God* 14.21–22 (CC 48:443–44) on the original divine plan for sexual reproduction in Paradise.

[38] Jerome's position on marriage, even in the *Adversus Jovinianum*, may not actually have been as extreme or as negative as the received wisdom has it (and has had it for centuries): see John Oppel, 'Saint Jerome and the History of Sex,' *Viator* 24 (1993), 1–22.

although it was contaminated by concupiscence.[39] The solemn nuptial blessing, spoken over the bride during the nuptial Mass, calls marriage 'the fellowship ordained from the beginning by that benediction which alone was not taken away, either by the punishment for original sin or by the sentence of the Flood.' Even the solemn blessing of virgins grants that 'no prohibitions have diminished the honor of marriage, and the founding blessing on holy wedlock remains,' although it naturally goes on to say that virginity is preferred as a life closer to the mystery sacramentally expressed by matrimony – the heavenly wedding of Christ and the Church.[40]

The association of marriage with Eden and the insistence that it had been established and blessed there can also be found in vernacular sermons, like John Mirk's *Sermo de Nupcijs*:

> Þis ordur was not furste fondon be erthely man, bot be þe holy Trenite of Heuen; Fadur and Sone and Holy Gost made hit in paradise erthely, and is in a place in þe est, and so heygh þat þe flode of Noe cam not nygh it. In þe whyche place is so myche ioy and blysse þat no tonge may telle, ne no herte may thenk. And for encheson þat þis ordur was made in þat mery place, ȝit holy chirch suffreth it to be made here in erthe wyth myrth þat is holy hymself, and wythoute vylony.[41]

Mirk goes so far as to suggest that entering the church for the nuptial Mass is a reversal of Adam and Eve's expulsion from Eden, almost paradise regained:

> Whan þei haddyn brokyn Goddys forbedyng, anone be Goddys bydyng an angel drof ham oute of paradyse into þys worlde. . . . *Herefore* þe prest takuth [the bride and groom] be þe hande and brynguth hem into chyrch þat is Goddys hous, as þilk þat han sworne and made an opon oth to lyvon in Goddys lawe, . . . and so setteth

---

[39] For this universally accepted belief, see Müller, *Paradiesesehe*; Peter Lombard, *Sentences* 4.26.2–3; ParsT 842, 918–21.

[40] *Manuale ad Usum Percelebris Sarisburiensis*, ed. A. Jefferies Collins, HBS 91 (Chichester, 1960), 54. For 'proof' that the blessing on marriage was not taken away by the Flood, medieval exegetes and theologians had God's words to Noe after the Deluge: repeating the Edenic blessing, God told Noe and his family to 'Increase and multiply and fill the earth' (Gen. 9:1; cf. Lombard, *Sent.* 4.26.3). For the blessing of virgins, see for instance the Pontifical of Roger de Martivall, Bp. of Salisbury, in *Liber Pontificalis Christopheri Bainbridge Archiepiscopi Eboracensis*, ed. William G. Henderson, SS 61 (Durham, 1875), 210. Like the nuptial blessing, this blessing of nuns at the solemn consecration was widely used throughout the Middle Ages; René Metz discusses its textual history in *La Consécration des vierges dans l'église romaine*, (Paris, 1954), 142–43, 151.

[41] *Mirk's Festial: A Collection of Homilies*, ed. Theodor Erbe, EETS e.s. 96 (London, 1905), 289. The notion that Eden was on a mountain so high the Flood did not reach it, which Mirk seems take as a metaphor for the 'high' holy mirth of marriage in Eden, occurs elsewhere in Middle English literature; e.g., *The Metrical Version of Mandeville's Travels*, ed. M. C. Seymour, EETS 269 (London, 1973), 2685–93 and n.

hem beforen þe auter as before Goddys awne faas. (p. 291, my emphasis)

Mirk's 'paradise erthely' echoes the references to marriage as a 'paradys (terrestre)' that may be found in contexts as distinct as the *Merchant's Tale* (l. 1332), *Cleanness* (l. 704), or other Middle English marriage sermons and pastoral guides. Thus, we find comments like the following sermon extract reported by G. R. Owst:

> One cawse [to honor matrimony] is ffor God hymselff was ffyrst fownder and maker of the sacrament of matrimonye. The secunde, for it was made and ordeyned off God in the most precious place that he wroghyt upon erthe, ffor it was 'in paradiso terestre.' The iiide cawse, for it was the ffirst sacrament that God ordeynde; and the iiiite, ffor holy chyrche hathe admytted it to be one of the vii sacraments off holy chyrche. And for thys cawse is the palle holden on theyr hedys in the messe time; for the palle representethe the dignite of matrimony. . . . [And] holy chyrche . . . ordenythe that bothe man and the woman be reconcylyd to clennes of lyffe by confessyon beforne the matrimony is solemnisyd ffor the encresynge and augmentynge off grace.[42]

Along similar lines, Susanna Fein notes the much-amplified and paradisal description of the garden owned by the married couple Joachim and Susannah in the *Pistel of Swete Susan*, a poem which she argues 'offers an inspiring example of marriage and wifehood for fourteenth-century women of noble birth.'[43] Three of the five texts of *The Pistel* occur in manuscripts also containing *Piers Plowman*, making the retold Old Testament tale second only to *Mandeville's Travels* as a companion text to *Piers*, and perhaps indicating the potential interest of both poems to devout lay audiences concerned with family (among other) virtues. An Englished version of the 'paradise terrestre' phrase even occurs in one of Langland's own earlier references to marriage, in a passus similarly filled with allusions to Genesis:

> The wif was maad þe wye for to helpe werche,
> And þus was wedlok ywroȝt wiþ a mene persone,
> First by þe fadres wille and þe frendes conseille,
> And siþenes by assent of hemself as þei two myȝte acorde;

---

[42] The same sermon tells the story of the creation of the sexes as reported by Genesis and describes the 'three bonds or yokes of God which should unite the wedded' in terms remarkably like Langland's: honest work; true, faithful love in life; and obedience and abiding together for ever. See *Preaching in Medieval England: An Introduction to Sermon Manuscripts of the Period c. 1350–1450* (1926; rpt. New York, 1965), 269–70. On the institution of marriage in paradise, see also Bromyard, *Summa Praed.*, s.v. 'Matrimonium,' § 1; de Burgh, *Pup. Oc.*, 122r; ParsT 918–21; 'Of Weddid Men and Wifis,' *Select English Works of John Wyclif*, ed. Thomas Arnold, 3 vols. (Oxford, 1869–71), 3:189.

[43] 'Fourteenth-Century Trinitarian Piety for Women in *The Pistel of Swete Susan*,' a paper presented at the 28th International Congress on Medieval Studies (May 1993).

Þe Trinite It Meneþ

And þus was wedlok ywroȝt and god hymself hit made.
In erþe þe heuene is; hymself was þe witnesse. (B.9.115-20)

To judge by medieval exegetical, theological, pastoral, and liturgical traditions, if one asked 'Which grade of chastity did the Father bless in Eden, when he made man and woman?' the most likely answer by far would be 'Matrimony.'[44] The fact that Langland speaks of the Father's blessing in particular may also be meant to make us think of marriage – in the parallel between the three grades and the Trinity, it is the Father who is associated with the married state, just as it is primarily the Father who is associated with Kynde the Creator ('fader and formour') in Wit's speech. As Abraham says in B.16:

> Might is in matrimoyne þat multiplieþ þe erþ
> And bitokneþ trewely, telle if I dorste,
> Hym þat first formed al, þe fader of heuene. (B.16.211-13)

I offer this extensive rationale for taking 'the fruit that the Father blessed' as matrimony because the rest of the argument advanced in this section turns directly upon such an interpretation. Instead of reading Liberum Arbitrium's answer in light of the long tradition of praising virginity, a tradition normally associated with ecclesiastical authors addressing celibate audiences (religious, clerical, or anachoritic), we should consider reading it in terms of the equally important tradition that affirmed the institution and blessing of marriage in Eden. While that tradition was also usually promulgated by ecclesiastics, its ultimate audience was the laity and its main goal was the maintenance of a proper respect for marriage conducted according to the Church's precepts. It would be entirely natural for Langland to draw on this latter, pro-matrimonial and pro-familial tradition in a poem so deeply addressed to the problems of pursuing spiritual ends while still within the secular world.

[44] At least in the West; Eastern Christianity emphasized the angelic, Edenic virginity of Adam and Eve and of Christian virgins more strongly than did the western branch of the Church. Examples of Eastern views of the pre-lapsarian state of humankind can be found in Müller, *Paradiesesehe*, 9-19; John Bugge, *Virginitas*, 5-35; and Cohen, 229-43. Bugge also examines Western reflexes of the Eastern viewpoint, especially in monastic spirituality. Such reflexes never completely fade away (Biggs cites examples from Augustine, Hugh of St Cher, and Vincent of Beauvais; ' "Aungeles peeris," ' 433), though they are naturally more common in discussions of virginity than of marriage.

Biggs also points out that 'Langland's sources are not always the most common' (' "Aungeles peeris," ' 433), which is true enough, and certainly makes it possible that the poet is using the Edenic scene to remind his audience of virginity. Of course, my own focus on marriage and family in this book naturally encourages me to make the matrimonial connection, but the likelihood of that connection does seem to be strengthened by the positive, Eden-recalling treatments of marriage elsewhere in C.18 and in Wit's speech (most explicitly in B.9.115-20).

133

Thus in the *Historia Scholastica* Peter Comestor remarks,

> *Increase and multiply*: Since this could not take place without their physical union, it is clear that God instituted the marriage of man and woman, whence those heretics are confuted who say that intercourse without sin is impossible. (*PL* 198:1064)

The concern about heretics expressed here was a recurring motive for defenses of matrimony, from Augustine's anti-Manichean arguments to Comestor's anti-Catharism and similar sentiments found in later writers. Over the centuries, positive treatments of marriage gradually became more common among both lay and clerical writers, as the Church gained more control over marriage, found a new need to defend it against heretics, acknowledged its sacramental and grace-conferring status, and addressed herself more fully to the growing numbers of devout laypersons. Although there was some jostling back and forth of rigorist and liberal viewpoints, the overall tendency was in fact to prepare the way for humanist and Protestant revaluations of marriage and celibacy. However, these eventual developments clearly go beyond the position of Langland and other serious late medieval writers on marriage, who do not question the superlative value of virginity for those who choose it, but simply focus their attention on the solid positive value of marriage for the many to whom it is physically, economically, or emotionally desirable.[45]

'Hit was þe furste fruyte þat þe fader of heuene blessed': if the 'fruyte' of this line is indeed matrimony, then we cannot take the word 'hit' as referring anaphorically back to virginity, the most recent possible antecedent. In fact, 'hit' does not refer back to an antecedent at all. Rather, Langland is using the introductory phrase 'hit was' to place the emphasis of the clause in line 91 directly on matrimony, the first fruit named by Liberum Arbitrium, and the object of the Father's Edenic blessing.[46] 'It was the *first* fruit (of those named),' Langland tells us, 'that the Father blessed.'

[45] A related development, though not one that affects Langland much, was the increasing late medieval devotion to the Holy Family, from the child Jesus, to Mary in ordinary household activities, to Sts Joseph, Anne, and Elizabeth. Useful discussions of changing medieval perspectives on marriage can be found in Jean Leclercq, *Le mariage vu par les moines au XIIe siècle* (Paris, 1983); Müller, *Paradiesesehe*; John T. Noonan, Jr., *Contraception: A History of Its Treatment by the Catholic Theologians and Canonists* (Cambridge, MA, 1965); Henry A. Kelly, *Love and Marriage in the Age of Chaucer* (Ithaca, 1975); David Herlihy, *Medieval Households* (Cambridge, MA, 1985); and Payer, *The Bridling of Desire*. On the 'holy kinship,' see Kathleen Ashley and Pamela Sheingorn, eds., *Interpreting Cultural Symbols: Saint Anne in Late Medieval Society* (Athens, GA, 1990).

[46] Line 91 is what Otto Jespersen calls a 'cleft sentence,' in *A Modern English Grammar on Historical Principles*, Vol. 7, completed by Niels Haislund (Copenhagen, 1949), 147–48. As Jespersen observes, sentences of this form are ambiguous in writing, although the

But marriage is not 'first' simply because of the ordering of Liberum Arbitrium's speech. Marriage is also, historically, the first of the three sexual estates that God blessed, a point made clear by the literal sense of Gen. 1:27-28. This is only fitting, since it is marriage that produces widows and virgins, as Wit suggests (A.10.135-38, B.9.111-14, C.10.204-05), and as Abraham states outright in comparing the Trinity to the three grades of chastity (B.16.216-19). For Langland, matrimony 'susteyneth' the world; it 'multiplieth þe peple' and 'þe erþe' (C.10.203, B.9.111; C.18.86; B.16.211). His 'multiplieth' may echo the *multiplicamini* of that first nuptial benediction. Yes, Adam and Eve were created as a virginal man and a virginal maid, but they were also created – and blessed with fertility – to be husband and wife. Virginity can quite properly be called the 'first-fruits,' plural, as in the Apocalypse; but the first *fruit*, singular, is better taken as matrimony.[47]

Thus, I would suggest that Langland's argument in lines 91-93 runs something like this: God blessed marriage first 'in menynge' that it should be honored as the 'furste thynge,' even by people in the fairer state of virginity. (To be sure, the literal 'first thing' was light, but of the three 'things' under discussion here, marriage was the first created; the rhetorical effectiveness of contrasting first thing and fairest thing easily justifies applying the phrase 'first thing' to marriage, if such justification is necessary.) An identification of the 'first thing' as marriage also resolves the syntactic ambiguity of line 93: it makes no sense to say that God blessed marriage as a sign that marriage should honor virginity, though such a reading is grammatically possible.

Interpreting both 'þe furste fruyte' and 'þe furste thynge' as marriage differentiates them from 'þe fayrest thyng,' accounts for the reference to 'a man and a maide,' and, most important, fits the usual reading of the biblical context of the passage better than taking the first fruit as virginity. The marital interpretation also develops Liberum Arbitrium's assertion that 'bothe two ben gode' by justifying the honor due marriage as first fruit, despite the existence of worthier and fairer states of life. 'Bothe two' need not mean only marriage and widowhood; given the

different meanings are differentiated orally by intonation. Other grammarians describe the construction in other terms (e.g., 'Introductory *it* with relative clause' or 'impersonal periphrasis'), but all recognize it as a means of expressing contrast or emphasis. For ME instances, including *Piers Plowman* B.15.311 (= K-D B.15.328), see Frederic Theodor Visser, *An Historical Syntax of the English Language*, 3 vols. (Leiden, 1963-73), 1:49-50.

[47] While virginity clearly was not the first of the three grades blessed by God, according to the literal sense of Gen. 1:27-28, it does come early in human history, with Abel who offered first-fruits and was first-fruits in himself. First inhabitant of the City of God, he was also the first human to die, by a virgin-martyr's death; though created after Adam and Eve, he was sweeter to God, sooner ripe, and soonest harvested.

'two lives' classification already mentioned, we might interpret 'two' as referring to marriage on the one hand and to *all* the 'bettere fruyte' above it on the other – the active fruit of wedlock in contrast to the contemplative, continent fruits of widowhood and virginity. In any event, 'bothe two ben gode' is not a parenthetical aside, but a principal point of Liberum Arbitrium's answer. Such gains in clarity and force argue strongly for identifying both the 'furste fruyte' and the 'furste thynge' as marriage.

One more ambiguous line in this knot of ambiguities still needs to be worked out, C.18.94. Let us review the whole cluster of lines 91–94:

> Hit was þe furste fruyte þat þe fader of heuene blessed,
> And bad hit be, of a bat of erthe, a man and a maide,
> In menynge þat the fayrest thyng the furste thynge shold honoure,
> And þe clennest creature furste creatour knowe.

The syntax of line 94, like that of 93, is formally ambiguous, thanks to the long-standing poetic license to invert subjects, verbs, and objects for the sake of meter, emphasis, or variety. As with line 93, we must examine the sense of the line to determine its proper subject and object. Like 93, to which it is coordinated by 'And,' line 94 explains the *menynge* of lines 91–92, with their description of the establishment and blessing of marriage. Its own meaning should therefore have some reasonably logical connection to that state of life or to the blessing on it, if at all possible.

Unravelling the meaning of line 94 begins fairly easily. 'þe clennest creature,' like 'the fayrest thyng,' must be virginity, which God honors above all else, just as earthly lords honor their 'cleanest and fairest' courtiers (C.18.95–100). Taking 'þe clennest creature' as virginity, and following Pearsall's emended text and glosses for line 94, we then have two basic alternatives for the general meaning of the line in its context:

1. (God blessed marriage as a sign that . . .) virginity should honor or acknowledge or know the Creator first;
2. (God blessed marriage as a sign that . . .) the Creator would honor or acknowledge or know virginity first.

Now it is perfectly true that virginity serves God more closely than the other grades of chastity, and so could be said to honor, acknowledge, or know him first. It is equally true that by giving virginity the highest rank among the three grades, God can be said to honor or acknowledge it first. But the truth of these two statements, even though supported by the following six lines, does not make them follow as a logical implication ('In menynge þat . . .') from the blessing on marriage. They are *non sequiturs,* and so do not explain the *menynge* of that blessing satisfactorily.[48]

I would suggest instead that we preserve the reading of Huntington MS. 143, the copy-text for Pearsall's edition, with *creature* in place of *creatour.*[49] If marriage can be called 'first thing,' then it can be called 'first creature,' a gloss which makes line 94 almost perfectly parallel to 93 in form and meaning: the fairest thing should honor the first thing; the cleanest creature should honor the first creature; virginity should honor matrimony. Such a reading, I would argue, improves the sense of Liberum Arbitrium's answer to Will's question about the three degrees and the two lives, and even fits that answer more tidily into the whole vision of the Tree of Charity. In this most Edenic of scenes in *Piers,* an allusion to the Edenic blessing on marriage is completely natural, and if one accepts that the 'fruyte þat þe fader of heuene blessed' is marriage, temporally the first fruit on the Tree of Charity, the rest follows. First fruit, first thing, first creature – all mean marriage, the honor of which no prohibitions have diminished, a life not to be condemned even if virginity is now preferred, the fellowship ordained from the beginning by the only blessing not taken away by Flood or Fall.

Let us turn now to the broader aims of Liberum Arbitrium's answer to Will. It is worth noting that he never really answers Will's question, never tells him exactly why, if there are two 'lives,' there should also be three 'degrees' of charity. Although he has already hinted that the three grades reflect the Trinity, he does not pursue that notion in any detail. Instead, like many of Will's other guides, he responds obliquely, redirecting the question so as to explain a distinction more central to a life of Trewe-love than the three grades. His main point here, to judge from his restatement of the degrees and the lives, is that married couples in their productive *Activa Vita,* and widows and virgins in their continent *Vita Contemplativa,* all participate worthily in humankind, in

---

[48] A third possible reading would involve assuming that line 94 somehow reveals the significance of God creating the first fruit from 'a bat of erthe, a man and a maide,' and would yield roughly the following sense: God blessed marriage as a sign that it should be honored even by people in the fairer state of virginity; and he created the first married couple in a state of virginity as a sign that virginity would know him first or most closely, or as a sign that he would acknowledge virginity before the other grades. A reading like this makes a loose kind of sense, though the logic is not as tight as it might be. But even allowing for Langland's willingness to employ loose rather than rigorous logic at times, the phrase 'a man and a maide' still seems more suggestive of sexual distinction than of sexless purity, and the interpretation just described rather strained.

[49] ME *creatour* can mean 'creature' as well as 'creator,' so one could even interpret the line as I am about to propose without changing Pearsall's emended reading here; however, reading the line as it stands in Huntington 143, with *creature* written twice, avoids unnecessary orthographic confusion.

Charity, and in the *Ymago-dei* planted in the world and in man's heart. He then goes on to show the source of matrimony's goodness, and the basis for the honor due to it – its ancient institution by divine blessing for the purpose of propagating the race. Finally, shifting to the epitome of contemplative life, he explains that virginity ministers directly to God, and hence is closest to him in heaven and fairest in his eyes on earth. The shift seems abrupt, but in fact makes sense if one sees his answer as a judicious, balanced explanation of the two lives as epitomized by marriage and virginity: both are honored by God, one with the sacramental blessing, the other with its special closeness to the Creator.

In responding to Will's question, Liberum Arbitrium may seem to give widowhood short shrift, but if widowhood is lived as a 'lyf of contemplacioun,' it too will give direct service to God and presumably be near him in heaven. Like virginity, and unlike marriage, widowhood is a life 'as in heuene' (C.18.88–89); to use St Paul's formulation, widows and virgins can give undivided attention to the things of the Lord, while married people must worry about worldly affairs and pleasing their spouses (1 Cor. 7:8, 32–35). Virginity, of course, is still more heavenly ('more vertuous and fayrest') thanks to its physical integrity, which neither widowhood nor marriage can claim. As Biggs has pointed out, the virgin state has a special symbolic status because of its eschatological approximation of angelic integrity. Like patient poverty, it undeniably participates in that perfection whose constant pull keeps tugging poet, characters, and readers forward and upward: the 'lyf of longing to be hennes' that beckons them to cast their worldly cares on God and follow him alone. However, the fact that Liberum Arbitrium names martyrs along with maidens as examples of those who 'serue for þe lord sulue' suggests to me that his praise for virgins is not merely based on their physical integrity but also on their whole-hearted service to God, a service which non-virgins can undertake as well.

It seems only right that Liberum Arbitrium, Actyf's leader, should point out and praise the sweet beauty of single-minded spirituality, so sharply in contrast with the multiple secular distractions of Actyf's life. Just as virginity should honor matrimony, so Liberum Arbitrium can be seen as honoring virginity in the name of marriage and '*Actiua* lyf.' From the midst of active responsibilities and temptations, the devout Christian may well find the contemplative life very attractive, even if it cannot be adopted – sometimes especially if it cannot be adopted. But the worldly anxieties attending an active, married life do not mean that such a life offers no service to God. On the contrary, the moist fruit of matrimony grows by divine command and blessing, bringing forth fruit and multiplying the people of God. The 'better fruit' of continence may be fairer than marriage, but both lives serve God and 'bothe two ben gode.'[50]

It has long been recognized that the Tree of Charity, like the child-bearing tree seen by Seth in the legends of the Cross, is a cosmological tree that prefigures the Cross, the Axis Mundi linking earth and heaven, bridging flesh and spirit, nature and grace, man and God. This linking role gives the Tree an intrinsic dichotomy in addition to its obvious triplicities. Langland takes advantage of both qualities, triplicity to stress the Triune image of God in man as an individual and as a race, and dichotomy to suggest the relations of several analogous conceptual pairs: earth/heaven, active/contemplative, sexual/asexual, *kynde*/grace, variability/soothfastness, imperfect/perfect modes of life.

These pairs are most clearly represented in Liberum Arbitrium's answer by the terms 'erthe' and 'heuene,' which appear three and four times respectively in C.18.85–100 (earth: 92, 97, 99; heaven: 88, 89, 91, 98, with aural reinforcement from 'euene' in 90). He plays the terms against each other, moving back and forth between them, not denigrating either but suggesting their complementarity. Direct contemplative service to God, through widowhood or virginity, is a life 'as in heuene' but lived on earth (88, 89, 97); spending a whole life in this service is what makes virginity fairest on earth and nearest God in heaven (98, 99). Marriage was formed 'of a bat of erthe,' but blessed by the Father of heaven, so that it might be honored for bringing forth the rest of the fruit on the Tree of Trewe-love (91–94). Liberum Arbitrium's phrase 'and fruyt forth brynge' (79) which describes marriage, is echoed in Will's remark that the entire Tree mysteriously ('priueliche') blooms and 'bryngeth forth fruyt, folk of alle nacion, / Bothe parfit and inparfit' (101–03), indicating the indispensability of marriage to the continuing growth of this world-tree of love and God's image in man.[51]

Langland does not doubt that true 'maydones and martres' are closest to God in heaven and earth. Contemplatives *can* serve God more

[50] For a similar analysis of the relative values of active and contemplative lives, with accompanying defense of the merits of the active life rightly lived, see *Dives and Pauper* 1/1, ed. Priscilla Heath Barnum, EETS 275 (London, 1976), 65–69: active and contemplative lives are associated with 'perfeccioun lesse and perfeccioun more.' Oppel suggests that medieval discussions of marriage from Jerome and Augustine to Erasmus 'all seem to have a lot to do with the dichotomy between the active and the contemplative life' ('Saint Jerome,' 14 n. 41). Further discussion of Langland's interest in 'the problem of how an ordinary Christian leading the active life should order his life' (Thomas D. Hill, *N&Q* 29 [1982], 241), can be found in Dunning, 'Action and Contemplation,' and Middleton, 'Public Poetry.'
[51] De Burgh distinguishes the two 'voluntary' sacraments, orders and matrimony, as being proper to the *perfecti* and *imperfecti* respectively (*Pup. Oc.*, 3r); Langland's continent contemplatives and married actives seem to be similarly distinguished.

immediately than actives, whose troubles we have seen in Haukyn's and Actyf's lives. But they should not lose their respect for the active life, nor for the fact that it usually involves the married state. As Grace will admonish in establishing the crafts, all estates should love each other, even though some are cleaner than others; 'he þat moest maistries can, [should] be myldest of berynge' (C.21.250-55, B.19.250-55). Marriage plays an essential role in Langland's world: it multiplies the people and Actyf's leader may take it if he has need. In part, Liberum Arbitrium 'needs' a remedy for fleshly desires (cf. B.9.182-86, C.10.281-85), but given the general emphasis on fruitfulness in the whole Tree of Charity episode, it seems likely that his primary need is to keep propagating the apples of Adam's tree, which he has been set to tend. While obeying *kynde* is not as clean and fair as serving the Lord directly, it nonetheless sustains the world. And insofar as *kynde*, nature, is the viceroy of Kynde, the Creator, wedded folk too 'live in law and in love do well':

> For of here kynde þey come, bothe confessours and martres,
> Prophetus and patriarkes, popes and maydenes.
> For god saith hymsulue, 'Shal neuere goed appel
> Thorw no sotil sciense on sour stok growe';
> And is no more to mene but men þat ben bygeten
> Out of matrimonye, nat moyloure, mowen nat haue þe grace
> That lele legityme by þe lawe may claymen.   (C.10.204-10)

Doing as *kynde* asks means following the flesh, but it also means following the Father's blessing-command 'Increase and multiply': bringing forth fruit, multiplying the people, making the Tree of Charity grow.

Betokening the Trinity

Abraham and the Three Degrees

With the sudden transformation of scene from the arboreal tableau of Charity to the swift-paced narrative of Christ's Incarnation and ministry, Langland leaves the three grades of chastity behind in order to lead us rapidly up to the very moment of Redemption. But Will needs more thorough doctrinal grounding before the sublime revelations of the Redeemer's actions in B.18/C.20, and the poet therefore offers a trivium of Faith, Hope, and Charity to provide the requisite instruction. The first teacher in this curriculum is Abraham, 'foot of [God's] feiþ,' and his lesson reinforces several of the major points illustrated by the

Tree of Charity: the Trinity's image within the human race, all or one of the grades of love, the devil's capture and imprisonment of Adam's progeny, and the promise of a Savior.

Abraham takes the schematic representations of these points in the vision of the Tree and expresses them in a more personal vein. The reflection of the Trinity within the race is described in terms of the affective experience and internal relationships of the various states of chastity; in testifying to his first-hand knowledge of God, Abraham talks about his own family and the promises which God made to him and his issue: an unbroken lineage which will receive 'land and lordshipe and lif wiþouten ende,' and 'mercy for oure mysdedes as many tyme as we asken' (B.16.240, 242, C.18.257, 259–60).

I shall limit my discussion here to the features of Abraham's discourse which pertain to matrimony and the other grades of chastity; other aspects of his speech are less central to the goals of this book, and have been more thoroughly explored by previous scholars.[52] Again, I shall begin with the B text, and then move on to the major changes introduced in C.

One of the most interesting features of Abraham's remarks in B is his comparison of the Trinity to the human race, as organized into the three sexually-defined estates of marriage, widowhood, and virginity.[53] Having briefly noted a familial parallel between the Trinity and 'Crist and cristendom and cristene holy chirche' (B.16.199; see below for further discussion), he moves on to his major figure for the tri-unity of God, the longest and most complex of his whole speech:

> And þat it [God's tri-unity] may be so and sooþ sheweþ it manhode:
> Wedlok and widwehode wiþ virginite ynempned,
> In tokenynge of þe Trinite, was taken out of a man,
> Adam, oure aller fader. (B.16.202–05)

---

[52] Usually in the context of the entire Abraham-Moses-Samaritan passage. See D. W. Robertson, Jr. and Bernard F. Huppé, *Piers Plowman and Scriptural Tradition* (Princeton, 1951), 198–211; John Lawlor, *Piers Plowman: An Essay in Criticism* (London, 1962), 156–63; Smith, *Traditional Imagery*, 74–93; Raymond St-Jacques, 'The Liturgical Associations of Langland's Samaritan,' *Traditio* 25 (1969), 217–30; Ruth M. Ames, *The Fulfillment of the Scriptures: Abraham, Moses, and Piers* (Evanston, 1970), 86–89, 178–84, and 'The Pardon Impugned by the Priest,' in *The Alliterative Tradition in the Fourteenth Century*, ed. Bernard S. Levy and Paul E. Szarmach (Kent, OH, 1981), 49–54; Lawrence M. Clopper, 'Langland's Trinitarian Analogies as Key to Meaning and Structure,' *M&H*, n.s. 9 (1979), 94–96; and Douglas Bertz, 'Prophecy and Apocalypse in Langland's *Piers Plowman*, B-Text, Passus XVI-XIX,' *JEGP* 84 (1985), 314–21. For iconographic analogues to Abraham's speech, see Avril Henry, 'Some Aspects of Biblical Imagery in *Piers Plowman*,' in *Langland, the Mystics and the Medieval English Religious Tradition: Essays in Honour of S. S. Hussey*, ed. Helen Phillips (Cambridge: Brewer, 1990), 39–55.

[53] Cf. Bloomfield, 'Three Grades,' 246–48.

The simile that follows is no easy one-to-one correspondence; indeed, its overlapping vehicles for the same tenor may have prompted the poet's revisions in the C version of this passage. In the B text, however, the complexity begins with what seems at first to be a relatively simple parallel – the three 'orders' of chastity all derive from one man and thus have one nature, just as the three Persons of the Trinity have a common nature and derive from the Father.[54] The problem lies in the fact that this simile creates two different analogues to the Father – wedlock (from which the other grades do derive, according to Wit's explanation of marriage as the source of saints) and Adam (from whom *all* human beings in or out of the three grades derive). These two analogues for the first divine Person, a group and an individual, will bifurcate Abraham's subsequent explanation of his Trinitarian simile.

Let us first follow up the individual dimension. Humanity can be anatomized into the three grades that come from one man, 'in tokenynge of þe Trinite':

> Adam, oure aller fader. Eue was of hymselue
> And þe issue þat þei hadde it was of hem boþe. (B.16.205–06)

Under this comparison, Adam is like the Father, and Eve was generated 'of hymselue' as the Son is generated of the Father; their issue proceeds 'of hem boþe' as the Spirit from Father and Son. Looking for analogues to widowhood and virginity in these lines seems to me to strain the sense of the text; the image of father, mother, and offspring is much more to the fore than any set of relations among the three grades.[55] In fact, the simile has digressed from three grades to a single grade, marriage, with emphasis on its three-fold, familial aspect. Abraham acknowledges this digression toward marriage in lines 207–10:

> And eiþer is oþeres ioye in þre sondry persones,
> And in heuene and here oon singuler name.
> And þus is mankynde and manhede of matrimoyne yspronge
> And bitokneþ þe Trinite and trewe bileue.

---

[54] See n. 20 above. Lyra justifies mankind's derivation *ex uno* as a reflection of the Deity: 'ut in hoc esset quaedam similitudo hominis ad deum propter dignitatem humanae naturae' (*Post.*, 1:34). Dronke suggests that Abraham's comparison offers a corrective to the hierarchical view of the three fruits on the Tree: 'now each of the three states signifies one of the three equal divine persons' ('Arbor Caritatis,' 213).

[55] If Abraham had specified Abel as the child of the archetypal family in B as he does in C, instead of using the generic term 'issue,' one might be able to argue a three grades parallelism more convincingly, since Adam, Eve, and Abel each died in one of the three degrees. See n. 60 and pp. 153–54, nn. 78–79 below.

In heaven and on earth one finds a 'family,' one in name and kind but three in the distinction of roles and persons, characterized by mutual, loving joy in each other. (Compare Wit's remark earlier that marriage 'in erþe þe heuene is,' B.9.120.) All humanity and humanness spring from the familial structure of marriage, and the family cell which thus structures the race bears the imprint of the Trinity.[56]

In the C text, this analogy will blossom into a much richer comparison between marriage and the Trinity, but for now Langland leaves it undeveloped so as to return to his initial point about the three grades. Adam is no longer at center stage; instead, matrimony itself is directly compared to the Father. The state of life which 'multiplieþ þe erþe . . . / bitokneþ trewely . . . / Hym þat first formed al, þe fader of heuene' (B.16.211-13). This is clear enough: marriage, established for the increase and multiplication of the race, is like the Father, who is especially associated with the act of creation. Similarly clear is the association of widowhood with the Son. The lines describing that association are remarkably rich in implication:

> The sone, if I dorste seye, resembleþ wel þe widewe:
> *Deus meus, Deus meus, vt quid dereliquisti me?*
> That is, creatour weex creature to knowe what was boþe.
> As widewe wiþouten wedlok was neuere ȝit yseyȝe,
> Na moore myȝte god be man but if he moder hadde.
> So widewe withouten wedlok may noȝt wel stande. (B.16.214-18)

As has long been recognized, these lines reflect Langland's theory of the Incarnation and Redemption through the shared natures, knowledge, suffering, and joy of God and man, a theology explored more fully later in the poem (B.18.203-29, C.20.208-38).[57] Likewise recognized has been the inevitable, generative link between marriage and widowhood; every widow or widower was once married, almost every marriage eventually yields a widowed relict (cf. 'dereliquisti' in

---

[56] Twentieth-century theologians of marriage are quite comfortable seeing an image of the Trinity in the family unit; thus Henri Rondet, *Introduction à l'étude de la théologie du mariage* (Paris, 1960), 6: 'Ce qu'il y a de plus profond dans l'amour conjugal nous transport donc au-delà du monde naturel, jusqu'au sein même de la Trinité et du mystère des échanges entre les personnes divines.' See also Bernard Häring, *Marriage in the Modern World*, trans. Geoffrey Stevens (Westminster, MD, 1965), 144-45. Similarly comfortable are some Trinitarian theologians; see Bertrand de Margerie, *The Christian Trinity in History*, trans. Edmund J. Fortman, Studies in Historical Theology 1 (Still River, MA, 1982), 274-92, and Leonardo Boff, *Trinity and Society*, trans. Paul Burns (Maryknoll, 1988), 105-06, and 164-212 *passim*.

[57] The importance of the shared divine and human experience of suffering, joy, and knowledge for Langland's soteriology has been indicated by Mary Clemente Davlin, '*Kynde Knowyng* as a Major Theme in *Piers Plowman B*,' *RES* n.s. 22 (1971), 11-14; Murtaugh, *Image of God*, 110-15, 119-21; and Mann, 'Eating and Drinking,' 40-43.

214α). But just what aspect of the Trinity that link corresponds to is more complicated than it might first seem.

At the simplest level, presumably, Abraham means that marriage generates widowhood, and the Father generates the Son; the pro-creative purpose of matrimony and the grief of widowhood parallel the creative might of the Father and the suffering of the Son in his human nature. But there is also a suggestion that the 'marriage' which generates the 'widowed' suffering of the Son is in fact the Incarnation itself, the sacred union between the two natures of Christ which took place in the *thalamus* of the Virgin's womb. Under such a reading, Christ's anguished cry on the cross reflects a sense of being abandoned, not by a father, but by a spouse – the impassible divinity which 'abandons' his humanity to solitary sorrow, pain, and death. The abandonment described here is Paul's *kenosis*, the emptying out of the divine so as to take on the form of a servant, the *similitudo* and *habitus* of a man, obedient even unto death on the cross (Phil. 2:5–8). Or, in Langland's words, following us in the likeness and apparel of a poor pilgrim.

Just as there can be no widow without wedlock, so there can be no God-become-man without Christ's birth through Mary: 'Na moore my3te god be man but if he moder hadde' (217). This last line may also be meant to remind us of the literal marriage of Mary to Joseph as well as the incarnational marriage of Christ's two natures in Mary's womb. Theologians often justified the Virgin's marriage on the grounds that the Savior had to be born in lawful wedlock so as to beguile the devil, protect Mary from slander and stoning, and give due honor to matrimony itself.[58]

The comparison of the Trinity to the three grades of chastity concludes somewhat amorphously; the final lines refer primarily to the Spirit, but the correlated term of the simile is not as obviously virginity as one would expect:

Ne matrimoyne withouten Mulerie is no3t muche to preise:
Maledictus homo qui non reliquit semen in Israel.
Thus in þre persones is parfitliche pure manhede,
That is man and his make and mulliere children;
And is no3t but gendre of a generacion bifore Iesu crist in heuene:
So is þe fader forþ with þe sone and fre wille of boþe,

---

[58] On the *causae convenientes* for Christ's mother to be married, see commentators on Lombard, *Sent*. 4.30.4 – e.g., Aquinas, *In IV Lib. Sent*. 4.30 q.2 a.1 (*Opera* 7/2:948–49), or Peter of Tarantaise (later Innocent V), *In IV Lib. Sent*. (Toulouse, 1651; rpt. Ridgewood, NJ, 1964), 4:314–15; so too the *Gl. Ord*. and Lyra on Mt. 1:18 (5:43–44, citing Ambrose and Origen), and from a popular perspective *Cursor Mundi* 10784–816.

Þe Trinite It Meneþ

Spiritus procedens a patre & filio &c,
Which is þe holy goost of alle, and alle is but o god. (B.16.219–24)[59]

The previous claim that the three grades of chastity signify the Trinity, taken together with the explicit associations of the Father and Son with marriage and widowhood, would seem to imply that these lines will be about virginity. Taken by themselves, however, they suggest a different equivalence: once again, that the Trinity is parallel to lawful, child-bearing marriage – 'man and his make and mulliere children.' At best, but desperately, one might argue that virgins are implicitly included among the 'mulliere children,' since they certainly would not be included among the married or widowed parents who have produced them. Langland himself seems to have realized – perhaps even in writing the B text – that the matrimonial figure for the Trinity fit his purposes better than the three grades of chastity. Certainly, when he came to revise this passage, the lines that he carried over into C were drawn mainly from these comments on the Holy Spirit (B.16.219, 219a, 220–21, and perhaps 223 becoming C.18.221, 223a, 234–35, and 232, where their application to marriage is unequivocal). In the revised version of the whole passus, the only definite trace of the three-grades analogy for the Trinity appears in the description of the Tree of Charity, when Liberum Arbitrium declares the closeness of virginity to the Holy Spirit.[60]

Two other features of Abraham's discourse, both of which pass over into C, deserve notice here.[61] First is the comment that Christ 'occupied' himself on earth until issue had sprung forth from Holy Mother Church. Interestingly, this is the only passage where Langland clearly employs the well-known metaphor of Christ's fruitful marriage to the Church, the *sacramentum magnum* of Eph. 5:32. Even in B.2 and C.2, where we hear of Holy Church's leman Leaute, it would take a few associative steps to interpret Leaute convincingly as Christ. After the beginning of

[59] Skeat's and Schmidt's gloss of *Mulerie* and *mulliere* as 'woman(kind)' in lines 219 and 221 should be corrected to 'legitimate offspring,' as in C.18.221 and in Theology's defense of Meed's birth. Cf. Henry Bradley, 'The Word 'Moillere' in *Piers the Plowman*,' *MLR* 2 (1906–07), 163–64; Alford, *Glossary of Legal Diction*, 102. On the rich denotational and connotational complexities of the difficult phrase 'gendre of a generacion,' as well as the relation of B.16.220–24 to Trinitarian theology, see my ' "Gendre of a generacion": *Piers Plowman* B.16.222,' *ELN* 27.2 (December 1989), 1–8.

[60] There may be another echo of the three grades in Abraham's C-text reference to Adam, Eve, and Abel as figures for the persons of the Trinity, since Eve was traditionally said to have died after Adam, making her the first widow, and Abel was believed to have been the first virgin martyr. See below, pp. 153–54.

[61] On Abraham's use of 'generative' metaphors for the Trinity and his further remarks on his own family later in the passus, see Britton J. Harwood, *Piers Plowman and the Problem of Belief* (Toronto, 1992), 113–14. Harwood also suggests that Abraham's metaphors tend to keep the human and divine levels separate, whereas the Samaritan will explain the Godhead in ways that suggest the intersection of the human and divine (115).

the poem, Langland usually presents Holy Church as a community, or a metaphorical tree or building – as Paul would say, 'Dei agricultura . . . Dei aedificatio' (1 Cor. 3:9).[62]

Here in Abraham's speech, however, Langland does describe the Church as mother of all the saints, from both the Old and New Testament, and implicitly as spouse of Christ. God, says Abraham,

> Sente forþ his sone as for seruaunt þat tyme
> To ocupie hym here til issue were spronge,
> That is children of charite, and holi chirche þe moder.
> Patriarkes and prophetes and Apostles were þe children,
> And Crist and cristendom and cristene holy chirche.
> (B.16.195–99, C.18.205–09)

The phrase 'children of charite' probably makes the best sense when it is taken to describe the mutual love of Christ and the Church, through which they beget spiritual offspring (though one could also identify Christ with charity so as to say that Christ/charity begets the offspring). In B, the passage concludes with two somewhat elliptical lines explaining the 'menynge' of the ecclesiological family, lines whose general sense is repeated more simply in their C reflex:

> . . . And Crist and cristendom and cristene holy chirche.
> In menynge þat man moste on *o god* bileue,
> And þere hym likede and he louede, in *þre persones* hym shewede.
> . . . And Crist and cristendoem and alle cristene, holy churche –
> Bitokeneth þe trinite and trewe bileue.
> (B.16.199–201, C.18.209–10; my emphasis)

In both texts these lines fairly clearly refer to a signification of the Trinity in terms of Christ, the Church or collective Christendom, and individual Christians: i.e., the spiritual family sprung from God's Son and the Spouse drawn forth from his side on Calvary.[63] The shared nature and separate but loving and similar 'persons' of this ecclesiastical family are what make it a suitable token of the Trinity. Through liking, likeness, and love, the members of these trinitarian families generate and manifest themselves and their common *kynde*.

---

[62] On ways in which the marriage of Christ and the Church is adumbrated in *Piers*, see Sigrid Pohl Perry, 'Trewe Wedded Libbynge Folk: Metaphors of Marriage in *Piers Plowman* and the *Canterbury Tales*' (Diss. Northwestern, 1981), 126–40, 158–66, 172–73.

[63] The common figural reading of Eve's creation from Adam's rib interpreted the event as a type of the Church being drawn out of Christ 'sleeping' in death on the Cross; Church and Christ then beget spiritual offspring. The inclusion of OT figures among the children of Holy Church is orthodox enough, since Ecclesia transcends time to include all members of the City of God from Abel onward. The syntactic ambiguities of B.16.198–201 and the corresponding passage C.18.208–10 are discussed by Schmidt, *B-Text*, 293, and Pearsall, C.18.208–09n.

Secondly, both B and C reveal Abraham's interest in yet another family: his own. Throughout the book of Genesis, God's relationship with his people is a relationship with holy men and their families, and Abraham is no exception. God tested Abraham through his heir Isaac (B.16.231–34, C.18.248–51); insisted that he demonstrate his faith by circumcising all the males of his tribal household (B.16.235–37, C.18.252–54); and made promises to him and his issue forever:[64]

> For hymself bihiȝte to me and to myn issue boþe
> Lond and lordshipe and lif wiþouten ende.
> To me and to myn issue moore yet he me grauntede,
> Mercy for oure mysdedes as many tyme as we asken.
> *Quam olim Abrahe promisisti & semini eius.*
> (B.16.239–42α; cf. C.18.256–60)

What God promised to Abraham and his seed, according to the Requiem Mass from which B.16.242α is drawn, was a most generous mercy indeed: the holy light and eternal life into which they might pass from hell, darkness, and death.[65]

The C text adds one more important detail to Abraham's description of God's mercy to his family, namely the very promise of a family itself. The visit of the three men to Abraham at Mambre, traditionally said to have been a manifestation of the Trinity, was also one of the occasions on which God promised that the aged Sarah would bear a son (Gen. 18:1–15 and C.18.240–46; the other occasion was at the original covenant of circumcision, Gen. 17:15–19). As we will see in the following pages, medieval audiences would have been unsurprised to find the Trinity involved in the making of a family, either at its sacramental initiation or in its fulfillment in children.

Lo, Treys Encountre Treys

Abraham's comparison of the Trinity to marriage has received a somewhat negative treatment at the hands of editors of *Piers Plowman*, much of it derived from Skeat's observation that Augustine had disapproved of such comparisons in the *De Trinitate*.[66] However,

---

[64] On God's grants of land and lordship to Abraham and his heirs, see James Simpson, 'Spiritual and Earthly Nobility in *Piers Plowman*,' *NM* 86 (1985), 474–75.

[65] J. Wickham Legg, ed., *The Sarum Missal Edited from Three Early Manuscripts* (1916; rpt. Oxford, 1969), 433.

[66] *De Trin.* 12.5.5–6.8 (*CC* 50:359–63; Skeat 2:240; Pearsall, C.18.215n; Schmidt, *B-Text*, 347. Augustine especially objects to finding the image of the Father-Son-Spirit in a father-son-mother relationship, as certain Gnostic sects attempted to do (cf. Irenaeus, *Contra Haereses* 1.30.1 (*PG* 7:694–95). For a general study of similarities between *Piers Plowman* and the *De Trinitate*, see Elaine M. Martin, 'Seek God's Face Evermore: A Study in Structure

Augustine's ideas on the suitability of the simile were neither the only nor the most familiar context in which a medieval audience could have viewed Abraham's remarks. There existed a number of other orthodox traditions in which the Trinity and marriage were quite often connected, including some theological works, the iconography of human creation, and, most importantly, the nuptial liturgy.

For instance, in the twelfth century, the theologians at the school of Laon produced a treatise on marriage, beginning 'In coniugio figura et uestigium trinitatis multipliciter inuenitur,' and going on to explain these multiple traces of the Trinity in human marriage.[67] The claim has some biblical support: the famous proof-text of the plurality of Persons in God, 'Faciamus hominem ad imaginem et similitudinem nostram' (Gen. 1:26), is followed by the description of man's creation as male and female and the pre-lapsarian blessing and institution of matrimony. 'Ad imaginem Dei creavit illum, masculum et feminam creavit eos. Benedixitque illis Deus, et ait: Crescite et multiplicamini, et replete terram' (Gen. 1:27-28).[68] More specifically, Aquinas compares the procession of the Holy Spirit from the Father and Son to the 'procession' of Abel from Adam and Eve. The Spirit proceeds from the Father both *immediate* and *mediate* – i.e., directly and through the Son; 'so also Abel proceeded from Adam immediately inasmuch as Adam was his father, and mediately inasmuch as Eve was his mother, who proceeded from Adam.' Although Aquinas qualifies the comparison by noting that material procession is not a very apt analogue for the immaterial procession of the divine persons, he must have seen it as carrying some force, since he uses it as part of the solution to an objection.[69] In Germany, Mechthild of Magdeburg suggests that the desire of the divine Persons for fruitfulness led to the creation of Adam and Eve in such a way that they could produce children 'in heiliger minne,' so that mankind could be the Deity's bride.[70] A fifteenth-century French

and Common Themes in Augustine's *De Trinitate* and Langland's *Piers Plowman*,' (Diss. Yale, 1988); Martin defends Langland's use of the matrimonial simile as being compatible with Augustine's thought on pp. 223-35.

[67] 'Est enim uir principium, unde mulier; uterque uero principium, unde procedit tertium'; *Anselms von Laon Systematische Sentenzen*, ed. Franz P. Bliemetzrieder (Münster, 1919), 112. For further references, see Heinrich J. F. Reinhardt, *Die Ehelehre des Anselms von Laon* (Münster, 1974), 36-37, and Valerie I. J. Flint, 'The "School of Laon": A Reconsideration,' *Recherches de Théologie Ancienne et Médiévale* 43 (1976), 89-110. Seamus P. Heaney notes that the Trinitarian metaphor for marriage in the 'In conjugio figura' is relatively rare, but raises no questions about its orthodoxy; see *The Development of the Sacramentality of Marriage from Anselm of Laon to Thomas Aquinas* (Washington, 1963), 5-6.

[68] On Gen. 1:28 as one of the two biblical reports of the divine institution of marriage before the Fall (Gen. 2:23-24 is the other), see Le Bras, 'Mariage,' *DTC* 9/2:2214-15.

[69] *ST* 1 q.36 a.3 (*Opera* 1:149).

[70] *Offenbarungen der Schwester Mechthild von Magdeburg*, ed. Gall Morel (1869; rpt.

depiction of the moment of conception associates the Trinity, the 'Faciamus' verse, and a three-person familial structure: the child's soul floats down a shaft of light from the Trinity, who are surrounded by a scroll bearing the 'Faciamus' verse, to its mother and father lyir.g together in bed.[71]

The Church's tacit acceptance of a special connection between the Trinity and marriage can be seen by her use, in northern Europe, of the Mass of the Trinity as the nuptial Mass. Additionally, when the groom placed the wedding ring on his bride's hand, he did so by setting it consecutively on the first, second, and third digit in the names of the three Persons of the Trinity respectively.[72] Not surprisingly, medieval observers recognized this Trinitarian dimension in the nuptial liturgy; in his 'Sermo de Nupcijs,' John Mirk explains that the Mass of the Trinity is said at marriages because 'þe holy Trynyte dyde alle þis offyce before sayde [i.e., the establishment of marriage]' (*Festial*, 291). Earlier in the *Festial*, in his sermon for Trinity Sunday, Mirk describes the Trinitarian image of God in humankind in terms of Adam, Eve, and their offspring, and connects that image with the wedding mass; citing the twelfth-century liturgist John Beleth, he notes:

> As a gret clerk, Ion Belet telleþ, þat þe forme trinite was fonden in a mon þat was Adam oure forme fadyr. As þys Adam was formet of erþe on person, and Eue of Adam the secunde person, and a mon of hom boþe þat was þe þryd person. Thys trinite was þus fonde yn man furst by worchyng of þe Trinite of Heuen. Wherfor þat man schulde haue mynde of þe Trynyte, holy chyrch ordeyneþe þat yn weddyng of mon and woman þat masse of þe Trinite ys songen. (*Festial*, 164; cf. Beleth, *Summa de ecclesiasticis officiis* 161, CC-CM 41:172 and 41A:317, on the Trinity being signified by Adam, Eve, and the 'homo procreatus . . . ex utroque.')[73]

Langland's decision to have Abraham describe the Trinity in terms of marriage, then, need not be seen as a sign of theological obtuseness in

Darmstadt, 1963) 3.9, 'Von dem angenge aller dinge, die got hat geschaffen,' pp. 68–70. Also available in Margot Schmidt's translation, *Das Fliessende Licht der Gottheit* (Einsiedeln, 1956), 139–41. I am grateful to Professor Petrus Tax for this reference.

[71] Paris, B.N. MS Arsenal 5206, fol. 174r. Reproduced in Eileen Power, *Medieval Women* (Cambridge, 1975), 51.

[72] See Jean-Baptiste Molin and Protais Mutembe, *Le Rituel du mariage en France du XIIᵉ au XVIᵉ siècle* (Paris, 1974), 159–69, 207–08; Korbinian Ritzer, *Formen, Riten und religiöses Brauchtum der Eheschliessung in den christlichen Kirchen des ersten Jahrtausends* (Münster, 1962), 189, n.144; Legg, *Sarum Missal*, 413–18; Collins, *Man. Sar.*, 48–59; and most other medieval English missals and manuals.

[73] In 'Trinitarian Piety,' Fein argues that the author of *The Pistel of Swete Susan* implies a Trinitarian element in the marriage of Susan and Joachim, figured by the couple together with the Spirit-filled child-prophet Daniel, and reinforced by a number of other triads present in the poem.

either the character or the author. To be sure, like Wit, Abraham is only the first in a series of teachers, and his lessons to the Dreamer must be supplemented with the teaching offered by subsequent guides – by Moses to some extent, and even more so by the Good Samaritan. However, again as with Wit, Abraham's understanding of the Trinity has been given less credit than it deserves. After all, Abraham is a type of Faith, and it is only through faith that the human mind and heart can know and accept the mystery of the Trinity. Furthermore, according to medieval tradition, Abraham was one of the few mortals to have knowingly witnessed a manifestation of the Trinity; as the Quinquagesima liturgy put it, speaking of Abraham's encounter with the Lord at Mambre, 'Tres vidit et unum adorauit.'[74] Langland recalls this tradition in order to emphasize the reliability of Abraham's testimony to the Trinity, by having Will question him after the marriage simile:

> 'Hastow ysey this?' y seyde, 'alle thre and o god?'
> 'In a somur y hym seyh,' quod he, 'as y saet in my porche,
> Where god cam gangynge a thre riȝt be my gate.'
> *Tres vidit et unum adorauit.* (C.18.240–42a)

But the best argument for taking Abraham's comparison of the Trinity to marriage as a sign of a genuinely significant understanding of the Trinity, instead of the 'limited' understanding which has been attributed to him, is the poetic depth and power of the comparison itself as it is worked out in the C text.

In both B and C, Abraham is intent on showing that the Trinity is reflected in the human race. In the B text, he has made the point via a pair of rather mixed similes, shifting back and forth between the three grades of chastity and the three members of the basic family cell as figures for the divine Persons. In C, he offers instead a single, clear comparison between the Trinity and fruitful matrimony, carefully structured and more explicitly connected with the great themes and images of the entire poem. The care with which the revised comparison has been constructed and the reinforcement it gives to a number of the major ideas in the poem strongly suggest that the poet intended us to take the comparison quite seriously, with full appreciation for the richness of its implications.

Let us turn then to the passage, and explore some of those implications. Langland organizes the new version of the simile straightforwardly enough: a brief prologue; the comparison proper,

---

[74] *Brev. Sar.*, 1:541 (Vespers), 546 (Matins).

with vehicle and tenor neatly set apart; and a final summary. He uses puns, alliteration, verbal echoes, parallelism, and *chiasmus* to formally reinforce such themes as the witnesses to divine truth, the importance of physical and spiritual fruitfulness, the *kynde* order underlying the similarity of God and man, and the ultimate union of man and his Maker that follows from that similarity. By emphasizing these themes in the passage, and by drawing on agricultural images in its description of marriage, he tightens the connections between Abraham's speech and other parts of the poem, notably Wit's discourse on good and bad marriages near the beginning of Dream 3. Both Wit and Abraham present marriage against the backdrop of the Creation, natural law, and the early days of the human race. But where Wit stresses the moral aspects of real-life marriage, Abraham treats it more as a figure of higher things: it is a *sacramentum magnum*, one of the major reflections of God in man, a sign betokening the Trinity from which all loving, fruitful societies take their origin.

Together with the Tree of Charity earlier in the passus, Abraham's discussion helps bring Will into a more clearly teleological series of events, linking his pilgrimage through the intellect and the individual moral self to his pilgrimage through salvation history – a pilgrimage more clearly oriented to the divine and to the more broadly social aspects of human life. As we have seen above, Abraham concludes his comparison of the Trinity and the family of man with a listing of the divine blessings and promises given to Abraham's own family (C.18.256–60) – a family that increases and multiplies to become the entire family of faith, which he has already identified as a figure of the Trinity:

> Patriarches and prophetes and apostles were the childrene,
> And Crist and cristendoem and alle cristene, holy churche –
> Bitokeneth þe trinite and trewe bileue. (C.18.208–10)

Within this familial frame, we find the matrimonial simile reproduced here. For ease of reference, I have added marginal notations to the text, indicating its rhetorical organization. Abraham – Faith – is speaking:

Prologue:
> 'O god almyhty þat man made and wrouhte
> Semblable to hymsulue ar eny synne were,
> A thre he is þer he is and hereof bereth wittnesse
> The werkes þat hymsulue wrouhte and this world bothe:
>   *Celi enarrant gloriam dei.*
> That he is thre persones departable y preue hit by
>   mankynde,
> And o god almyhty, if alle men ben of Adam.

Comparison: Eue of Adam was and out of hym ydrawe
     And Abel of hem bothe and alle thre o kynde;
     And thise thre þat y carp of, Adam and Eue
     And Abel here issue, aren bote oen in manhede.
     Matrimonye withoute moylere is nauht moche to preyse,
Vehicle: As þe bible bereth witnesse, a boek of þe olde lawe,
     That acorsede alle couples þat no kynde forth brouhte:
     Maledictus sit homo qui non reliquit semen in Israel.
     And man withoute a make myhte nat wel of kynde
     Multiplie ne moreouer withoute a make louye
     Ne withoute a soware be suche seed, this we seen alle.

     Now go we to godhede: in god, fader of heuene,
     Was þe sone in hymsulue in a *simile* as Eue
     Was, when god wolde oute of þe wey ydrawe.
Tenor: And as Abel of Adam and of his wyf Eue
     Sprang forth and spak, a spyer of hem tweyne,
     So oute of þe syre and þe sone þe seynt spirit of hem bothe
     Is and ay was and worþ withouten ende.

Summary: And as thre persones palpable is puyrlich bote o mankynde,
     The which is man and his make and moilere here issue,
     So is god godes sone, in thre persones the trinite.
     In matrimonie aren thre and of o man cam alle thre
     And to godhede goth thre, and o god is all thre.
     Lo, treys encountre treys,' quod he, 'in godhede and in
      manhede.' (C.18.211–39)

We begin with 'O': 'One God Almighty' (211). He made humankind 'semblable to hymsulue ar eny synne were' (212). Abraham testifies to his Lord by citing that Lord's greatest work, man, the *imago dei* that sin marred but could not destroy. If our memory is unusually good, we may hear echoes of C.10.157, where, after describing Do-wel's protection of Anima, Wit says that man is 'semblable in soule to god but if synne hit make.' And even an ordinary memory should not have forgotten that C.18 began with the tree *Ymago-dei* – also called Trewe-Love – planted in man's heart. It is this loving Image, likewise planted in man as a race, as *manhede*, that the next thirty lines will explore.

From 'O' we quickly move to 'thre': 'A thre he is þer he is' (213).[75] This simple assertion is immediately supported by Abraham's offer of witnesses – 'the werkes þat hymsulue wrouhte and this world bothe' (214) bear witness to God's nature just as the elements bear witness to Christ's nature later in the poem.[76] The theme of witness, highly appropriate in a speech by Faith about the deepest mysteries of belief, will recur several times in our passage. Here we learn that, while the

---

[75] Skeat notes that 'a thre' means 'in three' (2:239).
[76] See R. E. Kaske, 'The Speech of "Book" in *Piers Plowman*,' *Anglia* 77 (1959), 117–44.

heavens testify to God's glory, it is man's privilege, as the *imago dei*, to 'preue' that God is 'thre persones departable . . . / And o god almyhty' (215–16).[77]

With line 216, Langland concludes what I have called the prologue of the passage. He has stated his thesis – that God is triune – and indicated the basis of his argument for that thesis – humanity's resemblance to its creator. The next eleven lines set out marriage and offspring ('matrimonye' and 'moylere') as the vehicle of the simile by which God's triunity will be 'preued.' They also justify fruitful matrimony as a natural and lawful institution, and by implication, as a suitable figure for the Trinity. Interestingly, the archetypal family here is Adam, Eve, and Abel, not Adam, Eve, and Seth, as it had been in Wit's discussion of good and evil marriages. Langland does not elaborate his reasons for this change, but several possible explanations come to mind, none of them mutually exclusive. 'Abel,' of course, alliterates with 'Adam' and 'Eve,' and the closer phonetic link among the names may suggest a tighter family unit. The vocalic alliteration is also picked up in the word 'issue,' which harks back to the spiritual 'issue' of the Church in line 206 and forward to Abraham's physical and spiritual 'issue,' to whom the promise of salvation was made (246, 256, 258).

Beyond the alliteration, Langland may still have been thinking of the metaphor he had tried in the B version of the passage, comparing the Trinity to the three grades of chastity: Abel was the first virgin saint, and Adam was traditionally said to have died before Eve, making her the first widow.[78] Also, since Abel had no offspring, and Adam and Eve no parents, the Adam-Eve-Abel trinity has a self-containment that would

---

[77] Langland's profound interests in the image of God and in the Trinity have long been recognized, especially with respect to the sociohistorical or psychological reflexes of those topics. Among others, see Frank, *Scheme of Salvation*; Bloomfield, *Piers Plowman as a Fourteenth-century Apocalypse* (New Brunswick, NJ, 1962); Edward Vasta, *The Spiritual Basis of Piers Plowman* (The Hague, 1965); Ames, *Fulfillment of the Scriptures*; Sally Ann Mussetter, 'The Reformation of the Pilgrim to the Likeness of God: A Study of the Tropological Level of the *Divine Comedy* and *Piers Plowman B*,' (Diss. Cornell, 1975), 108–92; Murtaugh, *Image of God*; and Anna P. Baldwin, 'The Tripartite Reformation of the Soul in *The Scale of Perfection, Pearl*, and *Piers Plowman*,' in *The Medieval Mystical Tradition in England* 3, ed. Marion Glasscoe (Cambridge, 1984), 143–46.

However, only a few critics have discussed Langland's deliberate, extended metaphors for the Trinity in detail, and those who have usually focus on the metaphors given by the Good Samaritan in both B and C. The most thorough discussion I know of the Samaritan's metaphors is Clopper's 'Trinitarian Analogies,' 87–110. A riddle that remains to be solved is why Langland calls the Trinity 'thre persones departable' in C.18.215 and 188, and 'thre persones indepartable' in C.18.27 (if this earlier use is not simply a scribal error).

[78] On Adam's death, see 'The Books of Adam and Eve' and the 'Apocalypse of Moses' in *The Apocrypha and Pseudepigrapha of the Old Testament in English*, ed. R. H. Charles, 2 vols. (Oxford, 1913), 2:151–53. A ME version of the story appears in *The Wheatley Manuscript*, ed. Mabel Day, EETS 155 (London, 1921), 95–97.

be spoiled were Seth its third person, since Seth married and had children in his turn. Seth and his offspring are suitable exemplars for actual human marriages in Wit's speech, but Abel is more appropriate as a type of the Holy Spirit, who does not become the father of a trinity on his own.[79]

In 218, Abraham reminds us of the 'o kynde' found in a good family and so thoroughly explored in Wit's diatribe against *unkynde*, mixed marriages between young and old or good and evil partners. We will hear the word 'kynde' twice more in the next seven lines (223, 224). It is worth remembering that Langland has already added seven references to 'kynde' in his revisions at the beginning of C.18 (C.18.21, 57, 59, 62, 67, 70, 78); five of these references take some form of the phrase '(of) o kynde.' As noted earlier, this repetition of 'kynde' connects the one *kynde* of the three *shoriares* of the Tree of Charity, the one *kynde* of its threefold human fruit, and the one *kynde* of the family of man. In contrast, there are *no* uses of the noun 'kynde' in B's description of the Tree, and the adjective appears only once, or twice if we count 'vnkynde' in B.16.42. 'Kynde' thus unifies the C visions of the Tree and of Faith in ways that they are not unified in B.

The *kyndes* of C.18 are in turn bound up with other *kyndes* in the poem: the *kynde knowynge* and love recommended to the Dreamer, the good and bad *kyndes* of individual human natures, the *kynde* of human nature in general, the *kynde* which is Nature itself, and the Kynde who is Nature's Creator and the lover of Mansoul. As we have seen, Langland delights in pointing out how Kynde the Creator has ordered Nature so that 'kynde folweth kynde.' Good trees bear good fruit, bad trees bear bad, and, as demonstrated by the lineage of Lady Meed, trees of mixed kinds take after the inferior stock. Wit sets out the matrimonial corollary to this axiom of order and descent, arguing that *kynde* should wed *kynde*. Moreover, the marriage bond should be love, the natural attraction of like to like, not the desire for land and riches that leads to so many ill-matched mates (A.10.182–201, B.9.159–81, C.10.254–80). An even more important corollary is that the shared *kynde* of Christ and man is what makes the Redemption work: Jesus

---

[79] In *El fin y la significación sacramental del matrimonio desde S. Anselmo hasta Guillermo de Auxerre* (Granada, 1939), Pedro M. Abellán observes that the Trinitarian symbolism of the man-woman-child family cell 'finds its full realization only in the marriage of our first parents,' since only Eve was literally generated from her husband. But insofar as husbands and wives participate figurally in Adam and Eve, the symbolism continues in the marriages of their descendants (196). Both Aquinas (p. 148 and n. 69 above) and Langland seem to have come to a similar conclusion: i.e., that the marriage and holiest child of Adam and Eve constitute the fullest, most archetypal realization of the family metaphor for the Trinity.

will joust in Piers's helm and habergeon, his *humana natura*, for only as man can he amend man's misdeeds (B.18.22–26, 341, C.20.21–25, 389).[80] The bloody brotherhood that in a sense enables Christ to save man also makes him desire to do so: 'Ac to be merciable to man þanne my kynde it askeþ. . . . For I were an vnkynde kyng but I my kynde (C: kyn) helpe' (B.18.375, 398, C.20.417, 441). Thus, the new emphasis on shared *kynde* in C.18 knits up many of Langland's earlier themes, and prepares us for the upcoming passus of the Incarnation, Passion, and Redemption accomplished by the mingled divine and human *kyndes* of Christ.

After the picture of the first truly loving (or *trewe-louelich*) family as 'alle thre o kynde; . . . thre . . . bote oen in manhede' (C.18.218–20), Langland vindicates the whole institution of marriage on the basis of its fecundity. As pointed out earlier in this chapter, the first command given to humankind was 'Increase and multiply,' and that command cannot be lawfully fulfilled without marriage. Matrimony is not praiseworthy without 'moylere,' a legal term for 'legitimate offspring.'[81] Returning to the themes of witness and of *kynde*, Langland cites the ancient curse on infertility:

> As þe bible bereth witnesse, a boek of þe olde lawe,
> That acorsede alle couples þat no kynde forth brouhte:
> *Maledictus sit homo qui non reliquit semen in Israel.*
> And man withoute a make myhte nat wel of kynde
> Multiplie ne moreouer withoute a make louye
> Ne withoute a soware be suche seed, this we seen alle.
>
> (C.18.222–26)[82]

---

[80] Mary Clemente Davlin treats this sharing of *kyndes* in 'Kynde Knowyng,' 10–15, and 'Petrus, Id Est, Christus: Piers the Plowman as 'The Whole Christ,'' *ChauR* 6 (1972), 280–92, with special reference to the marital metaphor for such sharing on pp. 287–88. See also Chap. 4, pp. 198–200, below on Christ's sharing of human *kynde*.

[81] The procreative purpose and the *bonum prolis* of Christian marriage were not taken by theologians to imply that individual childless marriages were unblessed. They were careful to point out that the command to multiply applies to the species as a whole, not to individuals, and that the *bonum prolis* was not offspring *per se* 'but the hope and desire with which offspring are sought so that they might be raised in religious fashion' (Lombard, *Sent.* 4.31.2). For human kind as a whole, however, offspring are the primary and final cause of marriage, and have been ever since the initial blessing/command, 'Increase and multiply.'

[82] Editors have cited the apocryphal gospels of Mary's infancy as an approximate source for this allegedly biblical curse, but acknowledge that the modern editions of those gospels do not provide exact verbal parallels with C.18.223a. An exact parallel can be found, however, in the *lectiones* for the Feast of St Anne in the Hereford Breviary (but not in the Sarum or York Breviaries); see Walter H. Frere and Langton E. G. Brown, eds. *The Hereford Breviary, Edited from the Rouen Edition of 1505 with Collation of Manuscripts*, 3 vols., HBS 26, 40, 46 (London, 1904–15), 2:264, 266. See my ' ''Maledictus qui non reliquit semen'': The Curse on Infertility in *Piers Plowman* B.XVI and C.XVIII,' *MÆ* 58 (1989): 117–25.

In line 223, 'kynde' means 'kindred, children' in a natural specializa-
tion of the more general sense 'species, race.' In this particular sense,
'kynde' corresponds to 'semen' in line 223a; the literal meaning of the
Latin word evokes the great patterns of agricultural imagery in the
whole poem, and relates the charge of marital fruitfulness to the general
mandate to sow good seed and produce good fruit for the physical and
spiritual welfare of one's fellow man. As the plowing of the half-acre has
shown at greater length, all mankind is called to help Piers the
Plowman. We have seen Haukyn and Activa Vita endeavoring, though
not with complete success, to answer this call; in B, Liberum Arbitrium
has been introduced as Piers's undergardener; within its proper context,
the wedded state can also be considered 'Peres prentys' insofar as it
brings forth those who do well.

Both husbands and wives participate in this 'apprenticesł ¡. The
elliptical line 226 speaks explicitly of marital sowing: 'without a sower,
[there could] not be such seed.'[83] But Langland does not limit his
discussion to the husbandly act of insemination. Even before he
mentions sowing, he insists that without a *make*, a mate like himself, a
man cannot multiply his kind naturally ('of kynde' in line 224 can mean
'with respect to children' or 'by nature' or both). Equally important, a
man without a *make* cannot love. Wit has pointed this out more fully in
his discussion of Do-wel, asserting that mismatched couples will be
unloving couples. They will produce *unkynde*, morally defective
children, or no children at all, 'bute cheste and choppes hem bitwene'
(C.10.272, A.10.193, B.9.172). Likewise for Abraham, proper love and
proper generation both require a mate of one's own *kynde* (C.18.224–25).
So also Adam, understanding this requirement, said of Eve under
divine inspiration, 'This now is bone of my bone, and flesh of my flesh;
she shall be called woman, because she was taken out of man.
Wherefore a man shall leave father and mother, and shall cleave to his
wife: and they shall be two in one flesh' (Gen. 2:23–24).[84]

'And man withoute a make myhte nat wel of kynde / Multiplie ne . . .
louye, / . . . this we seen alle.' The closing words of Abraham's *apologia*
for marriage again call forth witnesses to its truth: not the speaking
elements, nor man as a *kynde*, nor the Bible, but we ourselves have seen
and attest to the praiseworthy purpose and necessity of loving, kindly,

---

[83] 'Kynde' can also mean 'semen' in the sense 'seminal fluid,' and the phrase 'don kynde'
means 'to engage in sexual intercourse' (*MED*, s.v. *kinde* n., 14a). Perhaps Langland is
alluding to the act of procreation literally, as well as through the more general notion of
bringing forth offspring and the transparent agricultural metaphor of sower and seed.
[84] That Adam's words were divinely inspired was proven, for medieval exegetes, by the
fact that when Christ quoted them in his prohibition of divorce, he attributed them to God
(Mt. 19:4–6).

and fruitful wedlock. By saying that 'we all' have seen how generation and love depend on the similarity between mates, Langland grounds Abraham's claim in common human experience; thus he directly involves his audience in the analogical exposition of the Trinity being set forth. 'We' know matrimony by experience. Marriage is the most common, the most 'familiar,' of the three grades of chastity, and hence the most easily identified with. The experiences of marriage and family – growing up in a family, starting and maintaining one's own, seeing family members disperse and die – would have been shared directly by many and indirectly by virtually all.[85] This near-universality of experience may have contributed to Langland's decision to use 'matrimonye with moylere' instead of the three grades as the vehicle for his explanation of the Trinity. By using a 'homelier' analogy, based on a state of life more common than dedicated virginity or even continent widowhood, the poet may well have hoped to bring his whole audience more fully into the argument at hand.

Langland maintains audience involvement as he passes to the tenor of his simile. 'Now,' says Faith, 'go *we* to godhede' (227), announcing the movement from *figura* to *res*, and hinting with powerful simplicity at our own ascending return to the loving Creator whose image we are, a reunion like that of Kynde and Anima, the 'lemman þat he louyeth ylyke to hymsulue' (C.10.132, A.10.6, B.9.6). Langland begins the explanation of his simile by showing the likeness of the Father and Son to Adam and Eve:

> in god, fader of heuene,
> Was þe sone in hymsulue in a *simile* as Eue
> Was, when god wolde oute of þe wey ydrawe. (C.18.227–29)

The phrase 'in a *simile*,' besides calling attention to the figure of speech underlying the whole passage,[86] has at least two distinct applications to the Father : Son :: Adam : Eve correspondence. First, the Son's existence in and generation from the Father are like Eve's being in and of Adam. That is, 'in a *simile* as' can be translated by a simple 'as';

---

[85] Not everyone started families in the Middle Ages, of course, but more people did than has sometimes been supposed – even in the resource-tight period before the Plague. In the late 14th century, some records show marriage rates as high as 85 to 95 per cent for certain groups (94 per cent for peasant farmers, 86 per cent among the knightly class; lower for artisans and servants); other sources suggest lower figures, perhaps because of economic factors in the areas they document. But while the evidence is mixed, it does show many couples setting up households, even with only a tiny plot of ground to their name, rather than remaining unmarried and at home with parents or siblings. See Barbara A. Hanawalt, *The Ties That Bound: Peasant Families in Medieval England* (New York, 1986), 96–100.
[86] Langland recognizes the term 'simile' as the name of a figure of speech: see C.19.159, where the Samaritan calls his comparison of the Trinity to a hand 'this *simile*.'

the Son was in the Father and came from the Father just as Eve was in Adam and came from Adam. Second, since Eve was an *adjutorium simile* to Adam (Gen. 2:18; cf. B.9.115), we might say that she was in Adam 'in a *simile*,' and that in the same way, the Son is in the Father 'in a *simile*.' This double likeness means that Eve's similitude to Adam is a similitude of the Son's similitude to the Father.

Chapter 2 has already indicated how seriously Langland takes likeness, reading it as many medieval thinkers did, as a sign of deeper, often ontological relationships. Theologically, the most important likeness mentioned by Wit is that between Anima and Kynde – the 'imago et similitudo Dei' in which man was created, to which Langland attaches the greatest significance. He relates that likeness to the Incarnation – Christ can be seen as the perfect image of God in man. He defines the *imago dei* as True Love, the Tree of Charity planted in the human heart. At one point in the B text, Langland even loosely equates the *imago dei*, the Incarnate Word, and Love; he says that God made his Son

> vs synfulle yliche:
> *Faciamus hominem ad ymaginem et similitudinem nostram;*
> *Et alibi, Qui manet in caritate in deo manet & deus in eo.* (B.5.486–86β)

By planting love in our hearts, God has made us like him; by living in love, we become still more Godlike, perhaps even to the point of sharing in his nature – abiding in love and thus abiding in God.

Man's likeness to God is not the only similitude that Langland invests with ontological significance. As we have seen, he believes that parents and children, and well-matched husbands and wives, share each other's *kynde* in a special way, which is reflected in their similarity. '*Bona arbor bonum fructum facit,*' 'goode sholde wedde goode,' and 'Eue of Adam was . . . / And Abel of hem bothe and alle thre o kynde' (C.2.29a, 10.242a; C.10.252, B.9.163; C.18.217–18). He does acknowledge the possibility of deceptive appearances, as when he compares false Christians to counterfeit coins, 'bad pennies with good print' (C.17.72–84, B.15.349–55). Yet he continues to believe that genuine likeness between things represents a near or complete sharing, perhaps even an identity, of their natures. Like attracts like, and like can become one with like, because their natures are the same. Similitude implies destiny: it is a dynamic and generative relation, not a static one. Woman comes from man by creation, man from woman by birth, and so they share 'o kynde'; therefore, they can fall in love and return to one flesh in marriage. The Son 'comes from' the Father by eternal generation, and 'returns' to him in the Spirit, who is love. Since humankind was made to the image of God, the Son can become man, but he eventually returns to the Father of whom he is the divine and human image. Human beings likewise have come from the 'o god almyhty' to whom they are 'semblable' through love, and to whom they are destined by love to return.[87] Similitude is the greatest trope of all.

Having explained how the Father and Son are similar to Adam and Eve, Langland goes on to compare the Spirit to Abel (230–33). He calls Abel a 'spyer' ('scion, blade of wheat'; 231) of Adam and Eve, and thus develops the agricultural imagery of seed and sowing yet further. The name 'seynt *spirit*' for the Holy Ghost (232) echoes 'spyer' semantically as well as aurally, for both words pertain to life, either in terms of sprouting vegetation or of breathing, speaking animation – Abel 'sprang forth and spak,' and the Spirit springs forth from heaven bringing the gift of tongues.[88]

Besides showing how Abel represents the Spirit, lines 230–33 set out the overall analogy between Adam's family and the Trinity. The lines unfold clearly, gracefully, and powerfully. With the lists of names and the quasi-doxology in 233, they are almost a litany:

> And as Abel of Adam and of his wyf Eue
> Sprang forth and spak, a spyer of hem tweyne,
> So oute of þe syre and þe sone þe seynt spirit of hem bothe
> Is and ay was and worþ withouten ende.

Alliteration binds each of the two sets of names more closely together within itself; the likeness of the initial letters points to the likeness of kind within each of the two trinities, showing that the ontological implications of similitude operate in language as well as in physical creation and supernatural reality.[89]

---

[87] The importance of similitude, especially the similitude of man to God, in *Piers* has been amply demonstrated by many scholars, some of whom are listed in note 77 above. Of the works cited there, several pay special attention to the renewal of God's image in the human soul and the consequent return of the soul to God: e.g., the studies of Vasta, Mussetter, and Murtaugh. Myra Stokes notes the principle of like-for-like in divine justice and mercy and the mirroring of that principle in human action, in *Justice and Mercy in Piers Plowman* (London, 1984), 1–6, 86–95, 154, and *passim*. See also Chap. 2, nn. 52, 75, and 83.

[88] For related earlier plays on the words 'spire,' 'grace,' 'Spirit,' and 'speech,' cf. B.9.103–04; B.12.59–63a, C.14.23–27a; C.12.178–84. On some of these word-plays, see R. A. Shoaf, ' "Speche þat Spire is of Grace": A Note on *Piers Plowman* B.9.104,' *YLS* 1 (1987), 128–33; and Mary Clemente Davlin, *A Game of Heuene: Word Play and the Meaning of Piers Plowman B* (Cambridge, 1989), 58–59.

[89] The seriousness with which Langland 'plays' with linguistic similitude has long been recognized. See Bernard F. Huppé, '*Petrus Id Est Christus*: Word Play in *Piers Plowman*, the B Text,' *ELH* 17 (1950), 163–90; Lawlor, *Essay in Criticism*, 265–74; A. C. Spearing, 'Verbal Repetition in *Piers Plowman* B and C,' *JEGP* 62 (1963), 722–37; Patricia M. Kean, 'Love, Law, and *Lewte* in *Piers Plowman*,' *RES* n.s. 15 (1964), 241–61. James P. Hala sets

Line 234 brings us to Langland's summary of his matrimonial metaphor for the Trinity. He first sketches the 'proof' of the theorem proposed in line 215, 'That he is thre persones departable':

> And as thre persones palpable is puyrlich bote o mankynde,
> The which is man and his make and moilere here issue,
> So is god godes sone, in thre persones the trinite. (C.18.234–36)

Three persons – man and his mate and their legitimate issue – are one mankind; putting it more prosaically, one could say that three classes of persons constitute the race when it is viewed in terms of familial structure – fathers, mothers, and children. So also, within the Godhead, God's Son is God (likewise the Spirit, by implication), just as the members of the human family are all human. Moreover, the Trinity consists of three persons with specific interrelationships analogous to the specific relations that link the three classes of persons which constitute mankind. *Quod erat demonstrandum*.

Using clausal parallelism, the next two lines of the summary (237–38) reveal, once more and emphatically, the trinitarian image of God in man. In addition, a chiastic relationship among the verbs works alongside the direct parallels among the nouns and adjectives, showing the dynamic implications of the *imago dei*:

> In matrimonie   aren thre and of o man cam   alle thre,
> And to godhede   goth thre and   o god is   all thre.

The sentence moves from multiple existence ('aren') which proceeded ('cam') from one human origin, to the return ('goth') to the one divine origin and end, the God 'Who Is.' The verbal echoes here reach back across the whole passage: 'is all thre' recalls 'A thre he is þer he is' (213); 'to godhede goth thre' repeats the phrasing of 'Now go we to godhede' (227). By echoing line 227, the first half of 238 suggests momentarily that it is the threefold family of man which 'goes to Godhead.' Strictly speaking, of course, the 'three' who go to Godhead are the persons of the divine Trinity, and the second half of 238 confirms this more orthodox assertion. Nevertheless, the looser hint of man's own return to his source, to the original of which he is the image, continues to echo in the mind's ear.

In the last line of this complex and powerful passage, we might hope for some kind of climactic, recapitulatory finish, and Langland does not disappoint us. 'Lo, treys encountre treys,' says Abraham as he ends his

Langland's word-play in a medieval rhetorical context in 'The Word Made Flesh: Word-Play in *Piers Plowman B*' (Diss. University of Michigan, 1984).

matrimonial explanation of the Trinity; the phrase has a formulaic ring, like the Latin lines strewn throughout the poem.[90] It sounds numerological, magical, metaphysical.[91] 'Encountre,' which may be two words rather than one, suggests balances, crossings, counterings, rather like the modern 'point counter point.' It seems particularly apt after the chiastic countering of man and God, threes and ones, in the preceding lines. But while the formula may sound mysterious, perhaps even foreign, Langland is careful to end in clear, English explication. How do 'treys encountre treys'? 'In godhede and in manhede.' The whole line looks back to the beginning of the passus, to the multiply threefold Tree of Charity, and ahead, with the faithful Abraham, to the encounter of *godhede* and *manhede* in the Incarnate Redeemer.

The marriage simile in C.18 is one of the finest pieces of discursive rhetoric in *Piers*: its rhythms are solemn, almost liturgical, in their balance, stately flow, rising energies, and final climax. Several of the themes from Wit's account of marriage and creation reappear, as deliberate echoes of the earlier material, or as necessary repetitions of natural expressions for the same set of ideas. The agricultural images of seed and scion also link the comparison to the rest of the poem, as do the ideas of *kynde*, of similitude, of the values of fertility, productivity, and love, and the use of word- and letter-play to indicate close relationships among persons, things, and concepts.

By revising Abraham's explanation of the Trinity as he does from B to C, Langland shifts the emphases of the passus, sharpening the images he uses for the Trinity and giving a more explicitly positive weight to matrimony. These changes, along with the expanded discussion of the fruits of Charity described above, shed a brighter light on his conceptions of marriage and the Trinity. To a certain extent, we can see those conceptions in B, but C expresses them more clearly and

[90] In Huntington Library MS 143 (Pearsall's copy-text), 'treys encountre treys' is underlined like the Latin lines in the poem; see R. B. Haselden and H. C. Schulz, eds., *Piers Plowman: The Huntington Manuscript (HM 143), Reproduced in Photostat* (San Marino, 1936), fol. 82r. The early 15th-century scribe evidently perceived the words as foreign, and Langland may well have meant them so. Even if we take them as English, they are all French loans, and 'treys' an unusual one, glossed by Pearsall as the equivalent of 'trey,' a throw of three at dice.

[91] Since the dice were sometimes used for divination, a dicing allusion here may not be completely out of place, and could even be seen as matching Langland's penchant for unexpected images. In the divinatory method known as the *Sortes apostolorum*, the divination is preceded by a three-day fast, the singing of the office of the Trinity, and an additional prayer, after which three dice were thrown simultaneously; see W. L. Braekman, 'Fortune-Telling by the Casting of Dice: A Middle English Poem and Its Background,' *SN* 52 (1980), 5–6. Or perhaps 'treys' is the contracted form of *trey-as* 'three-ace,' a throw of three and one (*OED*, s.v. *trey* sb., 1c); the word is attested in Gower, and would be an excellent linguistic icon for tri-unity.

powerfully. The C version of *Piers* is often damned with faint praise as being clearer but less poetic than its B counterpart, and such a characterization may be true of some passages. But in its treatment of marriage and the Trinity in Passus 18, C is not only clearer than B but also more forceful and esthetically more satisfying. What Donaldson has called Langland's 'large capacities, both intellectual and artistic' (*C-Text*, 197) are fully evident in the poet's revised, matrimonial simile for the Trinity.

And what conceptions does that simile illuminate? Most important is a clearer view of marriage as a deeply valuable institution, a worthy reflection of the Trinity within the whole race. To be sure, the value placed by the poet on marriage is visible before Abraham's speech. In the Third Dream, Wit presents the sacrament as part of the divinely established natural order, a *kynde* union epitomizing law, love, and the universal principles of like from like and like returning to like. Both doing well and ideal wedlock are at the root of the life of sanctity. Chaste widowhood and virginity grow out of it just as Do-bet and Do-best grow out of Do-wel. The Edenic institution of marriage and its exegetical association with the Trinitarian 'Faciamus' strengthen its credentials further and make it at least as honorable a metaphor for the Trinity as a hand or a taper.

The discussion of marriage in Wit's speech takes place on the natural level, in literal and moral terms. But Piers, Liberum Arbitrium, and Abraham/Faith move on a higher plane in both B and C; and in C, Langland shows that marriage points beyond earthly *kynde*, that it is a *sacramentum* which can turn our gaze upward to the Trinity. In making marriage a figure of the Trinity, Langland may have been struck by the 'mystère d'unité dans la multiplicité' which has been offered as a reason for the medieval use of the Mass of the Trinity as the nuptial Mass (Molin and Mutembe, *Le Rituel du mariage*, 208). We know that Langland was interested in unity, whether of man with man or of man with God. Thanks to Eph. 5:32, matrimony was regularly read as signifying Christ's union with the Church, a union which Langland also sees as 'betokening the Trinity' (C.18.210). Perhaps Abraham's discourse in C implies a loose, general analogy between family unity, Unity-Holy-church (in which we are all bloody brethren), and the Tri-unity figured both by the natural family and by Christ, the Church, and Christendom their offspring.[92]

---

[92] The standard explanation of the sacramental significance of matrimony involves concepts central to Langland's thought: the Church and Christ were said to be united in will and nature (or *kynde*), since he had 'assumed the form of human nature,' and this union is signified by the marital union of two souls and two bodies through 'conformity in love ["caritate"] and nature' (Lombard, *Sent.* 4.26.2; my emphasis).

More obviously important to Langland is the dynamic of love that operates in both the Trinity and the family. Based on the shared nature of separate but similar persons, such love effects a fruitful union which issues in similar offspring. In terms of this dynamic at least, 'matrimony with moilere' is a better image of the Trinity than Augustine's psychological model or the attributes of power, wisdom, and goodness, though Langland recognizes those analogues elsewhere. The family reveals similar but distinct persons joined in a loving, generative union much more directly than do the faculties and attributes of a single soul. (In fact, it is interesting to note that Langland's allegories of the soul's faculties often represent them as spouses or as members of a familial household.) The likeness and the love and the fruitfulness of well-married couples are what lead Langland to compare matrimony to the Trinity. The demonstration that likeness, love, and generation characterize the Godhead does not indicate a 'limited understanding' on Abraham's part, but rather a very Langlandian understanding of God's nature and its reflections in man.[93]

For Langland sees God's image in many aspects of human life. With Augustine, he sees it in the individual memory, intellect, and will; he sees it also governing the process of moral growth from Do-wel to Do-best. He finds it reflected in the three grades of chastity; he sees it structuring human history and society.[94] And he sees it in that small but most familiar society – fruitful marriage. Abraham's matrimonial simile is important in *Piers* because it, as much as any reflection of the Deity in mankind, reveals the active operation and effect of the *imago dei* planted within the race. Eve's generation from and likeness to Adam meant that the two would become one, joined and fruitful in love. Anima's creation by and likeness to Kynde means that they too will be united in love. The image of God in man, whether found in the individual, in the moral life, in the family, or in society and history, means that *godhede* and *manhede* must meet in loving Unity, in Christ and Christendom and Holy Church the mother. 'Lo, treys encountre treys': *Sacramentum hoc magnum est.*

---

[93] The modern theologian Bertrand de Margerie prefers the familial model of the Trinity to the psychological on grounds remarkably similar to the themes highlighted in Langland's poetic analysis (*Christian Trinity*, 289–92).
[94] Murtaugh, *Image of God*, 31–62; Bloomfield, *Fourteenth-century Apocalypse*, 98–126; Alan J. Fletcher, 'The Social Trinity of *Piers Plowman*,' *RES* n.s. 44 (1993), 355–58.

Conclusions

Unlike the Meed episode or Wit's speech, Passus B.16/C.18 displays extensive revisions in the matrimonial material handled by the two versions. The C text's changes in this material do not contradict Langland's treatment of marriage and family in the earlier version or in earlier passus, but they do add important new dimensions to that treatment. Thus the C text definitely has more to offer on the subject of matrimony than B, which itself has already added significantly to A's remarks on marriage through the simple act of carrying the poem on past the Third Dream.

The references to matrimony in B.16 are relatively thin, and their implications correspondingly sketchy, but even those sketchy hints can be seen to carry the germ of C's extended comments on the married state. The B version of the passus presents marriage as one of the three grades of chastity, which are in turn presented as fruits on the Tree of Love protected by the Trinity and (in Abraham's speech) as tokens of the Trinity itself. Thus the human race is shown as reflecting the triune Deity in its threefold sexual estates or vocations. Furthermore, the B text contains a preliminary version of the C text's comparison of the Trinity to matrimony alone, and it clearly establishes the importance of the family of faith – Abraham's issue and ultimately the Church – at the start of Will's journey through salvation history.

In C, all these ideas recur in one form or another. The three grades are discussed more fully, though their parallelism to the Trinity is somewhat de-emphasized. The *imago dei* theme is pointed up by alterations in the initial description of the Tree and in Abraham's matrimonial simile for the Trinity. Marriage itself is more explicitly honored, partly by its status as the divinely blessed institution for propagating all mankind and partly by the reflected glory of the Godhead to which it is compared. And in a slightly expanded form, we hear again of the family of faith – proximally fathered by Abraham, and ultimately by God the Father through his Son and servant Christ.

But the C text does more than develop ideas already available in B.[95] It adds a number of important references to *kynde*, thereby relating this passus more closely to other parts of the poem. It also participates in the C text's continuing exploration of the tensions between the active life of

---

[95] The way C adds to or verbally 'intensifies' themes already present in B is characteristic of its strategies of revision, as A. C. Spearing has demonstrated in his highly perceptive studies, 'Development of a Theme' and 'Verbal Repetition.'

working as the world asks and its contemplative counterpart in patient poverty, between imperfection and perfection, sexuality and continence, earth and heaven, *kynde* and grace. It is Langland's genius, and no doubt his sense of purpose and audience, that allow him to honor the complementary merits of both sides while still privileging the less worldly halves of these dichotomies. Indeed, his expanded description of the three fruits on the Tree lays greater emphasis on the value of *both* virginity and marriage, even as he expounds the sources of their relative worth. He explains virginity's closeness to the gracious warmth of the Spirit more fully and adds the fact of its direct service to God, while still insisting that honor is owed to marriage by virtue of its divine institution and its sacred function of bringing forth 'folk of alle nacion, / Bothe parfit and inparfit.' Langland may have read the old biblical gloss, 'marriages fill the earth, virginity heaven,' as a mark in favor of wedlock as well as virginity. Certainly, Wit's diatribe against the covetous barren marriages that have been made since the plague (whether reflective of social reality or not) places significant value on literal fruitfulness within loving marriages. Filling the earth through honest marriage is analogous to winning food for the *comune* by honest work, in so far as the former preserves the physical existence of the species while the latter preserves the bodily existence of individuals.[96] And, as Wit also notes, without saintly marriages, saintly virginity is likely to be hard to find.

The honor which the C text claims for marriage is really twofold: on the one hand, marriage deserves honor because of its original procreative purpose, its Edenic institution, and the divine blessing laid upon it; on the other, it deserves honor for the sake of the mysteries reflected in it – Christ and the Church, and the Trinity that founded marriage in the first place. The sacraments could be (and often were) ranked according to various criteria, such as the conferral of a sacramental character, the dignity of the minister of the sacrament, or the necessity of the sacrament. Not surprisingly, matrimony comes out near the bottom of many such lists. But in at least two rankings,

---

[96] This commonsense observation was not infrequently made in theological discussions of the purposes for marriage, and seems to be in harmony with the way Langland presents doing well in this world as a matter of good family relationships as well as honest work. See for example Augustine, *De Bono Coniugali* 16 (*CSEL* 41:210–12); Aquinas, *ST* 2-2 q.152 a.2, a.4 (*Opera* 3:504–05, 506); Lyra, *Post.*, 1:35. For a similar but literary analogy between the spiritual meanings of food and conjugality in *Cleanness*, see Charlotte Morse, *The Pattern of Judgment in the 'Queste' and 'Cleanness'* (Columbia, MO, 1978), 46–52; T. D. Kelly and John T. Irwin, 'The Meaning of *Cleanness*: Parable as Effective Sign,' *MS* 35 (1973), 234–43.

marriage stands right at the top: when judged by the place or time of its institution – in paradise before the Fall; and when judged by what it signifies – the mystical union of Christ and the Church.[97]

Passus C.18 of *Piers Plowman* appears to follow in the same tradition, save for its striking extension of the matrimonial *sacramentum* to include the Triune Deity itself as well as the Mystical Body. The respect which the passus pays to marriage should warn us that however much Langland saw or felt the desirability of the perfect life that forsakes family, world, and even one's 'ownere wil,' he still recognized the fundamental necessity and worth of the active life rightly lived and the social and spiritual dangers of devaluing that 'comune lyf.' For all the flaws of the actual marriages of his own day – and Wit's speech in C is even harsher in denouncing those flaws than in A or B – Langland knows that the solution is not and cannot be a universal rejection of marriage and the active life in favor of virginity, contemplation, patient poverty, and pure 'longing to be hennes.' All crafts and callings have been given by Grace. Instead of making an impossible plea for universal contemplation and continence, the poet recommends the taking up, by those who have need, of the active, married life as intended by God from the beginning, in reflection of his own nature. Even Piers the Plowman lives in honest wedlock until he turns pilgrim. And those who live lovingly under the *kynde* law of marriage will indeed bear fruit, earn grace, and do well.

---

[97] Thus Bromyard, *Summa Praed.*, s.v. 'Matrimonium,' § 1: 'Of all the sacraments, it was instituted by God first and in the most solemn place, i.e., in paradise. Thus it clearly has pre-eminence of place and of priority over the other sacraments.' Cf. de Burgh, *Pup. Oc.*, 2v–3r, for several ways of ordering the sacraments, and Kelly, *Love and Marriage*, 257, summarizing Joannes Andreae's 'reasons for the pre-eminence of the sacrament of matrimony.'

4

A Kind Familiarity

The principal extended treatments of marriage and family in *Piers Plowman* appear in the Meed episode, Wit's speech, Abraham's speech, and the C version of the Tree of Charity scene. As we have seen, those treatments move from the public to the private to the transcendent. But there are many lesser references to husbands, wives, children, sisters, and brothers throughout the poem, often made in pursuit of other subjects but still contributing to Langland's representation of family life and its place in the economies of society and salvation. Future in-depth analysis of these references on an individual basis is much to be desired; detailed attention could be given to such questions as their immediate narrative or rhetorical functions in the poem, or to more specific aspects of familial experience, such as its role in the construction of the social self (including gender) or in economic production, to name but a few possible directions. My goal in this chapter, however, is broader and more preliminary, a matter of bringing into critical view some of the most promising passages for such future work, as well as suggesting ways in which these materials work together to create a general representation of family life in *Piers Plowman* and how they relate thematically to other major issues raised in the poem.

Since Langland's briefer references to marriage and family occur in no particular order across the poem, an external organizing principle is a *sine qua non* for their analysis. They could be treated, for instance, according to their rhetorical mode – allegorical, typical, literal, and so forth; or along a spectrum of positive to negative instances; or possibly in terms of some sort of estates hierarchy. But the most convenient order is one intrinsic to the family experience itself: the human life-cycle, beginning with childhood and parent-child relations, and then moving through sexuality, the making of marriages, the familial affections that operate into and through adulthood, and finally, to old age and the transmission of worldly goods to the next generation.

In the following pages, I discuss many of the poem's references to marriage and family not covered in the three preceding chapters; they will be organized according to the phases of the life cycle just given. I have endeavored to include all thematically important references to the familial experience (e.g., passages dealing with fraternal affections, generation and sexuality, heirship, and family governance), adding a few secondary examples to round out the overall picture. What will be said below about the relations between parents, children, and siblings within a biological family can often be applied quite naturally to analogous communities, from small households with one or two servants or apprentices, to village or town communities, to the great aristocratic *meynees*, to the entire kingdom, Church, or human race. Since these analogies are by and large transparent, I have usually left their details to the reader; only a few of the many such extensions suggested in the poem will be noted in this chapter.

Childhood

Langland frequently depicts childhood in idealistic and sentimental terms. Children are loving, cheerful, innocent, chaste, humble, and obedient. Charity is 'a childissh þyng,' glad with those who rejoice and sad with those who sorrow; it is 'as a good child hende,' merry of mouth, light of speech, companionable and comforting (B.15.149, C.16.296; B.15.165–70, C.16.297–302; B.15.216–19). According to the B text, Truth sits in a chain of charity in the hearts of good men, as if they were children obedient to their father's will (B.5.606–08). When Holy Church needs a figure for pure chastity, she speaks of childhood. In A and B, it is a 'child þat in chirche wepiþ,' perhaps out of penitent sorrow, or simple squalling innocence. In C, the connotations are clearer – 'as chast as a child þat chyht noþer ne fyhteth' (A.1.154, B.1.180; C.1.176). The bloody brotherhood that men share in Christ means that they should 'loue [each other] as leue children,' sharing with each other in a kind, fraternal affection (B.11.209–13, C.12.115–117a).

These positive references to childhood do not mean that children need no moral guidance – the 'faunteltee' and 'wilde wantownesse' of youth must be grown out of, as Will learns after his encounter with Fortune and her maidens (B.11.42–45, C.11.312–15; B.12.6). He does take an inordinately long time to leave childish folly behind, however; forty-five is rather late to be abandoning *faunteltee*.[1] Charity's 'childisshnesse,' in

---

[1] On Will's wanton 'faunteltee' and the significance of forty-five as the start of old age,

contrast, is 'Wiþouten fauntelte or folie a fre liberal wille' (B.15.150). Several passages in the poem insist on the importance of teaching and correcting children so that they know *how* to do well and avoid *wantownesse*. For instance, in the ideal society outlined by Reason in Passus 4, 'childris cherisshing [will] be chastisid with ȝerdis' (A.4.103, B.4.117, C.4.112). And when Reason (Conscience in A) exhorts the multitude before the confessions of the Sins, a significant portion of his sermon is devoted to family discipline and draws on well-worn parental sayings:

Tomme Stowue he tauȝte to take two staues
And fecche Felice hom fro wyuen pyne.
He warnede watte his wif was to blame
That hire heed was worþ a marc & his hood noȝt a rote.
He bad Bette kutte a bouȝ ouþer tweye
And bete Beton þerwith but if she wolde werche.
He chargede Chapmen to chastiȝen hir children:
'Late no wynnyng forwanye hem while þei be yonge,
Ne for no poustee of pestilence plese hem noȝt out of reson.
My sire seide to me, and so dide my dame,
"Lo, þe leuere child þe moore loore bihoueþ";
And Salomon seide þe same þat Sapience made,
Qui parcit virge odit filium:
Whoso spareþ þe spryng spilleþ hise children.'
(B.5.28–40, A.5.28–33, C.5.130–39a)[2]

When carried 'out of reson,' softhearted treatment of children spoils them, even if it is rooted in natural parental affections. Langland recognizes the power of the plague to make people cherish their children to the point of coddling, and the tendency among the affluent to lavish their winnings on their children. Like Jean Gerson in the next generation, he sees the dangers in such misdirected and faulty expressions of love for one's children. But where Gerson will emphasize the danger to the parents, who are distracted from God and risk becoming idolaters of their own children, Langland focuses on the danger to the children, whose moral growth may be severely stunted.[3]

see John Burrow, 'Langland *Nel Mezzo Del Cammin*,' in *Medieval Studies for J. A. W. Bennett, Aetatis Suae LXX*, ed. P. L. Heyworth (Oxford, 1981), 25–34.
[2] In addition to having biblical roots (Prov. 13:24, quoted by Reason), the 'spare and spoil' theme is widespread in ME proverbs about children; cf. Whiting B13, C214–15, C199–200, F74, Y1. Myra Stokes notes the importance of images of children under discipline throughout B.5, in *Justice and Mercy in Piers Plowman: A Reading of the B Text Visio* (London, 1984), 164, 172, 184, 186.
[3] Cf. David Herlihy, 'Medieval Children,' in Bede Karl Lackner and Kenneth Roy Philp, eds., *Essays on Medieval Civilization*, The Walter Prescott Webb Memorial Lectures 12 (Austin, 1978), 122–26; Nicholas Orme, 'Langland and Education,' *History of Education* 11 (1982), 253–56. See also Barbara A. Hanawalt, *Growing Up in Medieval London: The*

The burden of responsibility for a child's moral development is on its parents, godparents, guardians, and teachers. As Reason's exhortation demonstrates, Langland expects that their teaching will include the use of the rod when necessary. Study, who devised 'gramer for girles,' also 'bet hem wiþ a baleis but ȝif þei wolde lerne' (A.11.132–33, B.10.180–81, C.11.123–24). According to Imaginatif in B, Will himself has been chastised by the 'bittre baleises' and comforting rod of a loving heavenly Father, as a way of moving him away from youthful wantonness. Interestingly, in responding to Imaginatif, the Dreamer defends his poetry-making by invoking a gentler instance of paternal instruction, Cato's advice to his son, 'Interpone tuis interdum gaudia curis' (B.12.6–22α).

In Chapter 2 we saw that godparents who do not concern themselves with their godchildren's physical and spiritual welfare 'Shul purchace penaunce in purgatorie but þei hem helpe. / For moore bilongeþ to þe litel barn er he þe lawe knowe / Than nempnynge of a name and he neuer þe wiser' (B.9.79–81). Langland recognizes that children lack a fully developed 'inwit,' or capacity for self-governance. But he does not think of children as innately vicious, and in A he even argues that

> in fauntis ne in folis þe fend haþ no miȝt
> For no werk þat þei werche, wykkide oþer ellis.
> Ac þe fadir & þe Frendis for fauntis shuln be blamid
> But þei witen hem fro wauntounesse whiles þei ben ȝonge.
>
> (A.10.64–67)

In response to parental and pedagogical discipline, children owe obedience and sufferance, youthful versions of the great virtue of patience which the poem recommends to all Christians. Thus, 'buxum speche' and the honoring of parents stand very near the beginning of the road to Truth, right after the Two Great Commandments (A.6.50–56, B.5.563–69, C.7.208–16a); buxom speech can also be found in the ideal cloister or school (B.10.305–08, C.5.152–55). The names of Piers's own daughter and son suggest the parallel importance of obeying both one's own parents and one's social elders: 'Do-right-so-or-thy-dame-shall-beat-thee' and 'Suffer-thy-sovereigns-to-have-their-will-and-deem-them-not-for-if-thou-dost-thou-shalt-buy-it-dear – Let-God-be-withal-for-so-his-word-teacheth' (A.7.71–74, B.6.79–82, C.8.81–83). Wit stresses the *suffraunce* of children and subjects in the pedagogically slanted mid-section of his speech in A (10.80–120α), and *suffraunce* is

Experience of Childhood in History (New York, 1993), 69–87, on child-rearing and education; Orme, 'Children and the Church in Medieval England,' *Journal of Ecclesiastical History* 45 (1944), 563–87; and Chap. 1 n. 5 and Chap. 2 n. 82 above.

again linked to the teaching of children when Reason rebukes Will for his arrogant impatience:

> 'Holy writ,' quod þat wye, 'wisseþ men to suffre:
> *Propter deum subiecti estote omni creature.*
> Frenche men and fre men affaiteþ þus hire children:
> *Bele vertue est suffrance; mal dire est petite vengeance.*
> *Bien dire et bien suffrir fait lui suffrable a bien venir.'*
> (B.11.383–86; cf. C.13.199–203)[4]

Family discipline actually extends beyond children; like Reason's Wat, Bette, and Tomme Stowue, heads of households are expected to teach, protect, and discipline their entire *familia*, including wives and servants as well as offspring. Thus Piers is not only concerned about the meagre food he has for his children before harvest, but also about the health of his servants (A.7.267, B.6.283, C.8.306; A.7.237–40, B.6.253–56, C.8.266–69), and Peace complains to the King about wrongs done to his family, servants, and even unprotected neighbor women (A.4.34–47, B.4.47–60, C.4.45–63). This responsibility is paralleled by the responsibilities that churchmen have to their flocks and the king to the *comune*. In Reason's sermon, the exhortation to family discipline is immediately followed by exhortations to prelates and priests that they 'lyue as [þei] leren vs' so that people will believe their preaching, to religious that they hold to their Rules, and to the king and the pope that they govern lovingly and justly (B.5.41–51, A.5.34–39, C.5.140–96). But the most moving example of the head of a household providing spiritual leadership occurs in an ordinary, simple family, when Will calls Kit and Calot to join him in celebrating the Redemption with the rest of the Christian community (B.18.424–31, C.20.470–78).

It is worth noting that several wives in the poem also have a significant measure of responsible authority. Dame Study and Dame Scripture are both sterner teachers than their husbands, to the humorous point of being depicted as scolding schoolmistresses. Like Holy Church earlier in the poem, or like Lady Philosophy or the Pearl Maiden, their authority is not undermined by their tone of voice or their gender, though some anxiety about female authority may be read into their characterization. The name of Piers's wife, Dame Work-when-time-is, suggests that she plays an important part in the economic productivity of the household (as medieval wives usually did) and she is apparently also responsible for disciplining their daughter 'Do-right-so-or-thy-dame-shall-beat-

---

[4] This passage appears only in two B-MSS, R and F; C gives the proverb but drops the line mentioning children. See K-D 66, 460.

thee.'⁵ Similarly, the women who help Piers and his workers on the half-acre do the important work of making cloth, sewing, and (in B) teaching their daughters to do the same. By working whenever there is time, except on holy days and vigils, they 'help[en] hem werche wiʒtly þat wynne [here] foode' (A.7.8–22, B.6.8–20, C.8.6–18). (There is a suggestion here of a gender-based division of the essential labor of society, with women providing *vesture*, and men providing *mete at meel*. Since God freely gives water for drink, Langland may intend us to see that all three of the basic material needs mentioned by Holy Church could be provided if only the whole *comune*, men and women alike, obeyed Piers's labor-statutes.)

The *educatio* owed to children does not always stop with moral development, though it must begin there. Will speaks nostalgically of the support his own 'fader and . . . frendes' gave him in putting him to school, though the schooling seems to have been cut short when the friends died (C.5.35–41). In the A text, Wit associates the *timor domini* theme, which traditionally had strong ties to the concept of filial fear, with scholars learning in school and being 'ywar for betyng of þe ʒarde' (A.10.81–87). In all three texts, Langland urges merchants to perform such corporal works of mercy as arranging for the schooling or apprenticing of needy young men, as well as endowing and supporting poor maidens and widows (A.8.31–34, B.7.29–32, C.9.33–35). This kind of social charity – in effect, the provision of a surrogate family – also fulfills an important social function: the creation of productive members of society, the making of 'winners' from potential 'wasters.'⁶

Unfortunately, families do not always function as they should, internally or with respect to their larger social contexts. For Langland, as for social critics throughout history, the breakdown of loving support and discipline in families or similar communities signifies a far more

⁵ Piers's wife's name can mean either 'Work whenever there is opportunity' or 'Work (literally and perhaps also sexually) when it is the right time,' or both. Barbara A. Hanawalt explores the economic and emotional dimensions of the 'partnership marriage' common among the medieval peasantry, in *The Ties That Bound: Peasant Families in Medieval England* (New York, 1986), 141–55, 205–19. Margaret E. Goldsmith suggests that the name of Piers's wife contains an allusion to Gal. 6:8–10, verses which stress sowing and reaping in the spirit, and doing well 'dum tempus habemus'; see *The Figure of Piers Plowman: The Image on the Coin* (Cambridge, 1981), 39. Such a reading would make Piers's wife a more eschatological figure, signifying 'working while there is (still) time.'

⁶ Such charitable works were a common feature of medieval wills; see Michael M. Sheehan, *The Will in Medieval England: From the Conversion of the Anglo-Saxons to the End of the Thirteenth Century*, Studies and Texts 6 (Toronto, 1963), 261–65; Jo Ann Hoeppner Moran, *The Growth of English Schooling 1340–1548: Learning, Literacy, and Laicization in Pre-Reformation York Diocese* (Princeton, 1985), 166; and Frederick J. Furnivall, *The Fifty Earliest English Wills in the Court of Probate, London. A.D. 1387–1439*, EETS 78 (London, 1882), 15, 23, 49–54, 80, 95, 133, etc.

general corruption in society at large. We find such breakdowns within families proper: the strife-bound, socially mixed marriages attacked by Wit, or the *up-so-doun* family of Glutton, in which the husband has completely surrendered his role as caretaker and corrector to his wife. We find them in the schools: Anima and Liberum Arbitrium warn that 'Grammer, þe ground of al, bigileþ now children' (B.15.372, C.17.107), echoing a topos of socio-educational complaint that stretches from the Greeks to modern pop grammarians. Analogous breakdowns occur in aristocratic *familiae*: by eating in private parlors and chimneyed chambers, lords and ladies violate the communal hospitality owed to their household and the local community; worse yet, such nobles encourage and imitate vagabond fiddlers and friars, who are 'homliche at oþere mennes houses and hatien hir owene' (B.10.93–103). Even the spiritual family of the Church has its failures: Wit excoriates bishops for being *unkynde* to their spiritual kin, for wasting their own time, speech, and Christ's patrimony on japers instead of feeding, clothing, and teaching those in need (B.9.82–106); as we saw in Chapter 2, these comments on episcopal obligations grow naturally out of earlier remarks in A.10 and B.9 on familial and godparental duties to dependent kin.

Langland blames these breakdowns mainly on the people who have been given the right to govern, rather than on their subordinates. His theory of governance is in many respects paternalistic, but he generally does not waste energy blaming the less powerful for the failures of those in power, though he recognizes that such failures may well bring harm to the governed as well as to the governors. In an important addition to the C Prologue, he reminds us that God punished Israel for the sins of the priests Ophni and Phineas, which were in turn due to the sin of their father, the high priest Heli:

> And for here syre sey hem synne and suffred hem do ille
> And chastisid hem noght þerof and nolde noght rebuken hem,
> Anon as it was tolde hym that þe children of Israel
> Were disconfit in batayle and *Archa domini* lorn
> And his sones slawe ther, anon he ful for sorwe
> Fro his chayere þer he sat and brake his nekke atwene;
> And al was for vengeance he bet noght his children.
> And for þei were prestis and men of holy chirche
> God was wel þe wrother and took þe raþer vengeance.
> Forthy y sey ʒe prestes and men of holy churche
> That soffreth men do sacrefyce and worschipe maumettes,
> And ʒe shulde be here fadres and techen hem betre,
> God shal take vengeaunce on alle suche prestis
> Wel hardere and grettere on suche shrewed faderes

173

Than euere he dede on Offnies and Fines his fader,
For ȝoure shrewed soffraunce and ȝoure oune synne.

(C.Pr.109–24)[7]

The paternal *soffraunce* described here undermines the right relation between children and parents, in which children obey and 'suffer' their parents' discipline and commands. This kind of 'vnsittynge soffraunce' on the part of those in authority may be what Langland has in mind in two other C-text additions, the first introducing the vice as a sister of Meed (C.3.207) and the second warning the King against such sufferance in his courts (C.4.189).[8]

Occasionally, Langland does point out particular childhood faults, sometimes but not always mentioning parental responsibilities for those faults. For instance, he warns of the danger that can come to a land when a child is king (B.Pr.194–96, C.Pr.204–06). The reference to the kitten *and* the cat in the rat-fable suggests that the kitten is being trained in its harmful behavior by the older and more dangerous cat. Will implies that he himself was a lazy child at his lessons, learning too little Latin in his youth (B.1.141–41α, C.1.139–40). In the C text, Pride's sins begin with disobedience to his parents and to the Church (C.6.15–19). Pride is one of the sins that Charity washes and 'beats out' of youth later in the poem, though 'youth' here may refer to young adulthood rather than childhood proper (B.15.188–92, C.16.328–32). In the confession of the Sins, we also find the comic vignette of the licking Wrath will get if he tells tales in a monastery – 'chalanged . . . as I a child were / And baleised on þe bare ers and no brech bitwene'; conversely, we learn that Covetise began his sinful career as an apprentice, learning his 'lessouns' and his 'donet' of deception from his masters (B.5.172–75, C.6.154–57; A.5.115–28, B.5.199–212, C.6.207–220). Yet even in these references to childish vice, Langland spends little time blaming children themselves for their *faunteltee* or *wantownesse*; he is more interested in triggering compunction in those who have already achieved responsible, adult Inwit.[9]

---

[7] On textual features of this passage, see Wendy Scase, 'Two *Piers Plowman* C-Text Interpolations: Evidence for a Second Textual Tradition,' *N&Q* n.s. 34 (1987): 456–63 and sources cited at p. 457 n. 3. Adducing the story of Heli's sons in discussions of parental responsibilities was commonplace, as Pearsall notes (C.Pr.115n); see for example *Handlyng Synne*, ed. Frederick J. Furnivall, EETS 119, 123 (London, 1901–03), 4919–5044; Bromyard, *Summa Praed.*, s.vv. 'Ab infantia,' § 20, and 'Correctio,' § 27; *Dives and Pauper* 4.10, ed. Priscilla Heath Barnum, EETS 275 (London, 1976), 324. It also had received canonical application to the prelatical duty of maintaining clerical discipline, in X 5.3 (*De Simonia*), c. 31 ('Licet Heli').

[8] On 'vnsittyng soffraunce,' cf. Skeat, 2:xxxiv, and Pearsall, C.3.207n; for connections between sufferance and the larger theme of Patience in the C text, see Lorraine K. Stock, 'Parable, Allegory, History, and *Piers Plowman*,' *YLS* 5 (1991), 151–55.

[9] Proverbial wisdom similarly combines an awareness of the need to discipline children

Langland's general sympathy toward children is sharply curbed in his comments on bastardy. He doesn't worry about the social disadvantages that might attend the state of bastardy, perhaps because those disadvantages were relatively minor, possibly even non-existent in many cases. Studies of medieval English villages suggest that there was little, if any, social or economic stigmatization of bastards in fourteenth-century England, at least in rural communities.[10] There were legal disadvantages to bastardy, of course, in both common and canon law, but such disadvantages would have come into play only in certain contexts, and many bastards may never have run into much practical difficulty on account of their birth.[11] So it need not surprise us if Langland pays little attention to the troubles that beset bastard children. What he does notice, and vigorously objects to, is the fact that bastardy *is* so easily overlooked, usually for covetous motives. This objection is especially strenuous in the C text, which depicts rich male bastards being given dispensations for the priesthood, and rich but illegitimate bondwomen being sought after as wives, even if they are old and unchaste and even when young, beautiful, moral, gentle – but poor! – maidens are available as potential brides (C.5.59–81, 10.254–67).

The high value Langland places on legitimacy can also be seen in his frequent use of the legal term *mulier(e)*; of the fifteen instances of the word cited by the *MED*, six occur in specifically legal contexts, five in *Piers*, two in Lovelich's works, and two in other literary pieces. This emphasis on legitimacy as legally defined has little to do with social snobbery on Langland's part. *Mulerie* – birth within wedlock which gives rights before the king's courts – is important to the poet because it represents love expressed through law. It is thus an appropriate issue to raise, albeit ironically, at the loveless, lawless marriage of Lady Meed (A.2.83, 96, B.2.119, 132, C.2.120, 145); it is even more suitably mentioned, with utter sincerity, in Abraham's explanation of the lawful

with an essentially sympathetic view of their nature; compare Whiting C193–97, C203–04, C213, 217, 229 (positive traits) and B3, C37, C206–07, F421, V37, W436 (negative traits) with those on discipline cited above (n. 2).

[10] Hanawalt, *Ties*, 72–73, 195–96, 212; Zvi Razi, *Life, Marriage and Death in a Medieval Parish: Economy, Society and Demography in Halesowen 1270–1400* (Cambridge, 1980), 64–66. For higher ranks, see Chris Given-Wilson and Alice Curteis, *The Royal Bastards of Medieval England* (London, 1984), 48–51. But see n. 29 below for evidence of negative emotional force to the epithet 'bastard' in at least some social contexts.

[11] On the legal situation of bastards, see Norma Adams, '*Nullius Filius*: A Study of the Exception of Bastardy in the Law Courts of Medieval England,' *University of Toronto Law Journal* 6 (1945–46), 361–84; R. H. Helmholz, 'Bastardy Litigation in Medieval England,' *American Journal of Legal History* 13 (1969), 360–83; and J. L. Barton, 'Nullity of Marriage and Illegitimacy in the England of the Middle Ages,' *Legal History Studies 1972*, Papers Presented to the Legal History Conference, Aberystwyth, 18–21 July 1972, ed. Dafydd Jenkins (Cardiff, 1975), 28–49.

and loving familial qualities of the Trinity (B.16.219, 221, C.18.221, 235; see also Wit's remarks at C.10.209–10). Bastardy, in contrast, offends Langland deeply as a simultaneous scorning of law and corruption of love.

We do find some sympathy for bastard children in one passage, but the sympathy is not based so much on their bastard state as on the unnatural cruelty of their fathers – false beggars who do not marry the women they deal with, who sire bastard children, and then cripple those children so as to make them more effective beggars. Such folk 'lyue nouȝt in loue, ne no lawe holden,' and thus violate the fundamental bonds of human society as established by God (A.8.72–81, B.7.90–99, C.9.166–74). Given the details of Langland's belief in the common notion that 'kynde follows kynde' – i.e., that children take after their parents in the moral realm as well as the physical, and that their nature also reflects the manner of their begetting and upbringing – we can see why he thinks most beggars' bastards will end up following in their parents' footsteps, unless grace intervenes to help them amend:

> Þat oþere gatis [than in wedlock] ben geten for gadelynges ben holden;
> And þat ben fals folk, & fals eires also, foundlynges & leiȝeris,
> Vngracious to gete loue or any good ellis,
> But wandriþ as wolues & wastiþ ȝif þei mowe;
> Aȝens dowel hy don euele, & þe deuil plesen,
> And aftir here deþ day shuln dwelle with þe same
> But ȝif god giue hem grace here to amende.
>   (A.10.209–15, B.9.195–201, C.10.294–300)

Indeed, the C version of the passage on beggars' brats goes so far as to label them 'bastardus, beggares *of kynde*' (C.9.168; my emphasis).[12]

Sexuality

Langland's attitudes toward sexuality are more complex than his treatment of bastardy, education, or childhood in general. Not surprisingly, the poet is caught in a bind that has pinched orthodox

---

[12] A century later, Sir John Fortescue would also have hard words on the *kynde* of bastards, whom he sees as contracting 'corruption and blemish from the sin of [their] progenitors' to a much greater degree than those engendered in the 'lawful and chaste embraces of married couples'; a bastard 'deserves to be called the son of sin rather than the son of sinners.' He quotes a 'proverbium tritum': 'If a bastard be good, it comes to him by accident, that is to say, by special grace; but if he shall be bad, it comes to him by nature.' *De Laudibus Legum Angliae*, ed. and trans. S. B. Chrimes (Cambridge, 1942), 99.

Christian moralists from Paul through Augustine down to the present. On the one hand, sexuality and generation are an aspect of creation, a part of the natural law, and essential to God's plan for multiplying the human race. On the other, they are frequently connected with worldly involvement and lechery, and thus distract the soul from its divine ends. It is this bind that led medieval theologians and canonists to develop the idea of the two principal purposes for marriage, the *officium* of procreation and the *remedium* for carnal concupiscence.[13]

Some moralists resolve the tension between these two aspects of human sexuality by denying or minimizing its positive role, seeing it as a necessary evil, even in the sacrament of marriage itself.[14] They lay great stress on the merits of virginity; when speaking of those already in the married state, they urge a minimal use and less enjoyment of marital sexuality. They draw on rhetoric stemming from the early days of the Church, days when the Second Coming seemed particularly imminent and withdrawal from ordinary earthly involvements particularly appropriate.[15] The withdrawal from worldly attachments continued to be valued within the Church, particularly in the form of the monastic ideal. Since the monasteries contributed greatly to the formation of medieval literary culture, it is hardly surprising that virginity and continence remained objects of high praise in much medieval literature, even in non-monastic writings, sometimes at the expense of the far more common married life.[16] As for sexuality itself, the fear and repugnance shown by many serious religious writers on that topic is stronger still, though we should remember that ecclesiastical attitudes toward

---

[13] Both of these purposes are recognized in Wit's discourse on marriage; cf. Chap. 2, pp. 79–80, 99–102 above. For canonistic and some theological background, see Rudolf Weigand, 'Die Lehre der Kanonisten des 12. und 13. Jahrhunderts von den Ehezwecken,' *Studia Gratiana* 12 (1967), 443–78.

[14] On rigorist and liberal or laxist approaches to marital sexuality, see the magisterial survey of John T. Noonan, Jr., *Contraception: A History of Its Treatment by the Catholic Theologians and Canonists*, enlarged ed. (Cambridge, 1986), 266–300 and *passim*; Thomas N. Tentler, *Sin and Confession on the Eve of the Reformation* (Princeton, 1977), 162–232; Brundage, *Law, Sex, and Christian Society in Medieval Europe* (Chicago, 1987), 364–69, 447–53, 503–09; Pierre J. Payer, *The Bridling of Desire: Views of Sex in the Later Middle Ages* (Toronto, 1993); and, with discussion of literary reflexes, Henry A. Kelly, *Love and Marriage in the Age of Chaucer* (Ithaca, 1975), 245–85.

[15] On attitudes toward sexuality in the social contexts of early Christianity, see Peter Brown, *The Body and Society: Men, Women and Sexual Renunciation in Early Christianity* (New York, 1988), Stevan L. Davies, *The Revolt of the Widows: The Social World of the Apocryphal Acts* (Carbondale, 1980), and Rosemary Ruether, 'Mothers of the Church: Ascetic Women in the Late Patristic Age,' in *Women of Spirit: Female Leadership in the Jewish and Christian Traditions*, ed. Rosemary Ruether and Eleanor McLaughlin (New York, 1979).

[16] However, as Jean Leclercq has reminded us, monastic culture was also quite capable of generating eloquent statements in praise of marriage, a number of which accept a loving, temperate marital sexuality without difficulty; he also points out similar views expressed

marriage and sexuality were not always completely adopted by medieval lay culture.[17] Langland has been deeply influenced by the ecclesiastical culture of his day, perhaps by monastic culture in particular.[18] He clearly recognizes and accepts the traditional priority of virginity over continent widowhood, and continent widowhood over marriage, as the fruits on the Tree of Charity demonstrate. Unlike many monastic authors, however, he is not writing solely or primarily for an audience of fellow celibates. Whatever Langland's own 'grade' of chastity may have been, he is interested in the problems of people in all grades, and interested in how they can do well in the vocations in which they were called – the great majority of which are non-celibate callings. He does not counsel virginity for all or many; his audience is simply too wide for that to be a practical suggestion, even if he thought it desirable. Indeed, he reminds his readers early on that 'chastite wiþoute charite worþ cheynide in helle' (A.1.162, B.1.194, C.1.184). Langland's vision has strong eschatological elements, but his recommended response to the coming doom is not so much a change in one's external status or craft (though that may happen for some) as an internal change of contrition and growth in love.

Besides avoiding strong negative language about non-virginal states of life, Langland displays a genuinely positive attitude toward sexuality in its proper time and place. As noted in Chapter 2, the C text associates

---

by non-monastic writers. See *Le Mariage vu par les moines au XII*ᵉ *siècle* (Paris, 1983), also available as *Monks on Marriage: A Twelfth-Century View* (New York, 1981).

Even the notorious Stoic maxim made familiar by Jerome, 'The too ardent lover of his wife is an adulterer,' could be explicated less pessimistically than its surface meaning might suggest, as a warning against treating one's wife merely as a depersonalized sex-object rather than against marital sexuality in general. Thus, Thomas of Chobham's widely-read manual for confessors defines the *ardentior amator uxoris* as one who uses his wife day and night as if she were a mattress (*quasi pro culcitra*). See *Thomae de Chobham Summa Confessorum*, ed. F. Broomfield (Louvain, 1968), 335. A generation earlier, in a similar vein, Egbert of Schönau had explained that the conjugal act need not be sinful, if performed with a temperance that showed reverence for God in one's wife ('si sobrie et temperanter cum illa est, et per omnia Dei reverentiam in ipsa custodit'; *Sermo V Contra Catharos*, PL 195:29). Cf. Payer, *Bridling of Desire*, 120–29.

[17] Georges Duby demonstrates this nonconformity for the noble classes of 11th- and 12th-century France, in *Medieval Marriage: Two Models from Twelfth-Century France*, trans. Elborg Forster (Baltimore, 1978) and *The Knight, the Lady and the Priest: The Making of Modern Marriage in Medieval France*, trans. Barbara Bray (New York, 1983). Jean-Louis Flandrin argues that disregard for several important elements of the Church's teaching on conjugal sexuality was common throughout the laity in the Middle Ages and later; see 'Contraception, mariage et relations amoureuses dans l'Occident chrétien,' *Annales: Économies Sociétés Civilisations* 24 (1969), 1370–90.

[18] As Morton Bloomfield argues, in *Piers Plowman as a Fourteenth-century Apocalypse* (New Brunswick, NJ, 1961), 68–97. See also John M. Bowers, *The Crisis of Will in Piers Plowman* (Washington, 1986), 21–23.

'lossumnesse abedde' with morally desirable brides and calls well-regulated conjugal intercourse 'godes werk.' Near the end of both B and C, Will's memories of his and Kit's lost *bedbourde* are couched in what appear to be genuinely affectionate, nostalgic terms, albeit with strong overtones of humorous self-deprecation (B.20.193–98, C.22.193–98; see below, pp. 209–12).

This is not to say that the poem presents sexual attraction only in positive terms. One need merely consider the various pairs of lemans scattered across its passus to see that Langland can attach positive or negative values to the lover-beloved relationship. On the one hand, we have Holy Church and Leautee, Kynde and Anima, Patience and Love, and Peace and Love. On the other, we have the priests' lemans maintained by Meed, Sloth lying abed with his leman, the lovely ladies and their leman knights who are felled by Death in the last passus, and Life's taking of Fortune as leman some fifty lines later. While most of these couples are allegorical figures, it is difficult to see how Langland could give some of them negative value if he viewed the relationship of lovers in a totally positive light, and vice versa. (I am not suggesting that Langland thinks of his positive lemans as engaging in sex, allegorical or otherwise, though such activity is clearly present among his negative examples. *Lemman*, for him, would appear to connote mutual desire and commitment, as well as a similarity in kind; but if the couple's kind is a wicked one, their desire is likely to lead to lecherous behavior. Such behavior may be literal, as with the priests' lemans and the bastards they conceive, or allegorical, as with Life and Fortune who beget the *gadelyng* Sloth.)

Indeed, Langland sees the dangers of misused sexuality quite clearly. Condemnations of the lustful occur throughout the poem – from lecherous lords and ladies, to incontinent clerics, to wanton minstrels and beggars, to Haukyn and his lights o' love, to married couples who 'work out of time,' to the metaphorical whoredom of false leeches and lawyers. Part of the case against Meed is that, besides being allegorically promiscuous herself, she encourages and defends literal promiscuity among the nobility and the clergy, and teaches wantonness to wives and widows in general. Although Lechery has only four lines in the AB Confession of the Sins, the C text expands those lines with Haukyn's admission of sexual 'work' at all seasons, 'as leef in lente as out of lente, alle tymes ylyche'; moreover, it adds new material on the deliberate use of titillation, baudery, sorcery, and force to achieve one's sexual objects, on seeking only sex and not love, and on taking pleasure in lecherous tales after losing 'þat kynde' through old age (A.5.54–57, B.5.71–74, C.6.170–95; cf. B.13.342–53).

Besides intentional abuses like these, there are the natural risks of human sexuality – Langland recognizes its power, especially in the young, and its capacity to overcome Reason if the will is not properly formed. Both Wit and *concupiscentia carnis* associate strong sexual urges with being 'yong and yeep,' with having one's 'wepene yet kene' (B.9.185, C.10.284; B.11.18, C.11.180); the wind of the Flesh attacks the Tree of Charity 'in flouryng tyme' (B.16.31, C.18.35). This sexual force is parallel in some ways to the wantonness of children who lack Inwit, since it is in a sense 'natural' to adolescents and young adults. However, it is not excusable in the way that children's wantonness is excusable. In fact, when Imaginatif rebukes Will for misspending his life up to 'myddel age' (presumably referring to the dalliance with Fortune and her maidens), it is in terms of Will's 'wilde wantownesse whiles [he] yong were' (B.12.6–7). Sexuality without *mesure* – inordinate, indiscriminate, out of time or place – is a genuine danger, especially for the young. Fortunately, the sexual drive can be moderated or channeled by lawful and loving marriage, in which these post-lapsarian natural urges are directed to their proper ends. As Wit puts it in C: 'whil þou art ȝong an ȝep and thy wepene kene / Awreke the þerwith on wyfyng, for godes werk y holde hit' (C.10.284–85).[19]

Looked at this way, of course, marriage is indeed the *remedium* spoken of by the theologians and canonists, desirable as a cure for a problem rather than as a good in itself – to modern audiences, one of the less attractive features of the medieval view of marriage. As we have seen, Langland explicitly acknowledges the remedial character of marriage in the B and C versions of Wit's speech, and hints at it in A; given his general orthodoxy, it is highly unlikely that he would even think of denying that character. Nonetheless, this acknowledgment need not be taken as a sign that he looks at marriage in a negative or condescending way, as having a merely passive prophylactic value. He spends much more time stressing the *officium* and active virtues of the sacrament – its

---

[19] Flandrin argues that the folk traditions of medieval peasant culture could have naturally encouraged the timing of sexual activity according to the seasons of the calendar or of one's life, analogous to choosing the proper times for various types of agricultural work; *Un temps pour embrasser: aux origines de la morale sexuelle occidentale (VIᵉ–XIᵉ siècle)* (Paris, 1983), 153–58. Langland's comparison of marital sowing 'out of time' to a servant sowing fallow ground against his lord's bidding (C.10.215–18) may similarly reflect a countryman's 'sens du temps.'

Douglas Moffat offers a general linguistic – rather than agricultural or literary – context for medieval English notions about sexual pleasure, both positive and negative, in 'Rage, Play, and Foreplay in Middle English Literature,' *NM* 94 (1993), 167–84. Moffat concludes by glancing at developments in medieval theological, canonistic, and medical views on sexual pleasure, and suggesting that the linguistic evidence suggests a wider 'interest in sexual pleasure in the later Middle Ages. . .than we may have imagined' (181).

role in the production of holy souls, the grace it confers on those in the married state, the way it simultaneously expresses both love and law. Aside from his insistence on timely sex, he doesn't seem to have worried very much about the too-ardent loving of one's spouse that Chaucer's Parson mentions. The marriages that trouble Langland are those that are love*less*, cold, avaricious, strife-bound, adulterous, or lax in family discipline.[20]

But the distinction between good sexuality within marriage at the proper times and bad sexuality otherwise is not the sum of Langland's thinking on the subject. He also seems to have been concerned about the fact that this natural element of human nature, an element which has divinely established ends and which functions perfectly well in the animal kingdom, should be the source of imperfection and sin for so many human beings. And his concern is strong enough for him to spend some 120-odd lines near the end of the third dream on Will's puzzlement over the problem. Having been set by Kynde to gaze about the Mountain (C: Mirror) of Middle-earth during his inner dream, Will turns to consider sexuality in the natural realm. He finds it quite admirable, especially in the reasonable, temperate quality of animal breeding.[21]

The model of animal restraint in sexual matters had been offered by Jerome, *Adv. Jov.* 1.49 (*PL* 23:293–94), whence Lombard and Gratian incorporate it into the *Sentences* 4.31.6 and the *Decretum* C.32 q.4 c.5, along with the dictum on the too-ardent lover of his wife. The model especially stresses animal abstinence during pregnancy: 'Surely, those who say that they have had intercourse with their wives for the sake of the commonwealth and the human race, and to procreate children, should at least imitate the beasts, and afterward, when the wife's womb

---

[20] Intramarital lust could be among the sins included in Meed's marriage charter, since lechery is among the properties settled on Meed and False. Such lechery may also be referred to in B.2.98 (Meed and False will 'breden as Burgh swin,' a phrase not in A or C), but if so, it is as closely associated with gluttony as with ardent passion, since the 'breding' occurs after Meed and False have stuffed themselves into stupefaction. On possible glosses for *breden* here, see n. 22 below.
[21] Langland's association of the positive use of sexuality with Kynde and Reason may derive in part from medieval traditions of Nature, Genius, and the 'good Venus'; on these traditions, see especially George D. Economou, *The Goddess Natura in Medieval Literature* (Cambridge, 1972); 'The Character Genius in Alan de Lille, Jean de Meun, and John Gower,' *ChauR* 4 (1970), 203–10; 'The Two Venuses and Courtly Love,' in *In Pursuit of Perfection: Courtly Love in Medieval Literature*, ed. Joan M. Ferrante and George D. Economou (Port Washington, NY, 1975), 17–50; and Jane Chance Nitzsche, *The Genius Figure in Antiquity and the Middle Ages* (New York, 1975). On Reason as natural law – the transcendent order of Creation – in the passage, see John A. Alford, 'The Idea of Reason in *Piers Plowman*,' in *Medieval English Studies Presented to George Kane*, ed. Edward Donald Kennedy et al. (Woodbridge, 1988), 210–14.

has begun to swell, let them show themselves not as lovers to their wives but as husbands, lest they ruin the children.' Or, to put it in Will's terms:

> And after cours of concepcion noon took kepe of oober,
> As whan þei hadde ryde in Rotey tyme anoon reste þei after;
> Males drowen hem to males al mornyng by hemselue,
> And femelles to femelles ferded and drowe.
> Ther ne was cow ne cowkynde þat conceyued hadde
> That wolde bere after bole, ne boor after sowe;
> Boþe hors and houndes and alle oþere beestes
> Medled no3t wiþ hir makes, saue man allone.
>
> (B.11.337–44, C.13.144–52)

Beasts and birds, unlike humans, observe the due seasons for mating. They know *mesure* instinctively, 'in etynge, in drynkynge and in engendrynge of kynde' (B.11.336, C.13.143).[22] Humans, on the other hand, often surfeit themselves on sex, just as they do in food and drink. After marvelling at the sensibleness of animal breeding and at other natural 'selkouþes,' Will turns to Reason and, with characteristic impatience, rebukes him for not governing humans as well as beasts: 'I haue wonder in my wit, þat witty art holden, / Why þow ne sewest man and his make þat no mysfeet hem folwe' (B.11.374–75, C.13.183–85).

Not surprisingly, Reason responds by chiding Will for his lack of sufferance, especially inappropriate here, where Will is impatient with Reason's (and God's) own sufferance of human behavior – rather like Jonah at Nineveh. Reason warns the Dreamer to consider his own imperfections before accusing others – perhaps as a reminder that human beings, unlike animals, have the gift of free will to *choose* their

---

[22] There are only a few places in the poem where animal sexuality has negative connotations: e.g., the coupling of 'wilde bestis wiþ wehe' to which the fornication of dishonest beggars is compared (A.8.73–75, B.7.91–93). There may also be a hint of willful sexuality in the B-text use of the 'make wehee' phrase to describe Reason's potentially unruly horse (B.4.23), which J. A. Burrow has argued may represent the human will, in need of saddling and bridling in order to be ridden by Reason; see 'Reason's Horse,' *YLS* 4 (1990): 139–44. As Pierre J. Payer has suggested, medieval writers found the image of the unruly horse particularly apt for discussions of post-lapsarian concupiscence; see Payer, *Bridling of Desire*, 59–60, 145.

The 'breeding' town pigs of B.2.98 may not in fact signify lechery but slothful or gluttonous behavior. Although Skeat, Bennett, Goodridge, and Schmidt take *breden* in this line to mean 'breed' (*MED breden* v.[3]), Donaldson's translation of B interprets it as 'grow portly,' a gloss based on *MED breden* v.(2) and followed by George Kane's ' "become broad in the beam, fat" . . . from the abundance of swill' ('A New Translation of the B Text of *Piers Plowman*,' *YLS* 7 [1993], 133–34). Lister Matheson suggests to me that an even better translation would be 'spread out, sprawl, wallow,' since *MED breden* v.(2) does not connote obesity so much as things (e.g., arms, boughs, hair, feathers, etc.) spreading or extending spatially.

actions. Yet he also seems to suggest that men cannot avoid imperfections, presumably because of their fallen nature:

> For is no creature vnder crist can formen hymseluen,
> And if a man my3te make laklees hymself
> Ech a lif wolde be laklees, leue þow noon oþer. . . .
> For man was maad of swich a matere he may no3t wel asterte
> That som tyme hym bitit to folwen his kynde;
> Caton acordeþ þerwiþ: *Nemo sine crimine viuit.*
>
> (B.11.389–91, 402–04, C.13.206–11)

Given the overall context of Reason's answer to Will's question, it is likely that the word 'kynde' refers specifically to 'sexual nature, sexuality,' as it does in Lechery's C-text confession (C.6.193) and in such ME phrases as 'werkes of kynde' or 'to don kynde' (cf. *MED*, s.v. *kinde*, n., 14a). Thus, the term does not carry the strongly positive connotations that it had in Wit's discourse, where the definition of Kynde as the creating God of Nature emphasized the divinely intended features of material and human nature. Instead we see human nature here in its post-lapsarian imperfection, tending to work against the good unless it receives the grace to mend its ways.[23]

Reason's answer marks a critical turn in the poem: Will is shamed by the rebuke, and his shame triggers his waking into the outer dream. Perhaps he has finally recognized himself and his faults, or at least some of them. His shame may also be figurally related to Adam and Eve's shame in the Garden, which Augustine had explained as being a part of the punishment for their disobedience along with the frequent disobedience of the genital organs to reason.[24] Once back in the outer dream, Will immediately encounters Imaginatif, who provides a relatively authoritative resolution to the problems raised in the third dream as a whole, especially those pertaining to the salvation of the righteous heathen and the respective merits of Clergy, Kind Wit, and Faith as ways of understanding how to do well.

We might think that the subject of natural sexuality was closed; Reason has clearly warned Will off and there seems to be no absolute need to return to the topic. Yet Imaginatif brings it up again, and Will also includes it in his brief recapitulation of Imaginatif's key points at the

---

[23] Hugh White gives a sensitive discussion of the 'problematic quality of the vision' of Middle-earth in *Nature and Salvation in Piers Plowman* (Cambridge, 1988), 71–78.

[24] *De Civ. Dei* 14.15–19 (CC 48:436–42). Pamela Gradon suggests that the vision of Nature here 'might reflect the late medieval debate on Pelagianism,' and thus be connected with the much longer Trajan sequence; see '*Trajanus Redivivus*: Another Look at Trajan in *Piers Plowman*,' in *Middle English Studies Presented to Norman Davis in Honour of His Seventieth Birthday*, ed. Douglas Gray and E. G. Stanley (Oxford, 1983), 112–13.

start of the fourth dream. Even so, Imaginatif's 'answer' to the problem of human sexuality is less of an explanation than we or Will might have hoped for. He does not really explain *why* Reason teaches sexual *mesure* to animals but not to mankind; as with the salvation of righteous pagans, he is forced to admit that the details of God's creative design are not always knowable. Using the term Kynde once again as Wit did – to mean God the Creator, acting through Nature – Imaginatif asserts that Kynde alone knows all 'þe whyes' that Will seeks after so persistently. Clergy and Kind Wit

> ne knew neuere þe cause,
> Ac kynde knoweþ þe cause hymself, no creature ellis.
> He is þe pies patron and putteþ it in hir ere
> That þere þe þorn is þikkest to buylden and brede;
> And kynde kenned þe pecok to cauken in swich a wise.
> Kynde kenned Adam to knowe hise pryue membres,
> And tauȝte hym and Eue to helien hem wiþ leues.
> Lewed men many tymes maistres þei apposen
> Why Adam hiled noȝt first his mouþ þat eet þe Appul
> Raþer þan his likame alogh; lewed asken þus clerkes.
> Kynde knoweþ whi he dide so, ac no clerk ellis.
>
> (B.12.225–35; cf. C.14.159–67)

Why animal sexuality functions as it does, and why human sexuality is a source of shame after a Fall through gluttony and disobedience, are divine mysteries which even Kind Wit and Clergy cannot entirely explain. Animal behavior is not so much something for us to understand as to use for moral 'ensamples' like those expounded in B.12.236–69 and C.14.168–90. But if Imaginatif does not give Will a full explanation of the differences between human and animal mating, he does at least affirm the operation of God's will in human sexuality, as in human salvation: 'Kynde knoweþ þe cause hymself'; 'Kynde . . . contreuede hit furst of his corteyse wille' (B.12.226; C.14.160). By giving this affirmative statement to an authoritative figure in the poem, Langland acknowledges the importance – despite the sometimes baffling qualities – of the sexual and procreative dimension of human experience.[25]

Imaginatif's other principal topics – the value of learning, the salvation of the unbaptized, and the related issue of works vs. grace – may or may

---

[25] The association of the divine 'contreuance' of sexuality with divine courtesy in C.14.160 is reminiscent of the themes of courtesy and rightly-used sexuality in *Cleanness* – the 'cortays' command of God to all creatures to go forth and multiply after the Flood (512–28), the 'kynde crafte' and sweet *drwry* of the 'play of paramorez' instituted by the Creator (697–708). See also A. V. C. Schmidt, '*Kynde Craft* and the *Play of Paramorez*: Natural and Unnatural Love in *Purity*,' in *Genres, Themes, and Images in English Literature from the Fourteenth to the Fifteenth Century*, ed. Piero Boitani and Anna Torti (Tübingen, 1988), 116–24.

not have impinged directly on the lives of most devout lay Englishmen in the fourteenth century,[26] but the management of sexuality according to God's will certainly would have done so. Simply recalling the important procreative ends and obligations of marriage should suggest the weight likely to be given to sexual behavior, whether good or bad, and late medieval confessors' manuals confirm its significance from an official point of view.[27] Langland found the topic important too, though not merely because of the sinful potential of sexuality or its affective power. Sex within marriage is the literal source of those who do well; they have to be born before they can be baptized or learn to live by God's law. On the other hand, human sexuality can be indulged in to excess, without the tempering force of *mesure*, and can thus give rise to those who do evil, 'gadelynges, . . . fals folk, & fals eires also, foundlynges & lei3eris' (A.10.209–10, B.9.195–96, C.10.294–95).

Because of the poet's concern over such issues, Will's third dream focuses on generation and sexuality at several points: we have Wit's speech on Kynde, the creation of mankind, and marriage; Will's own temptation to carnal and material excess in his encounter with Fortune and her two maidens, *concupiscentia carnis* and *covetise-of-eyen*; and finally, Will's interest in animal reproduction near the end of the dream. The sexual and procreative dimension of human life is not as central to Langland's poem as, say, truth or faith or the reformation of the will, but its nearly universal influence, its affective force, and its potential for good or evil all combine to make it a significant factor in the well-lived life of ordinary Christians, and thus a significant element in Will's third vision.

One last aspect of sexuality in the poem needs to be mentioned here, and that is its use in metaphorical contexts in the poem. We have

---

[26] Gordon Whatley convincingly argues that the theological issues raised by the story of Trajan would indeed have interested at least one group of devout laymen: the 'growing numbers of people who were disillusioned or disgusted with the ecclesiastical establishment and eager to find more meaningful ways to serve God and man.' See 'The Uses of Hagiography: The Legend of Pope Gregory and the Emperor Trajan in the Middle Ages,' *Viator* 15 (1984), 60–61.

[27] Tentler observes that the 'explicit concern and detailed analysis [of sexual sins in marriage] on the part of those who wrote on confession prove that they themselves considered this one of the most basic moral issues' (*Sin and Confession*, xix). In his stimulating *History of Sexuality* (Vol. 1: Introduction), Michel Foucault speculates that the confessional anatomization of motive and action may have eventually led to the modern hyper-awareness of sex, the body, personal relations, and the self, and even helped provide a much more nuanced language in which to conceive and talk about them (trans. Robert Hurley [New York, 1978], 58–70). The interest which Will's vision of nature may have had for Langland's audience is suggested by the fact that it receives one of the seven major *nota* signs in Bodl. MS Laud Misc. 581, as John Norton-Smith points out in *William Langland* (Leiden, 1983), 50–51.

already glanced briefly at several pairs of allegorical lemans, and noted that Langland makes sexual activity part of the allegorical figure in some of the negative pairs – Sloth lying abed with his leman, or Life and Fortune begetting *gadelyng* offspring. In presenting positive allegorical lemans, he focuses on the mutual commitment and similarity between the two partners rather than on any sexual behavior. More negative, and more explicitly sexual, are the metaphorical whoredoms that appear in a number of places in the poem. The most obvious example is Lady Meed, judged rightly and finally as a whore, common as a cartway, and available to all for the right price. But other instances of metaphorical prostitution can be found in the poem as well. The C text explicitly connects whores and false physicians, both of whom 'asken here huyre ar thei hit haue deserued' (C.3.301). Such *pre manibus* payment is the essence of Meed, according to Conscience; later, we learn that lawyers who insist on *pre manibus* payments shall have the least forgiveness in Piers's pardon from Truth (C.9.44–45). Considering Langland's repeated linking of lawyers and lechery, especially in the church courts where divorces and adulteries could be condoned for meed, we are clearly justified in lumping false lawyers together with false leeches, whores, and Meed herself, all of them intent on 'arse-winnings' of the literal or the figural kind.[28]

Langland clearly knows the emotional force of defamatory sexual epithets like 'queynt comune hore!' In contemporary English society, such accusations could easily lead to blows, the courts, and even murder.[29] Employing a time-honored tactic of abuse, he exploits the power of such language to emphasize the moral offensiveness of corrupt elements within society. Yet his point goes beyond merely indicating the general heinousness of certain activities by calling them whorish. For

[28] On the phrase *pre manibus*, see John A. Alford, 'More Unidentified Quotations in *Piers Plowman*,' *MP* 81 (1984), 283–85.

[29] Cases of defamation, at times with sexual content, may be found in ecclesiastical court records, episcopal registers, and visitation returns; some striking but relatively late examples appear among the cases collected by James Raine, *Depositions and Other Ecclesiastical Proceedings from the Courts of Durham Extending from 1311 to the Reign of Elizabeth*, SS 21 (London, 1845) and Paul Hair, *Before the Bawdy Court: Selections from Church Court and Other Records . . . 1300–1800* (London, 1972).
Zvi Razi tells of a family feud in the 1320's, based on a property dispute, involving repeated assaults between brothers, and between a son and mother, and the slinging of names like 'bastard' and 'bytch' back and forth (*Life, Marriage and Death*, 69). P. M. Kean points out literary and extraliterary uses of the abusive colloquial epithet 'stronge hoore' in the 14th and 15th centuries, in *Chaucer and the Making of English Poetry*, 2 vols. (London, 1972), 1:19–20. The suddenness and anger with which Chaucer's pilgrims *quite* each other's remarks also suggests, by way of fiction, how sensitive medieval egos were to real or supposed slurs; this predilection for antagonistic discourse is explored in detail in 'Conventions of a Narrative War,' Part Two of Carl Lindahl's study, *Earnest Games: Folkloric Patterns in the Canterbury Tales* (Bloomington, 1987), 71–155.

Langland, false lawyers, false leeches, whores, and Meed herself are all odious in the same way; they pervert and prostitute what should be highly positive elements of human life: the law, the healing arts, the act of *kynde*, and just reward.

Marriage

Most of Langland's comments on marriage as an institution or on the actual making of marriages occur in the five passus discussed in the previous chapters. However, there are some aspects of the poet's attitudes toward marriage which we have not yet examined, and this section will look briefly at three of them, namely his treatments of arranged marriages, love matches, and clandestine marriages. First, it is worth considering Langland's understanding of the proper relationship between individual choice and familial involvement in the decisions that lead to marriage. When Wit urges that love be the main bond between the marrying pair, he is not merely insisting on their consent to the marriage. The poet takes this latter criterion for granted, even in the negative examples he gives. Simony and Civil approve Meed's marriage with False after seeing 'hir boþer wille' (B.2.67, C.2.67).[30] At several points, Wit's counsel against covetous marriages is addressed directly to the couples themselves. For Langland, personal consent is essential to a marriage, whether good or bad; it would have been hard for him to have believed otherwise given the sacramental theology of his time. But consent to marriage is not the same as love, and it need not be arrived at solely through one's own evaluation of possible marriage partners. Indeed, the poet accepts – even assumes – the contemporary social fact that such consent may well be preceded by the advice and negotiations of one's parents, friends, and allies.

Langland has no objection to arranged marriages in themselves, as long as the couple agrees to the union and are of like *kyndes*, and as long as the motives for the marriage are primarily those of love rather than profit (for the couple or their families). The B text's description of the divine establishment of marriage makes it clear that the ideal marriage can indeed involve a 'mene persone,' whose original model is the fatherly will and friendly counsel of God himself, the Prime Matchmaker and First Witness of the sacrament:

---

[30] In the context of this passage, parodying ecclesiastical approval of a marriage, the phrase must refer to the couple, and not to some other pair of people, such as False and Favel, say.

The wif was maad the wye for to helpe werche,
And þus was wedlok ywroȝt wiþ a mene persone,
First by þe fadres wille and þe frendes conseille,
And siþenes by assent of hemself as þei two myȝte acorde;
And þus was wedlok ywroȝt and god hymself it made.
In erþe þe heuene is; hymself was þe witnesse. (B.9.115-20)

Where things go wrong with arranged marriages is when family or friends abuse the role they have in the matrimonial decision. Meed's marriage was evidently arranged by her wicked sire Wrong/False/Favel, with the helpful 'ledyng' and 'brocage' of his comrades-in-evil Favel, Guile, and Liar, who have 'enchaunted' and 'bi-gon' Meed into consenting to the marriage, even though it disparages the lady by marrying her to a bastard. Some of Wit's sharpest accusations are leveled at those who marry their children 'at meschief,' who have 'maugre of hir mariages [and] marie so hir children [as the Sethites did],' and who 'ȝiven a ȝong wenche to an old feble' or 'ȝeue her childrene / For coueytise of catel and connynge chapmen' (A.10.181; B.9.158; A.10.187, B.9.166; C.10.254-55). But when parents or guardians consider the spiritual as well as material welfare of their offspring, then arranged marriages and marital advice to children can in fact be perfectly fitting, especially in light of the poet's statements on the duty of people in authority to look after the physical needs and moral guidance of their dependents.

Although Langland accepts the social custom of families arranging marriages for their younger members, as long as the motives for those marriages are spiritually well-ordered, he also has a certain sympathy for love-matches, even when they run counter to familial advice and negotiations. Evidence for this sympathy can be found in Patience's simile for that rare rich man who gives up all his wealth to follow Poverty:

And as a mayde for mannes loue hire moder forsakeþ,
Hir fader and alle hire frendes, and folweþ hir make (C: and goth
    forth with here paramours) –
Muche is þat maide to loue of a man þat swich oon takeþ,
Moore þan a maiden is þat is maried þoruȝ brocage
As by assent of sondry parties and siluer to boote,
Moore for coueitise of catel þan kynde loue of boþe (C: of þe mariage).
                                            (B.14.265-70, C.16.105-10)

Of course, the very rarity of rich men who give up all their goods to follow Poverty suggests that maidens who forsake their family to follow their true loves are also quite rare, and that the normal state of affairs is to go along with one's mother, father, and friends. Given Langland's concern elsewhere for humility and obedience of children to parents, I suspect that this simile of world-well-lost elopement is not intended as advice for actual daughters trying to decide whether to obey their parents or follow their paramours, with the possible exception of cases where the parental negotiations are aimed solely at an *unkynde*, covetous union. If the simile recommends any actual marital behaviors at all (after its primary recommendation of holy poverty), those recommendations seem to be addressed more to the occasional husband whose wife has married him against her family's will and at the usual familial costs, reminding him how much he should treasure her love and her sacrifice.

Lest we view this hint of a 'romantic' sympathy in Langland's outlook too sentimentally, let us note an additional implication it carries. The passage is clearly related to Adam's words in Genesis 2:24, 'Wherefore a man shall leave father and mother, and shall cleave to his wife,' but it reverses the genders of that line so that it is the wife who is leaving family to follow her husband. This reversal (like those seen in the Books of Tobias and Ruth) reflects the virilocality or husband-centeredness of its cultural setting. Recent historical studies have shown that many medieval Englishwomen who married did in fact break most of their legal and economic ties with their natal families and turned to their husbands for such social support, whereas married men usually retained strong ties with their blood kin.[31] In Langland's image of a husband treasuring his wife's willingness to follow him for love, we can see clear traces of a pattern that has continued to influence Western marriage practices, the pattern that gives priority to the interests and social network of the husband over those of the wife. A saintly rich man may metaphorically follow after Lady Poverty, as did Francis of Assisi, but in doing so he would be more readily compared (at least for Langland) to 'a mayde [who] for mannes loue hire moder forsakeþ, / Hir fader and alle hire frendes, and folweþ hir make.' For Langland, as for his culture, marriage is husband-centered, even in its most romantic manifestations.

One last observation on Langland's presentation of the making of marriages: he never mentions clandestine marriage as a moral or legal

---

[31] Judith M. Bennett, 'The Tie That Binds: Peasant Marriages and Peasant Families in Late Medieval England,' *Journal of Interdisciplinary History* 15 (1984), 111–29. Virilocal marriage was explicitly supported by the pastoral handbooks; if a husband moved or was exiled, his wife was said to sin if she did not follow him, except when he wanted her with him as a companion in crime. See Chobham, *Summa Confessorum*, 340–41 ('In quibus casibus debeat mulier sequi virum suum'). De Burgh says that the husband must follow the wife if she moves for a *necessary* cause, but that she must follow him for any cause, unless he wants her to lead a sinful life with him; if he is a vagabond or minstrel, she need only follow him if she knew of his wandering life at their marriage (*Pup. Oc.*, 130r).

problem. Take the case of the maid who follows her mate. Although the text does not specifically refer to a secret marriage, it is hard to see how the requirements of the banns and marriage in the woman's parish could be fulfilled if her parents were powerful and opposed the union. Yet the poet gives no sign of viewing such a marriage as somehow tainted by the necessary secrecy of elopement.[32] When Langland attacks those who make false divorces, he may well be aware that collusive claims of prior clandestine marriage might be used to procure such divorces, but his attack remains focused on the vices of greed and deceit infecting the makers of divorce rather than straying to the side-issue of clandestine marriages themselves. When he speaks of false beggars who 'lyue nou3t in loue, ne no lawe holden / [And] wedde no womman þat hy wiþ delen,' there is no hint that these beggars have deceived women into sex by false clandestine vows, although ecclesiastical authorities recognized that some men offered clandestine marriage vows in bad faith simply to have their sexual way with women (A.8.72–73, B.7.90–91, C.9.166–67).[33] And we have already seen that the marriages most vigorously attacked by Langland are fully public affairs – Meed's marriage and the marriages made across age-lines for 'covetise of catel.'

It would appear that for Langland, clandestinity is not a serious enough moral and legal problem to warrant criticism in his poem. A couple either is married, for good or for ill and with the associated obligations to God and each other, or they are not. Certainly, obedience to the Church would call for the rules of publicity and solemnity to be observed, and Langland is highly unlikely to have favored clandestine marriages. Nonetheless, as with too-ardent marital loving, he is less worried about hot or hasty sins within the structure of marriage than about the cold, deliberate sins of unkindness and greed.

---

[32] The power of parental control to keep a woman from her desired spouse can be seen in the constraints imposed on Margery Paston by her mother before she was able to have her secret vows to Richard Calle recognized and in the violence used against Elizabeth Paston in connection with her marital wishes.

See Norman Davis, ed., *The Paston Letters and Papers of the Fifteenth Century*, 2 vols. (Oxford, 1971–76), nos. 203, 332, 446, 861 (1:341–44, 541–43; 2:31–33, 498–500); Ann S. Haskell, 'The Paston Women on Marriage in Fifteenth-Century England,' *Viator* 4 (1973), 466–68; and Colin Richmond, 'The Pastons Revisited: Marriage and the Family in Fifteenth Century England,' *Bulletin of the Institute of Historical Research* 58 (1985), 31–36.

Different tactics were employed by the family of Agnes Nakerer, in York around 1407, who tried to supersede a clandestine marriage between her and a travelling minstrel by putting her through a marriage ceremony with a more suitable groom. However, the minstrel, John Kent, successfully brought a suit of pre-contract for Agnes, despite harsh attacks on his own and his witnesses' personal character. It seems likely that Agnes too had to face actual or threatened violence from her family, and eventually forsake them to follow her chosen *make*. See R. H. Helmholz, *Marriage Litigation in Medieval England* (London, 1974), 133.

[33] X 4.1.26 (on which see Helmholz, *Marriage Litigation*, 42–44); Powicke and Cheney 87; de Burgh, *Pup. Oc.*, 126v.

Family Affections

The basic picture of ideal family affection in *Piers* is a conventional combination of loving obedience and wise governance in suitable balance, together with such associated traits as humility and filial dread, mutual buxumness among siblings, leal and benign speech within the family, and an active care for the spiritual and material welfare of the dependent members of the household. We have already examined the relations of parents and children in some detail, but other familial bonds remain to be considered: the conjugal bond uniting husband and wife and the affectionate ties between siblings.

In comparison to the more focused treatments of the making of marriages, the married state itself, and sexuality, references to family affections in *Piers Plowman* are relatively brief and scattered. However, taken together, they add up to a significant amount of material, much of which is essential or important to Langland's explanation of the Redemption. Before we proceed to examine that material, a few words on language and procedure will be useful.

First, the term 'affection(s)' in the following pages will include both positive and negative affective relationships between people, as well as the behavior that expresses those affective relations. Second, many of the references discussed below pertain to allegorical figures, and function mainly as a convenient shorthand for abstract relationships: the five wits that protect Anima are brothers and the sons of Inwit; Wit and Study, and Clergy and Scripture, are wedded couples; and so on. In order to have a wide range of family references for analysis, I have chosen to look at allegorical characters (e.g., Wit and Study, the daughters of God) as well as those which are more broadly figural (e.g., Will, Piers), typical (e.g., Glutton, Tom Stowue), or literal (e.g., the contemporary families that marry their children 'at meschief'). The decision carries some interpretive risks, since a poet's use of familial metaphors in figurative contexts need not accord with his beliefs about actual families. But I find no great dissonances between the figurative family relations among some of Langland's abstractions and the behaviors depicted in his more naturalistic family images or scenes, and the risk seems worthwhile for the sake of the fuller picture it allows.[34]

[34] For further analyses of the gendered roles and relationships of Langland's allegorical figures, see Priscilla Martin, '*Piers Plowman*: Indirect Relations and the Record of Truth,' in *Suche Werkis to Werche: Essays on Piers Plowman in Honor of David C. Fowler*, ed. Míceál F. Vaughan (East Lansing, 1993), 179–82; and Helen Cooper, 'Gender and Personification in *Piers Plowman*,' *YLS* 5 (1991), 31–48, especially 44–46. Cooper observes that 'sexual, family,

Conjugal Affections

Langland's references to husbands and wives, whether allegorical, typical, or literal, demonstrate a clear awareness of both the positive and negative features of conjugal life. Many of the positive features have been discussed in Chapters 2 and 3 – the mutual likeness, love, joy, and fruitfulness of wedded folk, working together to fulfill God's law and maintain the world. Like the canonists, Langland sees ideal marriage as characterized by a genuine *maritalis affectio*, beginning in the steadfast commitment to the marital estate with one's chosen partner, but with the not surprising capacity of developing into a more intimately emotional bond.[35] Thus, in the B text, Imaginatif defines Do-wel for married men as loving one's mate and living as law wills for as long as both shall live (B.12.33–34). On the negative side, Glutton's repellent inebriation is a major trial for his wife, who suffers 'al þe wo of þe world' in retrieving him from the tavern (A.5.199, B.5.357, C.6.415), after which she attempts to correct him in wifely ways not unlike those suggested by some medieval confessors' manuals.[36] Or we have Covetise and his wife Rose the regrater, who share the sin of avarice; presumably, these two typical figures in some ways reflect Langland's perceptions of actual bourgeois couples, equally eager for profits in whatever trades they follow. In their case, we see evil *kynde* wedded to and reinforcing evil *kynde*.

The spectre of the promiscuous wife can be seen in Love's judgment on Meed – any husband she may take can count on being a cuckold. And Meed 'teaches' her metaphorical wantonness to real wives, encouraging them to gain meed in exchange for literal sexual favors. Haukyn claims that some of the stains on his coat are the fault of his wife, servants, and children; his words 'I slepe þerInne o ny3tes' may carry sexual overtones, given the traditional associations of garments

---

or household relationships often determine the gender Langland gives to his personifications' (44–45).

[35] On the concepts involved in the term *maritalis affectio*, see John T. Noonan, Jr., 'Marital Affection in the Canonists,' *Studia Gratiana* 12 (1967), 479–509; Michael M. Sheehan, '*Maritalis Affectio* Revisited,' in *The Olde Daunce: Love, Friendship, Sex and Marriage in the Medieval World*, ed. Robert R. Edwards and Stephen Spector (Albany, 1991), 32–43 and 254–60; and, in the same volume, Erik Kooper, 'Loving the Unequal Equal: Medieval Theologians and Marital Affection,' 44–56 and 260–65.

[36] Most notably the *Summa Confessorum* of Thomas of Chobham, who counsels priests to teach wives to be 'predicatrices virorum suorum,' speaking sweetly to their husbands about Christian behavior, even in the bedroom, urging mercy, denouncing plunder, and exciting generosity (ed. Broomfield, p. 375). Cf. Sharon Farmer, 'Persuasive Voices: Clerical Images of Medieval Wives,' *Speculum* 61 (1986), 517–43, and Margaret Hallissy, *Clean Maids, True Wives, Steadfast Widows: Chaucer's Women and Medieval Codes of Conduct* (Westport, CT, 1993), 67–70.

and wives with man's fleshly nature (B.14.1–4).[37] We find more admirable couples in Wit and Study, Clergy and Scripture; their figurative marriages reveal, *inter alia*, the close likeness, inseparable union, and mutual support between natural intelligence and study, learning (with special stress on religious learning) and written texts (with special stress on the Bible). Nonetheless, Study's justified but humorous berating of Wit and Will and the tonal differences between Clergy's and Scripture's answers to Will are presented in terms that can remind us of the conflicts that arise even in honest wedlock.

Of course, characterizing Study and Scripture as stern, scolding wives serves several other purposes in the poem, most of which take precedence over the lessons on marriage that might be drawn therefrom. As Anne Middleton has pointed out, the relations among Will's teachers are metaphorically represented by 'human social roles that conventionally permit . . . contention,' rather than in 'comforting familial or ideally amicable roles'; cast in a stereotypically contentious socio-literary pattern, these and other conflicts in the poem embody the 'free-floating combative animus' which regularly drives the work forward.[38] The outbursts of Study and Scripture also add to the poem's humor, evoking the stereotypes of domineering or fussily pedantic wives even as they provide valid complementary instruction to balance that given by their allegorical husbands. This humor occurs at their own and their husbands' expense as well as Will's, perhaps to help us keep the real but finite powers of the whole Wit-Clergy family in proper perspective. Finally, the impatience shown by Study and Scripture toward Will bears generic resemblance to the asperity of some of their literary ancestresses toward other dull pupils – Lady Philosophy or Beatrice, for instance – though the case of Prudence and Melibee shows that an allegorical, wifely instructor could also be portrayed as exercising a good deal of tact as a 'predicatrix viri sui.'

The scolding wife appears in a more negative light later in the poem, at the end of the Good Samaritan's discourse. Adapting a familiar proverb from the anti-matrimonial and anti-feminist tradition, the Samaritan characterizes the flesh as a vituperative 'wikkede wif,' impelled by her nature to oppose her spouse the soul. Yet he is also

[37] On these associations, see John A. Alford, 'Haukyn's Coat: Some Observations on *Piers Plowman* B.XIV.22-7,' *MÆ* 43 (1974), 133–38, and 'The Role of the Quotations in *Piers Plowman*,' *Speculum* 52 (1977), 89–91. For an argument against the K-D emendation of B.14.28 from 'Haukyns wif' (in all MSS except F) to 'Haukyn wil' (found in no MS), see his review of Kane and Donaldson's edition in *Speculum* 52 (1977), 1003.
[38] 'Narration and the Invention of Experience: Episodic Form in *Piers Plowman*,' in *The Wisdom of Poetry: Essays in Early English Literature in Honor of Morton W. Bloomfield*, ed. Larry D. Benson and Siegfried Wenzel (Kalamazoo, 1982), 97–100.

willing to offer forgiveness to any soul that has 'cleaved to' this natural fleshly frailty, if there is genuine contrition and intention to amend – a mercy which cannot be granted for *unkyndeness*, the sin against the Holy Spirit:

> Thre þynges þer ben þat doon a man by strengþe
> For to fleen his owene hous as holy writ sheweþ.
> That oon is a wikkede wif þat wol no3t be chastised;
> Hir feere fleeþ hire for feere of hir tonge.
> And if his hous be vnhiled and reyne on his bedde
> He sekeþ and sekeþ til he slepe drye.
> And whan smoke and smolder smyt in his sighte
> It dooþ hym worse þan his wif or wete to slepe. . . .
> The wif is oure wikked flessh þat wol no3t be chastised
> For *kynde* clyueþ on hym euere to contrarie þe soule;
> And þou3 it falle it fynt skiles þat 'frelete it made,'
> And 'þat is lightly for3yuen and for3eten boþe
> To man þat mercy askeþ and amende þenkeþ.'
> The reyn þat reyneþ þer we reste sholde
> Ben siknesse and sorwes þat we suffren ou3te. . . .
> And þou3 þat men make muche doel in hir angre
> And ben inpacient in hir penaunce, pure reson knoweþ
> That þei han cause to contrarie by *kynde* of hir siknesse;
> And lightliche oure lord at hir lyues ende
> Haþ mercy on swiche men þat so yuele may suffre.
> Ac þe smoke and þe smolder þat smyt in oure eighen,
> That is coueitise and *vnkyndenesse* þat quencheþ goddes mercy.
>
> (B.17.321–28, 334–40, 342–48, C.19.296–303,
> 309–15, 317–23; my emphasis)

It is worth noting that the Samaritan counts these feminized fleshly sins and the perhaps masculinized impatient anger at divinely-sent tribulation as imperfections based in human *kynde*, and as less grievous than the blinding, choking smoke of *covetise* and *vnkyndenesse*. We should also observe that the Samaritan's forgiveness for frailties of the flesh – available if a sinner 'mercy askeþ and amende þenkeþ' – is quite different from that sought by Meed for lecherous courtiers, since Meed ignores the necessity of repentance (B.3.51–59, C.3.55–63). The very fact that the Samaritan indicates that fleshly sins can be forgiven softens the anti-feminist force of the original proverb, suggesting that some 'wikkede wives' might indeed be corrigible and not as absolutely intolerable as the saying usually implies. Langland uses anti-matrimonial and anti-feminist material here, but for a different goal than simply criticizing women, and with a bit more sympathy for the natural weaknesses of both men and women than is seen in many applications of the proverb.[39]

---

[39] E.g., by 'genial' Chaucer (*Mel* 1086; *WBPro* 378–80; *ParsT* 631–32) or Innocent III (*De Miseria Condicionis Humane* 1.16); for other occurrences of the saying, see *Mel* 1086n in the

An important example of the mix of good and bad in married life is Will's own marriage to Kit, referred to twice in B and three or four times in C. In both the B and C texts, Will shares his joy in the Resurrection with Kit and their daughter Calot, in his first truly social or altruistic action in the poem, and calls them to share in the larger communal action of the Easter liturgy (B.18.424–31, C.20.470–78). In so doing, he takes his proper role as head of the household in guiding his *familia* in their religious life, a function fulfilled by household heads at every social level.[40] Near the poem's end, Will mentions his wife again, but his tone of voice is understandably different as he ruefully acknowledges his inability to satisfy her desires after Elde's attacks and her demands on him (B.20.193–98, C.22.193–98). The C text adds another reference to Kit in the Dreamer's apologia, where we see her sharing his poor life in Cornhill (C.5.2). Later in the C Visio, Actif tells Piers that he cannot undertake the pilgrimage to Truth 'for a Kitte [who] cleueth on me' – i.e., on account of the 'wantowen,' 'lihtly chyd[ing]' wife who clings jealously to him; he thereby reminds us of the responsibilities, trials, and spiritual distractions of the active, married life (C.7.299–304a). It seems likely that the name of Actif's wife is a deliberate echo of Will's own wife's name, much as the depiction of Haukyn in B bears similarities to Will himself. Since the names Kit and Calot were frequently linked with each other and associated with women of low social or moral standing, Langland may have chosen to use the names to reinforce our awareness of Will and Actif as members of what Chambers called 'the whole body of sinning, penitent laity.'[41] But sinfulness and low repute, whether in Will and his family or Activa Vita and his, can

Riverside Chaucer and Pearsall C.19.297n. Cooper observes that *Piers Plowman* is 'remarkably free of the misogyny or the hatred of sex that stalk so many medieval homiletic works' ('Gender and Personification,' 44), a conclusion corroborated by Terence Dolan in 'Langland's Women,' in *A Wyf Ther Was: Essays in Honour of Paule Mertens-Fonck*, ed. Juliette Dor (Liège, 1992), 123–28.

[40] See R. G. K. A. Mertes, 'The Household as a Religious Community,' in *People, Politics and Community in the Later Middle Ages*, ed. Joel Rosenthal and Colin Richmond (New York, 1987), 123–39.

[41] *Man's Unconquerable Mind* (1939; rpt. New York, 1967), 152. For the connotations of 'Kit' and 'Calot,' see Malcolm Godden, *The Making of Piers Plowman* (London, 1990), 9–10, and Tauno F. Mustanoja, 'The Suggestive Use of Christian Names in Middle English Poetry,' in *Medieval Literature and Folklore Studies: Essays in Honor of Francis Lee Utley*, ed. Jerome Mandel and Bruce A. Rosenberg (New Brunswick, NJ, 1970), 72–74. Mustanoja takes 'Kytte' in C.7.304 to mean 'nothing more than "wife" ' (72), but Langland's penchant for refracting an idea into several similar characters representing different aspects of the original notion suggests that he may have intended a connection between the two Kits in C. Marta Powell Harley makes the interesting suggestion that Haukyn's own name is a rhyming variant of Dawkin, a diminutive of David, an archetypal repentant sinner, minstrel, and 'exempla[r] of the active life'; see 'The Derivation of *Hawkin* and Its Application in *Piers Plowman*,' *Names* 29 (1981), 97–99.

not keep the truly contrite from receiving the gracious benefits of the Redemption. Will can and should invite his wife and daughter – whether interpreted as human characters or as Will's fleshly nature or both – to share in the promise of the Resurrection. If we sum across all the direct and perhaps indirect references to the Dreamer's own marriage, then, we arrive at a mixed view of the married life, one that recognizes both its pros and cons, its shared spiritual and physical joys and its sufferings, disappointments, and entanglements, even for a loving couple.

Sibling Affections

Langland's treatment of sibling relations is less mixed than his references to conjugal affections. The tensions that can infect sibling interactions do not interest him as much as those attendant on the marriage bond; his references to brothers and sisters usually present idealized pictures of brotherly and sisterly love. Not that he displays only the positive aspects of the sibling relationship; early on, Holy Church reminds us of Cain's fratricide in her definition of Wrong's castle and nature (A.1.64, B.1.66, C.1.62), and other false brothers and sisters occasionally appear in the poem.[42] On the whole, however, the negative sibling relationships in *Piers Plowman* are outnumbered and outweighed by the positive ones, and even some of the false or corrupt kinships may result in mutual assistance toward shared evil ends.[43]

How then does Langland conceive of the ideal sibling bond? He roofs and bars the halls and chambers of Truth's court with love, lowliness, and (in C) leal speech and buxumness, and then qualifies these virtues with the phrase 'as breþeren of o wombe' (A.6.77–78, B.5.590–91, C.7.237–39).[44] The seven porters of the court are sister virtues – mainly

---

[42] E.g., Meed's sister 'Vnsittyng-soffraunce' (C.3.207); the whore who says she will claim to be the pardoner's sister (B.5.642); the *falsi fratres* explicitly warned against in the Banquet scene and all too visible and active at the siege of Unity (B.13.68–75, C.15.75–82; B.20.230ff., C.22.230ff.); and the lazy workers at the plowing of the half-acre who, unlike Piers, clearly are *not* fulfilling the fraternal obligations that should bind them together. On real socio-economic tensions within English village communities and reflected in Piers's interactions with his more recalcitrant brethren, see Christopher Dyer, 'Piers Plowman and Plowmen: A Historical Perspective,' *YLS* 8 (1994), 155–76.

[43] Cf. Ian Bishop's 'Relatives at the Court of Heaven: Contrasted Treatments of an Idea in *Piers Plowman* and *Pearl*,' in *Medieval Literature and Antiquities: Studies in Honour of Basil Cottle*, ed. Myra Stokes and T. L. Burton (Cambridge, 1987), 114–15, with examples both *in bono* and *in malo*.

[44] For B.5.591, almost all B MSS read 'lowe speche as breþeren' instead of 'lowenesse as breþeren of o wombe,' which K-D restore, evidently on the basis of A and C. C's expansion to 'lele-speche. / The barres aren of buxumnesse, as bretherne of o wombe' probably reflects some form of the 'lowe speche' reading in the B MS from which the revision was made. Schmidt retains 'lowe speche,' but restores 'of o wombe' with K-D (*B-Text*, 63).

for the allegorical purpose of establishing their relatedness, but with the added effect of heightening the homely warmth and familiar reception that awaits anyone who is 'sib to þis sistris': 'He is wondirliche welcome & faire vndirfonge' (A.6.104–11, B.5.618–26, C.7.270–79). A similar feeling of joyful fraternal warmth can be sensed in Scripture's A-text definition of Do-bet in terms of the works of mercy:

> To breke beggeris bred & bakken hem with cloþis,
> Counforte þe carful þat in castel ben fetterid,
> And seken out þe seke & sende hem þat hem nediþ,
> Obedient as breþeren & sustren to oþere,
> Þis beþ dobet; so beriþ witnesse þe sauter:
> *Ecce quam bonum & quam iocundum habitare Fratres in vnum.*
> Sike with þe sory, singe with þe glade,
> *Gaudere cum gaudentibus Et flere cum flentibus,*
> Dredles þis is dobet.   (A.11.188–94)

But brotherly love, in its fullest expression, must extend beyond the weak and suffering to one's enemies, and in this it transcends the understanding even of the learned Dame Study. It takes 'misty' Theology to teach the paradoxical lessons of Love's school:

> [To] ben as breþeren, & blissen oure enemys,
> And louen hem þat liзen on vs, & lenen hem at here nede,
> And do good agens euil.   (A.11.151–53, B.10.202–04; cf. C.11.132–36)

Another factor in fraternal relationships appears in Langland's casting of the five senses in the Castle of Caro as Inwit's five sons, full brothers born of Inwit's first wife. Again, as with the seven sister-virtues at Truth's court, the primary function of this filial and fraternal relationship is simply to show the relatedness and relative hierarchy of Inwit and the five wits. But one also gets a hint of brothers working together at a common task, in this case the protection of a more vulnerable member of the household, the ward of the lord Do-wel. A slightly different association of brotherly responsibility and custody of others appears in the B passage which replaces Scripture's A-text definition of Do-bet as the mutual care and obedience of brothers and sisters. In B, the speaker is Clergy, and he quite alters Scripture's A discussion of the three Do's; the fraternal reference now occurs in his explanation of Do-best as the correcting of others' faults, as long as one removes the beam in his own eye before worrying about the mote in his brother's (B.10.264–71). Fortunately, Scripture's attractive picture of Do-bet is not entirely lost from the poem. In the B and C texts, the performance of the corporal works of mercy and the willingness to rejoice and weep with others will reappear in the description of childlike Charity (B.15.169–74, 182–94,

C.16.300–309, 321–33a); the *Quam bonum* verse will recur at one of the most powerful moments of the poem, as we will see in a few pages.

Yet despite their lovely qualities of humility, leal speech, and mutual mercy, obedience, and guidance, none of these brotherly and sisterly relations can match the importance of the highest fraternal bond of all: the bloody brotherhood of humankind in and with Christ. For Langland, this brotherhood between God and Man is what makes the Redemption possible. Some aspects of the kinship among human beings and between humanity and God have been touched on in earlier chapters. The biological *kynde* shared by all descendants of Adam is one source of this kinship, as is the spiritual *kynde* which men share with God by virtue of being created in his image and by being granted 'the grace of þe holy goost, goddes owene kynde' (B.17.275, C.19.251). But there are still closer kinships between *godhede* and *manhede*. Thanks to the Incarnation, in which the Word was made flesh, Christ became half-brother to the human race *ex sanguine*, a brotherhood confirmed in the Redemption by his pouring out of that blood for his fallen brothers and sisters. Christians are even more closely related to Christ through Baptism, which makes him their full brother in grace.[45]

The consequences of this fraternal relationship go beyond a mere passive acceptance of salvation, as the poet makes clear in his references to this blood-kinship in Christ. In B and C, these references begin with Repentance's eloquent prayer on the redemptive implications of man's creation in God's image and Christ's Incarnation in human likeness. The prayer climaxes by begging God's mercy for sinners on the grounds that he is 'oure fadur and of flesch oure broþer.' But to receive this grace, *rybaudes* must 'repenten hem sore'; Christ suffered 'to solace synfole' and even the saints must confess their sinfulness to gain salvation (C.7.121–54a, B.5.478–509). A further consequence appears when Piers asks Hunger for advice on helping and controlling the beggars who will not work on the half-acre:

> And it ben my blody breþeren, for god bouȝte vs alle.
> Treuþe tauȝte me ones to loue hem ichone
> And helpe hem of alle þing aftir þat hem nediþ.
> Now wolde I wite, ȝif þou wistest, what were þe beste,
> And how I miȝte amaistrie hem & make hem to werche.
> (A.7.193–97, B.6.207–11; C.8.217–22)

---

[45] It would be interesting to try to estimate the frequency and quality of full- vs. half-sibling relationships in medieval English families, both as a question in itself and as a way of better understanding the affective implications of Langland's distinction between Christ's full- and half-brotherhood with Christians and non-Christians. Unfortunately, such a project is far beyond the scope of this study.

Brotherhood through Christ mandates Christlike brotherly love of others, even though it can be hard to know what is best to do for one's brothers, especially when they are not living up to their own fraternal responsibilities. The A and B texts present this question more or less identically, in the form just quoted; C intensifies the problem by inserting three even sterner lines just before the parallel passage:

'Hit is nat for loue, leue hit, thei labore thus faste
But for fere of famyen, in fayth,' sayde Peres.
'Ther is no filial loue with this folk, for al here fayre speche.'
(C.8.214–16)

In C, moreover, Piers's brethren must be 'amayster[ed] to louye' as well as to labor (8.221). In all three texts, but particularly in the last, the workers on the half-acre fall far short of the fraternal love and mutual aid exemplified by Christ himself.

In B and C, Hunger's answer to Piers's question includes the Pauline advice 'Alter alterius onera portate' (Gal. 6:2; B.6.221α, C.8.231a), which will recur in the next B-text discussion of humankind's bloody brotherhood in Christ. In that discussion, a speaker of uncertain identity reminds the Dreamer of the equality and spiritual wealth available to all people as 'breþeren as of oo blood, as wel beggeres as Erles'; he goes on to conclude that we should therefore love

as leue children shal, and ech man laughe of ooþer,
And of þat ech man may forbere amende þere it nedeþ,
And euery man helpe ooþer for hennes shul we alle:
Alter alterius onera portate.
(B.11.200, 209–11α; cf. C.12.108–10, 114–16)

In C, Rechelesnesse gives a slightly reduced version of this passage, saving the verse from Galatians until later in his speech (C.13.77); still, the message here of joyful, childlike willingness to help one's brothers in Christ continues to come through loud and clear. Langland's familiar and familial sense of the ultimate equality between all human beings is even inscribed in the sociolinguistic register of his poem, as David Burnley has shown. Taking on the role of a 'clergial,' poetic instructor of a king, Langland generally rejects the courtesy-form 'ye' and makes his poem 'throughout the greater part of its length . . . a *thou*-text; [his] expressed attitude to fellow man and woman is rather *leeve brother and sister* or even *goode men and wommen* than *sire* and *madame* or *lord* and *lady*.'[46]

---

[46] 'Langland's Clergial Lunatic,' in *Langland, the Mystics and the Medieval English Religious Tradition: Essays in Honour of S. S. Hussey*, ed. Helen Phillips (Cambridge, 1990), 35.

The fullest explanation of man's spiritual brotherhood is fittingly withheld until the Harrowing of Hell episode, and made by Christ himself. The richness of the metaphor has been building up across the poem: Repentance (in BC) notes that God's mercy is 'þe sikerer' since Christ is father and brother to sinners; Piers says that the folk are his brethren in blood, because God 'bou3te vs alle,' and that they should therefore have his loving help; the unnamed interlocutor and Rechelesnesse speak of helping our spiritual brothers and of the noble spiritual *kynde* we have gained by being 'ywonne' and newly 'sprung' out of Christ's blood on Calvary, paradoxically becoming both his brethren and his offspring. Christ expounds the still deeper mysteries of divine mercy by declaring his half-brotherhood with all men, his full brotherhood with the baptized, and his desire to show mercy to all who share his *kynde*, half- and whole-brothers alike.[47] And the *kynde* which he shares with men is now revealed as making them not merely 'gentil men echone,' but brothers to the King of Heaven himself (B.18.375–78a, 393–98, C.20.417–20a, 435–41).[48]

One last sibling relationship deserves mention: the sisterhood of the Four Daughters of God. Again the kinship is an allegorical one, a conventional schematic for the relatedness of Mercy and Truth, Righteousness and Peace. Both the kinship and the debate of these four virtues were well-established literary motifs by the time Langland composed his version of that debate. Even so, with his skill at dialogue and description, Langland manages to suggest a genuine interaction of distinct persons, and a sibling interaction at that, both in conflict and in reconciliation.

As *dramatis personae*, Langland gives us gentle, westerly Mercy – meek, benign, buxom of speech, a merry delighter in paradoxes like death destroying death or venom fordoing venom, an accepter of experience as authority; bright, easterly Truth – comely, clean, fearless, walking softly, but indignantly refusing to believe what she thinks is logically impossible based on reason and authoritative texts; cold, northerly Righteousness – older than either Mercy or Truth, fast of foot,

---

[47] On the audacious statement that Christ's mercy will be available to his unbaptized half-brethren as well as his baptized full brethren, see Donaldson's discussion of the *archana verba* of B.18.395a/C.20.438a, 'Langland and Some Scriptural Quotations,' in *The Wisdom of Poetry: Essays in Early English Literature in Honor of Morton W. Bloomfield*, ed. Larry D. Benson and Siegfried Wenzel (Kalamazoo, 1982), 71–72.

[48] James Simpson discusses the gentle *kynde* granted to man by Christ, in 'Spiritual and Earthly Nobility in *Piers Plowman*,' *NM* 86 (1985), 467–81; see also White, *Nature and Salvation*, pp. 108–10. On fraternal elements in the 'duel' or 'joust' between Longeus and Christ, see Nicole Clifton, 'The Romance Convention of the Disguised Duel and the Climax of *Piers Plowman*,' *YLS* 7 (1993), 123–28.

sternly insistent that justice be done on transgressing humanity; and finally warm, southerly Peace – richly clothed in patience, playing and dancing and singing poetry, Love's leman and confidante, reverenced even by Righteousness, an advocate of the *concordantia discordantium* and knowledge *per contraria*. (I have sometimes wondered if the reference to the relative age of Righteousness and her position opposite Peace imply an image of Peace as a much-indulged, much-loved youngest child.)

Each of the sisters declares her desire to end the dispute, but the varied ways in which they do so help characterize both the debaters and the dynamics of the debate. Not surprisingly, Truth hopes that Righteousness's older and greater knowledge will resolve the conflict, while Mercy looks for an illuminating special revelation from Love to Peace. Righteousness almost callously declares the justice of man's self-chosen punishment and then prays the others, in what could be construed as an elder-sisterly tone, for family solidarity among themselves: 'Forþi lat hem chewe as þei chosen and chide we noȝt, sustres, / For it is botelees bale, þe byte þat þei eten' (B.18.201–02, C.20.206–07). After the Harrowing is complete, Truth and Peace make the last, and finally effective, pleas for reconciliation and solidarity, which Righteousness confirms:

> 'Trewes,' quod Truþe, 'þow tellest vs sooþ, by Iesus!
> Clippe we in couenaunt, and ech of vs kisse ooþer.'
> 'And leteþ no peple,' quod pees, 'parceyue þat we chidde;
> For inpossible is no þyng to hym þat is almyghty.'
> 'Thow seist sooth,' seyde Rightwisnesse, and reuerentliche hire kiste:
> Pees, and pees hire, *per secula seculorum.* (B.18.416–21, C.20.462–67)

Although the revision from A.11 to B.10 eliminated the beautiful psalm-verse 'Ecce quam bonum' from the lessons of Clergy and Scripture, Langland has saved the line for a still more potent use by Peace's leman Love:

> *Misericordia & veritas obuiauerunt sibi; Iusticia & pax osculate sunt.*
> Truþe trumpede þo and song *Te deum laudamus,*
> And þanne lutede loue in a loud note:
> *Ecce quam bonum & quam iocundum [habitare fratres in vnum].*
> (B.18.421a–23a, C.20.467a–69a)

The affective power of the familial model in Langland's thought is nowhere as clear as here at the end of B.18/C.20. Since the Redemption turns on humanity's kinship in blood and faith to Christ, it is most appropriate for this splendid passus of reconciliation to conclude with three family reunions: first, at the level of spiritual history and vision, the reunion of God with long-lost humanity, won back through the Passion and the Harrowing of Hell; second, and also within the vision, the allegorical reconciliation of the four daughters of God; and third, at the physical and waking level, Will's summoning of his wife and daughter to join him in celebrating the Resurrection.[49]

Inheritance and Old Age

Sooner or later, each life cycle comes to an end and to new beginnings. Willy-nilly, the older generation gives way to the younger, fulfilling its purpose by passing on its duties, resources, and authority to its children. Some of that transmission occurs during life, some only after death. The breadth of Langland's spiritual concerns and social vision makes it natural for him to refer off and on to matters of inheritance, aging, and impending death. The following section will draw those references together and examine their position within the larger patterns of familial material already laid out in this study.

Inheritance

Allusions to inheritances and heirship in *Piers Plowman* fall into several classes. For instance, Langland echoes traditional complaints against executors, who were commonly accused of frustrating the intentions of testators, and of cheating rightful beneficiaries of estates out of their due (e.g., C.2.189; B.15.132, C.16.277; B.20.291, C.22.290; possibly B.5.263, C.6.254; C.12.215).[50] More frequent are descriptions of particular

---

[49] Simpson notes that 'the pattern of Will's waking moments here [at the end of B.18 and beginning of B.19] suggests that he is being drawn back into the institution [of the Church].' Instead of wandering at the margins of society, the Dreamer now 'wakes into a domestic world of his wife and daughter (l. 429), and at the beginning of the seventh vision, he is pictured as participating in the ritual life of the Church.' Simpson goes on to suggest that under Grace's dispensation after the Harrowing of Hell passus, social structures and relationships are reformed according to a familial and brotherly model, with the model including horizontal, urban structures like guild or craft relationships rather than the more hierarchical, feudal and manorial structures suggested at the beginning of the poem. See *Piers Plowman: An Introduction to the B-Text* (London, 1990), 219, 224–27; ' "After craftes conseil clotheth yow and fede": Langland and London City Politics,' *England in the Fourteenth Century: Proceedings of the 1991 Harlaxton Symposium*, ed. Nicholas Rogers (Stamford, 1993), 109–27.

[50] For instances of mistrust of executors, see *Handlyng Synne* 6229–6508; Bromyard, *Summa Praed.*, s.v. 'Executor'; Alford, *Piers Plowman: A Glossary of Legal Diction* (Cambridge, 1988), 53. In most cases, both executors and heirs are accused of wrongly appropriating bequests made for the benefit of the testator's soul – not an unexpected charge considering the clerical sources and conventional religious purposes of these works. Langland worries

blessings or curses descending on individuals and their heirs, much as properties and rights descend in law. Adam and Eve and their issue are punished and then saved; Abraham and his issue are blessed; Agag and his people must die 'for deeds of their elders'; Saul and his sons are destroyed for Saul's sins. The Jews and their children are to become thralls and churls; traitors' sons lose their inheritance by Westminster law; the marriage charter of Meed and False also applies to their heirs; Truth sends his pardon to Piers and his heirs. For Langland, a person's good or bad deeds will have consequences of weal and woe for others as well as for himself, and especially for those others about whom most people care most deeply – the offspring who carry on their name and kind. The hortatory strategy is straightforward: if a person will not amend for his own sake, perhaps he will leave the evil and choose the good for the sake of his children.[51]

In addition to this spiritual duty owed to one's heirs, Langland has a strong sense of the material duties owed them as well. He criticizes donations to religious orders because, among other things, the donations often impoverish the donors' heirs; charity should begin at home. The strongest statement of this principle appears in Liberum Arbitrium's discourse on Charity. After quoting and glossing Job 6:5 to prove that religious orders should live moderately, he comments:

Yf lewede men knewe this Latyn, a litel they wolden auysen hem
Ar they amorteysed eny more for monkes or for chanons.
Allas! lordes and ladyes, lewede consayle haue ȝe
To feffe suche and fede þat founded ben to þe fulle
With þat ȝoure bernes and ȝoure bloed by goed lawe may clayme!
For god bad his blessed, as þe boek techeth –
  Honora patrem et matrem –
To helpe thy fader formost byfore freres or monkes
Or ar prestes or pardoners or eny peple elles.
Helpe thy kyn, Crist bid, for þer bigynneth charite,

more about heirs being deprived of the means to live on than about the Church losing promised building-funds or mass-money (B.15.319–31, C.17.53–71).

Elaine Clark discusses actual arrangements made by 14th-century peasant testators for both the benefit of their souls and the well-being of their families in 'Deathbed Sales of Land in the Medieval Countryside,' a paper presented at the Social Science History Conference (October 1986). More generally, see Joel T. Rosenthal, *The Purchase of Paradise: Gift Giving and the Aristocracy, 1307–1485* (London, 1972); Furnivall, *Fifty Earliest English Wills*; Sheehan, *The Will*, 107–323, with special reference to complaints about executors on 219–20, and 'The Wife of Bath and Her Four Sisters: Reflections on a Woman's Life in the Age of Chaucer,' *M&H* n.s. 13 (1985), 33–35, on women's old age and will-making.

[51] Fortescue makes a similar argument, in defense of the common law's refusal to recognize pre-marital offspring as legitimate: 'the law which punishes the progeny of the delinquent prohibits the sin more effectively than the law which punishes only the guilty' (*De Laudibus Legum*, 95).

And afturward awayte ho hath moest nede
And þer help yf thow haste, and þat halde y charite.
(C.17.53–63; cf. B.15.319–25)

The inclusion of responsibilities to one's children and secondarily to the needy under the Fourth Commandment is a little surprising at first, though the logic of the extension is clarified by the phrase 'helpe thy kyn' in line 61. However, Langland is not alone in extending the commandment like this; the author of *Dives and Pauper* also views the Fourth Commandment as the natural starting point for his discussions of *parental* responsibilities and of almsgiving.[52] The B version of the passage, though briefer, contains lines implying that leaving property to one's heirs is itself a form of obeying one's own ancestors: 'lewed counseil haue ye / To ȝyue from youre heires þat youre Aiels yow lefte' (B.15.322–23). As Conscience suggests in the grammatical metaphor in C, the inheritance and bequeathing of family name and property from one generation to the next is 'resonable [and] rect' (C.3.366–69).

Similar sentiments occur in a section of Clergy's discussion of the three Do's in B.10, a passage transferred to Reason's sermon before the realm in C.5: 'Litel hadde lordes to doon to ȝyue lond from hire heires / To Religiouse þat han no rouþe þouȝ it reyne on hir Auters' (B.10.317–18, C.5.163–64). Barons, earls, and their children shall reprove the orders, reclaiming their rights; the 'heirs' of churchmen, like 'Gregory's godchildren' (the monks) and the issue or niece of the Abbot of Abyngdon, will be disendowed 'incurably' by a millennial king (B.10.322–35, C.5.168–79). To be sure, the references to inheritance are not the primary point of the passage, which mainly expresses Langland's standing concern over the infection of the Church by superfluous wealth, cast here in vivid eschatological language. The concern itself reflects the great medieval controversies of secular vs. ecclesiastical lordship, monastic and fraternal poverty and ownership, and the worldly endowments of the Church. Langland also stands in the long, specifically English tradition of resistance to irrevocable donations to the Church, a tradition most notably expressed in the Statute of Mortmain but retaining its vigor through Wyclif and later writers.[53]

---

[52] 4.10–11, 25–26 (EETS 275:324–28, 354–56). *Dives and Pauper* 4.5 (EETS 275:313–15) also observes that, 'be weye of kende,' parental love toward children should be greater than that of children toward parents, citing 2 Cor. 12:14 in support thereof ('Neither ought the children to lay up for the parents, but the parents for the children'). See also Siegfried Wenzel, ed. and trans., *Fasciculus Morum: A Fourteenth-Century Preacher's Handbook* (University Park, PA, 1989) I.xi, 'Humiliandum Parentibus,' in which the obligations of both children and parents are discussed in connection with the commandment (pp. 87–93).
[53] On the Statute of Mortmain and its operation, see Sandra Raban, *Mortmain Legislation*

These large issues are outside my purposes here, but it is noteworthy that Langland speaks of them in terms of their implications for donors' families; his perspective is not solely political or theological. Not only does he mention the injustice of endowing religious at the expense of one's heirs, he also leads into the passage with discussions that have already raised questions of family obligations: Clergy's definition of Do-best as the correction of one's brother and his warning against bad correctors like Heli, Ophni, and Phineas (B); Reason's exhortation to familial and ecclesiastical discipline (C). We should likewise note that the priority of one's heirs over religious orders is more than a simple matter of personal preference for one's kin. It is also a very practical consequence of Langland's views on the application of Charity to the entire *comune* – what might be called an ecological or 'system' approach to practicing Charity. First, all families should take care of their own, physically and spiritually; next, the needy without blood-kin to help them should be cared for by the Church and by those laypersons with the capacity to do so. But religious who are already well-off and who fail to serve the poor or the parish churches in their patronage deserve nothing but disendowment and enforced reformation.[54]

Even the call to spiritual perfection does not eliminate certain family duties. In preparation for the pilgrimage to Truth, Piers makes his will, bequeathing his soul, body, and goods to God, the Church, and his wife as the family executrix. His debts, he says, are all quit; when the half-acre is sown and reaped, he can set out on pilgrimage. Thus, when he throws his life in God's lap after tearing the Pardon (AB), his insolicitude for worldly meat need only affect himself, as would also have been the case had the pilgrimage to Truth actually taken place. Personal perfection must be founded on justice to others – kin, neighbors, lord; Do-best can only grow from Do-bet and Do-wel.

Old Age

Whether or not a person has any legacy to pass on to any heirs, his life must eventually come to an end, and the forerunners of that end are

---

and the English Church 1279-1500, Cambridge Studies in Medieval Life and Thought, 3rd ser. 17 (Cambridge, 1982). Wyclif's opposition to the endowment of the Church with material wealth can be found throughout his writings; see Pearsall, C.5.164n, 168–71n, 17.220n, 227n for numerous references to relevant material in Wycliffite works.
[54] *Dives and Pauper* 4.7–8 denounces covetous religious who refuse to help even their needy parents with the resources of their monastery (EETS 275:317–21). For further discussion of the theme of ecclesiastical and lay duties to give alms to the proper recipients, see my '*Piers Plowman* and the Liturgy of St. Lawrence: Composition and Revision in Langland's Poetry,' *SP* 84 (1987), 245–71.

often sickness and old age.[55] Langland occasionally alludes to literal details of old age: weakness and helplessness among the aged poor (A.8.82, B.7.100, C.9.175); the need of some widows for physical protection and support (B.9.71); the wooing of rich widows by covetous suitors even if the women are 'reueled for elde' (C.10.263, A.10.188, B.9.167); impotent lechery in old age (C.6.193–94); and Will's own baldness, deafness, toothlessness, gout, and sexual impotence (B.20.183–98, C.22.183–98; a subject to which we will return). His most interesting references to aging, however, are those which involve the personification Elde itself. Elde appears at several points in the B and C texts, all crucial for the narrator in one way or another. The first encounters occur in Will's dream-within-a-dream of Fortune and her maidens; the last in the final passus of the poem when Kynde, Death, and Elde attack the legions of Antichrist; in C, Elde makes yet another entry, replacing Piers as the harvester of apples from the Tree of Charity.

In each of these instances, Elde is a force for good, albeit a frightening one. As such, he stands in contrast to the flawed state of life represented by Elde in the *Parliament of the Three Ages*, a figure reminiscent of Will in his more unregenerate phases, able to complain about others' vices, but not to put his own spiritual house in order, as Donald Fry has shown.[56] Interestingly, Langland's Elde is far more taciturn than his garrulous namesake in the *Parliament*; Will is less influenced by Elde's few words than by actually experiencing his physical effects, both after the dalliance with Fortune and at the end of the poem. The intimate experience of age, rather than any authority it may have at a distance, seems to be what finally effects conversion in Will, a point that Hugh White also makes in connection with Will's interactions with Elde as a representative of Kynde.[57]

'Heuy of chere,' Langland's Elde first enters the poem to warn Will of Fortune's fickleness; he joins Holiness in bewailing the Dreamer's willingness to listen to Rechelesnesse and Faunteltee, and his pursuit of Covetise, Concupiscentia-carnis, and Pride of Life. Will's first instructive shock in the internal dream of Fortune and her maidens does indeed come from 'running into Elde,' as he had been warned, though he has several other such shocks to undergo before his conversion of life

---

[55] For a rich collection of analyses of old age in medieval European culture, see Michael M. Sheehan, ed., *Aging and the Aged in Medieval Europe* (Toronto, 1990); more particularly, see Alicia K. Nitecki, 'Figures of Old Age in Fourteenth-Century Literature,' pp. 107–16 in Sheehan, with special reference to *Piers* on pp. 111–12.
[56] 'The Authority of *Elde* in *The Parlement of the Thre Ages*,' in *Hermeneutics and Medieval Culture*, ed. Patrick J. Gallacher and Helen Damico (Albany, 1989), 213–21.
[57] *Nature and Salvation*, 55–59, 79–84.

begins in earnest (B.11.27–45, 59–62, C.11.189–98, 306–15, 12.1–2, 11–14). These 'manacing' encounters with Elde in the Third Dream are important enough to the Dreamer that he mentions them in his waking recapitulation of the vision just before the Fourth Dream (B.13.6, C.15.6).

In the C version of the Tree of Charity scene, Elde gathers apples from the Tree at Liberum Arbitrium's command, though the effects of his harvesting are suffering, death, and darkness and dread for the Old Testament saints *in limbo inferni*. Yet despite the grief that accompanies Elde's work, the results of that work are what moves 'moed *in magestate dei'* to go after the fiend who has stolen his fruit. Elde is associated with the fullness of time required for Christ to be born, and for the fruits of Charity to ripen:

> Iesus, a iustices sone, moste iouken in [Mary's] chaumbre,
> Til *plenitudo temporis* tyme ycome were
> That Elde felde efte þe fruyt, or full to be rype. (C.18.126–28)

The interplay of 'felde,' 'full,' and *plenitudo* here, along with the willed descent implied by 'iouken,' carries the same paradoxical richness as the plays on falling through leaping pride and heavy love in Holy Church's speech. The sin-derived power of *chronos* – manifested in age, the dark fall into death, and the steady deterioration of the world over time – can only be broken by Redemption's *kairos*, the ripe moment of fullness which humankind, caught in *chronos*, eagerly awaits. Only Christ's freely accepted death and descent into darkness – the submission of the eternal to the temporal – can bring about the transtemporal *kairos* of salvation, when time 'falls fully to be ripe.' It is virtually impossible to unpack the compressed syntax of these lines, but I take *full* as carrying both its literal sense as a preterite of *fallen* and a kind of 'hovering' adverbial sense which semantically echoes *plenitudo*. Thus, for the three lines, I tentatively translate as follows: 'Jesus, the son/sun of (a) justice, had to alight in Mary's womb/chamber until, (in the) fullness of time, it became time/*kairos* that Elde again felled the fruit (of the Tree, of Mary's womb) or that it (time/*kairos*) fell/befell (fully) to be ripe.' (I see no easy way to read *or* as 'before,' and take it as the simple coordinating conjunction 'or.') Old age and death are a terror and a grief, but *O felix dolor!*

In the last passus of the poem, we see even more clearly, and at a more personal level, why *unhende* Elde stands on the side of Holiness, Liberum Arbitrium, and the good. Like Kynde and Death, he assists Conscience in the war against Pride and Antichrist, Comfort, Fortune, Covetise, Lechery, and prideful Life. The forces of nature are creatures of God;

whether pleasant or painful, they work toward divine ends. And one of those ends is turning people away from worldly life and loves toward a perfect, heavenly love. It is a grim measure of the power of Antichrist and his allies – and of the undeniable frightfulness of Elde and Death – that so few sinners are willing to undertake that conversion, despite their certain vulnerability to the inevitable attacks of Kynde's agents.

However, at least one soul does respond appropriately to the assaults of Elde and the approach of Death: the Dreamer himself. Here at last we have the menacing final meeting with Elde foreseen in Will's dream of Fortune, and the menace turns out to be quite real. Elde gallops over the Dreamer's head and then attacks him, leaving him bald, deaf, toothless, gouty, and impotent as Death draws near:

> And Elde [rood] after hym; and ouer myn heed yede
> And made me balled bifore and bare on þe croune;
> So harde he yede ouer myn heed it wole be sene euere.
> 'Sire yuele ytauȝt Elde!' quod I, 'vnhende go wiþ þe!
> Siþ whanne was þe wey ouer mennes heddes?
> Haddestow be hende,' quod I, 'þow woldest haue asked leeue.'
> 'Ye, leue, lurdeyn?' quod he, and leyde on me wiþ Age,
> And hitte me vnder þe ere; vnneþe may ich here.
> He buffetted me aboute þe mouþ and bette out my wangteeþ;
> And gyued me in goutes: I may noȝt goon at large.
> And of þe wo þat I was Inne my wif hadde ruþe
> And wisshed ful witterly þat I were in heuene.
> For þe lyme þat she loued me fore and leef was to feele
> On nyghtes namely, whan we naked weere,
> I ne myghte in no manere maken it at hir wille,
> So Elde and heo hadden it forbeten.
> And as I seet in þis sorwe I sauȝ how kynde passede
> And deeþ drogh neiȝ me; for drede gan I quake,
> And cryde to kynde: 'out of care me brynge!
> Lo! Elde þe hoore haþ me biseye.
> Awreke me if youre wille be for I wolde ben hennes.'
>
> (B.20.183–203, C.22.183–203)

The verbs used for Elde's onslaught are forceful and terrifying – buffetting, beating, going and riding over men's heads, hitting and laying on and shackling those in his way, rather like the callous actions of a mounted soldier against unarmed civilians in his path – though the terror is mitigated somewhat by Will's comic, querulous objection, 'Since when was the road over men's heads? If you were polite, you would have asked leave!'

Elde's encounter with Will has generally been recognized for both its ironic humor and its dramatic personalizing of the allegorical action.[58] It

---

[58] Cf. Schmidt, *B-Text*, 356–57; Pearsall, C.22.183n; John Lawlor, *Piers Plowman: An Essay*

thrusts the narrator and reader directly into the poem's swift-paced conclusion; Will's sufferings are a starkly particular analogue to what Pearsall calls 'the vision of the world running down to destruction' (C.22.183n). These final events of the poem demand an immediate moral response from Will, just as the poem itself demands a moral response from its readers. Apocalypse is no spectator sport.

Before examining Will's response to Elde's attacks, we should look more closely at the last affliction laid upon him by his attacker. I take the mention of his impotence as something more than just another physical effect of old age. It receives six lines of description – as much as all the other afflictions together – and it gets the important final position in the list of Will's woes. But it is a difficult passage to interpret, since the allusion to the sexual desire of Will's wife might be read in malo or in bono, and one's understanding of the passage will be colored by one's understanding of that marital sexuality. Is it allied with Lechery, who has infiltrated 'alle manere men, wedded and vnwedded' (B.20.112, C.22.112)? Or still to be viewed as 'godes werk,' even if no longer achievable? Is the wish of Will's wife to see him 'in heuene' selfish or loving? Perhaps the line 'þe lyme þat she loued me fore and leef was to feele' accuses Will's wife of non-procreative motives in sex; the 'forbeting' which Elde and she have given to Will's sexual capacity could suggest an insistence on conjugal rights beyond mesure.[59] On the other hand, these remarks on her desires and demands may in fact refer to a genuine conjugal love, seen in the humorous light of some rueful bragging by Will as to how desirable he used to be, like Actif's slightly boastful complaint in C of how jealously his Kit cleaves to him. We are, after all, still subject to the perspective of our fallible narrator, whose old self-centeredness has just resurfaced in his complaints to Elde.[60] Will's

---

in Criticism (London, 1962), 181–82; Philippa Tristram, Figures of Life and Death in Medieval English Literature (London, 1976), 68. Elizabeth Salter notes a parallel passage in the Poema Morale, in 'Langland and the Contexts of "Piers Plowman," ' Essays and Studies 32 (1979), ed. Dieter Mehl, 22–23.

[59] De Burgh notes that the wife does not have the right to seek the conjugal debt if doing so would be counter to the husband's 'consistentia' or the health of his person; nor if he is impotent from rendering the debt already or from lawful causes like fasting (Pup. Oc., 128v). Presumably the impotence of old age would constitute a lawful cause as well, though I have not yet found a direct statement to that effect in canonical or pastoral sources.

[60] An interesting pair of readers' responses to this passage, from the sixteenth and early seventeenth centuries, may be found in Bodl. MS Digby 145, the Fortescue manuscript, which was written and presumably glossed by Adrian Fortescue in 1532, and later came into the possession of Kenelm Digby, who appears to have added further glosses. At the point of Elde's attack on Will, the sixteenth-century glosses read 'Nota the wyfe' (fol. 193r) and 'the wief is woo' (fol. 193v), comments to which the later hand responds 'ye but nota for what cause' (fol. 193r) and 'but why' (fol. 193v). Also of interest is the insightful

impotence itself could be read as a sign of his own or the *comune*'s backsliding into a debilitated *fainéantise*, the *acedia* to which old age could be particularly susceptible.[61]

My own sense of the passage is that it presents the past sexual bond between Will and his wife with affection, wistful nostalgia, and a certain element of comic self-deprecation. Given the poet's generally non-rigorist attitude toward marital sexuality and the well-ordered love expressed in the reference to Kit and Calot in B.18/C.20, a condemnatory stance here seems relatively unlikely. Will's physical weakness and sexual impotence after Elde's attacks are not so much judgments on his previous active, married life as God-sent warnings that the time has come for him to lay down the secular responsibilities of that life and turn himself wholly to heavenly pursuits. I also have difficulty seeing Will as spiritually impotent here – he does in fact heed Kynde's warning, entering Unity *via* contrition and confession late, but still in time. Perhaps the fact that Langland has Will come completely to the end of his natural capacities for physical love and fruitfulness is a way of emphasizing the point that those capacities are necessarily finite, by the law of nature itself. Earthly crafts and loves, even when they do well in this world, eventually must be left behind – and those who do well will leave them for the craft of heavenly love. Unlike Covetise, falsely departing leal matrimony for a mantle of miniver (B.20.138–39, C.22.138–39), death makes a true departing of marriage, and Elde simply starts to prepare Will for that parting a little sooner and more painfully than he himself might have liked.[62]

The notion that old age is a proper time for laymen to turn from the active life to a more spiritual orientation can be found elsewhere in medieval literature. Burrow observes that old age, like childhood, was sometimes viewed as a period of special sanctity, often in contrast with the carnal and worldly middle period of life.[63] In light of this observation, it is interesting to note that the inspired singers who welcome the Samaritan to Jerusalem are 'gerlis' and 'olde folk'; their joyous melodies of praise will be resoundingly echoed at the end of the

seventeenth-century gloss of Elde in C.22.173 and 202 as 'alias Tempus' and 'Tempus.' I am grateful to the late Judson Allen for directing me to these glosses.

[61] Bowers, *Crisis of Will*, 96.

[62] On Langland's propensity for using metaphors from earthly experience to explicate spiritual matters, and then revaluing the earthly term by comparison with its spiritual analogue, see James Simpson, 'The Transformation of Meaning: A Figure of Thought in *Piers Plowman*,' *RES* n.s. 37 (1986), 161–83, with special attention to 'craft' on 182–83.

[63] '*Mezzo Del Cammin*,' 34. For further discussion of medieval notions of the activities proper to old age and of Langland's Elde, see also Burrow's *The Ages of Man* (Oxford, 1986), 150–62, 178–88, and Mary Dove's *The Perfect Age of Man's Life* (Cambridge, 1986), 26–42, 103–17.

Easter Passus when adult brothers and sisters, husband and wife are reunited amidst the harmony of instruments, song, and worship. Perhaps one of the most eloquent expressions of the relation of age to holiness comes in the fourth tractate of Dante's *Convivio*, which analyzes the nobility of the soul and the ages of man. Having noted that the noble soul 'mak[es] use of her activities at the proper times and ages, according as they are adapted to produce her ultimate fruit,' Dante goes on to describe these proper acts for each of his four ages – Adolescence, Youth, Old Age, and Decline (Adolescenza, Gioventute, Senettute, and Senio). In Youth and Old Age, one's activities should be directed outward, to the profit of others; in Decline, the soul withdraws from this public life and returns to God:

> Just as a good mariner when he draws near to the harbour lets down his sails, and enters it gently with slight headway on; so we ought to let down the sails of our worldly pursuits, and turn to God with all our understanding and heart, so that we may come to that haven with all composure and with all peace. . . .

> And no one ought to excuse himself by reason of the marriage tie which still binds him in extreme age: for not only does he who assumes a habit and rule of life like that of St Augustine, or St Francis, or St Dominic, join the ranks of the professed, but a man may also become truly and properly professed while married, for God does not require us to be professed save in heart.

Finally, Dante compares the soul returning to God to Marcia returning to Cato, and saying to him

> 'Now that my womb . . . is weary, and I am exhausted for child-bearing, I return to thee, no longer fit to be given to another spouse,' that is to say, the noble soul discerning that she no longer has any womb to bear fruit, in other words, when her members feel that they have become enfeebled, turns to God, to Him who has no need of bodily members.[64]

Philippa Tristram has shown that most Middle English portrayals of Elde and Death, including Langland's, are much less serene than Dante's characterization of Decline as a tranquil letting down of life's sails.[65] Moreover, Langland's Elde is not identical with Dante's Senio, though he might be seen as a combination of Senettute and Senio. But despite these differences in the tone and details of the two poets' presentation of extreme old age, one can see that both Dante and Langland contemplate that age from a similar vantage point. Both read

---

[64] Trans. William Walrond Jackson (Oxford, 1909) 4.24, 4.26–28 (pp. 277, 283–94).
[65] *Life and Death*, 62–94.

Kindly Similitude

its effects as natural signals to turn away from the world – however well used at earlier stages of life – and set one's heart and mind entirely on God. Both invoke prior marital obligations, literally or figuratively, only to show that these obligations have been fulfilled or become peripheral to the soul's journey. Ideally, Will would respond to Elde as Piers does after his forty or fifty years serving Truth, calmly deciding that

> now I am old & hor & haue of myn owene
> To penaunce & to pilgrimage wile I passe with oþere;
> Forþi I wile er I wende do wryte my bequest.
> (A.7.75–77, B.6.83–85, C.8.92–94)

Tristram's comment on these lines sheds light on Will's situation at the poem's end:

> Piers' will divides the things of time from those of eternity; his soul is given to God, his goods to his wife, and his body to the Church, which, mediating temporal and eternal, will care for his 'caroyne' until the general Resurrection. . . . Piers, who comes to represent [Christ's] human nature, embraces the close of man's life, and redeems it by indicating its true purpose. To be 'old and hor' is not the end, but a new beginning: it is the time appointed to set out on the pilgrimage to Truth and to eternal life.[66]

Unfortunately, the Dreamer can only partially achieve the ideal exemplified by Piers. The right-meaning but still imperfect Will needs a certain amount of help in detaching himself from the distractions and temptations of the active life. Thus Elde's attacks on Will are a real answer to Conscience's cry for help against Antichrist, Pride, and 'likyng of body' (B.20.69–79, C.22.69–79), being not-so-gentle reminders that the *plenitudo temporis* 'to ben hennes' has come. The folk on the field would not help sustain the world without the grim stimulus of Hunger; Will would not abandon the world's evil uses until he had been frightened by Elde and shamed by Reason and Kynde; now Elde joins again with Kynde, forcibly inviting Will to leave behind even the lawful use of the world.

With little to hold him here, the Dreamer asks Kynde for release from his troubles and help in 'being hence.' He is directed through Contrition and Confession to Unity, to wait there until Kynde sends for him. The only craft he need follow now is leal love; he should 'leef alle oþere,' become as insolicitous as Piers for 'weede ne worldly mete, while . . . lif lasteþ' (B.20.199–213, C.22.199–213; cf. A.8.104–17, B.7.122–35). Kynde's promise to send for Will and the subsequent description of besieged

---

66 *Life and Death*, 77.

212

Unity under the constableship of Conscience recall Wit's depiction of Anima, guarded by Inwit from Sir Princeps Huius Mundi, waiting for Kynde to come or send for her. Elde may be one of Kynde's less courteous messengers, but his message should be good news for Will and his Anima, if they remain true: that they can soon expect their final summons home. However, the barn of Unity Holy Church is in far more immediate danger than Wit's Castle Caro ever seemed to be, assaulted from without by Antichrist's seven great giants and weakened internally by the treachery of flattering friars.

In such desperate straits, Death's delivery of Kynde's summons may be welcome indeed to the individual Will and the other holy fools who are still awake behind the walls of Unity. But for the *comune* as a whole, those embattled walls must be defended by Conscience until the eschatological *plenitudo temporis*, and his only hope for awakening the drug-bound folk therein lies in the aid of Kynde, Piers, and Grace, the manifestations among men of the three Persons of the Trinity.[67] Once again the call to pilgrimage is sounded in the poem – and therewith Will awakes.

Conclusions

The picture that emerges as one examines Langland's shorter references to marriage and family life is conventional enough, reflecting the social and religious conservatism that frequently marks his thinking. It can be differentiated from other expressions of the same conventions mainly in terms of the points which Langland emphasizes or does not emphasize, and by the way it is articulated into the larger framework of his spiritual and social vision. Thus it is interesting to note his special irritability over bastards, his general assumption of significant familial involvement in marriage-makings, his apparent unconcern over sexual ardency between spouses as long as the right *mesure* is observed in the times chosen for intercourse, and the way his chronic preoccupation with the uses of material goods frequently informs his analyses of problems within families. Drawing parallels as he does between the relations and organization of the family and those of larger societal structures is a familiar strategy for social criticism, by no means restricted to the Middle Ages and probably grounded in a certain amount of psychological and sociological truth – socialization *is* primarily accomplished within the family, even if it is easier to offer explanations of a particular adult's

---

[67] Cf. Schmidt, *B-Text*, 357.

socialization in retrospect than to predict the outcome for a child still being reared.

Langland's representations of the family's place in the economy of salvation are somewhat less commonplace than the place he gives it in the social economy. Not that he is unorthodox, but that fewer writers bother to go beyond noting that, spiritually speaking, matrimony helps to fill up the ranks of the blessed and provides a remedy for lust. Few attach the unflagging importance to the filial and spousal likeness between human souls and God, or to the special brotherhood between humankind and Christ, that we find in Langland's understanding of the Redemption. And fewer still would go beyond these pneumatological and soteriological family metaphors to Langland's matrimonial metaphor for the Trinity. The explanation of these multiple uses of family metaphors for spiritual truths resides, I believe, in a combination of the poet's desire to express those truths in ways that would deeply touch the experience of a wide range of people and his profoundly social sense of the spiritual life, at both the human level and the divine. Even though he vividly portrays the struggling search of the individual Will for salvation, and makes thoroughly clear the necessarily internal locus of doing well and of charity, he never lets us think of doing well or charity as something free from a social matrix – the need to help support the *comune*, to preach, to rule or obey, to render what one owes in justice and mercy, to love one's neighbor as well as God. And this social matrix for the spiritual life is ultimately rooted in the divine society of the Trinity itself, which humanity mirrors and has been created to share in.

Changes in Langland's shorter references to family and marriage cannot easily be viewed as part of a single, large program of revision. Since those references are usually only loosely connected with each other, and often occur in *ad hoc* service to some other topic, revisions that affect them will generally be only loosely connected as well. Nonetheless, smaller patterns or tendencies of revision within this family material can be found, if we are willing to settle for relatively limited claims, and those tendencies themselves may be symptomatic of broader trends in Langland's thought and poetic expression as his life's work grew.

For example, on matters of familial mores, we seem to find the poet expressing himself more and more emphatically on the rights and wrongs he finds in the behavior of contemporary families. Hence the increased frequency and severity of his references to bastards in the C text, as in the Dreamer's remarks on bastards and villains being made clerks by purchased dispensations, or the new phrase 'beggares of kynde' to describe the bastard children of dishonest beggars, or Wit's new attack on cross-status marriages to rich bastard bondwomen in C. Lechery's C-text confession is lengthened not only by importing material from Haukyn's speech in B, but also by the addition of several new lines, describing sins of baudery, rape, sexual sorcery, fulfillment of lust without love, and (with two lines for B's one) the taking of pleasure in obscene stories in impotent old age. Meed's character is successively darkened and made more whorish across all three versions, as we saw in Chapter 1, and it is C that caustically applies the phrase *pre manibus* to the harlotry of doctorly and lawyerly greed. In Reason's speech in both B and C, the opening remarks on family discipline are much longer than in A, while in C, failures in the discipline of literal and spiritual children are brought to our attention even sooner, with the expansion of the brief Ophni and Phineas allusion in B.10 and its transfer to the C Prologue. Piers accuses his workers of having 'no filial [*var.* final (Skeat)] loue' and of helping each other *only* for fear of famine in the C text, a charge much harsher than its AB predecessor. The B and C texts also lay respectively increasing stress on the importance of Inwit having control over Anima, and of the immorality of marriages for money rather than love, as noted in Chapter 2.

Offsetting these increasingly pessimistic remarks are the increasingly idealistic statements on marriage and family rightly used, most of which have been examined in Chapters 2 and 3. Indeed, the pessimism described in the preceding paragraph is but the converse of this idealism – as with the friars, *corruptio optimi pessima*. Thus we have the opening of Wit's marriage homily, which characterizes the fruits of lawful wedlock in more and more honorable and saintly terms, and describes marriage itself more and more in terms of loving fulfillment of law as well as profitable work. In the C version of that homily, at least, we even have an explicit touch of optimism about 'lossum' marital sexuality as God's work. An implied optimism could also be read into the honor proclaimed for marriage and family (*kyn, kynde*) in the Tree of Charity scene and even more in Abraham's familial simile for the Trinity. The rising frequency, over all three texts, of verbal associations between marriage and *kynde* also credits the institution with intrinsic value, although the capacity of human *kynde* to turn away from its divine model through frailty or deliberate *unkyndenesse* constantly threatens to stain or destroy that value, and in individual cases can succeed in doing so. But contrition is always possible. Actif-Haukyn can keep re-cleaning his earthly coat until it becomes his heavenly wedding-garment, and our imperfect Will and his perhaps likewise imperfect Kit and Calot can repent the willfulness and wantonness of weakened *kynde*, and participate in the grace of Easter.

215

Although a general discussion of the relations between Langland's familial references and the larger themes and purposes of the poem is best reserved for the next chapter, it is useful to call attention here to a few of the more important thematic connections of the material examined in this chapter. One such connection is with the theme of time in the poem. The natural rhythms of family life, from the growth and education of children into adults, to the timeliness of chaste marital sexuality, and especially to the experience of aging, embed the family experience in temporality more obviously than do less biological elements of human life. The church, the schools, government, the urban workplace – these institutions and environments leave a greater impression of perpetuity and a relatively steady state, though individuals within them come and go. Even in the rural workplace, where at least the annual cycle of seasonal change is visible, the years come around more or less the same each time. But to see children shoot up from infancy to adolescence, from childhood to adulthood, in what seem retrospectively like mere flashes of time – like Will's sudden jump through forty-five winters – is to sense one's own temporality. So too, and more imminently, the infirmities of age impress upon a person the linearity and irrevocability of one life's time.

The significance of time in *Piers Plowman* has been explored by a number of scholars, often in relation to connections between the various ages of salvation history, or to apocalyptic elements in the poet's vision.[68] Time is also an aspect of Nature, of the created universe; furthermore, together with speech it is one of the things that Langland worries most about wasting. Humankind was created in time, to work out its return to God in time; time must be used profitably and wisely – by laborers, husbands and wives, or preachers and poets. But all these profitable uses are designed to come to an end, in the lives of individuals and in the world's age; they are temporary as well as temporal. Times are not 'alle yliche,' as Haukyn and C's Lechery claim; the fullness of time opens some doors but closes others, and if one waits too long, it will be too late for 'alle tymes of [his] tyme to profit [to] turne' (C.5.101).

---

[68] Cf. Morton W. Bloomfield, *Piers Plowman as a Fourteenth-century Apocalypse* (New Brunswick, NJ, 1962); Ruth M. Ames, *The Fulfillment of the Scriptures: Abraham, Moses, and Piers* (Evanston, 1970); Katherine Bache Trower, 'Temporal Tensions in the *Visio* of *Piers Plowman*,' *MS* 35 (1973), 389–412; Robert Adams, 'The Nature of Need in "Piers Plowman" XX,' *Traditio* 34 (1978), 291–301; Mary J. Carruthers, 'Time, Apocalypse, and the Plot of *Piers Plowman*,' in Mary J. Carruthers and Elizabeth D. Kirk, eds., *Acts of Interpretation: The Text in Its Contexts 700–1200: Essays on Medieval and Renaissance Literature in Honor of E. Talbot Donaldson* (Norman, OK, 1982), 175–88; Douglas Bertz, 'Prophecy and Apocalypse in Langland's *Piers Plowman*, B-Text, Passus XVI to XIX,' *JEGP* 84 (1985), 313–27.

Thus the few but salient references to Elde at crucial moments in Will's history (BC) and salvation history (C) and the many references to Kynde in connection with marriage juxtapose the most immediate personal experiences of the temporally structured, natural order with the working out of salvation in time, with winning grace by not wasting time, and with recognizing the 'tempus plantandi, et tempus evellendi quod plantatum est; . . . tempus amplexandi, et tempus longe fieri ab amplexibus; . . . tempus nascendi, et tempus moriendi' (Eccles. 3:2, 5, 2).

Another important topic, or pair of topics, illuminated by the poet's references to family and marriage is that of individuals in relation to their social networks. By and large, Langland is more interested in the social network side of this relation, in both positive and negative manifestations – mutual support or conflict among siblings, covetous or wise family involvement in matrimonial decisions, an ideally loving and respectful hierarchy of authority within the family or a family in which children are over-coddled or a wife must compensate for her husband's total abdication of moral authority. Now and then, however, he portrays individuals breaking free of these societal structures; usually this breakout leads into disorderly lives, as with most minstrels and wanderers or the dishonest beggars who will neither work nor marry, but sometimes the fool or the eloping couple manage to serve truth better by refusing to follow loveless or lawless social expectations. The difficulties of choosing between responsibilities to oneself and to one's fellows, with whom one usually stands in some positive or negative relationship, is probably nowhere more common or complex than in families. It may be fairly easy to praise the painful moral decision made by the young girl who follows the man she loves instead of acquiescing to her parents' brokered marriage plans for her, even though we see that she is rejecting her natural social network. (The judgment is even easier in that the case is actually a metaphor for the rich man abandoning the world for Poverty and God.) It is harder to utterly condemn Haukyn/ Actif or Will for remaining so long with their dependent families, even if their wives and children are occasions of sin.

Finally, it is worth noting the frequency with which the poem's great themes of law and love are embodied in familial relations, not so much by the poet's contriving but by the very nature of marriage and family themselves. Serving ends both societal and personal, structured for the expression of authority and of affection, these two interlinked institutions naturally embody the sometimes conflicting, sometimes concordant demands of law and love, rational order and leal liking. They are not mere metaphors for the operation of love and law in society at large, but rather the central social arena in which love and law actually do or should operate.

Langland's judgments on particular marital or familial behaviors seem to be largely and often consciously shaped by the degree to which a given behavior conforms itself to both law and love: discipline with loving sympathy and care for children; marital desire fulfilled in orderly ways that respect the life of the spirit, and issuing in *muliere* children; lawful marriages, perhaps arranged by 'fader and frendes,' but with fruitful love in mind rather than the *brocage* of land and money. When parents are too easy with their children, or when bastards are born outside both love and law, or when marriages are made lawfully but out of cold *covetise*, then both the soul and society come under attack. Law is sapped by 'vnsittyng soffraunce' and sloth, which stupefy the hopeful fear needed for contrition and the restitution of all that one owes. Even worse, love – the special reflection of the divine Spirit in the soul – is quenched by *unkyndenesse*, the obdurate and unforgivable contempt for God's life in one's fellow human beings.

5

Kindly Similitude: Marriage and Family in *Piers Plowman*

Asking 'How many children had Lady Macbeth?' sheds no light on Shakespeare's play. Chaucer does not tell us whether his much-married archwife, Alice of Bath, had children or not. Langland, on the other hand, accounts for the families of his two principal characters, and depicts both of those characters fulfilling family responsibilities: Piers with his wife, son, and daughter, and Will with Kit and Calot. Although the characterization of the families of Will and Piers does not go much beyond the allegorical or typical connotations of their names, their very presence in the poem suggests that Langland conceives the basic human situation as being grounded in familial experience and structured by marital, parental, filial, and sibling bonds.

In the preceding chapters, we have examined many passages in which Langland explores these structural bonds or assumes them pursuant to his treatment of other issues. We have also noted, in *ad hoc* and local terms, the major revisions in marital and familial materials in *Piers*. However, it seems appropriate, given the wide range of particular passages and changes discussed above, to close this study by reviewing them globally, and then situating that review within the still larger framework of the poem's ruling themes. Since the patterns of change are suggestive of the direction and development of Langland's thought on marriage and family, I begin here with the revisions and then move on to the broader functions of the marital and familial elements in the poem as a whole.

Patterns of Revision

The largest wholesale changes in Langland's many references to marriage and family occur in the central portion of Wit's speech and in the Tree of Charity and Abraham episodes, discussed above in Chapters 2 and 3 respectively. In the former, we have seen the trend toward increasingly spiritualized notions of familial and vocational responsibilities, and the sharp decrease (especially from B to C) in concrete familial images. Indeed, the changes across the three texts are so great that, were it not for the mediation of the B text, A and C would appear to erect completely different bridges between the allegory of Castle Caro and Wit's homily on marriage. In contrast to this middle part of Wit's speech, with its general reduction of familial material from one text to the next, the changes from B.16 to C.18 expand the amount of verse devoted to the human family and lay greater stress on the essential worth of the married, family-producing state and its high spiritual significance as a positive source of grace and reflection of the Trinity. In both sets of revisions, however, we find a growing emphasis on the spiritual or metaphorical implications of familial relationships, an emphasis also visible in other, smaller revisions in the poem's treatments of marriage and family: e.g., the shifting focus of Wit's discussion of marriage as Do-wel, moving from honest work to a life of love and law; the increasingly saintly classes of people listed by Wit as the fruit of wedlock; the poet's increasingly negative associations of illegitimacy with evil *kynde* and behavior; and Conscience's inclusion of family relations in the grammatical metaphor for *relacioun rect*.

Although Langland stresses the spiritual aspects of marriage and family more and more from one version of *Piers Plowman* to the next, giving increasing emphasis to the work of grace in familial life, he also connects the two subjects more and more frequently to nature's work, to the theme of *kynde* in the poem. For example, we find the concept of the descent of virtue and vice along family lines implied by A.10 (Wit's speech), then stated more explicitly in terms of *kynde* in B.2 (Holy Church on Meed, quoting Mt. 7:17) and B.9 (Wit again, paraphrasing Mt. 7:17 and quoting Mt. 7:16). In C.2, Holy Church adds an Englished version of Mt. 7:16 to her comments on Meed, while Wit gives both biblical verses and adds the lapidary phrase 'kynde folweth kynde' in his C text speech. In all three texts, Wit's speech turns our attention to Kynde and the origins of moral *kynde* in human beings, but at the end of that speech, B and C bring in additional natural examples as evidence for parental transmission of character, modify the Noachian allusion to speak of all *kyndes* being saved in pairs, and remind us of the natural sexual drives upon which marriage can impose *mesure*. The C text pushes the theme of *kynde* still further, by sharpening the contrast between the *kyndes* found in mismatched, covetous marriages to the point of outraged hyperbole.

Later, both B and C set the mystery of human sexuality against the rational laws established by Kynde for all other animal kinds – a new topic in the poem, as Langland moves on past the conclusion or obstruction reached at the end of the A text. New allusions to *kynde* – divine and human – appear again in the description of the Tree of Charity and in Abraham's speech on the Trinity, especially in the C version of those passages: we have the 'o kyne colour and kynde' of the three *schoriares* of Charity, the common Adamic *kynde* of the apples on the Tree, the lower but still *kynde* need which leads most people to elect the active married state, and the shared *kyndes* found among the three divine persons and in human families. Elde, who shakes the Tree in C, reminds us that the tree of Adam's *kynde* is firmly rooted in the natural world, and is thus, since the Fall, subject to time and death even though its fruits and branches reach upward to the bright warmth of God's grace. As Will learns by experience in the final passus, family bonds and duties are unavoidably subject to dissolution, either in or before death. The only craft that retains its value at the end of life is the craft of love itself, a craft learned *en famille* but now to be aimed Godward, in the 'longing to be hennes.'

I have already noted the sharpened contrast between the mismatched *kyndes* who marry 'for coueytise of catel' according to Wit's C-text speech. This heightening of differences, even to the point of hyperbole, conforms to another pattern of revision in the familial references from one version of *Piers* to the next. On the one hand, the language in which the poet describes the positive aspects of marriage grows more and more idealistic, with increasing emphasis placed on its role in producing saintly offspring through 'godes werk'; its potential as a life of love, law, and *leaute*; its lesser but still highly honorable place on the Tree of Charity; and its signification of the Mystical Body and the Trinity. On the other hand, the language which he applies to abuses and abusers of marriage and family life grows increasingly condemnatory. Meed's character is shaded somewhat more negatively in each version, with slight but noticeable underscorings of her metaphorical promiscuity and her encouragement of literal promiscuity and whorish behavior among women and men. References to bastardy become harsher and harsher across the three texts: Meed's illegitimacy first appears in B; in C, Will complains about bastards and bondmen being ordained while noblemen's sons must become laborers; the bastards sired and crippled by undeserving beggars are said in C, but not in the earlier texts, to be 'beggares of kynde'; it is in C also that Wit accuses the old, rich, *vnlossum* women sought by young gentlemen of being bastard and bond, while fair, young, and gentle virgins go unwed. In B, and to a slightly lesser extent in C, Reason's sermon begins with more than twice as many lines on family discipline as the parallel sermon by Conscience in A. The C text also adds the exemplum of Ophni and Phineas to the Prologue (greatly expanded from the earlier allusion in B.10.285–88); the addition denounces the corruption of ecclesiastical leadership in terms of corruption in family discipline – the 'vnsittyng soffraunce' named as Meed's sister later in C.

This turning up of the emotional contrast makes a great deal of psychological sense. Impassioned idealism and the *saeva indignatio* of the satirist are natural obverses. Langland's revisions in the familial and matrimonial content of *Piers Plowman* reflect a steadily intensifying commitment to two closely-linked goals: first, to affirm the positive social and spiritual functions of marriage and family, and second, to demonstrate the familial dimensions of the evils that attack church, society, and soul alike. Over the course of the poem, these evils are shown to operate in many of life's arenas, but the familial demonstration has the special advantage of hitting quite literally close to home for a very large majority of the poet's audience.

Marriage and Family as Kindly Similitude

While Langland's treatment of marriage and family is not as overtly central to *Piers Plowman* as his explorations of salvation, work well-done, truth, law, perfection, and similar great themes, it nonetheless plays an important role in the poem. For one thing, family life is a large and intrinsic part of the active life for most adult lay Christians, and the proper use of family life is essential to maintaining and transmitting a well-lived *Activa Vita* within the whole Christian community. Hence Reason's and Conscience's early acknowledgments of the need for strict child-rearing practices; hence Wit's discourse on marriage near the start of Will's quest for Do-wel.

Hence also Liberum Arbitrium's defense of marriage in the C text as a state of life blessed by God, which multiplies the people, whether perfect or imperfect, on the Tree of Charity. Langland's 'public poetry' addresses itself not merely to problems of government and social economy, but also to the private, domestic economies on which public society is built. The married state is transcended by continence and contemplation, but only as Piers's honest physical work for the good of others is transcended by his prayers and penitence after he tears the Pardon.

In addition to recognizing the importance of literal family relations in the poem's larger scheme, we should remember that familial references

222

in *Piers* frequently apply to other social relations as well, by way of a natural metaphor, a 'kindly similitude.' The metaphor here is natural because it is only partially figurative: the social relations of mutual support, governance, obedience, and love are first learned within the family, so the figuring of society in familial terms has a sound etiological basis.

The principles of love, law, and *leaute* which bind society together are not merely symbolized by ideal marriage and family life, but also depend on good families for their transmission. Given this natural – indeed, well-worn – metaphor for social relationships, one can easily understand Langland's readiness to depict corrupted society in terms of corrupted marriages and families: the marriage of Meed, Wrong's attack on the household of Peace, the *covetise* of the Sethites in marrying their children to Cain's seed, or the lecherous couplings and descent of Life, Fortune, Sloth, Tom Two-tongue, and Wanhope.

A different kind of etiological basis underlies Langland's figurative uses of marriage and family to explain the Redemption and the Trinity: insofar as Langland goes beyond the commonplace analogy between family and society, it is in this theological application of familial terms and relationships. His familial expositions of theological mysteries implicitly extend Paul's insight that 'all paternity in heaven and earth' takes its name from the Father (Eph. 3:15). For Paul, creaturely fatherhood is not just a convenient device to explain the relation between the first and second persons of the Trinity, but actually derives from that divine and eternal relation. Langland's fraternal metaphor for Christ's redemptive relationship with humankind and his familial metaphors for the persons of the Trinity likewise imply such derived similitude. Because humanity bears the image of the Trinity, 'man and his make and moilere here issue' can help us partially understand the society of the Trinity; Christ's incarnate, brotherly relation to humankind is what establishes the right relationships between us and our human brothers and sisters, rather than the other way round.

Thus, we may hypothesize that Langland saw the ideal human family as a fulcrum or focal point between the Deity and human society at large. The moral and social relationships that should govern the *comune* – law and love, justice and mercy, truth and peace, fruitfulness and mutual delight – originate in the Godhead, receive their first human embodiment in conjugal and familial bonds, and can only then be extended successfully to the rest of society. As evidence for this hypothesis, one might cite Langland's frequent emphasis on the importance of love and legitimacy in wedlock, the associations of marriage with one or all persons of the Trinity in B.16/C.18, Wit's combined genetic and educational explanation of Do-wel's familial origins, and his analogical arguments for helping needy members of society as spiritual kin. The poem does not so much expound or defend such a view as simply assume it. From that assumption, the poet goes on to a wide variety of corollary allusions to marital or familial life, most of them very much in harmony with the basic axiom proposed here.

The frequent references to particular aspects of family life throughout *Piers Plowman* can be understood from a rhetorical perspective as well as a conceptual or thematic one. Whether or not Langland had fully articulated his understanding of marriage and family to himself, he clearly found the familial realm a fertile one for all manner of moral and theological examples. When he describes social relations, secular or spiritual, he very often does so in terms of familial experiences. Charity is as cheerful as a child in its dealings with others; care for our needy fellow-humans is like the care owed by parents and godparents to dependent family members; even the relations of the various faculties within the soul are seen as being like those among a noble household structured by bonds of both kinship and fealty. To be sure, the familial sphere is not the only area from which Langland draws examples and figures; the world of feudal loyalty just mentioned and the agricultural and legal realms are at least as important as sources for his imagery, figurative expression, and conceptualizing of spiritual issues. However, these other sources of image and idea have hitherto been explored more fully than the familial realm: an imbalance which the present study has endeavored to redress, at least in part.

Family life can also be usefully distinguished from these other sources of Langland's habitual forms of expression. Its most important characteristic as such a source is its near-universality, its very common-ness and homeliness. To illustrate one's points in familial terms is to touch on the direct experience of almost all one's audience, from growing up to marriage and child-rearing to the eventual breakup of families by filial marriages, parental aging, and death. Like the more exalted but less common bond of knightly fealty, that homely experience involves some of the most important affective dimensions in the lives of medieval men and women. Even granting the differences between medieval and modern households, and between medieval and modern attitudes on many subjects, it is hard to imagine how the positive or negative familial experiences of Langland and his audience could *not* have informed, in one way or another, their commitments, passions, and ethical values – the habits of their hearts.

Thus, for instance, Langland speaks of offenses against *treuthe* not only in terms of the traitor angels who refused to serve as 'goddes knyghtes,' but also in terms of those wrangling couples who 'plyhte treuthe to louye, / Ac . . . lyen lely, here neyther lyketh other' (C.1.103–10a, 10.269–70; cf. A.1.104–11, 10.191, B.1.105–19, 9.170). He explains the Redemption not only in terms of a chivalric jousting, or a cleverly-argued legal debate, or a divine hunger and thirst for human souls, but also as the inescapable outcome of a brother's love. He thinks of teaching and preaching not only as a sowing and harvesting of seeds, but also as a discourse that takes place within families, from those with knowledge and responsibility to those still in need of guidance, be they sons and daughters, servants, wives, indiscreet or sinful husbands, or the spiritual children of godparents and prelates. By presenting the economy of salvation in language drawn from the familial economy, Langland offers us a similitude which is kindly in the full sense of the word, and thus a way of *knowynge* which is deeply *kynde* for men and women of every estate.

In sum, Langland's references to marriage and family serve his poetic ends in a number of ways. First, as important literal elements in the life that leads the ordinary Christian to salvation; second, as a way of figuring forth other social relations; third, as a mode of explaining certain central theological mysteries, especially the Trinity, the Incarnation, and the Redemption; and fourth, as a strategy for driving home his arguments in some of the most familiar and affective terms available to him. His figurative extensions of family relations to social and theological matters reflect more than a convenient but coincidental similarity; for Langland, these metaphors are founded on genuine causal connections between the structures and relationships within the Deity, the human family, and the *comune* at large. While Langland may not be writing *about* marriage and family in the way he writes *about* salvation or society or the uses of learning, both marriage and family remain important means for expressing his passionate concerns on the latter and larger themes.

Indeed, the familial theme leads to a number of larger topics within *Piers Plowman*, as I have tried to show in the preceding chapters. Family life and marriage epitomize the frequent conflict and potential cooperation between Nature and Grace. They were founded by Kynde the Creator to transmit human *kynde*, which should but all too often does not imitate the divine *kynde* from which it takes its ultimate origin. Used in timely and measurable fashion – or, as Reason would put it, used 'kyndely' – they are a source of grace and well-doing among humankind. Abused by *immesure* of whatever sort, they are sources of ill-doing and shame. *Kynde* and grace are linked with marriage and with family from Wit's *kynde*-centered discourse onward, if not before. The creation of individual human *kyndes*, even after the Fall, is marked by God's gracious gifts – especially Anima herself, the God-like life of the human soul, and Inwit, closely related to God's grace and image within the individual. Matrimony, through which good human *kynde* is passed on, is at once rooted in nature and a source of positive grace; and it has been such from its primal institution in Eden. We also see, with increasing fullness as the poem progresses, how salvific grace is related to Christ's fraternal sharing of *kynde* with the human race.

Langland eventually fuses the notions of *kynde* and grace, when he has the Good Samaritan identify the Holy Spirit – God's grace and love – with 'goddes owene kynde' (B.17.275, C.19.251). The deepest sin against the Spirit, the unforgivable sin, is *unkyndeness* – violating the bonds of physical and spiritual kinship, being obdurately '*ingratus* to þi kynde' (B.17.257, C.19.218), and thus forfeiting all claim to the merciful warmth of God's own loving *kynde*. While families are not explicitly mentioned in the Samaritan's discourse, the affective force of that discourse is powerfully enhanced by all the preceding associations of nature and grace, and of love, life, and likeness, with both the Trinity and with virtuous human families.

The right and wrong uses of marriage constitute everyday examples of another large concern in *Piers Plowman*: the ordinate and inordinate use of physical goods, from natural bodily drives to the property that is involved in bringing up children, providing for their marriages, or making one's last will and testament. Similarly, the poem links marriage and family with worldly and spiritual work, both of which should be fruitful or productive. The medieval family was itself a major locus of economic production, whether in the country or the city; like the theoretical version of the feudal social contract, the family would have provided a prime instance of the mutually supportive division of labor which Langland sees as essential to the ideal *comune*.

The subject of good work and good works leads to the related question of using time rightly, which is juxtaposed with the poet's marital and familial remarks at several significant points. One of the key elements in Wit's discussion of marriage is his enjoining of married folk to observe the due times for sexuality; the injunction appears at both the beginning and end of his marriage 'homily.' Piers's wife is named Dame Work-when-time-is. Family life itself is unavoidably shaped by the effects of time – children growing, parents aging, physical powers passing away. In family life, we see something which is just as true (though perhaps more easily ignored) in the spiritual life of the individual: namely, that human beings are creatures of time, who must work out their lives and

226

their salvations within time. When the time is at hand for a given action, be it generating children, harvesting a field, or repenting of one's sins and converting one's life, then the action must be taken before the opportunity is lost. To misuse time is to bring forth spiritual monsters, cursed like Cain, or to waste it outright, perhaps losing its fullness forever. Time lost never returns, for Nature, Age, and Death inexorably bring all of our times and powers to an end. The best way for the Dreamer to find 'a tyme / That alle tymes of [his] tyme to profit shal turne' is to 'rape [him] to bigynne / The lyif þat is louable . . . . / 3e, and contynue' (C.5.100–04).

The experiences of marriage and of family life thus embody some of Langland's most significant themes. Marriage begins with a plighting of *treuthe*, and a consensus of wills; its union of bodies represents a sharing of like *kyndes*, and often results in the generation of new but still-similar natures. In healthy marriages, one finds a striking combination of a lawful, socially-directed institution with loving, personal relationships. Healthily functioning families combine well-ordered structures of governance with mutual affections and loyalties. Love, Law, and their *tertium quid* Leaute come together in ideal family life in a way recognizable to people at all levels of society, and essential for the sound functioning of society itself. As Wit puts it in C,

> Ho-so lyueth in lawe and in loue doth wel,
> As this wedded men þat this world susteyneth.

Bibliography

(This bibliography omits a number of biblical commentaries and a few Middle English works cited in footnotes as parallels to material discussed in the text; these works can be located by way of the general index below.)

Abellán, Pedro M. *El fin y la significación sacramental del matrimonio desde S. Anselmo hasta Guillermo de Auxerre.* Granada: Colegio de la Compañia de Jesús, 1939.

Adams, Norma. '*Nullius Filius*: A Study of the Exception of Bastardy in the Law Courts of Medieval England.' *University of Toronto Law Journal* 6 (1945–46), 361–84.

Adams, Robert. 'Langland's Theology.' In *A Companion to Piers Plowman*, ed. John A. Alford, 87–114. Berkeley: University of California Press, 1988.

———. 'Langland's *Ordinatio*: The *Visio* and the *Vita* Once More.' *YLS* 8 (1994), 51–84.

———. '*Mede* and *Mercede*: The Evolution of the Economics of Grace in the *Piers Plowman* B and C Versions.' In *Medieval English Studies Presented to George Kane*, ed. Edward Donald Kennedy et al., 217–32. Woodbridge: Brewer, 1988.

———. 'The Nature of Need in "Piers Plowman" XX.' *Traditio* 34 (1978), 273–301.

———. 'Piers's Pardon and Langland's Semi-Pelagianism.' *Traditio* 39 (1983), 367–418.

Aers, David. 'Class, Gender, Medieval Criticism, and *Piers Plowman*.' In *Class and Gender in Early English Literature: Intersections*, ed. Britton J. Harwood and Gillian R. Overing, 59–75. Bloomington: Indiana University Press, 1994.

———. *Piers Plowman and Christian Allegory*. New York: St Martin's, 1975.

Albertus Magnus. *Opera Omnia*. Ed. Bernhard Geyer et al. Münster, Westf.: Aschendorff, 1951– .

Alford, John A., ed. *A Companion to Piers Plowman*. Berkeley: University of California Press, 1988.

———. 'The Design of the Poem.' In *A Companion to Piers Plowman*, ed. John A. Alford, 29–65. Berkeley: University of California Press, 1988.

———. 'Haukyn's Coat: Some Observations on *Piers Plowman* B.XIV.22-7.' *MÆ* 43 (1974), 133–38.

———. 'The Idea of Reason in *Piers Plowman*.' In *Medieval English Studies Presented to George Kane*, ed. Edward Donald Kennedy et al., 199–215. Woodbridge: Brewer, 1988.

———. 'More Unidentified Quotations in *Piers Plowman*.' *MP* 81 (1984), 278–85.

———. *Piers Plowman: A Glossary of Legal Diction*. Cambridge: Brewer, 1988.

229

──────. Review of George Kane and E. Talbot Donaldson, eds., *Piers Plowman: The B-Version. Speculum* 52 (1977), 1002–05.

──────. 'The Role of the Quotations in *Piers Plowman.' Speculum* 52 (1977), 80–99.

Allen, David G. 'The Dismas *Distinctio* and the Forms of *Piers Plowman* B.10–13.' *YLS* 3 (1989), 31–48.

Ames, Ruth M. *The Fulfillment of the Scriptures: Abraham, Moses, and Piers.* Evanston: Northwestern University Press, 1970.

──────. 'The Pardon Impugned by the Priest.' In *The Alliterative Tradition in the Fourteenth Century*, ed. Bernard S. Levy and Paul E. Szarmach, 49–54. Kent, OH: Kent State University Press, 1981.

Aquinas, Thomas. *Opera Omnia.* 25 vols. Parma, 1852–73; rpt. with introd. by Vernon J. Bourke, New York: Musurgia, 1948–50.

Archibald, Elizabeth. 'The Flight from Incest: Two Late Classical Precursors of the Constance Theme.' *ChauR* 20 (1986), 259–72.

Ashley, Kathleen, and Pamela Sheingorn, eds. *Interpreting Cultural Symbols: Saint Anne in Late Medieval Society.* Athens: University of Georgia Press, 1990.

Atkinson, Clarissa W. *The Oldest Vocation: Christian Motherhood in the Middle Ages.* Ithaca: Cornell University Press, 1991.

Audelay, John. *The Poems.* Ed. Ella Keats Whiting. EETS o.s. 184. London: Humphrey Milford, 1931.

Augustine. *De Civitate Dei Libri XXII*, ed. Bernhard Dombart and Alfons Kalb. CC 47–48. Turnhout: Brepols, 1955.

Baldwin, Anna P. *The Theme of Government in Piers Plowman.* Cambridge: Brewer, 1981.

──────. 'The Tripartite Reformation of the Soul in *The Scale of Perfection, Pearl*, and *Piers Plowman.'* In *The Medieval Mystical Tradition in England* 3, ed. Marion Glasscoe, 136–49. Cambridge: Brewer, 1984.

Barnes, Joshua. *The History of that Most Victorious Monarch Edward IIId.* Cambridge: John Hayes, 1688.

Barnes, Ralph, ed. *Liber Pontificalis of Edmund Lacy, Bishop of Exeter.* Exeter: Roberts, 1847.

Barney, Stephen A. 'The Plowshare of the Tongue: The Progress of a Symbol from the Bible to *Piers Plowman.' MS* 35 (1973), 261–93.

Barnum, Priscilla Heath, ed. *Dives and Pauper.* EETS o.s. 275, 280. London and Oxford: Oxford University Press, 1976–80.

Barratt, Alexandra. 'The Characters "Civil" and "Theology" in *Piers Plowman.' Traditio* 38 (1982), 352–64.

Barron, Caroline M. 'William Langland: A London Poet.' In *Chaucer's England: Literature in Historical Context*, ed. Barbara A. Hanawalt, 91–109. Minneapolis: University of Minnesota Press, 1992.

Barton, J. L. 'Nullity of Marriage and Illegitimacy in the England of the Middle Ages.' In *Legal History Studies 1972*, Papers Presented to the Legal History Conference, Aberystwyth, 18–21 July 1972, ed. Dafydd Jenkins, 28–49. Cardiff: University of Wales Press, 1975.

Bennett, Judith M. 'Medieval Peasant Marriage: An Examination of Marriage License Fines in *Liber Gersumarum.'* In *Pathways to Medieval Peasants*, ed. J. A. Raftis, 193–246. Papers in Mediaeval Studies 2. Toronto: Pontifical Institute, 1981.

──────. 'The Tie That Binds: Peasant Marriages and Peasant Families in Late Medieval England.' *Journal of Interdisciplinary History* 15 (1984), 111–29.

──────. *Women in the Medieval English Countryside: Gender and Household in Brigstock Before the Plague.* New York: Oxford University Press, 1987.

Bennett, Michael J. *Community, Class and Careerism: Cheshire and Lancashire Society in the Age of Sir Gawain and the Green Knight.* Cambridge Studies in Medieval Life and Thought. 3rd ser. 18. Cambridge: Cambridge University Press, 1983.
————. 'Spiritual Kinship and the Baptismal Name in Traditional European Society.' In *Principalities, Powers, and Estates: Studies in Medieval and Early Modern Government and Society,* ed. L. O. Frappel, 1–13. Adelaide: Adelaide University Union Press, 1979.
Benson, C. David. 'The Function of Lady Meed in *Piers Plowman.*' *English Studies* 61 (1980), 193–205.
Bertz, Douglas. 'Prophecy and Apocalypse in Langland's *Piers Plowman*, B-Text, Passus XVI to XIX.' *JEGP* 84 (1985), 313–27.
Biblia Sacra cum Glossa Ordinaria . . . et Postilla Nicolai Lyrani [ac Moralitatibus]. 6 vols. Douai and Antwerp, 1617.
Biggs, Frederick M. ' "Aungeles Peeris": *Piers Plowman*, B 16.67–72 and C 18.85–100.' *Anglia* 102 (1984), 426–36.
Biller, P. P. A. 'Birth-Control in the West in the Thirteenth and Early Fourteenth Centuries.' *Past and Present* 94 (1982), 3–26.
Bishop, Ian. 'Relatives at the Court of Heaven: Contrasted Treatments of an Idea in *Piers Plowman* and *Pearl.*' In *Medieval Literature and Antiquities: Studies in Honour of Basil Cottle,* ed. Myra Stokes and T. L. Burton, 111–18. Cambridge: Brewer, 1987.
Bliemetzrieder, Franz, ed. *Anselms von Laon Systematische Sentenzen.* Münster: Aschendorff, 1919.
Bloomfield, Morton W. '*Piers Plowman* and the Three Grades of Chastity.' *Anglia* 76 (1958), 227–53.
————. *Piers Plowman as a Fourteenth-century Apocalypse.* New Brunswick: Rutgers University Press, 1962.
————. *The Seven Deadly Sins: An Introduction to the History of a Religious Concept, with Special Reference to Medieval English Literature.* East Lansing: Michigan State College Press, 1952.
Boff, Leonardo. *Trinity and Society.* Trans. Paul Burns. Maryknoll: Orbis Books, 1988.
Boswell, John. *The Kindness of Strangers: The Abandonment of Children in Western Europe from Late Antiquity to the Renaissance.* New York: Pantheon, 1988; rpt. New York: Vintage, 1990.
Bowers, A. Joan. 'The Tree of Charity in *Piers Plowman*: Its Allegorical and Structural Significance.' In *Literary Monographs 6,* ed. Eric Rothstein and Joseph Anthony Wittreich, Jr., 1–34, 157–60. Madison: University of Wisconsin Press, 1975.
Bowers, John M. *The Crisis of Will in Piers Plowman.* Washington: Catholic University of America Press, 1986.
Bracton, Henry de. *De legibus et consuetudinibus regni Angliae.* Ed. George E. Woodbine, rev. and trans. Samuel E. Thorne. 4 vols. Cambridge: Harvard University Press, 1968–77.
Bradley, Henry. 'The Word "Moillere" in *Piers the Plowman.*' *MLR* 2 (1906–07), 163–64.
Braekman, W. L. 'Bollard's Middle English Book of Planting and Grafting and Its Background.' *SN* 57 (1985), 19–39.
————. 'Fortune-Telling by the Casting of Dice: A Middle English Poem and Its Background.' *SN* 52 (1980), 3–29.
Britton, Edward. *The Community of the Vill: A Study in the History of the Family and Village Life in Fourteenth-Century England.* Toronto: Macmillan, 1977.

Bibliography

Bromyard, John. *Summa Praedicantium*. Venice, 1586.

Brooke, C. N. L., and M. M. Postan, eds. *Carte Nativorum: A Peterborough Abbey Cartulary of the Fourteenth Century*. Northamptonshire Record Society 20. Oxford: Oxford University Press, 1960.

Brooke, Christopher N. L. *The Medieval Idea of Marriage*. Oxford: Oxford University Press, 1989.

Brown, Peter. *The Body and Society: Men, Women and Sexual Renunciation in Early Christianity*. New York: Columbia University Press, 1988.

Brundage, James A. *Law, Sex, and Christian Society in Medieval Europe*. Chicago: University of Chicago Press, 1987.

———. 'Widows as Disadvantaged Persons in Medieval Canon Law.' In *Upon My Husband's Death: Widows in the Literature and Histories of Medieval Europe*, ed. Louise Mirrer, 193–206. Ann Arbor: University of Michigan Press, 1992.

Bugge, John. *Virginitas: An Essay in the History of a Medieval Ideal*. The Hague: Nijhoff, 1975.

Burgh, John de. *Pupilla Oculi*. Strassburg, 1514.

Burnley, David. 'Langland's Clergial Lunatic.' In *Langland, the Mystics and the Medieval English Religious Tradition: Essays in Honour of S. S. Hussey*, ed. Helen Phillips, 31–38. Cambridge: Brewer, 1990.

Burrow, J. A. *The Ages of Man*. 1986; rpt. Oxford: Clarendon, 1988.

———. 'Chaucer's *Knight's Tale* and the Three Ages of Man.' In *Essays on Medieval Literature*, 27–48. Oxford: Clarendon, 1984.

———. *Essays on Medieval Literature*. Oxford: Clarendon, 1984.

———. 'Langland *Nel Mezzo Del Cammin*.' In *Medieval Studies for J. A. W. Bennett: Aetatis Suae LXX*, ed. P. L. Heyworth, 21–41. Oxford: Clarendon Press, 1981.

———. *Langland's Fictions*. Oxford: Clarendon, 1993.

———. 'The Portrayal of Amans in the *Confessio Amantis*.' In *Gower's Confessio Amantis: Responses and Reassessments*, ed. A. J. Minnis, 5–24. Cambridge: Brewer, 1983.

———. 'Reason's Horse.' *YLS* 4 (1990), 139–44.

———. ' "Young Saint, Old Devil": Reflections on a Medieval Proverb.' In *Essays on Medieval Literature*, 177–91. Oxford: Clarendon, 1984.

Burton, Dorothy Jean. 'The Compact with the Devil in the Middle-English *Vision of Piers Plowman*, B.II.' *California Folklore Quarterly* 5 (1946), 179–84.

Campbell, Bruce M. S. 'Population Pressure, Inheritance and the Land Market in a Fourteenth-Century Peasant Community.' In *Land, Kinship and Life-Cycle*, ed. Richard M. Smith, 87–134. Cambridge: Cambridge University Press, 1984.

Carlson, Paula J. 'Lady Meed and God's Meed: The Grammar of "Piers Plowman" B 3 and C 4.' *Traditio* 46 (1991), 291–311.

Carruthers, Mary J., and Elizabeth D. Kirk, eds. *Acts of Interpretation: The Text in Its Contexts 700–1600: Essays on Medieval and Renaissance Literature in Honor of E. Talbot Donaldson*. Norman, OK: Pilgrim Books, 1982.

Carruthers, Mary. *The Search for St. Truth: A Study of Meaning in Piers Plowman*. Evanston: Northwestern University Press, 1973.

———. 'Time, Apocalypse, and the Plot of *Piers Plowman*.' In *Acts of Interpretation: The Text in Its Contexts 700–1600: Essays on Medieval and Renaissance Literature in Honor of E. Talbot Donaldson*, ed. Mary J. Carruthers and Elizabeth D. Kirk, 175–88. Norman, OK: Pilgrim Books, 1982.

Chambers, R. W. *Man's Unconquerable Mind: Studies of English Writers, from Bede to A. E. Housman and W. P. Ker*. 1939; rpt. New York: Haskell, 1967.

Bibliography

Charles, R. H., ed. *The Apocrypha and Pseudepigrapha of the Old Testament in English*. 2 vols. Oxford: Clarendon Press, 1913.

Chaucer, Geoffrey. *The Riverside Chaucer*, 3rd ed. Ed. Larry D. Benson. Boston: Houghton Mifflin, 1987.

Cheney, C. R. *Notaries Public in England in the Thirteenth and Fourteenth Centuries*. Oxford: Clarendon, 1972.

Clark, Elaine. 'The Custody of Children in English Manor Courts.' *Law and History Review* 3 (1985), 333–48.

———. 'Deathbed Sales of Land in the Medieval Countryside.' Paper presented at the Social Science History Conference (October 1986).

———. 'The Decision to Marry in Thirteenth- and Early Fourteenth-Century Norfolk.' *MS* 49 (1987), 496–516.

———. 'Some Aspects of Social Security in Medieval England.' *Journal of Family History* 7 (1982), 307–20.

Clark, Elizabeth A. ' "Adam's Only Companion": Augustine and the Early Christian Debate on Marriage.' In *The Olde Daunce: Love, Friendship, Sex, and Marriage in the Medieval World*, ed. Robert R. Edwards and Stephen Spector, 15–31, 240–54. Albany: SUNY Press, 1991.

Clifton, Nicole. 'The Romance Convention of the Disguised Duel and the Climax of *Piers Plowman*.' *YLS* 7 (1993), 123–28.

Clopper, Lawrence M. 'Langland's Trinitarian Analogies as Key to Meaning and Structure.' *M&H* n.s. 9 (1979), 87–110.

Cohen, Jeremy. *'Be Fertile and Increase, Fill the Earth and Master It': The Ancient and Medieval Career of a Biblical Text*. Ithaca: Cornell University Press, 1989.

Collins, A. Jefferies, ed. *Manuale ad Usum Percelebris Ecclesiae Sarisburiensis*. HBS 91. Chichester: Moore and Tillyer, 1960.

Coolidge, Sharon Ann. 'The Grafted Tree in Literature: A Study in Medieval Iconography and Theology.' Diss. Duke, 1977.

Cooper, Helen. 'Gender and Personification in *Piers Plowman*.' *YLS* 5 (1991), 31–48.

Cornelius, Roberta D. *The Figurative Castle: A Study in the Mediaeval Allegory of the Edifice*. Bryn Mawr: Bryn Mawr College, 1930.

———. '*Piers Plowman* and the *Roman de Fauvel*.' *PMLA* 47 (1932), 363–67.

Crow, Martin M., and Clair C. Olson, eds. *Chaucer Life-Records*. Austin: University of Texas Press, 1966.

Cursor Mundi. Ed. Richard Morris. EETS o.s. 57, 59, 62, 66, 68, 99, 101. London: Kegan Paul, Trench, Trübner, 1874–93.

Dante Alighieri. *Dante's Convivio*. Trans. William Walrond Jackson. Oxford: Clarendon, 1909.

Davies, R. R. *Lordship and Society in the March of Wales, 1282–1400*. Oxford: Clarendon, 1978.

Davies, Stevan L. *The Revolt of the Widows: The Social World of the Apocryphal Acts*. Carbondale: Southern Illinois University Press, 1980.

Davis, Norman, ed. *The Paston Letters and Papers of the Fifteenth Century*. 2 vols. Oxford: Clarendon Press, 1971–76.

Davlin, Mary Clemente. *A Game of Heuene: Word Play and the Meaning of Piers Plowman B*. Cambridge: Brewer, 1989.

———. 'A Genius-Kynde Illustration in Codex Vat. Pal. Lat. 629.' *Manuscripta* 23 (1979), 149–58.

———. '*Kynde Knowyng* as a Major Theme in *Piers Plowman B*.' *RES* n.s. 22 (1971), 1–19.

———. '*Kynde Knowyng* as a Middle English Equivalent for "Wisdom" in *Piers Plowman B*.' *MÆ* 50 (1981), 5–17.

233

———. 'Petrus, Id Est, Christus: Piers the Plowman as "The Whole Christ." ' ChauR 6 (1972), 280–92.

———. 'Piers Plowman and the Books of Wisdom.' YLS 2 (1988), 23–33.

d'Avray, D. L., and M. Tausche. 'Marriage Sermons in ad status Collections of the Central Middle Ages.' Archives d'histoire doctrinale et littéraire du moyen âge 47 (1981), 71–119.

Day, Mabel, ed. The Wheatley Manuscript. EETS o.s. 155. London: Humphrey Milford, 1921.

DeWindt, Edwin B. Land and People in Holywell-cum-Needingworth: Structures of Tenure and Patterns of Social Organization in an East Midlands Village, 1252–1457. Studies and Texts 22. Toronto: Pontifical Institute, 1972.

Dolan, Terence. 'Langland's Women.' In A Wyf Ther Was: Essays in Honour of Paule Mertens-Fonck, ed. Juliette Dor, 123–28. Liège: Département d'anglais, Université de Liège, 1992.

Donahue, Charles, Jr. 'The Canon Law on the Formation of Marriage and Social Practice in the Later Middle Ages.' Journal of Family History 8 (1983), 144–58.

———. 'The Policy of Alexander the Third's Consent Theory of Marriage.' In Proceedings of the Fourth International Congress of Medieval Canon Law, Monumenta Iuris Canonici, Series C: Subsidia, Vol. 5, ed. Stephan Kuttner, 251–81. Vatican City: Biblioteca Apostolica Vaticana, 1976.

Donaldson, E. Talbot. 'Langland and Some Scriptural Quotations.' In The Wisdom of Poetry: Essays in Early English Literature in Honor of Morton W. Bloomfield, ed. Larry D. Benson and Siegfried Wenzel, 67–72. Kalamazoo: Medieval Institute, 1982.

———. Piers Plowman: The C-Text and Its Poet. 1949; rpt. Hamden: Archon, 1966.

Dove, Mary. 'Perfect Age and Piers Plowman.' Parergon 1 (1983), 55–67.

———. The Perfect Age of Man's Life. Cambridge: Cambridge University Press, 1986.

Dronke, Peter. 'Arbor Caritatis.' In Medieval Studies for J. A. W. Bennett, Aetatis Suae LXX, ed. P. L. Heyworth, 207–53. Oxford: Clarendon, 1981.

Duby, Georges. The Knight, the Lady and the Priest: The Making of Modern Marriage in Medieval France. Trans. Barbara Bray. New York: Pantheon Books, 1983.

———. 'Le mariage dans la société du haut moyen âge.' In Il Matrimonio nella Società Altomedievale, 2 vols. Proceedings of the 1976 Spoleto Conference 1:15–39. Spoleto: Centro Italiano di Studi sull' Alto Medioevo, 1977.

———. Medieval Marriage: Two Models from Twelfth-Century France. Trans. Elborg Forster. Baltimore: Johns Hopkins University Press, 1978.

Dunning, T. P. 'Action and Contemplation in Piers Plowman.' In Piers Plowman: Critical Approaches, ed. S. S. Hussey, 213–25. London: Methuen, 1969.

———. Piers Plowman: An Interpretation of the A Text, 2nd ed. Rev. T. P. Dolan. Oxford: Clarendon Press, 1980.

Dyer, Christopher. Lords and Peasants in a Changing Society: The Estates of the Bishopric of Worcester, 680–1540. Cambridge: Cambridge University Press, 1980.

———. 'Piers Plowman and Plowmen: A Historical Perspective.' YLS 8 (1994), 155–76.

Eaton, Roger. 'Langland's Malleable Lady Meed.' Costerus n.s. 80 (1991), 119–41.

Economou, George D. 'The Character Genius in Alan de Lille, Jean de Meun, and John Gower.' ChauR 4 (1970), 203–10.

———. The Goddess Natura in Medieval Literature. Cambridge: Harvard University Press, 1972.

Bibliography

————. 'The Two Venuses and Courtly Love.' In *The Pursuit of Perfection: Courtly Love in Medieval Literature*, ed. Joan M. Ferrante and George D. Economou, 17–50. Port Washington: Kennikat, 1975.

Elliott, Dyan. *Spiritual Marriage: Sexual Abstinence in Medieval Wedlock*. Princeton: Princeton University Press, 1993.

Emerson, Oliver F. 'Legends of Cain, Especially in Old and Middle English.' *PMLA* 21 (1906), 831–929.

Esmein, Adhémar. *Le mariage en droit canonique*, 2nd ed. Rev. R. Génestal and Jean Dauvillier. 2 vols. Paris: Sirey, 1929–35.

Farmer, Sharon. 'Persuasive Voices: Clerical Images of Medieval Wives.' *Speculum* 61 (1986), 517–43.

Fein, Susanna. 'Fourteenth-Century Trinitarian Piety for Women in *The Pistel of Swete Susan*.' Paper presented at the 28th International Congress on Medieval Studies, Kalamazoo, Michigan, May 1993.

Fischer, Boniface, ed. *Novae Concordantiae Bibliorum Sacrorum Vulgatam Versionem Critice Editam*. 5 vols. Stuttgart: Frommann-Holzboog, 1977.

Flandrin, Jean-Louis. 'Contraception, mariage et relations amoureuses dans l'Occident chrétien.' *Annales: Économies Sociétés Civilisations* 24 (1969), 1370–90.

————. *Un temps pour embrasser: aux origines de la morale sexuelle occidentale (VI⁺-XI⁺ siècle)*. Paris: Seuil, 1983.

Fletcher, Alan J. 'The Social Trinity of *Piers Plowman*.' *RES* n.s. 44 (1993), 343–61.

Flint, Valerie I. J. 'The "School of Laon": A Reconsideration.' *Recherches de Théologie Ancienne et Médiévale* 43 (1976), 89–110.

Fortescue, Sir John. *The Governance of England*. Ed. Charles Plummer. 1885; rpt. Westport, CT: Hyperion, 1979.

————. *De Laudibus Legum Angliae*, ed. and trans. S. B. Chrimes. Cambridge: Cambridge University Press, 1942.

Foucault, Michel. *The History of Sexuality*. Vol. 1: Introduction. Trans. Robert Hurley. New York: Pantheon, 1978.

Fradenburg, Louise O. *City, Marriage, Tournament: Arts of Rule in Late Medieval Scotland*. Madison: University of Wisconsin Press, 1991.

Frank, Robert Worth, Jr. 'The "Hungry Gap," Crop Failure, and Famine: The Fourteenth-Century Agricultural Crisis and *Piers Plowman*.' *YLS* 4 (1990), 87–104.

————. 'The Number of Visions in *Piers Plowman*.' *MLN* 66 (1951), 309–12.

————. *Piers Plowman and the Scheme of Salvation: An Interpretation of Dowel, Dobet, and Dobest*. New Haven: Yale University Press, 1957.

Frere, Walter H., and Langton E. G. Brown, eds. *The Hereford Breviary, Edited from the Rouen Edition of 1505 with Collation of Manuscripts*. 3 vols. HBS 26, 40, 46. London: Harrison and Sons, 1904–15.

Friedberg, Emil, ed. *Corpus iuris canonici*. 2 vols. Vol. 1: *Decretum Magistri Gratiani*; Vol. 2: *Decretalium collectiones*. Leipzig: Tauchnitz, 1879–81; rpt. Graz: Akademische Druck- und Verlagsanstalt, 1955.

Frost, Michael H. 'Symbolic Buildings in *Piers Plowman*: A Reading.' Diss. SUNY-Binghamton, 1984.

Fry, Donald K. 'The Authority of *Elde* in *The Parlement of the Thre Ages*.' In *Hermeneutics and Medieval Culture*, ed. Patrick J. Gallacher and Helen Damico, 213–21. Albany: SUNY Press, 1989.

Furnivall, Frederick J., ed. *Robert of Brunne's Handlyng Synne*. EETS o.s. 119, 123. London: Kegan Paul, Trench, Trübner, 1901–03.

————. *The Fifty Earliest English Wills in the Court of Probate, London: A.D. 1387–1439*. EETS o.s. 78. London: Trübner, 1882.

Galloway, Andrew. 'Two Notes on Langland's Cato: *Piers Plowman* B I.88–91; IV.20–23.' *ELN* 25 (1987), 9–12.

Genders, Roy. *The Complete Handbook of Fruit Growing*. London: Ward Lock, 1976.

Gerson, Jean. 'Le profit de savoir quel est péché mortel et véniel.' In *Oeuvres Complètes*. 10 vols. Ed. Palémon Glorieux. 7/1: 370–89. Paris: Desclée, 1960–73.

Gies, Frances and Joseph. *Marriage and the Family in the Middle Ages*. New York: Harper & Row, 1987.

Gilbert, Beverly Brian. ' "Civil" and the Notaries in *Piers Plowman*.' *MÆ* 50 (1981), 49–63.

Given, James Buchanan. *Society and Homicide in Thirteenth-Century England*. Stanford: Stanford University Press, 1977.

Given-Wilson, Chris, and Alice Curteis. *The Royal Bastards of Medieval England*. London: Routledge & Kegan Paul, 1984.

Glanville, Ranulf de (attrib.) *Tractatus de legibus et consuetudinibus regni Angliae qui Glanvill vocatur*. Ed. and trans. G. D. G. Hall. London: Nelson, 1965.

Godden, Malcolm. *The Making of Piers Plowman*. London: Longman, 1990.

Godwin, Frances G. 'An Illustration to the *De Sacramentis* of St Thomas Aquinas.' *Speculum* 26 (1951), 609–14.

Goldsmith, Margaret E. *The Figure of Piers Plowman: The Image on the Coin*. Cambridge: Brewer, 1981.

Gollancz, Israel, ed. *A Good Short Debate between Winner and Waster*. London: Humphrey Milford, 1930.

Gottlieb, Beatrice. *The Family in the Western World from the Black Death to the Industrial Age*. New York: Oxford University Press, 1993.

Gower, John. *The Complete Works of John Gower*. Ed. G. C. Macaulay. 4 vols. Oxford: Clarendon Press, 1899–1902.

Gradon, Pamela. '*Trajanus Redivivus*: Another Look at Trajan in *Piers Plowman*.' In *Middle English Studies Presented to Norman Davis in Honour of His Seventieth Birthday*, ed. Douglas Gray and E. G. Stanley, 93–114. Oxford: Clarendon, 1983.

Green, Richard Firth. *Poets and Princepleasers: Literature and the English Court in the Late Middle Ages*. Toronto: University of Toronto Press, 1980.

Haas, Louis. 'Social Connections between Parents and Godparents in Late Medieval Yorkshire.' *Medieval Prosopography* 10/1 (Spring 1989), 1–21.

Hair, P. E. H. *Before the Bawdy Court: Selections from Church Court and Other Records Relating to the Correction of Moral Offences in England, Scotland, and New England, 1300–1800*. London: Elek, 1972.

Hala, James P. 'The Word Made Flesh: Word-Play in *Piers Plowman B*.' Diss. University of Michigan, 1984.

Hallissy, Margaret. *Clean Maids, True Wives, Steadfast Widows: Chaucer's Women and Medieval Codes of Conduct*. Westport, CT: Greenwood, 1993.

Halliwell, J. O. *Early English Miscellanies*. London: Warton Club, 1855.

Hanawalt, Barbara A. 'Childrearing among the Lower Classes of Late Medieval England.' *Journal of Interdisciplinary History* 8 (1977), 1–22.

———. *Crime and Conflict in English Communities, 1300–1348*. Cambridge: Harvard University Press, 1979.

———. *Growing Up in Medieval London: The Experience of Childhood in History*. New York: Oxford University Press, 1993.

———. *The Ties That Bound: Peasant Families in Medieval England*. New York: Oxford University Press, 1986.

————. 'The Widow's Mite: Provisions for Medieval London Widows.' In *Upon My Husband's Death: Widows in the Literature and Histories of Medieval Europe*, ed. Louise Mirrer, 21–45. Ann Arbor: University of Michigan Press, 1992.

Hanna, Ralph III. *William Langland*. Authors of the Middle Ages 3. Aldershot: Variorum, 1993.

Harbert, Bruce. 'A Will with a Reason: Theological Developments in the C-Revision of *Piers Plowman*.' In *Religion in the Poetry and Drama of the Late Middle Ages in England*, ed. Piero Boitani and Anna Torti, 149–61. Cambridge: Brewer, 1990.

Häring, Bernard. *Marriage in the Modern World*. Trans. Geoffrey Stevens. Westminster, MD: Newman Press, 1965.

Harley, Marta Powell. 'The Derivation of *Hawkin* and Its Application in *Piers Plowman*.' *Names* 29 (1981), 97–99.

Harvey, John. *Mediaeval Gardens*. Beaverton, OR: Timber Press, 1981.

Harwood, Britton J., and Gillian R. Overing, eds. *Class and Gender in Early English Literature: Intersections*. Bloomington: Indiana University Press, 1994.

Harwood, Britton J. ' "Clergye" and the Action of the Third Vision in *Piers Plowman*.' *MP* 70 (1973), 279–90.

————. 'Dame Study and the Place of Orality in *Piers Plowman*.' *ELH* 57 (1990), 1–17.

————. 'Langland's *Kynde Knowyng* and the Quest for Christ.' *MP* 80 (1983), 242–55.

————. 'Langland's *Kynde Wit*.' *JEGP* 75 (1976), 330–36.

————. '*Liberum Arbitrium* in the C-Text of *Piers Plowman*.' *PQ* 52 (1973), 680–95.

————. *Piers Plowman and the Problem of Belief*. Toronto: University of Toronto Press, 1992.

————, and Ruth F. Smith. 'Inwit and the Castle of *Caro* in *Piers Plowman*.' *NM* 71 (1970), 648–54.

Haselden, R. B., and H. C. Schulz, eds. *Piers Plowman: The Huntington Manuscript (HM 143), Reproduced in Photostat*. San Marino, CA: Huntington Library, 1936.

Haskell, Ann S. 'The Paston Women on Marriage in Fifteenth-Century England.' *Viator* 4 (1973), 459–71.

Hatcher, John. *Plague, Population and the English Economy, 1348–1530*. London: Macmillan, 1977.

Hauréau, Barthélemy. 'Les filles du diable.' *Journal des savants*, April 1884, 225–28.

Heaney, Seamus P. *The Development of the Sacramentality of Marriage from Anselm of Laon to Thomas Aquinas*. Washington: Catholic University of America Press, 1963.

Helleiner, Karl F. 'The Population of Europe from the Black Death to the Eve of the Vital Revolution.' In *The Cambridge Economic History of Europe*, Vol. 4, ed. E. E. Rich and C. H. Wilson, 1–95. Cambridge: Cambridge University Press, 1967.

Helmholz, R. H. 'Bastardy Litigation in Medieval England.' *American Journal of Legal History* 13 (1969), 360–83.

————. *Marriage Litigation in Medieval England*. London: Cambridge University Press, 1974.

Heltzel, Virgil B. *Fair Rosamond: A Study of the Development of a Literary Theme*. Northwestern University Studies in the Humanities 16. Evanston: Northwestern University Press, 1947.

Bibliography

Henderson, W[illiam] G., ed. *Liber Pontificalis Christopheri Bainbridge Archiepiscopi Eboracensis*. SS 61. Durham: Andrews, 1875.
——, ed. *Manuale et Processionale ad Usum Insignis Ecclesiae Eboracensis*. SS 63. Durham: Andrews, 1875.
Henry, Avril. 'Some Aspects of Biblical Imagery in *Piers Plowman*.' In *Langland, the Mystics and the Medieval English Religious Tradition: Essays in Honour of S. S. Hussey*, ed. Helen Phillips, 39–55. Cambridge: Brewer, 1990.
Henry of Lancaster. *Le Livre de Seyntz Medicines: The Unpublished Devotional Treatise of Henry of Lancaster*. Ed. E. J. Arnould. ANTS 2. Oxford: Blackwell, 1940.
Herlihy, David. 'Medieval Children.' In *Essays on Medieval Civilization*, The Walter Prescott Webb Memorial Lectures 12, ed. Bede Karl Lackner and Kenneth Roy Philp, 109–41. Austin: University of Texas Press, 1978.
——. *Medieval Households*. Cambridge: Harvard University Press, 1985.
Higden, Ranulf. *Polychronicon*. Ed. Joseph Rawson Lumby and Churchill Babington. Rolls Series 41. 9 vols. London: Longman, 1865–86.
Hill, Thomas D. Review of Priscilla Martin, *Piers Plowman: The Field and the Tower*. *N&Q* 29 (1982), 240–41.
——. 'Seth the "Seeder" in *Piers Plowman* C.10.249.' *YLS* 1 (1987), 105–08.
Holdsworth, William S. *A History of English Law*. 3rd ed. 12 vols. Boston: Little, Brown, 1922–38. Book 3: The Mediaeval Common Law.
Holmes, G. A. *The Estates of the Higher Nobility in Fourteenth-Century England*. Cambridge: Cambridge University Press, 1957.
Hugh of St Cher. *Opera Omnia in Universum Vetus et Novum Testamentum*. 8 vols. Venice, 1600.
Huppé, Bernard F. '*Petrus Id Est Christus*: Word Play in *Piers Plowman*, the B-Text.' *ELH* 17 (1950), 163–90.
Hussey, S. S., ed. *Piers Plowman: Critical Approaches*. London: Methuen, 1969.
Innocent III. *De Miseria Condicionis Humane*, ed. Robert E. Lewis. Athens: University of Georgia Press, 1978.
Jefferies, P. J. 'Social Mobility in the Fourteenth Century: The Example of the Chelreys of Berkshire.' *Oxoniensia* 41 (1976), 324–36.
Jerome. *Adversus Jovinianum Libri Duo*. PL 23: 221–352.
Jespersen, Otto. *A Modern English Grammar on Historical Principles*. 7 vols. Completed by Niels Haislund. Heidelberg: Winter; Copenhagen: Munksgaard, 1909–49.
Josephus, Flavius. *Jewish Antiquities*. Ed. Franz Blatt. *Acta Jutlandica* 30:1. Copenhagen: Munksgaard, 1958.
Jusserand, J. J. '*Piers Plowman*: The Work of One or Five.' *MP* 6 (1909), 271–329.
Kane, George. 'A New Translation of the B Text of *Piers Plowman*.' *YLS* 7 (1993), 129–56.
Kaske, R. E. 'Holy Church's Speech and the Structure of *Piers Plowman*.' In *Chaucer and Middle English Studies in Honour of Rossell Hope Robbins*, ed. Beryl Rowland, 320–27. London: Allen & Unwin, 1974.
——. 'The Speech of "Book" in *Piers Plowman*.' *Anglia* 77 (1959), 117–44.
Kaulbach, Ernest. '*Piers Plowman* B IX: Further Refinements of Inwitte.' In *Linguistic and Literary Studies in Honor of Archibald A. Hill*, 4 vols., ed. M. A. Jazavery et al., 4: 103–10. The Hague: Mouton, 1979.
Kean, P. M. *Chaucer and the Making of English Poetry*. 2 vols. London: Routledge and Kegan Paul, 1972.
——. 'Love, Law, and *Lewte* in *Piers Plowman*.' *RES* n.s. 15 (1964), 241–61.
Kelly, Henry Ansgar. *Love and Marriage in the Age of Chaucer*. Ithaca: Cornell University Press, 1975.

Kelly, T. D., and John T. Irwin. 'The Meaning of *Cleanness*: Parable as Effective Sign.' *MS* 35 (1973), 232-60.

Kirk, Elizabeth D. *The Dream Thought of Piers Plowman.* New Haven: Yale University Press, 1972.

——. 'Langland's Plowman and the Recreation of Fourteenth-Century Religious Metaphor.' *YLS* 2 (1988), 1-21.

Knight, S. T. 'Satire in *Piers Plowman.*' In *Piers Plowman: Critical Approaches*, ed. S. S. Hussey, 279-309. London: Methuen, 1969.

Kooper, Erik. 'Loving the Unequal Equal: Medieval Theologians and Marital Affection.' In *The Olde Daunce: Love, Friendship, Sex and Marriage in the Medieval World*, ed. Robert R. Edwards and Stephen Spector, 44-56, 260-65. Albany: SUNY Press, 1991.

Krueger, Paul, Theodore Mommsen, and Rudolf Schoell, eds. *Corpus iuris civilis.* 3 vols. Berlin: Weidmann, 1872-99.

Kruger, Steven. 'Mirrors and the Trajectory of Vision in *Piers Plowman.*' *Speculum* 66 (1991), 74-95.

Långfors, A., ed. *Roman de Fauvel.* SATF. Paris: Didot, 1914-19.

Langland, William. *The Vision of William concerning Piers the Plowman in Three Parallel Texts.* Ed. Walter W. Skeat. 2 vols. 1886; rpt. with additional bibliography, Oxford: Clarendon, 1969.

——. *Piers the Plowman: A Critical Edition of the A-Version.* Ed. Thomas A. Knott and David C. Fowler. Baltimore: The Johns Hopkins Press, 1952.

——. *Piers Plowman: The A Version.* Ed. George Kane. 1960; rev. ed. London: Athlone, 1988.

——. *Piers Plowman: The Prologue and Passus I-VII of the B Text.* Ed. J. A. W. Bennett. Oxford: Clarendon Press, 1972.

——. *Piers Plowman: The B Version.* Ed. George Kane and E. Talbot Donaldson. 1975; rev. ed. London: Athlone, 1988.

——. *The Vision of Piers Plowman: A Critical Edition of the B-Text.* Ed. A. V. C. Schmidt. New ed. London: Dent, 1987.

——. *Piers Plowman.* Ed. Elizabeth Salter and Derek Pearsall. York Medieval Texts. Evanston: Northwestern University Press, 1967.

——. *Piers Plowman: An Edition of the C-Text.* Ed. Derek Pearsall. London: Arnold, 1978.

Langlois, Charles-Victor. *Saint Louis, Philippe le Bel, les derniers Capétiens directs, 1226-1328.* 1901; rpt. Paris: Tallandier, 1978.

Laslett, Peter. *Family Life and Illicit Love in Earlier Generations: Essays in Historical Sociology.* Cambridge: Cambridge University Press, 1977.

Lawlor, John. *Piers Plowman: An Essay in Criticism.* London: Arnold, 1962.

Le Bras, Gabriel. 'Mariage (III), La Doctrine du mariage chez les théologiens et les canonistes depuis l'an mille.' *DTC* 9/2: 2123-2317.

Leclercq, Jean. *Monks on Marriage: A Twelfth-Century View.* New York: Seabury Press, 1982. Also published as *Le Mariage vu par les moines au XIIᵉ siècle.* Paris: Éditions du Cerf, 1983.

Lees, Clare A. 'Gender and Exchange in *Piers Plowman.*' In *Class and Gender in Early English Literature: Intersections*, ed. Britton J. Harwood and Gillian R. Overing, 112-30. Bloomington: Indiana University Press, 1994.

Legg, J. Wickham, ed. *The Sarum Missal Edited from Three Early Manuscripts.* 1916; rpt. Oxford: Clarendon, 1969.

Lehmann, Paul. *Die Parodie im Mittelalter*, 2nd ed. Stuttgart: Hiersemann, 1963.

Lerer, Seth. 'Artifice and Artistry in *Sir Orfeo.*' *Speculum* 60 (1985), 92-109.

Lindahl, Carl. *Earnest Games: Folkloric Patterns in the Canterbury Tales.* Bloomington: Indiana University Press, 1987.

Littlehales, Henry, ed. *English Fragments from Latin Medieval Service-Books.* EETS e.s. 90. London: Kegan Paul, Trench, Trübner, 1903.

Lombard, Peter. *Libri IV Sententiarum.* Ed. Collegium S. Bonaventurae. 2nd ed. 2 vols. Florence: Collegium S. Bonaventurae, 1916.

Lumiansky, R. M., and David Mills, eds. *The Chester Mystery Cycle.* EETS s.s. 3. London: Oxford University Press, 1974.

Lunz, Elisabeth. 'The Valley of Jehoshaphat in *Piers Plowman.*' *Tulane Studies in English* 20 (1972), 1-10.

Lynch, Joseph H. *Godparents and Kinship in Early Medieval Europe.* Princeton: Princeton University Press, 1986.

Madox, Thomas. *Formulare Anglicanum.* London: Tonson and Knaplock, 1702.

Maguire, Stella. 'The Significance of Haukyn, *Activa Vita*, in *Piers Plowman.*' *RES* o.s. 25 (1949), 97-109.

Manly, John M. 'The Authorship of *Piers Plowman.*' *MP* 7 (1909), 83-144.

Mann, Jill. *Chaucer and Medieval Estates Satire: The Literature of Social Classes and the General Prologue to the Canterbury Tales.* Cambridge: Cambridge University Press, 1973.

———. 'Eating and Drinking in "Piers Plowman."' *Essays and Studies* 32 (1979), 26-43.

———. 'The Power of the Alphabet: A Reassessment of the Relation between the A and the B Versions of *Piers Plowman.*' *YLS* 8 (1994), 21-50.

Margerie, Bertrand de. *The Christian Trinity in History.* Trans. Edmund J. Fortman. Studies in Historical Theology 1. Still River, MA: St Bede's Publications, 1982.

Martin, Elaine M. 'Seek God's Face Evermore: A Study in Structure and Common Themes in Augustine's *De Trinitate* and Langland's *Piers Plowman.*' Diss. Yale, 1986.

Martin, Priscilla. *Piers Plowman: The Field and the Tower.* London: Macmillan, 1979.

———. '*Piers Plowman*: Indirect Relations and the Record of Truth.' In *Suche Werkis to Werche: Essays on Piers Plowman in Honor of David C. Fowler*, ed. Míceál F. Vaughan, 169-90. East Lansing: Colleagues Press, 1993.

McIntosh, Angus, et al. *A Linguistic Atlas of Late Mediaeval English.* 4 vols. Aberdeen: Aberdeen University Press, 1986.

McKisack, May. *The Fourteenth Century, 1307-1399.* Oxford History of England. Oxford: Clarendon, 1959.

Mechthild of Magdeburg. *Das Fliessende Licht der Gottheit.* Trans. Margot Schmidt. Einsiedeln: Benziger, 1956.

———. *Offenbarungen der Schwester Mechthild von Magdeburg.* Ed. Gall Morel. 1869; rpt. Darmstadt: Wissenschaftliche Buchgesellschaft, 1963.

Mellinkoff, Ruth. *The Mark of Cain.* Berkeley: University of California Press, 1981.

Mertes, Kate. *The English Noble Household, 1250-1600: Good Governance and Politic Rule.* Oxford: Blackwell, 1988.

Mertes, R. G. K. A. 'The Household as a Religious Community.' In *People, Politics and Community in the Later Middle Ages*, ed. Joel Rosenthal and Colin Richmond, 123-39. New York: St Martin's Press, 1987.

Metz, René. *La Consécration des vierges dans l'église romaine.* Paris: Presses Universitaires, 1954.

Meyer, Paul. 'Notice du MS. Rawlinson Poetry 241 (Oxford).' *Romania* 29 (1900), 1-84.

Bibliography

Middleton, Anne. 'The Idea of Public Poetry in the Reign of Richard II.' *Speculum* 53 (1978), 94-114.

———. 'Narration and the Invention of Experience: Episodic Form in *Piers Plowman*.' In *The Wisdom of Poetry: Essays in Early English Literature in Honor of Morton W. Bloomfield*, ed. Larry D. Benson and Siegfried Wenzel, 91-122. Kalamazoo: Medieval Institute, 1982.

———. 'William Langland's "Kynde Name": Authorial Signature and Social Identity in Late Fourteenth-Century England.' In *Literary Practice and Social Change in Britain, 1380-1530*, ed. Lee Patterson, 15-82. Berkeley: University of California Press, 1990.

Mills, David. 'The Rôle of the Dreamer in *Piers Plowman*.' In *Piers Plowman: Critical Approaches*, ed. S. S. Hussey, 180-212. London: Methuen, 1969.

Mirk, John. *Mirk's Festial: A Collection of Homilies*. Ed. Theodor Erbe. EETS e.s. 96. London: Kegan Paul, Trench, Trübner, 1905.

Moffat, Douglas. 'Rage, Play, and Foreplay in Middle English Literature.' *NM* 94 (1993), 167-84.

Molin, Jean-Baptiste, and Protais Mutembe. *Le Rituel du mariage en France du XIIe au XVIe siècle*. Paris: Beauchesne, 1974.

Moran, Jo Ann Hoeppner. *The Growth of English Schooling 1340-1548: Learning, Literacy, and Laicization in Pre-Reformation York Diocese*. Princeton: Princeton University Press, 1985.

Morgan, Gerald. 'Langland's Conception of Favel, Guile, Liar, and False in the First Vision of *Piers Plowman*.' *Neophil* 71 (1987), 626-33.

———. 'The Meaning of Kind Wit, Conscience, and Reason in the First Vision of *Piers Plowman*.' *MP* 84 (1987), 351-58.

———. 'The Status and Meaning of Meed in the First Vision of *Piers Plowman*.' *Neophil* 72 (1988), 449-63.

Morse, Charlotte C. *The Pattern of Judgment in the 'Queste' and 'Cleanness.'* Columbia: University of Missouri Press, 1978.

Müller, Michael. *Die Lehre des hl. Augustinus von der Paradiesesehe und ihre Auswirkung in der Sexualethik des 12. und 13. Jahrhunderts bis Thomas von Aquin*. Regensburg: Pustet, 1954.

Murray, James A. H., ed. *The Romance and Prophecies of Thomas of Erceldoune*. EETS o.s. 61. London: Trübner, 1875.

Murtaugh, Daniel Maher. *Piers Plowman and the Image of God*. Gainesville: University Presses of Florida, 1978.

Mussetter, Sally Ann. 'The Reformation of the Pilgrim to the Likeness of God: A Study of the Tropological Level of the *Divine Comedy* and *Piers Plowman B*.' Diss. Cornell, 1975.

Mustanoja, Tauno F. 'The Suggestive Use of Christian Names in Middle English Poetry.' In *Medieval Literature and Folklore Studies: Essays in Honor of Francis Lee Utley*, ed. Jerome Mandel and Bruce A. Rosenberg, 51-76. New Brunswick: Rutgers University Press, 1970.

Myers, A. R., ed. *English Historical Documents IV: 1327-1485*. London: Eyre and Spottiswoode, 1969.

Neugebauer, Richard. 'Treatment of the Mentally Ill in Medieval and Early Modern England.' *Journal of the History of the Behavioral Sciences* 14 (1978), 158-69.

Nicholas of Lyra. *Postilla [ac Moralitates]*. In *Biblia Sacra cum Glossa Ordinaria*. Douai and Antwerp, 1617.

Niles, Philip. 'Baptism and the Naming of Children in Late Medieval England.' *Medieval Prosopography* 3/1 (Spring 1982), 95-107.

241

Nitecki, Alicia K. 'Figures of Old Age in Fourteenth-Century English Literature.' In *Aging and the Aged in Medieval Europe*, ed. Michael M. Sheehan, 107–16. Toronto: Pontifical Institute, 1990.

Nitzsche, Jane Chance. *The Genius Figure in Antiquity and the Middle Ages*. New York: Columbia University Press, 1975.

Noonan, John T., Jr. *Bribes*. New York: Macmillan, 1984.

———. *Contraception: A History of Its Treatment by the Catholic Theologians and Canonists*. 1965; enlarged ed. Cambridge: Harvard University Press, 1986.

———. 'Marital Affection in the Canonists.' *Studia Gratiana* 12 (1967), 479–509.

———. 'Power to Choose.' *Viator* 4 (1973), 419–34.

Norton-Smith, John. *William Langland*. Leiden: Brill, 1983.

Oberman, Heiko A., and James A. Weisheipl, eds. 'The *Sermo Epinicius* ascribed to Thomas Bradwardine (1346).' *Archives d'histoire doctrinale et littéraire du moyen âge* 25 (1958), 295–329.

O'Driscoll, Philomena. 'The *Dowel* Debate in *Piers Plowman* B.' *MÆ* 50 (1981), 18–29.

Olsson, Kurt. 'Natural Law and John Gower's *Confessio Amantis*.' *M&H* n.s. 11 (1982), 229–61.

Olszewska, E. S. 'Middle English *fader and frendes*.' *N&Q* 20 (1973), 205–07.

Oppel, John. 'Saint Jerome and the History of Sex.' *Viator* 24 (1993), 1–22.

Orme, Nicholas. *From Childhood to Chivalry: The Education of the English Kings and Aristocracy, 1066–1530*. London: Methuen, 1984.

———. 'Children and the Church in Medieval England,' *Journal of Ecclesiastical History* 45 (1994), 563–87.

———. 'Langland and Education.' *History of Education* 11 (1982), 251–66.

Orsten, Elisabeth M. '*Patientia* in the B-Text of "Piers Plowman."' *MS* 31 (1969), 317–33.

Owst, G. R. *Literature and Pulpit in Medieval England*. 2nd ed. 1961; rpt. Oxford: Blackwell, 1966.

———. *Preaching in Medieval England: An Introduction to Sermon Manuscripts of the Period c. 1350–1450*. 1926; rpt. New York: Russell and Russell, 1965.

Paull, Michael R. 'Mahomet and the Conversion of the Heathen in *Piers Plowman*.' *ELN* 10 (1972), 1–8.

Payer, Pierre J. *The Bridling of Desire: Views of Sex in the Later Middle Ages*. Toronto: University of Toronto Press, 1993.

———. 'Early Medieval Regulations Concerning Marital Sexual Relations.' *Journal of Medieval History* 6 (1980), 353–76.

———. *Sex and the Penitentials: The Development of a Sexual Code, 550–1150*. Toronto: University of Toronto Press, 1984.

Perry, Sigrid Pohl. 'Trewe Wedded Libbynge Folk: Metaphors of Marriage in "Piers Plowman" and the "Canterbury Tales."' Diss. Northwestern, 1981.

Peter of Tarantaise (Innocent V). *In IV Libros Sententiarum Commentaria*. 4 vols. Toulouse, 1649–52; rpt. Ridgewood, NJ: Gregg, 1964.

Plucknett, Theodore F. T. *A Concise History of the Common Law*. 5th ed. Boston: Little, Brown, 1956.

Pollock, Frederick, and Frederic William Maitland. *The History of English Law Before the Time of Edward I*. 2 vols. Cambridge: Cambridge University Press, 1899.

Postan, M. M. *The Cambridge Economic History of Europe*. Vol. 1, rev. ed. Cambridge: Cambridge University Press, 1966.

———. *The Medieval Economy and Society: An Economic History of Britain in the Middle Ages*. London: Weidenfeld & Nicolson, 1972; Pelican, 1975.

Bibliography

Pounds, N. J. G. *The Medieval Castle in England and Wales: A Social and Political History*. Cambridge: Cambridge University Press, 1990.

Power, Eileen. *Medieval Women*. Ed. M. M. Postan. Cambridge: Cambridge University Press, 1975.

Powicke, F. M., and C. R. Cheney, eds. *Councils & Synods, with other Documents Relating to the English Church II: 1205-1313*. 1 vol. in 2 parts. Oxford: Clarendon Press, 1964.

Procter, Francis, and Christopher Wordsworth. *Breviarium ad usum insignis ecclesiae Sarum*. 3 vols. Cambridge: Cambridge University Press, 1879-86.

Quilligan, Maureen. 'Langland's Literal Allegory.' *Essays in Criticism* 28 (1978), 95-111.

Quirk, Randolph. 'Langland's Use of *Kind Wit* and *Inwit*.' *JEGP* 52 (1953), 182-88.

Raban, Sandra. *Mortmain Legislation and the English Church 1279-1500*. Cambridge Studies in Medieval Life and Thought, 3rd ser. 17. Cambridge: Cambridge University Press, 1982.

Raftis, J. A. *A Small Town in Late Medieval England: Godmanchester, 1278-1400*. Studies and Texts 53. Toronto: Pontifical Institute, 1982.

Raine, James, ed. *Depositions and Other Ecclesiastical Proceedings from the Courts of Durham, Extending from 1311 to the Reign of Elizabeth*. SS 21. London: Nichols and Son, 1845.

Ratcliff, S. C., et al., eds., *Legal and Manorial Formularies Edited from Originals at the British Museum and the Public Record Office, In Memory of Julius Parnell Gilson*. Oxford: Oxford University Press, 1933.

Ravensdale, Jack. 'Population Changes and the Transfer of Customary Land on a Cambridgeshire Manor in the Fourteenth Century.' In *Land, Kinship, and Life-Cycle*, ed. Richard M. Smith, 197-225. Cambridge: Cambridge University Press, 1984.

Raw, Barbara. 'Piers and the Image of God in Man.' In *Piers Plowman: Critical Approaches*, ed. S. S. Hussey, 143-79. London: Methuen, 1969.

Raymo, Robert R. 'A Middle English Version of the *Epistola Luciferi ad Cleros*.' In *Medieval Literature and Civilization: Studies in Memory of G. N. Garmonsway*, ed. D. A. Pearsall and R. A. Waldron, 233-48. London: Athlone, 1969.

Raymond of Pennafort. *Summa de Poenitentia et Matrimonio cum glossis Joannis de Friburgo*. 1603; rpt. Farnborough, Eng.: Gregg, 1967.

Razi, Zvi. *Life, Marriage, and Death in a Medieval Parish: Economy, Society and Demography in Halesowen, 1270-1400*. Cambridge: Cambridge University Press, 1980.

———. 'The Myth of the Immutable English Family.' *Past & Present* 140 (August 1993), 3-44.

Reinhardt, Heinrich J. F. *Die Ehelehre der Schule des Anselm von Laon*. Münster: Aschendorff, 1974.

Richmond, Colin. 'The Pastons Revisited: Marriage and the Family in Fifteenth-Century England.' *Bulletin of the Institute of Historical Research* 58 (1985), 25-36.

Ritzer, Korbinian. *Formen, Riten und religiöses Brauchtum der Eheschliessung in den christlichen Kirchen des ersten Jahrtausends*. Münster: Aschendorff, 1962.

Robbins, Rossell H., ed., *Historical Poems of the XIVth and XVth Centuries*. New York: Columbia University Press, 1959.

Robert of Flamborough. *Liber Poenitentialis*. Ed. J. J. Francis Firth. Studies and Texts 18. Toronto: Pontifical Institute, 1971.

Robertson, D. W., Jr., and Bernard F. Huppé. *Piers Plowman and Scriptural Tradition*. Princeton: Princeton University Press, 1951; rpt. New York: Octagon, 1969.

Bibliography

Rokeah, Zefira Entin. 'Unnatural Child Death Among Christians and Jews in Medieval England.' *Journal of Psychohistory* 18 (1990), 181–226.

Rondet, Henri. *Introduction a l'étude de la théologie du mariage*. Paris: Lethielleux, 1960.

Rosenthal, Joel T. *Patriarchy and Families of Privilege in Fifteenth-Century England*. Philadelphia: University of Pennsylvania Press, 1991.

———. *The Purchase of Paradise: Gift Giving and the Aristocracy, 1307–1485*. London: Routledge & Kegan Paul, 1972.

Ruether, Rosemary. 'Mothers of the Church: Ascetic Women in the Late Patristic Age.' In *Women of Spirit: Female Leadership in the Jewish and Christian Traditions*, ed. Rosemary Ruether and Eleanor McLaughlin, 71–98. New York: Simon and Schuster, 1979.

Russell, G. H. 'The Salvation of the Heathen: The Exploration of a Theme in *Piers Plowman*.' *Journal of the Warburg and Courtauld Institutes* 29 (1966), 101–16.

———. 'Some Aspects of the Process of Revision in *Piers Plowman*.' In *Piers Plowman: Critical Approaches*, ed. S. S. Hussey, 27–49. London: Methuen, 1969.

Sajavaara, Kari, ed. *The Middle English Translations of Robert Grosseteste's 'Château d'Amour'*. Mémoires de la Société Néophilologique de Helsinki 32. Helsinki: Société Néophilologique, 1967.

Salter, Elizabeth. 'Langland and the Contexts of "Piers Plowman." ' *Essays and Studies* 32 (1979), ed. Dieter Mehl, 19–25.

Scase, Wendy. 'Two *Piers Plowman* C-Text Interpolations: Evidence for a Second Textual Tradition.' *N&Q* n.s. 34 (1987), 456–63.

Schillebeeckx, Edward. *Marriage: Human Reality and Saving Mystery*, trans. N. D. Smith. London: Sheed and Ward, 1976.

Schmidt, A. V. C. *The Clerkly Maker: Langland's Poetic Art*. Cambridge: Brewer, 1987.

———. '*Kynde Craft* and the *Play of Paramorez*: Natural and Unnatural Love in *Purity*.' In *Genres, Themes, and Images in English Literature from the Fourteenth to the Fifteenth Century*, ed. Piero Boitani and Anna Torti, 105–24. Tübingen: Narr, 1988.

———. 'Langland and Scholastic Philosophy.' *MÆ* 38 (1969), 134–56.

———. 'Langland's Pen/Parchment Analogy in *Piers Plowman* B.IX.38–40.' *N&Q* 27 (1980), 538–39.

———. 'Langland's Structural Imagery.' *Essays in Criticism* 30 (1980), 311–25.

———. '*Lele Wordes* and *Bele Paroles*: Some Aspects of Langland's Word-Play,' *RES* n.s. 34 (1983), 137–50.

Searle, Eleanor. 'Seigneurial Control of Women's Marriage: The Antecedents and Function of Merchet in England.' *Past and Present* 82 (1979), 3–43.

Severs, J. Burke, and Albert E. Hartung, gen. eds. *A Manual of Writings in Middle English*. Vol. 7. Hamden: Archon, 1986.

Seymour, M. C., ed. *The Metrical Version of Mandeville's Travels*. EETS o.s. 269. London: Oxford University Press, 1973.

———, et al., eds. *On the Properties of Things: John Trevisa's Translation of Bartholomaeus Anglicus De Proprietatibus Rerum: A Critical Text*. 3 vols. Oxford: Clarendon, 1975–88.

Shahar, Shulamith. *Childhood in the Middle Ages*. London: Routledge, 1990.

Sheehan, Michael M., ed. *Aging and the Aged in Medieval Europe*. Toronto: Pontifical Institute, 1990.

———. 'Choice of Marriage Partner in the Middle Ages: Development and Mode of Application of a Theory of Marriage.' *Studies in Medieval and Renaissance History* n.s. 1 (1978), 3–33.

————. 'The Formation and Stability of Marriage in Fourteenth-Century England: Evidence of an Ely Register.' *MS* 33 (1971), 228–63.

————. '*Maritalis Affectio* Revisited.' *The Olde Daunce: Love, Friendship, Sex and Marriage in the Medieval World*, ed. Robert R. Edwards and Stephen Spector, 32–43, 254–60. Albany: SUNY Press, 1991.

————. 'Marriage Theory and Practice in the Conciliar Legislation and Diocesan Statutes of Mediaeval England.' *MS* 40 (1978), 408–60.

————. 'The Wife of Bath and Her Four Sisters: Reflections on a Woman's Life in the Age of Chaucer.' *M&H* n.s. 13 (1985), 23–42.

————. *The Will in Medieval England: From the Conversion of the Anglo-Saxons to the End of the Thirteenth Century.* Studies and Texts 6. Toronto: Pontifical Institute, 1963.

————, and Jacqueline Murray, comps. *Domestic Society in Medieval Europe: A Select Bibliography.* Toronto: Pontifical Institute, 1990.

Shoaf, R. A. ' "Speche þat spire is of grace" ': A Note on *Piers Plowman* B.9.104.' *YLS* 1 (1987), 128–33.

Simpson, James. ' "After craftes conseil clotheth yow and fede" ': Langland and London City Politics,' *England in the Fourteenth Century: Proceedings of the 1991 Harlaxton Symposium*, ed. Nicholas Rogers, 109–27. Stamford, Lincolnshire: Watkins, 1993.

————. *Piers Plowman: An Introduction to the B-text.* London: Longman, 1990.

————. 'The Role of *Scientia* in *Piers Plowman*.' In *Medieval English Religious and Ethical Literature: Essays in Honour of G. H. Russell*, ed. Gregory Kratzmann and James Simpson, 49–65. Cambridge: Brewer, 1986.

————. 'Spiritual and Earthly Nobility in *Piers Plowman*.' *NM* 86 (1985), 467–81.

————. 'Spirituality and Economics in Passus 1–7 of the B Text.' *YLS* 1 (1987), 83–103.

————. 'The Transformation of Meaning: A Figure of Thought in *Piers Plowman*.' *RES* n.s. 37 (1986), 161–83.

Skeat, Walter W., ed. *The Book of Husbandry by Master [Anthony] Fitzherbert.* English Dialect Society 37. London: Trübner, 1882.

Smith, Ben H., Jr. *Traditional Imagery of Charity in Piers Plowman.* The Hague: Mouton, 1966.

Smith, D. Vance. 'The Labors of Reward: Meed, Mercede, and the Beginning of Salvation.' *YLS* 8 (1994), 127–54.

Smith, Richard M. 'Hypothèses sur la nuptialité en Angleterre aux XIIIᵉ-XIVᵉ siècles.' *Annales: Économies Sociétés Civilisations* 38 (1983), 107–36.

Spalding, Mary Caroline. *The Middle English Charters of Christ.* Bryn Mawr: Bryn Mawr College, 1914.

Spearing, A. C. 'The Development of a Theme in *Piers Plowman*.' *RES*, n.s. 11 (1960), 241–53.

————. 'Verbal Repetition in *Piers Plowman* B and C.' *JEGP* 62 (1963), 722–37.

Starkey, David. 'The Age of the Household: Politics, Society and the Arts, c. 1350–c. 1550.' In *The Later Middle Ages*, ed. Stephen Medcalf, 225–90. New York: Holmes and Meier, 1981.

St-Jacques, Raymond. 'The Liturgical Associations of Langland's Samaritan.' *Traditio* 25 (1969), 217–30.

Stock, Lorraine Kochanske. 'Parable, Allegory, History, and *Piers Plowman*.' *YLS* 5 (1991), 143–64.

Stokes, Myra. *Justice and Mercy in Piers Plowman: A Reading of the B Text Visio.* London: Croom Helm, 1984.

245

Szittya, Penn R. 'The Trinity in Langland and Abelard.' In *Magister Regis: Studies in Honor of Robert Earl Kaske*, ed. Arthur Groos et al., 207–16. New York: Fordham University Press, 1986.

Tavormina, M. Teresa. ' "Bothe two ben gode": Marriage and Virginity in *Piers Plowman* C.18.68–100.' *JEGP* 81 (1982), 320–30.

———. 'The Chilling of Charity: Eschatological Allusions and Revisions in *Piers Plowman* C.16–17.' In *Art and Context in Late Medieval Narrative: Essays in Honour of R. W. Frank, Jr.*, ed. Robert R. Edwards, 51–77. Cambridge: Brewer, 1994.

———. ' "Gendre of a generacion": *Piers Plowman* B.16.222.' *ELN* 27.2 (December 1989), 1–9.

———. 'Kindly Similitude: Langland's Matrimonial Trinity.' *MP* 80 (1982), 117–28.

———. ' "Maledictus qui non reliquit semen": The Curse on Infertility in *Piers Plowman* B.XVI and C.XVIII.' *MÆ* 58 (1989), 117–25.

———. '*Piers Plowman* and the Liturgy of St. Lawrence: Composition and Revision in Langland's Poetry.' *SP* 84 (1987), 245–71.

Tentler, Thomas N. *Sin and Confession on the Eve of the Reformation*. Princeton: Princeton University Press, 1977.

Thomas of Chobham. *Thomae de Chobham Summa Confessorum*. Ed. F. Broomfield. Analecta Mediaevalia Namurcensia 25. Louvain: Nauwelaerts, 1968.

Thompson, M. W. *The Rise of the Castle*. Cambridge: Cambridge University Press, 1991.

Tierney, Brian. '*Natura id est Deus*: A Case of Juristic Pantheism?' *Journal of the History of Ideas* 24 (1963), 307–22.

Titow, J. Z. 'Some Differences Between Manors and Their Effects on the Condition of the Peasant in the Thirteenth Century.' *AgHR* 10 (1962), 1–13.

Triggs, Oscar L., ed. *The Assembly of the Gods*. EETS e.s. 69. London: Kegan Paul, Trench, Trübner, 1896.

Tristram, Philippa. *Figures of Life and Death in Medieval English Literature*. London: Elek, 1976.

Trower, Katherine Bache. 'Temporal Tensions in the *Visio* of *Piers Plowman*.' *MS* 35 (1973), 389–412.

Tuck, J. A. 'Richard II's System of Patronage.' In *The Reign of Richard II: Essays in Honour of May McKisack*, ed. F. R. H. du Boulay and Caroline M. Barron, 1–20. London: Athlone, 1971.

Twomey, Michael W. 'The Anatomy of Sin: Violations of *Kynde* and *Trawþe* in *Cleanness*.' Diss. Cornell, 1979.

Tyssen-Amherst, Alicia M. [Mrs. Evelyn Cecil, Baroness Rockley]. 'A Fifteenth Century Treatise on Gardening.' *Archaeologia* 54 (1894), 157–72.

———. *A History of Gardening in England*. 3rd ed. New York: Dutton, 1910.

Vasta, Edward. *The Spiritual Basis of Piers Plowman*. The Hague: Mouton, 1965.

Visser, Frederic Theodor. *An Historical Syntax of the English Language*. 3 vols. Leiden: Brill, 1963–73.

Waldron, R. A. 'Langland's Originality: The Christ-Knight and the Harrowing of Hell.' In *Medieval English Religious and Ethical Literature: Essays in Honour of G. H. Russell*, ed. Gregory Kratzmann and James Simpson, 66–81. Cambridge: Brewer, 1986.

Walker, Nigel. *Crime and Insanity in England*. 2 vols. Edinburgh: Edinburgh University Press, 1968. Vol. 1: The Historical Perspective.

Walker, Sue Sheridan. 'Feudal Constraint and Free Consent in the Making of Marriages in Medieval England: Widows in the King's Gift.' In *Canadian*

Historical Association Papers (1979 Meeting), 97–110. Ottawa: Canadian Historical Association, 1979.

———. 'The Feudal Family and the Common Law Courts: The Pleas Protecting Rights of Wardship and Marriage, c. 1225–1375.' *Journal of Medieval History* 14 (1988), 13–31.

———. 'Free Consent and Marriage of Feudal Wards in Medieval England.' *Journal of Medieval History* 8 (1982), 123–34.

———. 'The Marrying of Feudal Wards in Medieval England.' *Studies in Medieval Culture* 4 (1974), 209–24.

———. 'Proof of Age of Feudal Heirs in Medieval England.' *MS* 35 (1973), 306–23.

———. 'Violence and the Exercise of Feudal Guardianship: The Action of "Ejectio Custodia." ' *American Journal of Legal History* 16 (1972), 320–33.

———. 'Widow and Ward: The Feudal Law of Child Custody in Medieval England.' *Feminist Studies* 3 (1976), 104–16. Also in *Women in Medieval Society*, ed. Susan Mosher Stuard, 159–72. Philadelphia: University of Pennsylvania Press, 1976.

Walther, Hans, comp. *Lateinische Sprichwörter und Sentenzen des Mittelalters in alphabetischer Anordnung.* 9 vols. Göttingen: Vandenhoeck & Ruprecht, 1963–86.

Waugh, Scott L. *The Lordship of England: Royal Wardships and Marriages in English Society and Politics, 1217–1327.* Princeton: Princeton University Press, 1988.

Weigand, Rudolf. *Die Naturrechtslehre der Legisten und Dekretisten von Irnerius bis Accursius und von Gratian bis Johannes Teutonicus.* Münchener Theologische Studien: Kanonistische Abteilung 26. Munich: Hueber, 1967.

———. 'Die Lehre der Kanonisten des 12. und 13. Jahrhunderts von den Ehezwecken.' *Studia Gratiana* 12 (1967), 443–78.

Wentersdorf, Karl P. 'The Clandestine Marriages of the Fair Maid of Kent.' *Journal of Medieval History* 5 (1979), 203–31.

Wenzel, Siegfried, ed. and trans. *Fasciculus Morum: A Fourteenth-Century Preacher's Handbook.* University Park: Pennsylvania State University Press, 1989.

Whatley, Gordon. 'The Uses of Hagiography: The Legend of Pope Gregory and the Emperor Trajan in the Middle Ages.' *Viator* 15 (1984), 25–63.

White, Hugh. *Nature and Salvation in Piers Plowman.* Cambridge: Brewer, 1988.

Whiting, Bartlett J., and Helen Wescott Whiting, comps. *Proverbs, Sentences, and Proverbial Phrases from English Writings Mainly Before 1500.* Cambridge: Harvard University Press, 1968.

Wilkins, David. *Concilia Magnae Britanniae et Hiberniae.* 4 vols. London: Gosling, 1737.

Williams, David. *Cain and Beowulf: A Study in Secular Allegory.* Toronto: University of Toronto Press, 1982.

Wimbledon, Thomas. *Wimbledon's Sermon 'Redde rationem villicationis tue': A Middle English Sermon of the Fourteenth Century.* Ed. Ione Kemp Knight. Duquesne Studies, Philological Series 9. Pittsburgh: Duquesne University Press, 1967.

Wittig, Joseph S. ' "Piers Plowman" B, Passus IX–XII: Elements in the Design of the Inward Journey.' *Traditio* 28 (1972), 211–80.

———. 'The Dramatic and Rhetorical Development of Long Will's Pilgrimage.' *NM* 76 (1975), 52–76.

Wright, Thomas, ed. *The Vision and Creed of Piers Ploughman.* 2nd rev. ed. 2 vols. London: John Russell Smith, 1856.

247

Wyclif, John (attrib.). *Select English Works of John Wyclif.* Ed. Thomas Arnold. 3 vols. Oxford: Clarendon Press, 1869–71.

Yunck, John A. *The Lineage of Lady Meed: The Development of Mediaeval Venality Satire.* Notre Dame: University of Notre Dame Press, 1963.

Index of Lines Cited

The following index lists the citations of lines and passus in *Piers Plowman* in the text and notes of this book. When parallel passages from two or more versions have been cited, the parallelism is indicated with parentheses or the letter-combinations ABC, AB, or BC. Note that this index does not identify all parallelisms among the passages listed here, but only those cited in the course of the discussions above.

Index of Biblical Citations

General Index

This index includes the names of all authors and anonymous works mentioned in the notes and text, other than Langland.

Lightning Source UK Ltd.
Milton Keynes UK
UKOW031805190112

185701UK00001B/21/P